# UNIX and XENIX

*A Step-by-Step Guide*

Publishing Director: David Culverwell
Acquisitions Editor: Chris Williams
Production Editor/Text Design: Michael Rogers
Art Director/Cover Design: Don Sellers
Assistant Art Director: Bernard Vervin
Photography: George Dodson
Manufacturing Director: John Komsa

Typesetter: Compolith Graphics, Indianapolis, IN
Printer: R. R. Donnelley and Sons Co., Harrisonburg, VA
Typefaces: Aster (text), Helvetica (display), OCR-B (computer material)

# UNIX and XENIX

## *A Step-by-Step Guide*

Douglas W. Topham
Hai Van Truong

Brady Communications Company, Inc.
*A Prentice-Hall Publishing Company*
*Bowie, MD 20715*

UNIX and XENIX: A Step-by-Step Guide



**Library of Congress Cataloging in Publication Data**
Topham, Douglas,W.,
UNIX and XENIX.

Includes index.
1. UNIX (Computer operating system) 2.XENIX (Computer operating system) I. Truong, Hai Van,
II. Title. III. Title: U.N.I.X. and X.E.N.I.X.
QA76.6.T664 1985 001.64'2 84-24371

ISBN 0-89303-918-7

Prentice-Hall of Australia, Pty., Ltd., *Sydney*
Prentice-Hall Canada, Inc., Scarborough, *Ontario*
Prentice-Hall Hispanoamericana, S.A., *Mexico*
Prentice-Hall of India Private Limited, *New Delhi*
Prentice-Hall International, Inc., *London*
Prentice-Hall of Japan, Inc., *Tokyo*
Prentice-Hall of Southeast Asia Pte. Ltd., *Singapore*
Editora Prentice-Hall Do Brasil LTDA., *Rio de Janeiro*
Whitehall Books, Limited, Petone, *New Zealand*

Printed in the United States of America

85 86 87 88 89 90 91 92 93 94 95 1 2 3 4 5 6 7 8 9 10

## Contents

## About the Authors

Douglas W. Topham received his M.A. from Stanford University before serving as an officer in the U.S. Air Force. After teaching math courses at the high school and college levels, he wrote a set of programs to provide live displays for ABC's "Password" show. Later he wrote the **WordStar Training Guide** and designed the screen displays for Version 3.0 of WordStar. He is now a member of the technical staff of Zentec Corporation in Santa Clara, California.

Hai Van Truong attended Saigon University before attending the Naval Academy (Nha Trang) and serving in the Navy of the Republic of Vietnam. After teaching math and electronics at the high school and college levels, he began working in the electronics industry as a test engineer. Later he worked at different times as a UNIX system diagnostics engineer, a hardware design engineer, and a software design engineer. He is now a member of the technical staff of Zentec Corporation in Santa Clara, California.

## Limits of Liability and Disclaimer of Warranty



## Note to Authors

Have you written a book related to personal computers? Do you have an idea for developing such a project? If so, we would like to hear from you. Brady produces a complete range of books for the personal computer market. We invite you to write to David Culverwell, Publishing Director, Brady Communications Company, Inc., Bowie, MD 20715.

## Registered Trademarks

# Introduction

In writing this book, we've made every effort to take the approach that the late William Strunk, Jr. took when he wrote **The Elements of Style** (William Strunk, Jr. and E. B. White, The Macmillan Company, 1959.) According to E. B. White, "Will felt that the reader was in serious trouble most of the time, a man floundering in a swamp, and that it was the duty of anyone attempting to write English to drain this swamp quickly and get his man up on dry ground, or at least throw him a rope."

If you feel that this book gives you a rope to grasp, hang on and don't let go. If you think that the ground under you is starting to feel solid, get up on your feet as fast as you can. If you're having a good time while you're learning UNIX, rejoice!

We'd like to thank Bill Potts and Jim Edele for reviewing certain key chapters for accuracy. We also thank Michael Rogers, Paula Huber, and the Brady Art Department for the effort they put into this book. The people at Brady Communications Company have been very helpful and cooperative every step of the way, and we appreciate it.

# I

# Fundamentals

# 1

# Introduction to UNIX

## About This Book

### *Why You Need a Step-by-Step Guide*

This book is about the UNIX operating system. If you are new to UNIX, you need a book like this. Using UNIX after using one of the earlier operating systems for microcomputers is like using a single-lens reflex camera after using a simple aim-and-shoot camera. There are more features than you know what to do with, and it's very difficult to figure out where to begin.

Even though the reference manuals for UNIX seem to come in truckloads, they often leave out essential information. You read page after page about a feature you have to use, only to find that the basic facts you need have been left out. The programmers who wrote them assume that you already know what the feature is for and that you know how to use it. The result is text that is COIAK (clear only if already known). To make matters worse, the earlier books written about UNIX are based on the original manuals.

This book departs from the programmers' manuals by explaining all the basics. In this book, the fundamental facts are given to you, not assumed. There's also another advantage to reading this book: it's fairly entertaining. It isn't quite as funny as it could have been, but it isn't too bad. And this book gives you real examples, not hand-waving. Since these examples have been simplified to bring out the intended concepts, you will be prepared to move on to more complex examples.

### *Organization of This Book*

The main text of this book is divided into five parts, each more or less independent of the others. Within each part, the discussion begins with simpler topics, then builds to more involved concepts in subsequent chapters. Unix commands that appear in the right margin are grouped by section, with section one near the top of the page and section v at the bottom. We hope this makes it a little easier for you to select the material you need and get the most out of this book.

I. **Fundamentals**. These chapters, intended for all readers, give you basic instruction in using UNIX for the first time and finding out how it works.

II. **Text Editing with ed**. These chapters show you how to use the original UNIX editor to create and modify text for memos, letters, programs, and information. **ed** embodies many of the basic features of UNIX.

III. **Text Editing with vi and ex**. These chapters show you how to use two newer, more versatile editors. Some readers may want to read either Part II or Part III, but not both.

IV. **Text Processing and Formatting**. These chapters show you how to sort, rearrange, format, and otherwise process text files, usually in preparation for printing.

V. **Programming the UNIX Shell**. These chapters, intended for more experienced users, provide you with the tools for designing your own procedures and customizing your UNIX system. If you just want to learn how to use UNIX and have no desire to change the way the basic system works, you may not be interested in these chapters.

The appendices summarize information presented in the main text and provide some technical reference material. You will find many of these appendices helpful for quick reference.

We have done everything possible to try to ensure that each topic has been introduced before being mentioned in connection with other topics. In nearly every instance we were able to do this. However, because of the way concepts are interrelated in UNIX, we faced many "chicken or egg" dilemmas in arranging the topics. As a result, there are a handful of instances where a topic is mentioned shortly before being described in full.

Feel free to turn directly to the parts of the book that are of greatest interest to you. We think you will enjoy learning about UNIX from this book.

## Operating Systems

### *What Is an Operating System?*

Having an operating system running on your computer is like living in a modern home, where all you have to do to receive running water is to twist the handle of a faucet and all you have to do to receive electricity is to turn a switch. Without the extensive utility systems that make water and electricity available so effortlessly, you would have to do a lot more work to obtain these basic resources. In a way, you would be like one of the pioneers of an undeveloped land, who had to dig their own wells, cut down their own trees to gather building materials and fuel, and plant and grow their own crops to produce food.

Similarly, the pioneers of the computer era had to go to enormous efforts to accomplish things that computer users can do with relative ease today. What has brought us out of the pioneering stage has been the development of programs called operating systems that handle a great deal of the ordinary, day-to-day tasks involved in operating a computer system.

What would it be like to have to use a computer without an operating system? To begin with, you would have to keep a giant logbook that told you exactly where you had everything stored in the computer's memory. Without an operating system to keep track of this for you, you would have to write down where your program was, where your data was, and where you were going to store the results of your program.

You would have to write a special program any time you wanted to use any of the computer's peripheral equipment: its keyboard, its video screen, or its disk drives. And you'd need another logbook for each disk drive. Without an operating system to handle these things for you, you would have to take care of every detail of the operation of these devices. You would also have to devise a filing scheme, so that you could store programs and text documents in some orderly way. Without an operating system to set up a filing system for you, you would have to set it up yourself.

A computer provides basic resources to allow you to complete a task (accounting, writing, information management, programming, and so on). However, it takes an elaborate program called an operating system to make these resources readily available to you and your programs. With an operating system, all you have to do is press a few keys to have a file transferred from the computer's memory to one of its disk drives—a task of considerable complexity.

This is what an operating system is: a program that allows you to use a computer's resources with relative ease. To do this, an operating system must provide, at a minimum, some means for developing and running programs on the computer, a means for managing the computer's memory space, some means for accessing the computer's peripheral devices, and some kind of filing system.

In addition, a more sophisticated operating system may provide other conveniences to make the computer even easier to use: a way of allowing many different people to use the computer at the same time (**time-sharing**), some means of communication between these different users, a way of allowing many different programs to run at the same time (**multi-**

**tasking**), tools for processing and maintaining files, tools to ease the task of software development, tools for entering and processing written text, and some kind of security measures.

### *What Is the UNIX Operating System?*

Now that you have some general notion of what an operating system is, what unique characteristics does UNIX have to distinguish it from other operating systems? Here are some of the most prominent:

- structured file system with multiple levels
- features that allow many users to work from the same computer at the same time (making UNIX a **multi-user** system)
- a feature that allows any of the users active on the computer to run more than one program at a time (this is called **multi-tasking**)
- mechanisms that allow one program to pass its results directly to another program, making it unnecessary to use extra storage space
- a scheme that allows any user to redirect the results of a program from one peripheral device to another (for example, from a display terminal to a disk drive)
- a built-in command interpreter and language (known as the **shell**)
- a structured language called C for systems programming
- extensive tools for writing and developing programs in C and other programming languages
- extensive tools for entering, changing, and processing written text and preparing it for printing.

## UNIX and Its Derivatives

One of the questions people always ask about UNIX is, "How does it differ from XENIX and other derivatives?" This section gives a brief answer.

### *The Beginnings*

The development of UNIX began with two engineers employed by Bell Telephone Laboratories in 1969 who had trouble working with the operating system available to them. The Murray Hill Computer Center (New Jersey), where they worked, was running a General Electric 645 mainframe under the Multics operating system, one of the first multi-user, interactive systems designed. Before Multics, only batch-oriented operating systems (often using punched cards for input and listings for output) were in widespread use.

Following the batch-processing tradition, Multics emphasized isolating users from one another with several layers of protection. This kept them from inadvertently altering each other's disk files. Since file-sharing among a team of programmers was the emerging software project style at Bell Labs, Ken Thompson set out to design a more appropriate operating system. The final result, UNIX, was not written all at once; it evolved over a period of years as Thompson addressed specific needs along the way.

Thompson's "Space Travel" program, which simulated the movement of the major celestial bodies in the solar system, provided much of the impetus for the development of UNIX. Since it cost 75 dollars to run the program on the GE mainframe, Thompson turned to a little-used Digital Equipment Corporation (DEC) PDP-7 with a good display processor to rewrite "Space Travel."

The project illustrated how difficult program development can be on a computer that lacks an adequate operating system. Initially, programs for the PDP-7 were developed on the GE 645 and carried to the DEC machine on paper tape. Thompson soon grew tired of this, and began to develop a rudimentary operating system and then an assembler for the PDP-7, both written entirely in assembly language (a low-level computer language that uses mnemonics that are parallel to primitive machine codes). This task started him thinking about the kind of file system that would encourage cooperative programming projects. As he implemented these concepts, he suggested the name UNIX, a play on the name "Multics."

## Further Development

As more people began to use UNIX, and as Thompson responded to requests to its early users for more features, UNIX continued to evolve into its current form: For example, the interest of Bell's Patent Department in UNIX resulted in the inclusion of extensive text-processing capabilities. In fact, a major part of the early work with UNIX was centered around text-processing, which explains why UNIX's ability to handle text is so highly developed today.

The lack of a high-level language for the growing system impelled Thompson to write a language called **B** just before the entire system was transported to one of the first PDP-11/45 systems ever made. He wrote a few utilities in **B** (an enhanced version of MIT's **BCPL**), but it soon became evident that an interpretive language like **B** with neither structure nor data-typing would not be suitable for rewriting UNIX.

Finally, as the burden of system maintenance grew steadily, Dennis Ritchie wrote a new language based on **B** called **C** to help shape UNIX into a more manageable form. The new C language evolved along with the overall UNIX project, making it possible to add multi-processing to UNIX and to transport UNIX to other machines. Now one of the most widely accepted structured programming languages in existence, C is largely responsible for the widespread use of UNIX in so many multiuser sites.

## Distribution to the Academic World

Since American Telephone and Telegraph, Bell's parent company, was then in the communications business, not the computer business, AT&T was not permitted to sell UNIX commercially. So UNIX spread most rapidly during the 1970s to universities and research institutions. (With the break-up of the telephone system in 1984, AT&T is just now beginning to sell UNIX.) Because UNIX was available for a relatively low license fee and because it was designed to be used by many users engaged in program development, it became one of the most widely used systems in the academic world.

Of all the institutions that acquired UNIX, the one that stands out is the University of California in Berkeley. Here significant enhancements to the original system were made: the **ex** and **vi** text-editing combination, the C shell, a Pascal compiler, a LISP interpreter, and a data base management system called INGRES. The major versions of Berkeley UNIX are called **2BSD** for DEC PDP-11 systems and **4BSD** for DEC VAX systems ("BSD" stands for "Berkeley Software Distribution"). In this book, Berkeley features are marked by the picture of Sather Tower shown here.

## The Emergence of UNIX Derivatives

Evolving as it did in the world of research and academics, UNIX lacked some of the features required for use in a business environment. A number of software developers have offered their own commercial versions of UNIX, usually scaled down to some extent. You may be familiar with some of these systems (Idris, Cromix, Coherent, Onyx, and XENIX). One of the most widely known of these, XENIX, was developed by Microsoft in the late 1970s and early 1980s to offer a full implementation of UNIX with commercial features. In 1984, IBM introduced a system called PC/IX to run on its PC-XT, followed by VM/IX to run on its mainframes. (For a more detailed discussion of UNIX variants, see Appendix I, "Different Versions of UNIX.")

## How Does UNIX Work?

If you run an application program under UNIX, three programs will be working together. The program that interacts directly with the computer is called the **kernel**. As an everyday user of UNIX, you will seldom be aware of the kernel's presence. You will be more aware of the program that interprets what you type at your keyboard and arranges for other programs to run—the **shell**. Strictly speaking, the shell is just another program, and shouldn't be distinguished from other programs. However, it is customary to depict the shell as a "middle layer" between the kernel and applications (as shown in Figure 1-1). This is because the shell plays such an important role in interacting with users and because the shell can be almost completely concealed from users if desired.

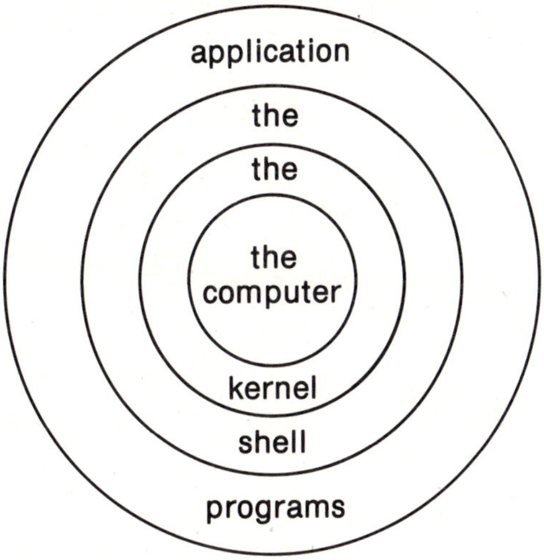


Figure 1-1. The different parts of UNIX.

### *The Kernel*

The kernel program allocates hardware resources, such as disk drives, tape drives, and internal memory, to each command program. Because the kernel interacts directly with the hardware, it is different for each computer. Since the kernel is such a small part of UNIX, it is relatively easy to produce a new version of UNIX for a different machine. (A program that can be run on a variety of machines is said to be **portable**. Portability is discussed later in this chapter.)

### *The Shell*

It is the shell that greets you when you begin a session with UNIX, and it is the shell that accepts instructions from you and carries them out. The shell is UNIX's command interpreter, a program that runs as a software layer over the kernel. The shell presents you with a prompt on the screen, followed by a cursor, like this:

```
$ _
```

When you type a command after this prompt, the shell begins a UNIX **process**. This process may be a simple routine to display today's date and time on the screen, or it may be a sophisticated text-editing system (the shell itself is also a process). You activate any process, large or small, by typing a command and letting the shell take care of carrying it out. If anything goes wrong while you are **invoking** the process, the shell will display an error message on your screen. Once a process has completed, the shell returns to display another prompt on your screen, indicating that it is ready for your next command.

Actually, there is more than one shell available for UNIX. First, there is the original shell developed for UNIX at Bell Telephone Laboratories by Stephen R. Bourne (known as the **Bourne shell**). Then there is another version of the shell that was developed at the University of California by William N. Joy in the late 1970s (known as the **C shell**). Finally, because the shell can be modified by any user with a license for the source code, there are many other variations of the shell at different installations around the world. As you will learn later in the book, you can customize the operation of your shell.

## Application Programs

Because of the increasing popularity of UNIX, the list of application programs available to run under UNIX is growing every day. There are word processing programs, spreadsheet programs, data base management programs, compilers for BASIC, FORTRAN, COBOL, C, and other programming languages, and assemblers. Many of the most popular programs for microcomputers are being rewritten in C, so that they can be offered to users of UNIX. In addition, sophisticated applications are being moved from mainframes and minicomputers down to microcomputers running UNIX.

Before long, it will be possible to run most of the programs that became popular under CP/M, MS-DOS, and PC-DOS, while at the same time enjoying the versatility and power of UNIX. Until a year or so ago, microcomputers simply could not provide the extensive computing resources required by UNIX. They couldn't match the large amounts of internal memory and the fast, large-capacity disks of the minicomputers. But with recent technical advances in both areas, microcomputers have quickly become powerful enough to assume the rigors of running UNIX.

### C and Portability

UNIX was originally written for the DEC PDP-7 minicomputer. Later it was modified to run on other minicomputers, and then finally on microcomputers. This has increased the popularity of UNIX and the portability of C, the language in which most UNIX programs and utilities are written. Many of the early programs for microcomputers were written in low-level assembly language, close to machine code, to obtain maximum performance. Later on, applications programs were written in high-level languages like BASIC and Pascal to achieve portability. Yet C is a sort of middle-level language, combining the high performance of a low-level language with the portability and ease of use of a high-level language. UNIX was the first major operating system that was **not** written primarily in assembly language.

Originally associated closely with UNIX and part of the development of UNIX, C has recently become recognized as a useful product in its own right. Over a dozen versions of C are being sold to microcomputer owners. Because of the portability of C, the task of moving UNIX applications (written in C) to a new UNIX system is greatly simplified.

## UNIX and This Book

### Versions of UNIX

UNIX has gone through many revisions over the past 15 years. The first one was called Version 1, the second one was called Version 2, and so on up to Version 7. Then, just to make things interesting, they decided to call the next revision "System III" instead of "Version 8." The original releases of XENIX and PC/IX were both based on Version 7, with some features borrowed from System III. By the time this book is published, there may be a new release of XENIX based entirely on System III. The latest version of UNIX as of this writing is System V, the version offered with the new AT&T computers. (System IV was never released outside of AT&T.)

### UNIX as a Whole

If you step back and take a look at the vast array of programs that comprise UNIX as a whole, you could probably place most of them in the following broad categories:

- **General Purpose**: Programs that give you access to the system, allow you to work with files, control program execution, get information, keep records, make computations, and communicate with other users

- **Text Editing**: Programs that allow you to enter, modify, and process text
- **Document Formatting**: Programs that allow you to format text to be printed and prepare manuscripts for typesetting
- **Program Development**: Programs that allow you to check and compile both high-level and low-level programs, and to develop your own language compilers and processors
- **Administration and Maintenance**: Programs that allow you to add and remove user accounts, and back up, restore, and maintain the file system
- **Miscellaneous:** Programs that allow you to plot graphs, play games, and quiz yourself.

## *The Scope of This Book*

This book concentrates on general-purpose programs, text editing and formatting, and one area of program development (shell programming). There is also some basic information on configuring your terminal. C programming and software development are vast subjects, and are beyond the scope of this book. After reading this book, however, you should be well prepared to go on to books that cover these other areas. Graphing is an interesting subject to discuss. However, because UNIX graphing requires a special graphics terminal (which most people don't have), we decided to omit graphing.

For a comprehensive treatment of UNIX commands, you have to turn to one of the detailed reference works, such as the two-volume **UNIX Programmer's Manual** from Bell Telephone Laboratories. Volume 1 (about 400 pages) contains comprehensive information about, but few examples of, commands and files. Each command or file is described in one of eight sections in a standard format: Name, Synopsis, Description, [Related] Files, See Also, and Bugs. Volume 2 (about 600 pages) contains scholarly articles by the creators of UNIX in six broad areas: General Works; Getting Started; Document Preparation; Programming; Supporting Tools and Languages; and Implementation, Maintenance, and Miscellaneous.

In printed form, a two-volume set costs about 75 dollars. However, at many installations, a copy of the manual is included with UNIX on disk. Whenever we reach the limits of the scope of this book, we refer to this manual—by whatever name it may be known at your installation. With the break-up of AT&T, Bell Telephone Laboratories is now called AT&T Bell Laboratories, and the manual is now called the **UNIX User's Manual.**

Which version of UNIX does this book apply to? Although we have used Version 7 for most of our test programs, we have also tried a few on BSD 4.2 and System III systems for extra verification. Since there are so many variations in UNIX systems, we have tried to minimize the "version issue." (Considering the relatively minor differences between versions in use today, the "version issue" should not be a major concern for new users.) No matter what we do, there will be some commands in this book that will not run on your system, and some commands on your system that are not documented in this book. The best we can do is offer Appendix I to try to clarify some of the many differences.

# 2

# Getting Started with UNIX

In this chapter you will learn these basic things about UNIX:

- Preliminary set-up procedures
- Logging in and logging out
- Editing a command line
- Running processes (commands)
- Using the calculators
- Aids to learning.

## Preliminary Set-up Procedures

If you have been using a single-user operating system like CP/M, MS-DOS, or PC-DOS, then you have become accustomed to simply turning on the computer, possibly entering the date and time, and going to work. However, with a multi-user system like UNIX, you have to consider that a number of different people can gain access to the computer at any given time from a number of different terminals. So before you can begin using UNIX, you have to be make sure that UNIX can recognize you as a user on the system and that it can communicate with the terminal you are using.

### *Identifying Yourself to UNIX*

You will be able to use UNIX only after your name has been added to a list of users. If you are working in a company or an institution, there is probably a system administrator designated to take care of new users. If so, this administrator will assign you an identifier, a password, and a terminal. The identifier assigned to you (also known as an "account name," "login name," or "user name") will probably be either one of your names or your initials. The password is designed to prevent anyone else (except a system administrator) from using the system under your name. In most cases, the terminal will provide you with a keyboard for entering information and a video screen for receiving information back from the system.

### *Identifying Your Terminal*

If your UNIX system has already been customized for your machine, then you probably won't have to do anything to identify your terminal. If not, you may have to make sure that the various settings for your terminal are compatible with the settings for your computer. Otherwise, your terminal and computer won't be able to communicate with each other. It's like making sure that you and another person both speak the same language before you try to begin a conversation.

Basically, you have to make sure that the terminal and computer are both sending information to each other at the same speed, that both are using the same convention for sending and receiving, that both are using the same scheme to check for errors, and that both interpret special characters the same way. To find out whether they have been set correctly, just log in and see what happens. If you see double characters on the screen (or no characters), random characters (also known as "garbage"), or no response to the RETURN key, the settings for your terminal may be incorrect—get help from your system administrator. If you don't have any problems, the settings are fine. Later on, after you become more familiar with UNIX, you can learn to use a command called **stty** (set teletype) to make adjustments.

## Logging in and Logging Out

### *Logging In*

Once you have an identifier, a password, and a working terminal, you are ready to log in. Logging in is what gives you access to the UNIX operating system. Let's go through the basic procedures (which may vary from one system to another) shown here.

1. Establish connection between the computer and your terminal.

   a. This is the part that can vary the most. For your system, it may mean dialing a telephone number, flipping a switch on your terminal, or typing something at the keyboard. Find out from your system administrator exactly what is required.

   b. Once you have taken the necessary action, UNIX will first make itself known to you by a short, simple message in the upper left-hand corner of your screen like this:

```
login: _
```

2. Identify yourself (the characters you type in are shown here enclosed in boxes).

   a. In the space after the "login" prompt, type your system identifier (or user name) and press RETURN.

   b. UNIX will probably respond by asking for your password:

   ```
   login: robin
   Password: _
   ```

3. Give your secret password.

   a. In the space after the "Password" prompt, type your password (which will not appear on the screen) and press RETURN.

   b. In the interest of security, the characters you type will not appear on the screen. After a brief pause, you will see something like this:

   ```
   login: robin
   Password:

   Last login: Sun Feb 5 20:17:26 on tty03

   * * * * * * * * * * * * * * * * * * * * * * * * *
   *                                               *
   *   Welcome to U N I X System III January 1985  *
   *                                               *
   * * * * * * * * * * * * * * * * * * * * * * * * *

   $ _
   ```

Congratulations! You have just successfully logged in. The dollar sign ($), percent sign (%), or other symbol in front of the cursor is called the UNIX shell prompt. Later in the book, we'll explain why it has that name. We'll also show you how you can change it to something else. For now you can think of the UNIX shell prompt as similar to the prompt you see on the screen when you use CP/M, MS-DOS, or PC-DOS (A>). It tells you that UNIX is ready for you to type a command and go to work.

A system administrator can log in as a **super-user** to perform special tasks that require extraordinary privileges. Such a user will have a special prompt that looks like a pound sign (#).

## Typing Commands

Just to verify that you have actually gained access to UNIX, try a few simple UNIX commands.

1. Let's begin with the command that tells you the day of the week, the date, and the time of day.

   a. Type *date* and press RETURN.

   b. UNIX will respond with a display like this:

```
$ date
Mon Jan 17 09:02:37 EST 1985
$ _
```

2. Next, let's find out who is logged in right now.

a. Type *who* and press RETURN.

b. UNIX will respond with a display like this:

```
$ who
janis         tty03   Jan 17   08:12
alex          tty05   Jan 17   08:39
jkl           tty07   Jan 16   21:16
robin         tty12   Jan 17   09:02
guapo         tty16   Jan 17   08:57
$ _
```

Each line of this display gives a user's identifier (like "janis"), a terminal number (like "tty03"), and the date and time the user logged in (like "Jan 17 08:12"). When UNIX was developed in the late 1960s, it was common to use a Teletype[R] hardcopy display (printing) device as a terminal. This is why UNIX says "tty" (from *tel*e*ty*pe) to mean "terminal."

3. Finally, let's type a command that UNIX doesn't know and see what happens.

a. Type *why* and press RETURN.

b. UNIX will respond with a message like this:

```
$ why
why: not found
$ _
```

## *Logging Out*

When the time comes to end a session with UNIX, you can't just turn off your terminal. You have to **log out**. If you don't log out, UNIX will still consider you logged in, even though your terminal is disconnected.

For most systems, all you have to do is to type Control-D (hold the CTRL key down with one finger and press D with another). Since Control-D often means end-of-file or end-of-transmission to UNIX, there may be times when you will have to type Control-D several times to log yourself out. Some systems may require that you also press other keys. If you are using the C shell and the variable called "ignoreeof" is set, you have to type *logout* and press RETURN. (Some systems, such as System III systems, require *exec login.*)

```
$                              [Press Control-D—nothing displayed]
login: _
```

When you have successfully logged out, what happens? The "login" prompt appears on the screen. Does this mean that UNIX doesn't like to see a user log out? It could mean that, but you only have to remember one simple thing: "login" tells you that you are logged out.

At this point you can either log in again or stay logged out. Since we have some more things to do, let's log back in and go on to the next section.

### Changing Your Password

Since your password gives you some measure of security under UNIX, you may want to change it from time to time. Changing it will make it more difficult for others to log in under your system name. For practice, try changing your password right now. Just type *passwd* and press RETURN:

```
$ passwd
Changing password for robin
Old password: _
```

Type your current password in the space provided (you won't see it on the screen). Next, UNIX will ask you to type your new password (up to eight characters), then type the new password a second time to confirm it:

```
$ passwd
Changing password for robin
Old password:
New password:
Retype new password:
$ _
```

If you really want to make your password difficult for anyone to guess, you can mix upper- and lowercase letters with numbers and other characters. The more unusual (and longer) you make it, the harder it will be for another user to stumble across it by trial and error. It's usually best to avoid things like your nickname, your license plate number, your social security number, or your cat's name.

## Entering a Command Line

Earlier in this chapter you used two simple commands, **date** and **who**. To carry out any action under UNIX, you have to execute a command (type a command line and press RETURN). In the case of the **date** command, the four letters *date* make up the entire command line. In the case of the **who** command, the three letters *who* make up an entire command line.

Although these two commands required nothing more than the name of the command, there are many other commands that also require additional information about the command's options and any files to be processed by the command. Such information, if required, follows the command's name on the command line. For example, the **who** command can be executed by itself to list the users currently logged in. But there is also another form of the command:

```
$ who am i
robin      tty05 Jan 17 09:02
$ _
```

If you should forget your system identifier or if you have to log in under more than one identifier, you can use this form of the command to find out which identifier you are currently logged in under. The extra words added to the command ("am i") form an **argument** to the command, which modifies the way the command works.

Until you press RETURN, it's still possible to make changes to a command line. The rest of this section discusses ways to make such changes.

## *Erasing a Character* CTRL-H

To erase a single character on the command line, use CTRL-H (hold down the CTRL key with one finger and press H with another). On some keyboards, there may be a key called BACKSPACE that performs this function. Here is how a typical correction might look in steps:

| | |
|---|---|
| `$ whoo_` | [ Extra *o* typed at the end of *who*] |
| `$ who_` | [Type #, CTRL-H, or BACKSPACE] |

Now you can press the RETURN key to have the command line executed.

## *Erasing an Entire Command Line* @

To erase the entire command line and start all over, use the at-sign (@), usually SHIFT 2. Again, there may be a different key for this function on your system. Assuming it's @, here is another typical correction:

| | |
|---|---|
| `$ fate_` | [You typed *fate* instead of *date*] |
| `$ fate` | [Press @ to erase the line. In most cases, you won't actually see the line erased; the cursor will simply drop down to the next line] |
| `_` | |
| `$ fate` | |
| `date_` | [Retype the line] |

Now press the RETURN key to have the command line executed. In this simple example, pressing the key to erase the line (@) instead of erasing the four characters separately (CTRL-H four times) saved you only three keystrokes. However, on a long command line, it would save you many more keystrokes.

### *Restoring the Prompt* **DEL**

Sometimes, after you have started a process, the process hangs and the UNIX shell prompt ($) does not return to the screen. If this happens, press DEL to terminate the process and restore the prompt:

```
$ who
            [Press DEL—nothing will be displayed]
$ _
```

## Process Control

Once you have typed a command line correctly, there are several things you can do to control the resulting process: you can run the process in the background, request a list of processes currently running, abort a process, or halt screen output from a process.

### *Running a Process in the Background* **&**

Once you execute a command, the shell usually waits for the process to complete, then displays another shell prompt. This is called **foreground processing**. Unless you instruct UNIX otherwise, any process that you initiate will run in the **foreground** by default. That is, the process will tie up your terminal while it is running, making it impossible for you to do anything else with UNIX until the process is complete.

By instructing UNIX to run a process in the **background**, you can free your terminal and proceed to another task immediately. To run a process in the **background**, type an ampersand (&) at the end of the command line before pressing RETURN. (The & is SHIFT 7 on most keyboards.) **Background processing** is usually most suitable for commands that take a long time to execute. For example, to begin formatting and printing a large file called "mammoth", type

```
$ pr mammoth | lpr &
2167
$ _
```

UNIX will respond by displaying a process identification number (PID) and then reissuing another shell prompt. With the job running in the **background** and the shell prompt on the screen, you are now free to enter another command line (which may be another **background process**), without having to wait for the printing of *mammoth* to be completed. While **background processing** is convenient for certain tasks, there are disadvantages to consider:

- A background process can't accept keyboard input
- Any output from a background process to your screen will disrupt whatever you are typing at that moment
- You have less control over a background process than you have over a foreground process
- If you try to initiate too many background processes at once, you may run the risk of over-loading your system.

DEL
&
ps
DEL
kill

## *Finding Out What Processes Are Running* **ps**

If you are running processes in the background, there is another UNIX command to find out which ones are still running at a particular moment and which have been completed. The **ps** (process status) command lists all processes currently running, displaying for each process its assigned process identification number (*PID*), the terminal on which it was initiated (*TTY*), the amount of time it has been running (*TIME*), and something to indicate the command line used to initiate it (*CMD*), as in this example:

```
$ ps
  PID   TTY   TIME CMD
 1905   12    1:16 -sh
 2132   12    2:18 ed
 2167   12    4:02 -sh
 2218   12    0:58 ps
$ _
```

## *Aborting a Process* **DEL kill**

Sometimes it may be necessary to terminate a process before it has been completed. To abort a **foreground process**, press the DEL key. To abort a **background process**, use the **kill** command. Type *kill*, followed by the PID for the process you are terminating. For example, to abort the printing of *mammoth* described above (process identification 2167), you could use

```
$ kill 2167
2167: terminated        [UNIX responds with a message]
$ _
```

As long as you know the PIDs, you can abort more than one process with a single command line:

```
$ kill 1905 2132 2167
1905 2132 2167: terminated
$ _
```

Some systems allow you to issue a **kill** to terminate **all** processes initiated from your terminal. However, since such a command can also log you out of the system, it's usually best not to try it—at least not now.

### *Halting Screen Output*

At times you will find that a screen display is scrolling up the screen faster than you can read it. To halt the scrolling temporarily, press *CTRL-S* to make the display pause. Then, after you've had a chance to read the display, you can press *CTRL-O* to resume scrolling.

## Using the Calculators

**CTRL-S**

UNIX provides a calculator (and a preprocessor for that calculator) that you can use right at your terminal.

### *Using the Desk Calculator*

**dc**

Use the **dc** command to call up a simple interactive desk calculator. Here is a typical session with **dc**, with comments to the right of each line:

```
$ dc      Call up the desk calculator
3         Enter 3
4         Enter 4
+         Perform addition
p         Display the result
7
3+p       Add 3 and display the result
10
4*p       Multiply by 4 and display the result
40
2/p       Divide by 2 and display the result
20
5-p       Subtract 5 and display the result
15
q         Exit the desk calculator
```

Other features include number bases, scaling, functions, subscripts, and logical control. For further details, see the **UNIX Reference Manual**.

### *Using the High-Precision Calculator*

**bc**

UNIX offers another calculator called **bc** that is patterned after the C language. This calculator allows unlimited precision for computations.

Use the **bc** command to call up this calculator, which is actually a preprocessor for **dc**. You can assign values to simple variables, functions, and arrays. When you invoke **bc**, you can also invoke a mathematical library, which includes six functions: sine, cosine, arctangent, exponential, logarithm, and Bessel function.

In general, **bc** allows you to write a mathematical subroutine for **dc**, using rules of syntax very similar to those used in C language programming. The program can handle input from files or from the standard input (the keyboard). For details, see the **UNIX Reference Manual.**

**CTRL-S**
**dc**
**bc**
**learn**
**man**

## Aids to Learning

Many UNIX systems have two aids to learning about UNIX: a computer-aided instruction course and an on-line copy of the **UNIX Programmer's Manual.**

### *Computer-Aided Instruction* **learn**

If this feature is available on your system, you can execute the **learn** command to initiate a beginner's course on the UNIX system. This course will take you through a series of instructions, followed by a series of questions on various topics. This can be a useful aid, but there are disadvantages to consider:

- You never receive any advance warning on how much time a particular lesson is going to take (one may take 15 minutes, the next may take over an hour)
- If you answer a question incorrectly, there is nothing to explain why your answer is wrong—just a message telling you it's wrong
- If you are interrupted in the middle of the course, it is difficult to resume where you left.

### *On-Line Manual* **man**

If this feature is available on your system, you can execute the **man** command to display a section of the **UNIX User's Manual.** Simply type *man*, followed by the name of a UNIX command. For example, to see the section on the **who** command, you could use

```
$ man who
```

This will give you a detailed description of the command, including all the different modifiers that can be used with the command.

# Summary of Chapter 2

In this chapter you learned some basic things about UNIX: preliminary set-up procedures, logging in and logging out, and running processes.

## *Preliminary Set-Up Procedures*

Before you can begin using UNIX, you have to have an identifier, a password, and a terminal, which will be assigned to you by the system administrator for your system.

## *Logging In and Logging Out*

**Logging in**: To log in to a UNIX system, establish connection with the computer, type your identifier, and type your password.

**Logging out**. To log out, type CTRL-D (possibly more than once) or type *logout* or *exec login* (System III) and press RETURN.

**Changing your password**. To change your password, use the **passwd** command.

## *Editing a Command Line*

**General**. To begin a **process** under UNIX, type a command line and press RETURN. The command line may contain either just the command by itself or the command plus modifiers.

**Erasing a character**. To erase a single character on a command line, use CTRL-H (or possibly BACKSPACE).

**Erasing an entire command line**. To erase an entire command line and start over again, use the at-sign (@) (or possibly some other character).

**Restoring the prompt**. To restore the shell prompt after running a process, press DEL.

## *Process Control*

**Running a process in the background**. To run a process in the background, type an ampersand (&) at the end of the command line.

**Finding out what processes are running**. To find out what processes are running on UNIX at a particular moment, use the **ps** (process status) command. The system will respond with a list of processes that shows the process identification number, the terminal on which it was initiated, the amount of time it has been running, and the command line itself.

**Aborting a process.** To abort a process running in the foreground, use the DEL key. To abort a process running in the background, use the **kill** command, along with the process identification number.

**Halting screen ouput.** To halt a rapidly moving screen display, press CTRL-S; to resume scrolling, press CTRL-Q.

## *Using the Calculators*

**Using the desk calculator.** To use the desk calculator, enter the **dc** command and enter "computational lines," with operations following the operands. Use the **q** command to exit.

**Using the high-precision calculator.** To use the high-precision calculator, enter the **bc** command and enter program statements.

## *Aids to Learning*

**Computer-aided instruction.** To take a course of instruction in UNIX at your terminal, execute the **learn** command.

**On-line manual.** To display a section of the **UNIX User's Manual** at your terminal, execute the **man** command. Type *man*, followed by the name of the command you wish described, then press RETURN.

# 3

# The UNIX File System

## What is a File System?

If you have used any kind of library, then you are already familiar with the concept of a **filing system**. A library offers you books kept on shelves, together with a **directory** that you can use to locate a particular book. In a library, the directory is called a card catalogue. Usually placed in an open area that is easy to find, the card catalogue gives you the location of each book in the library, together with brief information about the book.

Every operating system has a **file system** that works about the way a library's filing system works. In an operating system, the items stored are **files**, not books. Computer files can store text, data, graphics information, programs, and also directories to catalogue the other files. Each item in a typical directory provides a file's name, location, size, type, and possibly information about the file's accessibility to users. (In UNIX, only the file's name is in the directory itself; the rest of the information is kept somewhere else. But this introductory chapter is not the place to discuss that.)

If you have been using one of the common operating systems for microcomputers, then you have probably been using an unstructured file system. In an unstructured file system, there is one large directory to catalogue files, with all files named in this one directory. With no structure to relate the files in any particular way, the directory simply lists the files directly.

## A Structured File System

In the UNIX file system, there are many directories, not just one. Furthermore, there is a clearly-defined structure that places some directories within other directories and that may place different kinds of files in different directories. As a user of a UNIX system, you have your own personal directory, whose name is identical to the identifier that you type when you log in. Your directory, like other directories, may contain both files and other directories, allowing you to store related files together. Before we begin to discuss specific directories and files, there is one more point to consider: UNIX regards peripheral devices like terminals, printers, and disk drives as **files**. The procedure for accessing one of these devices is the same as the procedure for accessing any other file in the system.

A directory called **usr** contains the directories of all users of the UNIX system. (On very large systems, there may be several user directories, with names like **usr1**, **usr2**, or some other variation.) Your directory is known as your **home directory**. This is the directory that the system administrator assigns to you, the directory in which you begin working whenever you log in. Within this directory, you can create as many subdirectories as you need to organize your work. You can create one directory for your text files, one directory for your program files, one directory for your messages, and so on. Some of the other directories on a typical UNIX system are as follows:

- **bin**—contains the system's binary files, also known as executable object code files (most commands reside here)
- **dev**—contains the files representing the system's devices (terminals, printers, disk drives, and so on)
- **tmp**—contains the system's temporary storage files
- **etc**—contains miscellaneous files that are primarily used for system administration.

These five major directories all belong to a primal directory called the **root directory** (or simply the **root**), forming the main branches of a tree. It is customary to depict this tree upside down, with the root at the top and the branches pointing downward. Part of a simple UNIX file system is shown in Figure 3-1, with home directories for users Dan, Robin, and Ann.

UNIX, then, has a structured file system that contains three kinds of files: **directories**, which store the names of other files (including other directories); **ordinary files**, which store text, source programs, and object code; and **special files**, which correspond to peripheral devices. In the rest of this chapter, we'll discuss how directories and files are named, how to use pattern-matching characters to select files, how to work with files, how to work with directories, and how to grant or deny access to your directories and files.

## *Naming Directories and Files*

The **root** directory is identified by a single character: / (slash). To name one of the major directories directly under root, type a slash (/) to repre-

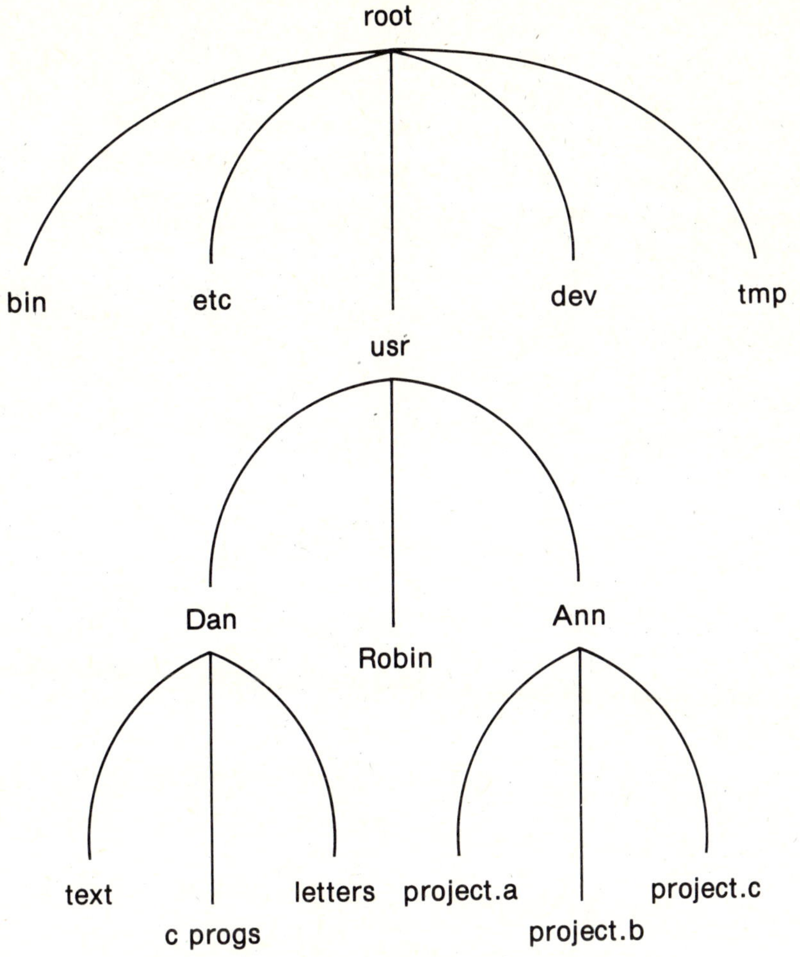


Figure 3-1. Part of a typical UNIX file system.

sent root, followed by the directory's own name, as in */usr*. The slash in front of *usr* tells you that **usr** is a subdirectory of root. Referring to Figure 3-1, here is how you would identify root and the major directories:

| | | | |
|---|---|---|---|
| / | root directory | **/usr** | user directory |
| **/bin** | binary directory | **/dev** | device directory |
| **/etc** | miscellaneous directory | **/tmp** | temporary directory |

To identify one of the user home directories, type another slash after /*usr*, followed by the account name, as in */usr/dan* and */usr/ann*. In each case here, the first slash refers to the root, while the second indicates that *dan* and *ann* are subdirectories of *usr*. (In UNIX terminology, *usr* is the **parent directory**, while *dan* and *ann* are **subdirectories**.)

To identify the subdirectories under *dan* and *ann*, we continue with the same conventions. We can identify Dan's *text* directory as */usr/dan/text* and Ann's *project.a* directory as */usr/ann/project.a.* Referring again to Figure 3-1, here is how you would identify all their directories:

| | |
|---|---|
| */usr/dan/text* | */usr/ann/project.a* |
| */usr/dan/c progs* | */usr/ann/project.b* |
| */usr/dan/letters* | */usr/ann/project.c* |

Suppose Dan has three C programs called *enter.c, files.c,* and *proc.c* and Ann has three files under *project.b* called *intro, search,* and *restore.* Then we could look at another part of the UNIX file system in Figure 3-2.

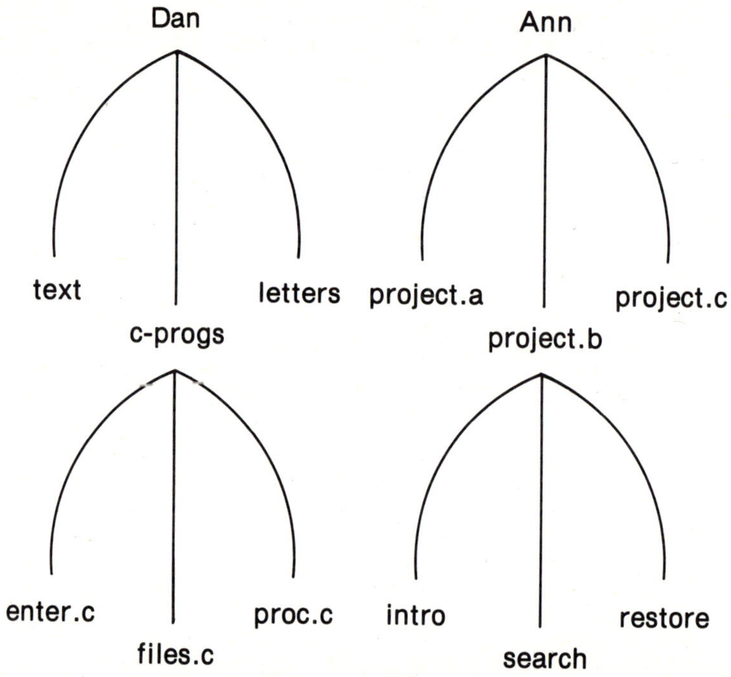


Figure 3-2. User files in a UNIX file system.

To identify these six files, you could give their full **pathnames**:

| | |
|---|---|
| */usr/dan/c progs/enter.c* | */usr/ann/project.b/intro* |
| */usr/dan/c progs/files.c* | */usr/ann/project.b/search* |
| */usr/dan/c progs/proc.c* | */usr/ann/project.b/restore* |

Ann (and other users) would have to use the names in the left-hand column to refer to Dan's files; Dan (and other users) would have to use the names in the right-hand column to refer to Ann's files. However, when

Dan and Ann refer to their own files in their own directories, they can use these shorter names (**partial pathnames**):

*c progs/enter.c*

*c progs/files.c*

*c progs/proc.c*

*project.b/intro*

*project.b/search*

*project.b/restore*

Later in this chapter, we'll show you how to "move around" the file system from one directory to another (change directories). If Dan should move from his own home directory to Ann's, then he could use the shorter names that Ann uses when she is working from her own home directory; if Ann should move from her own home directory to Dan's, then she could use the shorter names that Dan uses when he is working from his own home directory.

Furthermore, if Dan should move from his home directory to his own subdirectory *c__progs* and Ann should move from her home directory to her own subdirectory *project.b,* then they can use even shorter names for their files:

*enter.c*

*files.c*

*proc.c*

*intro*

*search*

*restore*

## *Rules for Naming and Accessing Files*

The rules for naming and accessing files (including directories) are closely related to the structure of the UNIX file system:

- The root directory is identified by a slash (/).
- A simple filename can be any combination of 1-14 characters **other than** slashes (/), asterisks (*), question marks (?), quotation marks (" or '), square brackets ([ or ]), or control characters.
- A pathname is a sequence of directory names, possibly followed by a simple filename, with each pair of names separated by a slash (/).

To avoid misinterpretation, the safest characters to use for simple filenames are letters of the alphabet, numbers, periods (.), hyphens (-), and underlines (__). Note: In UNIX, upper- and lowercase letters are **not** the same (for example, *newfile* is not the same as *NEWFILE*).

The directory permanently assigned to you is called your **home directory**; this is the directory to which you log on. Any directory to which you should move after logging on (including your home directory) will be called your **current directory**, or **working directory**, for as long as you remain in that directory. The directory in which your current directory belongs is called the **parent directory**. UNIX provides shorthand symbols to indicate your current directory (.) and your parent directory (..).

If a pathname, used to access a file, begins with a slash (/), then the search for the file begins at the **root directory**. Such a pathname is called an **absolute pathname** (or **full pathname**), since it always begins with the **root directory**. If a pathname begins with a simple filename, then the search for the file begins at your current directory. Such a pathname is called a **relative pathname**, since the file is accessed with respect to your current directory.

Later in this chapter we'll discuss procedures for giving other users **permission** to access your directories and files. It goes without saying that you can access only those directories and files for which you have permission.

## Working With Files

Whether you are composing letters, performing calculations, or writing programs, you spend much of your time on a computer dealing with files. It's always helpful to know how to display, combine, copy, and otherwise manipulate files. In this section we discuss such ways of working with UNIX files.

### *Creating a File*

**>**

As a general rule, UNIX creates files as needed by commands as they are executed. Therefore, it is not ordinarily necessary to create a file before executing a command that requires it for storing its output. However, if it should ever become necessary to create an empty file (say *put.into*), you can use the redirection symbol (>), as in the following example. You may want to do this to ensure that the creation time of the file is set **before** execution of a command, rather than **after**. Here is an example:

```
$ >put.into
```

### *Displaying the Contents of a File*

**cat**

To display the contents of any file, use the **cat** (concatenate) command. The **cat** command simply displays the contents of a file (or several files) on the screen, as in this example:

```
$ cat file.3
This is a very short file
```

```
$ cat file.1 file.2
This is "file.1"
```

```
that contains two lines.     This is "file.2"
$ _                          $ _
```

## Combining Files **cat**

Another function of the **cat** command is to combine, or concatenate, files with the result usually stored in another file. In this example

```
$ cat file.1 file.2 > file.1+2
$ _
```

the contents of files *file.1* and *file.2* are concatenated and stored as a single file called *file.1+2*. In using the **cat** command, avoid storing the result of a concatenation in one of the original files, since this will cause the original file to be overwritten. For example, in the command

```
$ cat file.1 file.2 > file.1          [no good—don't do this!]
$ _
```

*file.1* simply becomes *file.2*, which is not at all the intended result.

## Renaming a File **mv**

You can use the **mv** (move) command either to rename a file or to move it from one directory to another. To change the name of a file, enter a command like this:

```
$ mv old.name new.name
$ _
```

This command will change a file's name from *old.name* to *new.name* (you can then no longer access *old.file*).

## Moving a File **mv**

To move a file (or several files) from one directory to another (without changing their names), give the name of the new directory last on the command line, as in

```
$ mv file.3 file.4 text
$ _
```

This command will move *file.3* and *file.4* from your current directory to a subdirectory called *text*. You can verify this with the **ls** command:

```
$ ls test
file.3
file.4
$ _
```

You can also rename a file during a move by using a partial pathname. For example, to move *file.3* to subdirectory *text* and rename it *entries*, you could use this:

```
$ mv file.3 text/entries
$ _
```

## *Copying a File*

**cp**

To make a duplicate copy of a file, use the **cp** (copy) command illustrated here:

```
$ cp file.one FILE.ONE
$ _
```

This command will make a copy of *file.one* called *FILE.ONE*, so that the same file is now accessible by either name. (A reminder to users of other operating systems: In UNIX, *file.one* and *FILE.ONE* are **different** names.)

To copy a file (or several files) from one directory to another, use the **cp** command from the directory that contains the files, as shown here:

```
$ cp letter_a letter_b letter_c correspondence
$ _
```

This command will copy *letter_a*, *letter_b*, and *letter_c* from the current directory to a subdirectory called *correspondence*.

You can also rename a file as you copy it. For example, to copy *letter_c* to *correspondence* and rename it *ltr.04-16-85*, you could use this:

```
$ cp letter_c correspondence/ltr.04-16-85
$ _
```

## *Deleting a File*

**rm**

To delete a file (or several files), use the **rm** (remove) command, as shown here:

```
$ rm intro.1 intro.2 intro.3
$ _
```

This command will delete the files *intro.1*, *intro.2*, and *intro.3* from the current directory. Note: In UNIX, the files will be deleted immediately; there will be no warning like, *Are you sure you want to delete these files?* And once they're gone, you can't recover them—unless (1) another user has a **link** to these files or (2) they have been saved on a back-up tape.

## Linking a File

**ln**

A **link** is a directory entry that refers to a file. In UNIX, a given file may have several links to it, meaning that it belongs to several different directories (with the same size, contents, and other information that characterize the file). A link to a file cannot be distinguished from its original directory entry, meaning that any changes made to such a file will be in effect for each name by which the file may be known.

For example, if Dan should execute the following **ln** (link) command from his subdirectory *letters*, then he will be able to access the file *intro* from his own subdirectory *letters*, using the same name (*intro*)—provided that he has access to *intro*:

```
$ cd letters
$ ln /usr/ann/project.b/intro intro
$ _
```

If Dan prefers another name for the file, he can give the preferred name at the end of the **ln** command line. In the following example, Dan makes the same link as in the previous example, but this time the file will become known as *discover* to Dan (see Figure 3-3):

```
$ ln /usr/ann/project.b/intro discover
$ _
```

It is not possible to link a directory to another directory or to link a file in a different file system.

## Matching a Character

**?**

If you ever have to move, copy, or delete a large number of files, you can save time and keystrokes by using one of the UNIX "wildcard" characters for matching filenames. There are three varieties, and they generally have the same meanings throughout UNIX.

To match any single character in a filename, you can use a question mark (?) in the desired position in the filename. For example, to delete existing files *intro.1*, *intro.2*, and *intro.3*, as in the example above, you could use a command like this:

```
$ rm intro.?
$ _
```

If these are the only existing files with names that begin with *intro.* and end with a single character, then this command is equivalent to the command shown above under *Deleting a File.*

If *letter_a*, *letter_b*, and *letter_c* are the only existing files with names that begin with *letter_* and end with a single character, you can use the command

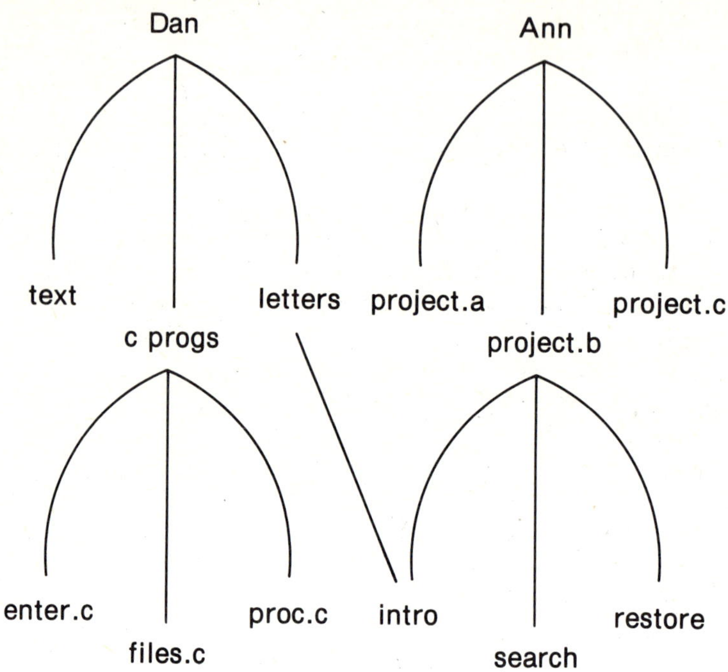


Figure 3-3. Linking file *intro*.

```
$ cp letter_? correspondence
$ _
```

to copy all three of them to directory *correspondence*.

In each example above, we have spoken of "existing files." You can never use a wildcard character like "?" to refer to a file that does not yet exist.

## *Matching Specific Characters* [ ]

To narrow the selection process to a specific set of characters and then match one of these characters in a filename, enclose the desired characters within square brackets in the appropriate position in the filename. For example, suppose you have files in your working directory with these names:

```
writer.0    writer.3    writer.6    writer.9
writer.1    writer.4    writer.7    writer.10
writer.2    writer.5    writer.8    writer.11
```

To delete *writer.5*, *writer.7*, and *writer.9*, you could use the following command:

```
$ rm writer.[579]
$ _
```

The three numbers inside the brackets let you select the three files desired.

You can also give a range of letters or numbers in brackets. For example, to delete *writer.1*, *writer.2*, *writer.3*, and *writer.4*, you could use this command:

```
$ rm writer.[1-4]
$ _
```

### *Matching Any Number of Characters* *

To match any number of characters in a filename, you can use the asterisk (*) in the desired position in the filename. (To match the entire name, use the asterisk alone.) For example, suppose you have the following files in your working directory:

| | | | |
|---|---|---|---|
| info.a | info.ab | info.abc | info.test |
| info.b | info.23 | info.new | info.old |

Then you could change to the parent directory and use the following command to move all of these files from directory *obsolete* to a subdirectory called *information*.

```
$ mv obsolete/info.* information
$ _
```

To use another example, suppose you have the following C programs in subdirectory *text*:

| | | | |
|---|---|---|---|
| enter.memo | files.dept | wide_col.c | news.ltr |
| F_327.c | a_file.text | new_compare.c | get_number.c |

You could use a command like this to copy all of the files that end in *.c* to a subdirectory called *C_programs*:

```
$ cp text/*.c C_programs
$ _
```

Be very careful when you use the asterisk (*), especially in a **rm** command. If you don't type the command exactly right, you may delete files unintentionally.

## Working With Directories

This section shows you how to work with UNIX directories using six common commands.

## Displaying the Contents of a Directory **ls**

To sort and display the names of all the directories and files that reside in your current directory, use the **ls** command, as illustrated here:

```
$ ls
file.1
file.2
letters
memos
specs
$ _
```

This doesn't show which names refer to files and which refer to directories. However, there is another form of this command that you can use to distinguish files from directories (and also to display a lot of other information). Just add the **-l** ("hyphen el" or "minus el") option to get a more detailed "long listing," as shown here:

```
$ ls -l
total 501
-rw-r-----   1 robin     108  Apr  5  14:33  file.1
-rw-r-----   1 robin     123  Apr  9  09:17  file.2
drwx-x----   2 robin     301  Mar 27  08:04  letters
drwx-x----   1 robin      87  Mar 15  13:42  memos
drwx-x----   2 robin     428  Mar 11  15:31  specs
$ _
```

We'll discuss this listing in greater detail in the next section. Here is a quick summary of the information given for each file or directory:

- Type of file: ordinary (-) or directory (d)
- Permissions (discussed in the next section)
- Number of **links** in the file system to other users
- Owner, or creator, of the file
- Size of the file in bytes (characters)
- Date and time of last modification of the file
- Name of the file.

## Changing Your Working Directory **cd**

To change your working directory (that is, to move to another directory), use the **cd** (change directory) command, as in

```
$ cd /usr/harold
$ _
```

If you have been given access, you can now operate within Harold's home directory. To return to your home directory from any other directory, use the **cd** command without a name following, as shown here:

```
$ cd
$ _
```



## *Finding Out the Name of Your Working Directory* pwd

To find out the name of your current working directory at any moment, use the **pwd** (print working directory) command, as in

```
$ pwd
/usr/robin
$ _
```

## *Creating a New Directory* mkdir

To create a new subdirectory within your current working directory, use the **mkdir** (make directory) command, as in

```
$ mkdir messages
$ _
```

This command will create a new subdirectory called *messages*. In setting up your home directory, try to find the right balance between too few subdirectories and too many. With too few, you fail to take advantage of the structure of the UNIX file system; with too many, you create a maze for yourself. Somewhere between five and 15 main subdirectories is usually optimal, but there may be exceptions.

## *Removing an Existing Directory* rmdir

To remove an existing directory from your working directory, move to the target directory, delete all its files, move back to the parent directory, and then use the **rmdir** (remove directory) command. For example, suppose you would like to delete a directory called *useless*. You could follow the procedure illustrated here:

```
$ cd /usr/useless      [Move to directory useless]
$ pwd                  [Make sure you are in the right directory]
/usr/useless
$ rm *                 [Delete all files in useless]
```

```
$ cd ..              [Move to the parent directory]
$ rmdir useless      [Delete directory useless—now empty]
$ _                  [The directory and its files are gone]
```

On many systems you may be able to use one of the following shorter methods instead of the above:

```
$ rm /usr/useless/*      [Delete all files in directory useless]
$ rmdir /usr/useless     [Delete directory useless]
$ _
```

```
$ rm -r /usr/useless     [Delete files in useless, then delete
$ _                       directory useless itself]
```

## *Renaming a Directory* **mv**

To change the name of a directory, use the **mv** (move) command. For example, to change the name of a directory from *old.name* to *new.name*, use this command:

```
$ mv old.name new.name
$ _
```

# File and Directory Permissions

As noted in Chapter 2, UNIX allows you to access other directories and files in the system, but only if you have permission from the owners of those directories and files. This section deals with the UNIX system of permissions, which apply to individual owners, groups of users, and other users.

## *Determining Permissions* **ls -l**

To determine the permissions associated with a given file or directory, use the **ls -l** command described in the previous section. The permissions are indicated by the nine characters that follow the first character:

```
$ ls -l
total 501
-rw-r-----   1 robin    108  Apr  5  14:33  file.1
-rw-r-----   1 robin    123  Apr  9  09:17  file.2
drwxr-x---   1 robin     87  Mar 15  13:42  memos
drwxr-x---   2 robin    301  Mar 27  08:04  letters
drw-rw----   1 robin    216  Mar  3  11:56  proposals
drw-r-----   2 robin    428  Mar 11  15:31  specs
```

The first character, as noted before, indicates the type of file:

- **-** ordinary file
- **b** block-type special file
- **d** directory
- **c** character-type special file

The remaining nine characters represent three sets of three characters: one set for the individual user (or **owner**), one for the user's working group (if any), and one for all other users. Taking the display in the example and spreading out the characters to show groupings, we get something like this:

**mv**
**ls-l**

| **Type** | **User** | **Group** | **Others** | |
|---|---|---|---|---|
| - (file) | r w - | r - - | - - - | file.1 |
| - (file) | r w x | r - x | - - - | file.2 |
| - (file) | r w x | r - x | - - - | memos |
| - (file) | r w - | r - - | r - - | letters |
| d (directory) | r w - | r w - | r w - | proposals |
| d (directory) | r w - | r - - | r - - | specs |

In each of these three groups of characters, there is one permission for reading, one for writing, and one for executing. *Reading, writing,* and *executing* have different meanings for ordinary files and directories:

For an **ordinary file:**

- **read** permission means you may look at the contents of the file
- **write** permission means you may change the contents of the file
- **execute** permission means you may type the name of the file in a command line as if the file were a UNIX command.

For a **directory:**

- **read** permission means you may see the names of the files in the directory
- **write** permission means you may add files to and remove files from the directory
- **execute** permission means you may change to the directory, search the directory, and copy files from it.

The characters used to represent these permissions are as follows:

- **r** read permission
- **w** write permission
- **x** execute permission
- **-** permission denied

Putting this all together, here are the nine characters for directory *memos* in the display above:

| **Owner** | **Group** | **Others** | **File** |
|---|---|---|---|
| `r w x` | `r - x` | `- - -` | `memos` |

This shows that the owner of *memos* has permission to read (*r*), write (*w*), and execute (*x*); members of the owner's group have permission to read (*r*) and execute (*x*), but not to write (-); and all other users are denied access of any kind (- - -).

Here are the nine characters for *file.1*:

| **Owner** | **Group** | **Others** | **File** |
|---|---|---|---|
| `r w -` | `r - -` | `- - -` | `file.1` |

This shows that the owner of *file.1* has permission to read (*r*) and write (*w*), but not to execute (-); members of the file's working group have permission only to read (*r*), but not to write (-) or execute (-); and all other users are denied access of any kind (- - -).

## *Changing Permissions* **chmod**

You can make changes to permissions by entering a **chmod** (change [access] mode) command. The **chmod** command allows the owner of the file to add (+) or remove (-) any of the three types of access for any of the three categories of UNIX users, using one letter symbols in the following order (left to right):

| | | | | | |
|---|---|---|---|---|---|
| **u** | owner (user) | + | add permission | **r** | to read |
| **g** | File's group | - | remove permission | **w** | to write |
| **o** | all others | = | absolute permission | **x** | to execute |
| **a** | all (default) | | | | |

For example, suppose you wanted to grant permission to write for members of your working group and permission to read and write for all other UNIX users for *file.1*. You could use these expressions in a **chmod** command:

**g+w** Add permission (+) to write (**w**) to your working group (**g**)

**o+rw** Add permission (+) to read (**r**) and write (**w**) to all other users (**o**)

Then, using the **ls -l** command to display "before" and "after," you could incorporate these expressions into a **chmod** command, as shown in the following sequence. Note: You must type the command line for **chmod** exactly as shown, with a comma between *g+w* and *o+rw* and no spaces surrounding the comma.

```
$ ls -l file.1
-rw-r-----   1 robin     108  Apr  5  14:33  file.1
$ chmod g+w,o+rw file.1
$ ls -l file.1
-rw-rw-rw-   1 robin     108  Apr  5  14:33  file.1
$ _
```

To remove permissions currently in effect, simply use a minus sign (-) in place of a plus sign (+), and then form a **chmod** command in the same way. For example, suppose you wanted to remove permission to write for members of your working group and permission to read and write for all other UNIX users for *file.1* (that is, revoke the permissions granted in the previous example). You could use these expressions in a **chmod** command: **chmod**

**g-w** Remove permission (-) to write (**w**) to your working group (**g**)

**o-rw** Remove permission (-) to read (**r**) and write (**w**) to all other users (**o**)

Then, using the **ls -l** command to display *before* and *after,* you could incorporate these expressions into a **chmod** command, as shown in the following sequence:

```
$ ls -l file.1
-rw-rw-rw-   1 robin     108  Apr  5  14:33  file.1
$ chmod g-w,o-rw file.1
$ ls -l file.1
-rw-r-----   1 robin     108  Apr  5  14:33  file.1
$ _
```

**Caution:** It's possible for you to lock yourself out of one of your own files with the **chmod**. Be careful when you type it.

## Summary of Chapter 3

After a brief introduction to file systems, this chapter discusses the structure of the UNIX file system, followed by basic procedures for working with files, directories, and permissions.

**What is a file system?** A computer file system may be compared to the filing system used in a library, where the card catalogue roughly corresponds to a **directory** and the books roughly correspond to **files**. In UNIX, a directory is also a file itself.

**A structured file system.** UNIX has a structured file system, with a primal directory called **root** at the top and at least five major directories branching out from the root directory. Five major directories are as follows:

**usr** the user directory

**bin** the directory for binary files

**dev** the directory for device files

**tmp** the directory for temporary files

**etc** the directory for miscellaneous files

Each UNIX user has a **home directory** in the **usr** directory (or in a user directory with another name). The name for this home directory is the same as the identifier with which the user logs on. The user may create as many subdirectories in his or her home directory as necessary.

**Naming directories and files.** The full pathname of every file begins with root (/), then includes the name of the major directory, followed by a subordinate directory, and so on, down to the name of the file itself.

**Rules for naming and accessing files.** The slash (/) is the symbol that represents the root directory. The slash is also used to separate directory names and the simple filename from each other, as in the example above. A simple filename consists of 1-14 characters other than the following (and control characters):

/ * ? " ' []

After you log in to your home directory, you can then move from one directory to another, provided you have permission. Any directory from which you are operating at a particular moment is known as your **working directory**, or **current directory**.

While a **full pathname**, like the one used above can be given from any directory, you can also use a **relative pathname**—a pathname relative to your current directory.

## *Working with Files*

**Creating a file.** To create an empty file, use the redirection symbol (>) in front of the name of the file.

**Displaying the contents of a file.** To display the contents of a file, use either **cat** or **more**.

**Combining files.** To combine, or concatenate, files, use the **cat** command with redirection of output to the target file (>).

**Renaming a file.** To rename a file, use the **mv** command, the old name, then the new name.

**Moving a file.** To move a file (or files) from one directory to another, use the **mv** command, the name(s) of the file(s), then the pathname of the new directory.

**Copying a file.** To make a copy of a file within the same directory, use the **cp** command this way:

```
$ cp original copy
```

To copy a file (or files) from one directory to another, use the **cp** command this way:

```
$ cp file_1 file_2 file_3 /usr/directory
```

**Deleting a file.** To delete a file (or files), use the **rm** command, followed by the name(s) of the file(s).

**Linking a file.** To **link** a file (that is, to attach a file to a different directory), use the **ln** command, giving the full pathname of the file being linked and optionally giving the file a different name for use in its new directory.

## *Using Wildcard Characters*

**Matching a character.** To match any single character in a filename, use a question mark (?) in the desired position.

**Matching specific characters.** To match one of a set of characters in a filename, enclose the character with square brackets ([ ]) in the desired position.

**Matching any number of characters.** To match any number of charcters in a filename, use an asterisk (*) in the desired position.

## *Working with Directories*

**Displaying the contents of a directory.** To display a sorted list of the names of all directories and files in your current directory, use the **ls** command (with **-l** for more details).

**Changing your working directory.** To change your working directory (that is, to move from one directory to another), use the **cd** command, followed by the name of the new directory (no name for your home directory).

**Finding out the name of your working directory.** To find out the name of your current working directory, use the **pwd** command.

**Creating a new directory.** To create a new subdirectory within your working directory, use the **mkdir** command.

**Removing an existing directory.** To remove an existing directory from your working directory, move to the target directory, delete all its files, move back to your working directory, and then use the **rmdir** command. (You may also be able to use **rmdir -r**.)

**Renaming a directory.** To change the name of a directory, use the **mv** command with the new name last.

## *File and directory permissions*

**Determining permissions.** To determine permissions associated with a file or directory, use the **ls -l** command. The first character indicates whether the entry is an ordinary file (-) or a directory (**d**). The next nine characters indicate whether permission to read (**r**), write (**w**), or execute (**x**) has been granted to the owner, the file's working group, or other users.

**Changing permissions.** To change permissions for a directory or file, use the **chmod** command, either adding (+) or removing (-) permission to read (**r**), write (**w**), or execute (**x**) for the owner (**u**), the file's group (**g**), all other users (**o**), or all users (**a**).

# 4

# Using UNIX Commands

Now that you are familiar with the UNIX file system, you are ready to learn more about UNIX commands. This chapter begins with a general discussion of command lines; then covers methods of interacting between UNIX processes; and concludes with descriptions of commands for displaying text on the screen, processing text files, and using line printers.

## Constructing a Command Line

### *Command Lines in General*

In general, a command consists of three parts, although not every command requires all three parts:

name of command        options        name(s) of file(s)

There isn't much to say about the command's name, except that most UNIX commands have short names. Command options are usually designated by a hyphen (or minus sign), followed by a single letter (sometimes called a **switch**). Sometimes you can type more than one letter after a single minus sign (to indicate multiple options); sometimes you can't. In a few instances, command options are designated by plus signs instead of minus signs. Many commands allow one or more input files to be named. (Output files are generally, but not always, designated by an output option switch like **-o**. Another method of designating an output file will be discussed later in this chapter.) The various options and filenames that follow the command are referred to collectively as **arguments**.

### *An Example*

As an example, consider the **ls** (list contents of directory) command, discussed in Chapter 3. The **UNIX Programmer's Manual** (or **UNIX**

**User's Manual**) shows 11 possible options for this command, which is described under *Syntax* as follows (spread out here with headings added for easier reading):

| **Name** | **Command Options** | **File(s)** |
|---|---|---|
| *ls* | *[ -ltasdrucifg ]* | *name . . .* |

The name of the command is **ls** (*list*). There are eleven different option switches you can use: **-l** (long format), **-t** (time of last modification), **-a** (all entries), **-s** (give size), **-d** (name only for directories), **-r** (reverse order), and so on (some of the others are unsuitable for this discussion). The brackets (which are not to be typed on a command line) indicate that all option switches are optional, never required. The compression of the 11 letters into a single word indicates that more than one letter can be typed after a single minus sign. (Don't bother trying to learn how to pronounce the word.) In the case of this command, some options turn off other options. Finally, the word *name*, followed by ellipses indicates that you can type at least one directory name after the options.

Given this information, here are a few of the command lines that can be constructed with the **ls** command:

| | |
|---|---|
| $ **ls** | List the contents of the current directory |
| $ **ls -l ..** | List the contents of the parent directory (long listing) |
| $ **ls -als /usr/paul** | List all entries (long listing), giving file sizes, of the contents of */usr/paul* |
| $ **ls -a /etc /bin** | List all entries in */etc*, then all entries in */bin* |

In this book, we won't even try to provide a complete description of each command. (The paragraph above doesn't come close to describing all the features of **ls**). It is the responsibility of the **UNIX Programmer's Manual** (or **UNIX User's Manual**) to provide this information. The purpose of this section is merely to make you aware of the structure of a command line (and also to show you how to interpret a syntax statement).

## Redirection of Input and Output

The entire operation of a computer can be summed up in three phases:

- Input—the user supplies a computer program with information to process
- Processing—the computer program performs a set of functions on the information received from the user

- Output—the computer program returns the results of processing to the user.

Although most of this takes place electronically, the basic procedure is similar to what happens when you step up to a window in a bank to make a deposit. You hand the teller an endorsed check with a deposit slip (input); the teller makes a record of the deposit and stamps a receipt (processing); then the teller hands you the stamped receipt to keep for your records (output).

When you deal with your computer through UNIX, it is common for you to submit input via your terminal's keyboard and to receive output via your terminal's video screen. In fact, UNIX regards your keyboard as its **standard input** and your screen as its **standard output**. For example, UNIX will ordinarily assume that the command **date** will be typed at your keyboard and that the information requested by **date** (date, day of the week, hour, minute, and second) is be be displayed on your screen.

However, with most UNIX commands, you can at any time **redirect** the input or output of a command. For example, you can have a UNIX command receive input from a file instead of from the keyboard. Or you can have a UNIX command send output to another terminal instead of to your own. (Keep in mind that UNIX regards peripheral devices like terminals as **files**.) The symbols used in a command line to request redirection are the *less than* sign (<) and the *greater than* sign (>) (SHIFT comma and SHIFT period, respectively, on most keyboards). You can think of these symbols as arrowheads pointing in the direction of the flow of information.

## *Redirection of Input*

As an example, the UNIX **mail** command that takes the text that you supply as input and places it in the directory of each user you name after *mail* in a command line. One way to send a letter to Mary, John, Sandy, and Paul would be to type the following after the UNIX shell prompt and then type the letter at your keyboard:

```
$ mail mary john sandy paul
```

Suppose you use the line editor **ed** to write your letter and then store the text in a file named *letter_5*. You could then send this letter to these same users on your UNIX system using the **mail** command with redirection of input. Then, to send your letter to Mary, John, Sandy, and Paul, you could type the following after the UNIX shell prompt and press RETURN:

```
$ mail mary john sandy paul < letter_5
```

The direction of the "arrowhead" tells you that *letter_5* is the input file, which is taking the place of your keyboard.

### Redirection of Output

Just as you can use the input symbol (<) to redirect **input**, you can also use the output symbol (>) to redirect **output**. For example, the command line

```
$ ls
```

will list all the files in your directory on your screen. UNIX also allows you to modify the command line

```
$ ls > files
```

to redirect the output of **ls** from your screen to a file named *files*. If *files* does not exist when you issue the **ls** command, it will be created by the shell; if *files* does already exist, its contents will be overwritten.

A common use of redirection of output is the joining together, or **concatenation** of several files, using the UNIX **cat** command. To concatenate files *file_1*, *file_2*, and *file_3* and store the resulting text in another file called *combine*, type the following after the UNIX shell prompt and press RETURN:

```
$ cat file_1 file_2 file_3 > combine
```

Then, to concatenate three more files and add the resulting text to *combine*, rather than overwrite it, use another redirection symbol (>>). For example, to concatenate *file_4*, *file_5*, and *file_6* and **add** the resulting text to *combine*, type the following after the UNIX shell prompt and press RETURN:

```
$ cat file_4 file_5 file_6 >> combine
```

If the file doesn't exist, >>, like >, causes the shell to create a new file; but if the file already exists, >> always adds to the end of it, never overwriting it.

## Pipelines

As noted in the previous section, UNIX regards the keyboard as the **standard input** and the video screen as the **standard output** for most commands being executed, or **processes**. (In UNIX terminology, a command that is currently being executed is called a **process**.) In addition to **redirection**, there is another way to alter the standard way of dealing with input and output: connecting two processes with a **pipe** (or **pipeline**), so that the output of one process becomes the input for another. The symbol for a pipe is the vertical bar (|), which is usually placed in different locations on different keyboards.

Ordinarily, if you wanted to use the output of one process as the input for another, you would have to go through a roundabout procedure. For example, suppose you had three small text files called *part_d*, *part_e*, and *part_f*. You would like to keep the files separate in UNIX, but when you print them on the lineprinter, you would like to see all the text on one page, rather than spread over three different pages. To accomplish this, first concatenate the files and store them in a fourth file:

```
$ cat part_d part_e part_f > temp_file
```

Then use this new file as input for the **lpr** command, which sends text to the lineprinter:

```
$ lpr temp_file
```

Finally, use the **rm** (remove) command to delete the temporary file that you used to store the combined files:

```
$ rm temp_file
```

With a pipeline, you can connect **cat** and **lpr** directly, eliminating the need for an intermediate file, like this:

```
$ cat part_d part_e part_f | lpr
```

The pipe symbol (|) allows you to take the output from **cat**, which otherwise would have gone either to a file or to the screen, and use it as the input for **lpr**. This will accomplish the desired result with one command line instead of three: the three files will be concatenated, then the resulting text will be sent to the lineprinter to be printed.

Commands that appear in pipe statements may include all the usual options and file designations. For example, the **pr** (print) command displays text on the screen. (The reason that it's called "print" instead of "display" is that the original terminals for UNIX were printing Teletype machines, not video display terminals.) In its modified form, the command **pr -4** displays text in four columns.

The **ls** (list) command provides a list of the files in your directory. To see a list of your files displayed on the screen in four columns, you could connect **ls** and **pr** with a pipe (|). Then include the four-column option (**-4**), along with the five-line option (**-5**) and the "throw out headers and footers" option (**-t**):

```
$ ls | pr -t -l5 -4
.excr        c_programs     grid          z1051
.profile     c_progs        link.mod      z1052
a.out        char.set_6     points        z1053
asm_progs    etc            termcap
bin          graphs         text_files
$ _
```

This gives you a nice, compact display. You will have to vary the number of lines (-l5, "el five") and columns (-4) according to the number of files in your directory, but the results will be similar. (Be sure the product of the number of lines and number of columns exceeds the number of files.) By adding the -t option, you can also get rid of a little extra clutter in the display.

You can also set up multiple pipelines. For example, to have your files printed in three columns on a line printer, rather than displayed on the screen (assuming you have more than 150 files in your directory), you could enter a command like this:

```
$ ls | pr -3 | lpr
```

In this command line, **ls** provides the list of files, **pr -3** formats the list in three columns, and **lpr** prints the formatted list on the line printer.

Having at your disposal all the commands of UNIX, plus the pipeline feature to connect them in various ways, is like sitting on the floor in front of a box of tinker toys. You can construct all kinds of clever new commands out of the existing commands. The combinations are endless. Here are a few more examples, using just a handful of commands: the **who** command to list all users currently logged on the system, the **sort** command to alphabetize lines of text, the **ls** command to list your files, and the **wc** (word count) command to count the number of lines, words, and characters in a file.

| Command Line | Purpose |
|---|---|
| `$ who \| sort` | To see a list of users in alphabetical order |
| `$ who \| wc` | To see how many users are currently logged on |
| `$ ls \| wc` | To see how many files are in your directory |

Note that, because of the way different commands work, many conceivable pipeline combinations are not possible to construct. For example, neither **who** nor **ls** could ever be on the receiving end of a pipe; these processes gather their information from within the system, never from external input. On the other hand, **lpr** could even be on the originating end of a pipe; this process must receive input to be able to function.

## Displaying Text on the Screen

In Chapter 3 you learned that you can use the **cat** (concatenate) command to display text on your screen. In this section you will learn more about **cat**, and also learn about other commands that you can also use to display text: **more**, **head**, **tail**, and **sp** (space).

## Entering Text into a File

**cat**

Using the concept of redirecting output, you can use the **cat** command to perform simple text entry. All you have to do is redirect the output of **cat** from the screen to a file. Then type the text, pressing CTRL-D after the last line to indicate to **cat** that you have no more to type. In the following example, we enter the text shown into a file called *enter*:

```
$ cat > enter
Here is a short message
to show what we can do
with the cat command.
                          [Press CTRL-D—nothing will be
                          displayed]
$ _
```

**cat**

Now we can use **cat** without redirection to display the text we have just entered:

```
$ cat enter
Here is a short message
to show what we can do
with the cat command.
$ _
```

If you are using a microcomputer with communications software as a terminal to a UNIX system, you can also use the **cat** command in the way just shown to **capture** text and store it on one of your own disk files. (This is also called **downloading** data.) Just start the capture feature in your communications program, log into UNIX, and execute a **cat** command like the one just shown to display text on the screen.

To send text from your microcomputer to UNIX (that is, to **upload** it), log into UNIX, move to the desired directory, and type a **cat** command line that will redirect output to the desired file, like this:

```
$ cat > micro.text
```

Then use the feature in your communications software that sends out the contents of a disk file, which should then be displayed on your screen. After all the text has been sent, remember to type **CTRL-D** to tell **cat** that you have no more text.

When you upload text to UNIX in this way, you may end up with undesired double-spacing. If this happens, don't worry. There's a C program presented in Chapter 10 that can help you. With a slight modification, this program will remove the unwanted blank lines for you. (The "slight modification" is to change *2* to *1* in line 12.)

## Displaying Text a Screen at a Time

**more**

A variation of the **cat** from Berkeley, called **more**, also displays text on your screen, but instead of letting the text race past you, it pauses after each screenful, displaying something like this on the bottom line:

```
--More-- (6%) _
```

Now you have several choices, such as these four:

- press the RETURN key to display one more line
- press the space bar to see the next screenful
- type /*text* to search for *text*
- type *Q* to exit.

## Displaying Part of a File

**head**
**tail**

A pair of commands, **head** and **tail**, allow you to display only the opening (or closing) segment of a file. (**head** is from Berkeley; **tail** is not.) Unless you request otherwise, the amount displayed will be ten lines. However, with either command, you can request another amount; with **tail** only, you can request an amount in characters (**c**), lines (**l**), or blocks (**b**). (A **block** in UNIX is usually 512 characters.) For example, to see only the last 17 characters of *enter*, you could use this:

```
$ tail -17c enter
the cat command.
$ _
```

## Spreading Out a Screen Display

**sp**

Sometimes you have a file that contains a long list of words (or numbers or something). If you try to display this file with **cat**, you see your words on the left side of the screen but nothing on the rest of the screen. You feel you'd like to use some of that open space on the screen to display your list, and view more items at the same time. Well, there's a UNIX command called **sp** (space) that can help you. By sending your text to **sp** via a pipeline, you can have it spread across the screen. Here is a brief example, using text you've already seen:

```
$ cat enter                    [without sp]
Here is a short message
to show what we can do
```

```
with the cat command.
$ _
$ cat enter | sp            [with sp]

Here is a short message to show what we can do  with the cat command.
$ _
```

more
head
tail
sp
file

The reason for the extra space after *do* is that **sp** positions items on tab stops, which are eight columns apart. You can use **sp** to view the names of all your files with **ls** at the same time:

```
$ ls | sp
begin   current file.1  file.2  file.3  file.4  file.5  garage.sale
help    late.items      memo_jan.23     memo_feb.12     memo_feb.17
memo_mar.06     notes   prep_d36a       prep_d36b       prep_d36c
prep_36d        quotes.wrap     quotes.build    quotes.dwgs
repair  store
$ _
```

# More on Working With Files

## *Determining the Contents of a File*

**file**

Sometimes we lose track of our files. We look at the directory and ask ourselves, "What's 'enter'? When did I create a file called 'enter'?" Most UNIX systems have a command called **file** that determines (or at least tries to determine) the general type of a file, which may give you some information about it very quickly. Here are three brief examples:

```
$ file enter
enter: English text
$ _

$ file ch.set_6
ch.set_6: ascii text
$ _

$ file FOCUS
FOCUS: commands text
$ _
```

This isn't an enormous amount of information about your file (and it isn't always correct), but at least it gives you something to start with.

## Sorting a File

**sort**

Sorting allows you to put lines of text in order. It is probably the most common form of text processing. For example, suppose you have used **cat** to enter two files named *fruits* and *animals* with the contents shown:

```
$ cat > fruits
bananas
oranges
apples
cherries
pears
                [CTRL-D]
$ _
```

```
$ cat > animals
horses
cats
dogs
birds
lizards
                [CTRL-D]
$ _
```

To sort *fruits* and display the results across the screen, use the **sort** command (with the results piped to **sp**):

```
$ sort fruits | sp
apples bananas cherries      oranges pears
$ _
```

To sort *animals* and display the results across the screen, use the **sort** command with **sp** again:

```
$ sort animals | sp
birds    cats    dogs    horses    lizards
$ _
```

As mentioned earlier, you can also sort the list of system users and display it on the screen this way:

```
$ who | sort
dave      tty11    Feb 2    15:56
elaine    tty04    Feb 3    09:58
manny     tty07    Feb 3    08:05
$ _
```

The **sort** command will be described in greater detail in Chapter 18, "Processing Text and Numbers."

## Dealing with Repeated Lines

**uniq**

Let's take an **extremely** simple example of a common task that often needs to be performed after you've sorted a list of items. Suppose that, for some strange reason, you decide to keep a list of the different animals that show up in your yard over a period of time. And, of course, you keep this list in a file on your UNIX system. (Ah, the wonders of modern technology! And you were wondering if you could find a good, practical reason to learn UNIX?)

Well, at the end of one eventful day, you rush to your terminal and add the following to your *animals* file:

```
$ cat >> animals       [Remember, two symbols (> >) to add text]
birds
raccoons
dogs
birds
cats
                       [Press CTRL-D—nothing will be displayed]
$ _
```

**sort**
**uniq**

Now comes the moment you've been waiting for: it's time to sort your list. Use the **sort** command (you don't want to use **sp** this time), and get the list on the left. If you don't want all those repeated items, you can pipe your list to a command called **uniq** to get the new list on the right.

```
$ sort animals
birds
birds             $ sort animals | uniq
birds             birds
cats              cats
cats              dogs
dogs              horses
dogs              lizards
horses            raccoons
lizards           $ _
raccoons
$ _
```

As you can see, the **uniq** command in its plainest form condenses a **sorted list** by listing each item only once, no matter how many times it appears in the original list.

The **uniq** command also has several options, one of which is to precede each item in the final list with the number of times it appeared in the original list (**-c**). Here is an example of **uniq** with the **-c** option:

```
$ sort animals | uniq -c
  3 birds
  2 cats
  2 dogs
  1 horses
  1 lizards
  1 raccoons
$ _
```

## *Preparing Text for Processing* **prep**

If you have a file with ordinary text in sentences and paragraphs and you would like to study the individual words in the file, you may be able to use the **prep** command (if it's available on your system) to list each word on a separate line. Here is an example, using a new file called *words*:

```
$ cat > words
The more you study, the more you learn.
                                   [CTRL-D]/

$ prep words
the
more
you
study          [The words are displayed without punctuation
the            or capitalization.]
more
you
learn
$ _
```

You could also sort this list and use **uniq** to determine how many times each word occurs in the file. First place each word on a separate line with **prep**; sort the list with the **sort** command; then get a count by word with **uniq** (using the **-c** (count) option):

```
$ prep words | sort | uniq -c
  1 learn
  2 more
  1 study
  2 the
  2 you
$ _
```

## *Counting Lines, Words, and Characters in a File* **wc**

Sometimes you need to have a few statistics on a file. If you're writing a program, you may want to know how many lines of code you have. If you're writing an article, you may want to know how many words you've written. The **wc** (word count) command tells you how many lines, words, and characters there are in a file (in that order). Words are assumed to be separated by either punctuation marks, spaces, tabs, or newlines. To obtain a complete count for *enter*, enter the following:

```
$ wc enter
          3      15      69 enter
$ _
```

If you would rather have one of the three numbers given by itself, you can use one of these options with the **wc** command:

- **-l** (lines only)
- **-w** (words only)
- **-c** (character only)

Here are examples of commands to obtain each of the separate counts:

```
$ wc -l enter
      3 enter   [There are 3 lines in enter]
$ wc -w enter
     15 enter   [There are 15 words in enter]
$ wc -c enter
     69 enter   [There are 69 character in enter]
$ _
```

## *Searching for a Pattern in a File* **grep**

If you need to find some key word or phrase in a file, you can use the **grep** command. In UNIX, any sequence of characters that you are looking for is called either a "search pattern" or a "regular expression." (If you're curious about such things, **grep** is an acronym that stands for "globally find regular expressions and print"—more or less. They didn't want to call it *gfreap,* so they settled on **grep.** Now you know.) For example, to display all lines in *enter* that contained the letters *cat,* you could use a command like this:

```
$ grep cat enter
with the cat command. [There was only one line.]
$ _
```

If you wanted to find out who was logged in on terminal *tty15,* you could use a command like this:

```
$ who | grep tty15
manny    tty15    Feb 3    10:05
$ _
```

Finally, suppose you have a file named *phone.list* that contains thousands of names, addresses, and phone numbers for employees in your company. Suppose that you are also trying to locate the entry for someone named Ted who works in the Los Angeles office. You could use **grep** to locate the desired entry with a command line like this:

```
$ grep Ted phone.list | grep 'Los Angeles'
Ted Peterson  1200 Fairfax Blvd., Los Angeles, CA 90104  (213) 657-1000
$ _
```

This command illustrates piping the result from a command to another instance of the same command. Note that Los Angeles required quotations marks because it is two separate words. The **grep** command will be discussed in greater detail in Chapter 18, "Processing Text and Numbers."

## *Finding Misspelled Words* **spell**

With the UNIX **spell** command, you can check spelling in a file by comparing the spelling of words against entries in a large on-line dictionary. In the process, you can also check derivatives of words in the dictionary. For example, suppose you have a file named *lines* that contains the following text:

```
$ cat > lines
Now is the tyme for all good men to
come to the ade of there country.
                                   [CTRL-D]
$ _
```

To check this file, use this command line:

```
$ spell lines
tyme
ade
$ _
```

Note that *there* isn't listed, even though it's incorrect. The **spell** program can determine whether a word is misspelled, but it can't determine whether or not the word is used correctly.

## *Comparing Files Line by Line* **diff**

There are many times when you find yourself with one copy of a file and also an *updated* version in the same directory. *Which one is more recent? Are they the same?* you ask yourself. One UNIX command that can help you is **diff**. To show how it works, let's create a simple file called *wildlife.1*, then modify it to create a second file called *wildlife.2*:

```
$ cat > wildlife.1
1 antelope
2 bear
3 coyote
4 deer
5 elk
```

```
$ cat > wildlife.2
1 antelope
2 buffalo
3 coyote
4 elk
5 fox
```

Comparing these two files with **diff**, we get the output shown below, which indicates how the second file differs from the first:

```
$ diff wildlife.1 wildlife.2

2c2              [Line 2 has been changed:
< 2 bear           • The first file (<) contains 2 bear
---
> 2 buffalo        • The second file (>) contains 2 buffalo]
4,5c4,5          [Lines 4 and 5 have been changed:
< 4 deer           • Line 4 of the first file is 4 deer
< 5 elk            • Line 5 of the first file is 5 elk
---
> 4 elk            • Line 4 of the second file is 4 elk
> 5 fox            • Line 5 of the second file is 5 fox
$ _
```

The **diff** program uses *c* to indicate a change, *d* to indicate a deletion, and *a* to indicate an addition, along with < to indicate a line in the first file and > to indicate a line in the second file. The hyphens (---) are inserted when a line from the first file is compared with a line from the second.

The **diff** command also has several options, such as ignoring blank spaces in the two files (**-b**) and providing a list of the **ed** commands required to change the first file to the second (**-e**). We'll have to move on now to another command for comparing files.

## *Displaying Lines Common to Two Files* **comm**

To obtain a different view of the differences between two files, you can use the **comm** (common) command. This command displays three columns on the screen, one for lines unique to the first file, a second for lines unique to the second, and a third for lines common to the two files. Here is how the output for **comm** would look for *wildlife.1* and *wildlife.2*:

```
$ comm wildlife.1 wildlife.2
                    1 antelope    [Common to both files]
2 bear                            [First file only]
          2 buffalo               Second file only]
```

```
                    3 coyote       [Common to both files]
4 deer                             [First file only]
          4 elk                    [Second file only]
5 elk                              [First file only]
          5 fox                    [Second file only]
$ _
```

As you can see, the three columns give you a graphic display that is easy to read. (If you look closely, though, you see that **comm** made a mistake: it first listed *elk* as being unique to *wildlife.2*, then as being unique to *wildlife.1*.) The **comm** command also allows you to suppress a column (or a pair of columns), using **-1** to suppress the first column, **-2** to suppress the second column, **-3** to suppress the third column, and combinations like **-13** to suppress the first and third columns. Here is how you could select lines common to both files (third column):

```
$ comm -12 wildlife.1 wildlife.2
1 antelope [Common to both files]
3 coyote   [Common to both files]
           [We missed elk again]
$ _
```

The option **-12** ("minus one two") in the above example told **comm** to suppress the first and second columns (that is, to output only the third column).

For comparison of program files, you may also be interested in the **cmp** command, which compares two files **character by character (byte by byte)**.

## *Translating Characters* **tr**

There may be times when you will want to change certain characters every place they occur in a file. For example, suppose you have used numbers to indicate the steps of a procedure you have written. Then you decide (or possibly you receive a request) to use letters of the alphabet instead. With the **tr** command, you can make the change fairly easily. Here's a file:

```
$ cat > five. steps
1. Turn on the machine.
2. Start the program.
3. Request the P option.
4. End the program.
5. Turn off the machine.
                          [CTRL-D]
$ _
```

To make the translation described, type the command (*tr*), a space, the set of characters to be translated, another space, then the set of characters into which to translate the original characters (in the order desired), using redirection to accept the input from *five.steps*:

```
$ tr 12345 abcde < five.steps
a. Turn on the machine.
b. Start the program.
c. Request the P option.
d. End the program.
e. Turn off the machine.
$ _
```

tr

This **tr** command translated *1* into *a*, *2* into *b*, *3* into *c*,and so on. On many systems, **tr** would allow you to use range notation to enter the command this way to accomplish the same thing:

```
$ tr 1-5 a-e < five.steps
a. Turn on the machine.
b. Start the program.
c. Request the P option.
d. End the program.
e. Turn off the machine.
$ _
```

If so, you could use the following **tr** command to translate all lowercase letters into uppercase letters:

```
$ tr a-z A-Z < five.steps
1. TURN ON THE MACHINE.
2. START THE PROGRAM.
3. REQUEST THE P OPTION.
4. END THE PROGRAM.
5. TURN OFF THE MACHINE.
$ _
```

This **tr** command line translates *a* into *A*, *b* into *B*, *c* into *C*, and so on. If your system doesn't allow this kind of range notation, you can place the two ranges within pairs of brackets (and then place the brackets within double quotation marks to keep them from being interpreted as parts of the sets of characters), as shown here:

```
$ tr "[a-z] [A-Z]" < five.steps
1. TURN ON THE MACHINE.
2. START THE PROGRAM.
3. REQUEST THE P OPTION.
4. END THE PROGRAM.
5. TURN OFF THE MACHINE.
$ _
```

We can also use the **tr** command to delete characters by including the **-d** (delete) option. For example, we could use the following command to delete the step numbers:

```
$ tr -d 12345 < five.steps
. Turn on the machine.
. Start the program.
. Request the P option.
. End the program.
. Turn off the machine.
$ _
```

On the other hand, if we wanted to delete the explanations and just leave the step numbers, we could also include the **-c** (complement) option to delete everything **except** the numbers:

```
$ tr -cd 12345 < five.steps
12345$ _
```

The reason that the numbers (and the prompt) appear together on the same line is that the characters that separate lines from each other (called **newlines** in UNIX) have been deleted along with the visible characters. Here's a similar command line. See if you can explain what is happening here:

```
12345$ tr -cd A-Z < five.steps
TSRPET$ _
```

In the two examples above, the two options **c** and **d** were placed together behind the same minus sign. In UNIX, this is referred to as **bundling** options. Some UNIX commands allow bundling of options, some do not.

The **tr** command also has a *squeeze* option that you can use to compress characters.

## Using Line Printers

You can use the UNIX command **lpr** to print the contents of a file on the system line printer. (Actually, the file is placed in a queue, and, depending on system demand for printing, won't necessarily be printed immediately.) For example, to print the contents of a file called *section_4*, you could use

```
$ lpr section_4
$ _
```

## Variations of the Command — lpr

Using some of the techniques you learned earlier in this chapter, you can do more than just print one file on the lineprinter. You can also print a series of files like this:

```
$ lpr section_1 section_2 section_3
$ _
```

lpr
lpr
ls-l

By piping text from **pr** to **lpr**, you can take advantage of some the formatting options of **pr** before starting to print. For example, to paginate text and arrange it in two columns before printing, you could use

```
$ pr -2 text_5 | lpr
$ _
```

Using two pipes, one from **sort** to **pr** and another from **pr** to **lpr**, you could sort and paginate lines of text in a file before printing:

```
$ sort data_15 | pr | lpr
$ _
```

## Options for the Command — lpr

Two of the options available for the **lpr** command can be helpful. The **-c** (copy) option makes a copy of the text to be printed, as a precaution against loss of the text in the queue like this:

```
$ lpr -c section_5
$ _
```

The **-m** (mail) option (if available on your system) reports to you by mail when your printing job has been completed, like this:

```
$ lpr -m section_5
$ _
```

## Finding Out What Is Queued for Printing — ls -l

In a multi-user system like UNIX, you have to share the system's resources (like the line printer and the disk drives) with other users. Therefore, UNIX must have procedures to arrange for sharing. For example, any time you initiate the **lpr** command to print a file, **lpr** places the name of the file in a queue. It's just like waiting in line at a bank. The names of the files are moved through the queue as the files are printed one at a time. Once a file has been printed, its name is removed from the queue.

The queue is kept in a UNIX directory, and the name of the directory is often */usr/spool/lpd*. Therefore, to find out which files are currently in the queue for printing, all you have to do is to display the contents of this directory file on your screen, using the **ls** (list) command (with the **-l** (long) option added here to give more detailed information):

```
$ ls -l /usr/spool/lpd
total 40
-rw-rw-r-- 1 robin   19658   Jul 3 09:39 cfA25956
-rw-rw-r-- 1 robin      50   Jul 3 09:39 dfA25956
---------- 1 robin       0   Jul 3 09:39 lock
```

It's possible that someone may have set up a shorter command for your system. Check with your system administrator to find out.

## Summary of Chapter 4

In this chapter you have learned about command lines, redirection and pipelines, and commands for displaying text, working with files, and using line printers.

**Constructing Command Lines.** To begin a **process** under UNIX, type a command line and press RETURN. The command may contain either just the command by itself or the command plus modifiers.

### *Redirection and Pipelines*

**Redirection in general.** Unless you instruct UNIX otherwise, UNIX regards your keyboard as its **standard input** and your video screen as its **standard output**. But you can **redirect** either input or output elsewhere.

**Redirection of input.** To have a UNIX command take its input from a file, instead of from your keyboard, use the *less than* sign (<) in front of the name of the file.

**Redirection of output.** To have a UNIX command send its output to a file, instead of to your video screen, use the *greater than* sign (>) in front of the name of the file. If the file does not exist, it will be created; if it does exist, it will be overwritten.

To **add to** the contents of the output file, rather than overwrite the contents of the file, use a pair of *greater than* signs (> >) in front of the name of the file.

**Pipelines.** To connect two processes, so that the output of one becomes the input of the other, use the vertical bar (|) between the names of the commands (with or without surrounding spaces).

## *Displaying Text on the Screen*

**Uses for cat.** You can use the **cat** command for entering text into a file, downloading to your microcomputer, or uploading to UNIX.

**Other display programs.** If you have Berkeley features on your UNIX system, you can use **more** to display text one screenful at a time, **head** to display only the opening lines of the text, or **tail** to display only the closing lines.

## *More on Working with Files*

**Determining the contents of a file.** To determine what kind of characters are in a file, you can use the **file** command.

**Sorting a file.** To sort a file by lines, use the **sort** command, followed by the name of the file. As with many other commands, the results of the **sort** command can also be redirected to a new file.

In addition, **sort** can receive its input from the standard input (the keyboard) or another command via a pipe.

**Dealing with repeated lines.** To eliminate repeated lines in a sorted list, use the **uniq** command. One option of this command (**-c**) also gives you an item count.

**Preparing text for processing.** To have each word of text in a file placed on a separate line for further processing, use the **prep** command. One option of this command (**-d**) also precedes each word with a number.

**Counting lines, words, and characters in a file.** To obtain the total number of lines, words, and characters in a file, use the **wc** command either by itself to display all three statistics or with one of three options (**-l**, **-w**, **-c**) to display one. (Combinations such as **-lw** and **-wc** are also allowed.)

**Searching for a pattern in a file.** To search for a pattern in a file, use the **grep** command, followed by the pattern and then the name of the file. You can also pipe input from another command (in which case the filename becomes unnecessary).

**Finding misspelled words in a file.** To see a list of misspelled words in a file, use the **spell** command, followed by the name of the file.

**Comparing two files.** To compare the contents of two files line by line, use the **diff** command. (There is also a program called **diff3** that compares three files at a time and another called **cmp** that compares two files character by character.)

**Finding common lines.** To determine which lines are common and which are unique to each of two files, use the **comm** (common) command.

**Translating characters.** To translate one set of characters into another set, use the **tr** command. You can also use this command to delete characters.

## *Using Line Printers*

**The basic command.** To have a file sent to the system's line printer to be printed, use the **lpr** command, followed by the name of the file(s).

**Variations of the command.** You can also use other commands and pipes with **lpr** to format the output before printing it.

**Options for the command.** The **-c** (copy) option informs **lpr** to make a copy before printing; the **-m** (mail) option informs **lpr** to notify you by mail when printing has completed.

**Finding out what is queued for printing.** To find out which files have been queued for printing on the line printer, use the **ls -l** command to examine directory */usr/spool/lpd*.

# 5

# Communication with UNIX

mail

In this chapter you will learn how to communicate within and outside of UNIX. We'll start by communicating with other users on your own system, then discuss communicating with other UNIX systems.

## Communicating With Other Users

To allow various forms of communication between users on the same system, UNIX provides three facilities: electronic mail, an automatic reminder service, and direct messages.

### *Sending Mail* **mail**

To send electronic mail to any user on your UNIX system, use the **mail** command. Just type mail, a space, the other user's identifier, and press RETURN. For example, to send a message to Janice, you could use

```
$ mail janice
```

Once you have pressed the RETURN key, UNIX may respond with a *Subject* prompt on the next line (Berkeley versions). If so, type the subject of your message, press RETURN, and begin typing the text. Type a period and press RETURN after the last line of text to conclude the message and return to the shell prompt. If there is no *Subject* prompt, just begin your message. Here is an example:

```
$ mail ralph laura peter sara
Subject: Design Review Meeting [This line may not appear]
There will be a meeting at 2:00 pm today to review the design
of the Rattlesnake. Bring the specifications you received from
```

```
Engineering last week.
.
$ _
```

Each recipient will be notified of the existence of this message when he or she logs on.

## Receiving Mail

**mail**

If another user has sent you any mail, you will see the message

```
You have mail
```

the next time you log on. This is known as the You have mail **message.** To find out what has arrived, type the **mail** command without any arguments:

```
$ mail
```

The *mail* command will then display a heading for each item you have received. Press RETURN to see the text of the first item displayed. Then press RETURN each time you are ready to read the next item (or type *d* to delete the item you have just read or type *p* to repeat the item). There are many other options too numerous to discuss here. So refer to the **UNIX User's Manual** for information about them.

One way to set up a reminder system is to use the **mail** command to send messages to yourself. Here is an example:

```
$ mail robin
Subject: Self-Improvement                [This line may not appear]
Avoid falling asleep when Wally starts talking about his pet frog,
avoid talking in a loud, boisterous voice, and avoid arguments.

.                                        [A period ends the message]
$ _
```

## Automatic Reminder Service

**calendar**

Another way to remind yourself of things is to use the automatic reminder service that UNIX provides with the **calendar** command. At a regular interval (usually daily), UNIX uses the **calendar** command to examine each user's home directory for a file named *calendar,* whose contents may look something like this:

```
Mar 21   Planning meeting at 9:30 in the conference room
Apr 17   Jennifer's wedding in Hendersonville
```

```
Apr 28   Awards dinner at the Blackjack Inn
May 3    Presidential primary
```

Other forms of dates, such as *March 21* and *3/21*, are also allowed. The **calendar** command extracts from this file each line that contains either today's date or tomorrow's date and mails it to you. You can also call up the **calendar** manually like this:

```
$ calendar
```

UNIX will search your home directory for a file named *calendar* to look for any pertinent items to display.

**mail**
**calendar**
**write**

## *Writing Directly to a User* **write**

The **write** command allows you to send a message directly to another user's terminal, where it will immediately appear on the screen. Here is an example of initiation of a **write** command, which is similar to sending mail:

```
$ write paul
How are you doing on your project? -o-
                        [CTRL-D—not displayed on the screen]
$ _
```

Here is what Paul will see on his screen immediately after this command line is initiated:

```
Message from robin tty07
How are you doing on your project? -o-
EOF
```

At this point, Paul can respond with a **write** command of his own, and begin a terminal-to-terminal dialogue:

```
$ write robin
It's about two-thirds completed. How about yours? -o-
                        [CTRL D—not displayed on the screen]
$ _
```

To avoid confusion during a dialogue (that is, wondering if the other party is about to say more), you can set up a simple protocol to let the other party know when you have completed your current message. For example, each user could type *-o-* for *over* at the end of each message and *-oo-* for *over and out* at the conclusion of the dialogue.

If you're the kind of fun-loving person who can't resist pulling pranks on other users, then **write** is one command you'll want to add to your repertoire immediately. Unfortunately, however, there is also a command called **mesg** that allows people who are less fun-loving to shut out **write** messages. All they have to do is to add the **n** (no) option, and the fun is over:

```
$ mesg n
$ _
```

To allow **write** messages again, add the **y** (yes) option, and you're back in business:

```
$ mesg y
$ _
```

Finally, to find out whether **write** messages are allowed or prohibited on your terminal at a given moment, type **mesg** without an argument:

```
  $ mesg
{ 0  yes   }
{ 1  no    }   [Three responses possible]
{ 2  error }
$ _
```

## Communicating Outside Your System

You can communicate with someone outside your UNIX system with one of two different UNIX commands: **cu** (call up) and **uucp** (UNIX-to-UNIX copy). Before you can use either of these commands, your system administrator must first set up certain system files and connect the different systems with the necessary cabling. We'll take the two commands one at a time.

### *Calling Outside Your UNIX System* — cu

The **cu** (call up) command allows you to dial a telephone number (or use a direct connection via wire) and talk to one of the following:

- another UNIX system
- a terminal
- a non-UNIX system.

Once a connection is established, you can carry on an interactive conversation as if you were using a terminal connected directly to the other system and possibly transfer files back and forth. If the telephone number of the other system is 345-6000 and both sides are set up to communicate at a speed of 1200 bit/s, you could type this:

```
$ cu 3456000 -s 1200
```

With connection established, you will probably see a login message:

```
login: _
```

You can now log into the other system as you would log into your own. Having logged in, you can use cu to send a file called *message* to the other side with a command like this:

```
~<message
```

If you are connected to another UNIX system, the **stty** (set teletype [terminal]) command on both systems specifies the same characters for *erase* and *kill*, and the **cat** command is active on both systems. Another way to send *message* to the other side is to type a command like this:

**cu**
**uucp**

```
~%put message
```

If you are connected to another UNIX system and the **echo** and **tee** commands are active on both systems, you can copy a file on the other to your working directory with a command like this:

```
~%take reply
```

To conclude your conversation, type one of the following:

```
~.
```

```
~CTRL-D
```

## *UNIX-to-UNIX Copying*

**uucp**

In Chapter 3 you learned about the **cp** (copy) command that you can use to make a copy of a file either in your working directory or in another directory. There is a similar command called **uucp** (UNIX-to-UNIX copy) that you can use to copy a file to or from another UNIX system. For example, if two microcomputers called *CATFISH* and *MOONDOG* both belong to a common network, then a user can execute a command like this from *CATFISH*:

```
$ uucp latest MOONDOG!/usr/robin/news
$ _
```

This command will take the contents of a file called */usr/leslie/latest* on CATFISH (assuming that **/usr/leslie** is the current directory) and make a copy called */usr/robin/news* on MOONDOG. An exclamation point (!) is used to separate the name of the microcomputer from the name of the file. Otherwise, **uucp** is quite similar to **cp**. Note that if you're using the C shell, you have to type a backslash (\) in front of each exclamation point, as shown here:

```
% uucp latest MOONDOG\!/usr/robin/news
% _
```

If you don't know the exact name of the recipient's directory, you can use a tilde (~) in front of the recipient's user name to have **uucp** search for the directory, as shown here:

```
$ uucp latest MOONDOG!~robin/news
$ _
```

To have **uucp** mail the originator a message after the copy has been made, include the **-m** option in the command line, as shown here:

```
$ uucp -m latest MOONDOG!~robin/news
$ _
```

To have **uucp** also mail the recipient a message after the copy has been made, add the **-n** option with the recipient's user name appended (if this option is available on your system), as shown here:

```
$ uucp -m -nrobin latest MOONDOG!~robin/news
$ _
```

In the following example, a user logged into MOONDOG transfers all files whose names end in the suffix *.c* to a directory named */usr/leslie* on CATFISH. (Since source programs in the **C** language have names like list.c, post.c, enter.c, and so on, this user is sending all the C programs in the user's working directory.)

```
$ uucp *.c CATFISH!/usr/leslie
$ _
```

Since the user who executed this command was logged into MOONDOG when the command was executed, it wasn't necessary for the user to type *MOONDOG!*. However, *MOONDOG!*.c* also would have been correct in place of **.c*. (The wildcard construction shown here may not be allowed on all UNIX systems.)

Actually, **uucp** is just one of a family of UNIX commands. Another member of the family is **uux** (UNIX-to-UNIX execute), which can be used to execute commands on another computer in the network. For example, to format the contents of a file called **raw.text** and then have it printed on MOONDOG's printer, you could execute a command like this from another computer in the network:

```
$ pr -2 raw.text | uux - MOONDOG!lpr
$ _
```

Except for the **uux** command, the hyphen, the name of the other computer, and the exclamation point (*uux - MOONDOG!*), this command is quite similar to a command for performing the same function on your own system. (The hyphen tells **uux** to take data from the pipe and send it to the other system.)

Although it is quite simple to execute commands like these once a network has already been set up, the task of setting up the original network is much more complex. Unfortunately, we won't be able to cover that in this book. At least you are now aware of these programs and some of their possible uses. Note that the **uucp** network, with over 3,000 sites, is tied into other networks, such as Ethernet and ARPANET.

## *Encrypting Information* crypt

crypt

If you have sensitive information that you would like to keep secret, you may want to consider encrypting certain files with the UNIX **crypt** command. In general, an encryption program takes the original text that you provide (the **cleartext**), transforms it with a sequence of characters (the **key** or **password**), and produces an encrypted version of the original (the **cyphertext**). You will have to remember the key (or write it down on a slip of paper) to be able to retrieve the cleartext at a later time.

### *Encrypting a File*

First we need a file that contains text. Let's use the **cat** command to enter the following. (I know, you're going to say that this text has already been encrypted.)

```
$ cat > remark
''I would not like to make a value judgment on that
other than to say that I have no comment.''
                              --Alexander Haig     [Four tabs]
                                       [CTRL-D to terminate text]
$ _
```

Now use the **crypt** command to perform the actual encryption, to which UNIX will respond immediately with a request for the key. We'll use *convolution.*

```
$ crypt < remark > remark.crypt
Enter key: convolution         [You won't see the key on the screen]
```

Redirection is used on this command line for both input and output. The **crypt** takes its input from the file you just typed (*remark*), then sends its output to a file called *remark.crypt.*

The next logical step is to remove the original file (*remark*); otherwise, it doesn't make much sense to have it encrypted:

```
$ rm remark
$ _
```

Don't let curiosity get the better of you and try to take a peek at *remark.crypt.* You'll just cause trouble for your terminal, which will probably beep and go blank trying to read the various things in the file.

## Viewing the Cleartext

To view the cleartext on the screen at a later time, use the crypt command again with the same key:

```
$ crypt < remark.crypt
Enter key: convolution          [The key won't appear on the screen]
''I would not like to make a value judgment on that
other than to say that I have no comment.''
                                    --Alexander Haig
$ _
```

## Printing the Cleartext

To print the cleartext on the system's line printer at a later time, use the **crypt** command with the same key, sending the output through **pr** to **lpr** via pipelines:

```
$ crypt < remark.crypt | pr | lpr
Enter key: convolution          [The key won't appear on the screen]
$ _
```

## Comments on Encrypting Files

The security of an encrypted file depends to a large degree on the invulnerability of the key that you select. For our simple example here, we have not really made a very good choice. If you really want your encrypted files to be secure, you should select a complex string of characters that cannot be readily determined. Here are two excellent candidates:

```
H7u_%3Sa:Ym5-x#p
,6gU*W1+ce5Q'')T\v;Kz
```

It goes without saying, but we'll say it anyway: If you're concerned about your encrypted files, don't store your key anywhere on the UNIX system. Either memorize it or write it on an unmarked slip of paper.

Both of the major UNIX text editors (**ed** and **vi**) have features for handling encrypted files.

# Some of the Basics of Communication

If you drive a car, it's very difficult to avoid terms like *disc brakes, rack-and-pinion steering, turbo-charger,* and so on. Likewise, as soon as you begin to think about using a computer, you find yourself confronted with new terms. Often the most perplexing terms for many people seem to be related to communication. For those interested, here are a few basic concepts. This is the *spinach* of the book: you may not enjoy it too much, but it will be good for you.

## Units of Information

The smallest amount of information that a computer handles is a binary digit (or **bit**), which can be one of two things: 1 or 0, in the language of the software engineers who write programs; high or low, in the language of the hardware engineers who design the machinery. At any rate, 8 of these bits form a **byte**, which is the unit by which information is usually stored in a computer. A byte corresponds to one character (of text, of data, or of program code).

Inside the computer, information is sent in groups of bits, depending on the machine's design capacity. For most microcomputers, information is sent in groups of 8, 16, or 32 bits at a time. Outside the computer, information may be sent either in groups of bits (**parallel** transmission) or one bit at a time (**serial transmission**).

## Communicating with Local Devices

A computer is constantly communicating. Every computer spends a considerable percentage of its time sending messages back and forth to various pieces of equipment. From the computer's point of view, the disk drives, printers, and terminals connected to it are external, or *peripheral,* devices. There must be something connecting them together, and there must be a common method for exchanging messages.

Any device in the same building can usually be connected to a computer with a cable (either parallel or serial). To make things a little easier for everyone, most computers and peripheral devices have plugs for widely-accepted types of cable connectors. One type of serial connector commonly used is called an **RS-232C** connector. The "RS" stands for "recommended standard," and the *232C* is the designator that some committee came up with. Your printer and terminal may both be attached with these cable connectors.

A newer **RS-422/423** standard is beginning to overtake **RS-232C** in serial transmission as we approach the mid 1980s.

## Communicating with Remote Devices

A computer can also be connected with another computer or a terminal at another location. However, since most people don't have miles of cables lying around (and since the cable wouldn't be able to carry signals far enough anyway), something else has to be used. That something is the vast network of cables used to handle telephone service.

There's one slight problem, however. Computers and telephones don't use the same kind of signals. Computers use **digital** signals, while telephones use **analog** signals. To see what this means, compare a watch with number displays to a watch with moving hands. The watch with number displays uses **digital** signals to tell us the time; the watch with moving hands uses **analog** signals. As another example, compare a thermometer with number displays (digital) to a thermometer with a column of mercury (analog).

We have a solution to the the problem of differences between computers and telephones, however: an electronic device that converts digital signals to analog (modulator) and also converts analog signals back to digital (demodulator). This modulator/demodulator is usually called a **modem** for short (or a **data set**). According to some predictions, around the beginning of the 21st century, a large part of the telephone system will have been converted to digital operation, and modems will be obsolete.

## Compatibility

Whether a cable or a telephone is used to connect them, a computer and another device must be in agreement about a number of things before they can start sending messages back and forth to each other: they have to be sending and receiving by the same timing method, at the same speed, with the same protocol, in the same **duplex mode**, and in the same coding system. Let's take a quick look at each of these, one at a time.

## Timing Method

One problem a computer must solve when it sends information back and forth is how to determine where a character (or byte) in transit begins and ends. One solution, usually used by larger computers, is to have both sides send messages back and forth to synchronize the transmission, and then release a continuous stream of information. This is called **synchronous** communication.

Another method, usually used by small computers and printers, is to *wrap* each individual byte between a pair of bits (a **start bit** and a **stop**

**bit**). This method, used where characters are usually sent sporadically and at irregular intervals, is called **asynchronous** (or **start-stop**) communication.

Another term used here relates to error-checking during transmission. An extra bit is often added to the character, start, and stop bits (the **parity bit**). The object is to make the total number of bits either even (**even parity**) or odd (**odd parity**).

## *Data Rate*

**Data rate** (often referred to incorrectly as **baud rate**) is the speed at which a computer sends or receives information. This speed is measured in bits per second (bit/s), and is sometimes classed as **slow** (110, 150, 300, or 600 bit/s), **medium** (1200, 1800, 2400, 3600, or 4800 bit/s), or **high speed** (9600 and 19,200 bit/s). A data rate of 1200 is the most common speed used by microcomputers today.

## *Protocol*

Communication requires a set of rules to determine which side is supposed to send information and when. On larger computers, such a set of rules is called a **protocol** (or **line discipline**), and is based on synchronous transmission. Such protocols are classed as either **byte-synchronous** or **bit-synchronous**. One byte-synchronous protocol, IBM's BSC (binary synchronous communication), uses timing signals from the sending and receiving sides to synchronize groups of characters being transmitted. One bit-synchronous protocol, IBM's SDLC (synchronous data link control), relies on standard data formats for synchronization.

On smaller, asynchronous computers, the protocol is often implemented within an application program. One of the most common protocols is called **XON/XOFF**. By this method, the sending side continues to send information until a temporary storage area (or **buffer**) on the receiving side approaches capacity. The recipient sends an XOFF signal to the sending side to halt transmission momentarily. Then, when the recipient's buffer gets low, it sends an XON signal to the sending side asking for more.

## *Transmission Mode*

The directional capability of the line connecting two commmunicating parties can be classed as

- **simplex**, meaning that transmission is possible in one direction only (similar to a one-way street)

- **half-duplex**, meaning that the two sides may take turns sending to each other, but that transmission may take place in only one direction at a time (similar to a street that is either one-way south or one-way north, depending on a flagman's directions.)
- **full-duplex**, meaning that transmission may take place in both directions at the same time (similar to a two-way street).

In discussing terminals, duplex mode is part of another issue: What happens to the characters you type at the keyboard? There are only two choices for a terminal: Process the characters locally at the terminal or send them to the host computer for processing. When a terminal processes only, it is said to be in **block mode**; when it transmits to the host only, it is said to be in **full-duplex mode**. When it does both, it is said to be in **half-duplex mode**; when it does neither, it is said to be **locked**. On the UNIX system, communication with terminals is typically carried out in **full-duplex mode**.

## *Coding System*

The final topic relates to the way information is coded by a computer. You may have learned Morse code at some time; it's a coding system that assigns one code for each letter of the alphabet. The entire operation of a computer and its related devices (including communication between them) is carried out through codes. Every letter of the alphabet, every number, and every instruction is known to a computer by a code.

Large computers use IBM's EBCDIC (extended binary-coded decimal interchange code), an 8-bit system with a total of 256 codes. Smaller computers use ASCII (American Standard Code for Information Interchange), a 7-bit system with a total of 128 codes. The entire coding system includes all the display characters found on a typewriter-style keyboard (letters, numbers, and symbols), plus a collection of control characters. Here is how a typical ASCII code looks when we represent it in binary digits (bits):

1101001

Since this isn't very easy to read, people usually represent numbers like this in a different number system. Our decimal system (base 10) is a little difficult to translate to binary (base 2), so it's customary to use either octal (base 8) or hexadecimal (base 16) to represent ASCII codes. Here's how all four systems look side-by-side for the letter *i*.

| Binary | Octal | Hexadecimal | Decimal | Symbol |
|---|---|---|---|---|
| 1101001 | 151 | 69 | 105 | i |

The five columns you see above show five different ways to interpret the same character. These are the codes used by UNIX, usually interpreted in octal (base 8). If you type *i* at your keyboard, the computer sees only *1101001* transmitted, although we could write this code in any of the number systems shown.

## The ASCII Table

Individual characters like *i* are customarily arranged in four columns of 32 characters each (or in eight columns of 16 characters). So far we have focused on one character (*i*). To gain a little more perspective, let's look at a complete row of ASCII characters from a table—the row that contains *i*. We'll assume that this is a four-column ASCII table.

| | | | | | | | |
|---|---|---|---|---|---|---|---|
| HT | 011 | ) | 051 | I | 111 | i | 151 |

Here we see four entries, each followed by its octal representation:

| | | |
|---|---|---|
| HT (horizontal tab) | octal code 011 | (commonly known as *TAB*) |
| ) (right parenthesis) | octal code 051 | |
| I (uppercase I) | octal code 111 | |
| i (lowercase i) | octal code 151 | |

There are several things to note about this arrangement of characters:

- Uppercase I and lowercase i are listed side-by-side on the same row
- I, i, and ) are **display characters** (characters that appear on the screen when you type them)
- HT (TAB) is a **control character** (a character that causes action).

To relate this discussion to your keyboard, there are two more things about the arrangement of these characters in the ASCII table:

- Pressing the key labeled *I* alone produces lowercase *i*
- Pressing *I* and the SHIFT key together produces uppercase *I*
- Pressing *I* and the CTRL key together produces HT (TAB), which causes the cursor to move across the screen to the next tab stop

HT (TAB) is called a **control character** because it causes an action that controls the way your terminal works. You could say that it's also called by this name because it's that code that results when you press the CTRL key and the I key at the same time. Pressing CTRL and i together (sometimes referred to as *pressing CTRL-I*) is equivalent to pressing the TAB key.

To view the ASCII table on the UNIX system, you can display the contents of the file */usr/pub/ascii* with the **cat** command, like this:

```
$ cat /usr/pub/ascii
```

**Table 5-1. ASCII Table.**

| *Character* | *Octal* | *Hex* | *Character* | *Octal* | *Hex* |
|---|---|---|---|---|---|
| NUL | 000 | 0 | [sp] | 040 | 20 |
| SOH | 001 | 1 | ! | 041 | 21 |
| STX | 002 | 2 | “ | 042 | 22 |
| ETX | 003 | 3 | # | 043 | 23 |
| EOT | 004 | 4 | $ | 044 | 24 |
| ENQ | 005 | 5 | % | 045 | 25 |
| ACK | 006 | 6 | & | 046 | 26 |
| BEL | 007 | 7 | ’ | 047 | 27 |
| BS | 010 | 8 | ( | 050 | 28 |
| HT | 011 | 9 | ) | 051 | 29 |
| NL | 012 | A | * | 052 | 2A |
| VT | 013 | B | + | 053 | 2B |
| FF | 014 | C | , | 054 | 2C |
| CR | 015 | D | - | 055 | 2D |
| SO | 016 | E | . | 056 | 2E |
| SI | 017 | F | / | 057 | 2F |
| DLE | 020 | 10 | 0 | 060 | 30 |
| DC1 | 021 | 11 | 1 | 061 | 31 |
| DC2 | 022 | 12 | 2 | 062 | 32 |
| DC3 | 023 | 13 | 3 | 063 | 33 |
| DC4 | 024 | 14 | 4 | 064 | 34 |
| NAK | 025 | 15 | 5 | 065 | 35 |
| SYN | 026 | 16 | 6 | 066 | 36 |
| ETB | 027 | 17 | 7 | 067 | 37 |
| CAN | 030 | 18 | 8 | 070 | 38 |
| EM | 031 | 19 | 9 | 071 | 39 |
| SUB | 032 | 1A | : | 072 | 3A |
| ESC | 033 | 1B | ; | 073 | 3B |
| NP | 034 | 1C | < | 074 | 3C |
| GS | 035 | 1D | = | 075 | 3D |
| RS | 036 | 1E | > | 076 | 3E |
| US | 037 | 1F | ? | 077 | 3F |

Unfortunately, the display will be *sideways*, with the control characters at the top of the table and the display characters on the bottom. The display will show 16 rows of eight characters each. It is more common to show an ASCII table with control characters on the left and display characters on the right, as shown in Table 5-1.

**Table 5-1. ASCII Table continued.**

| *Character* | *Octal* | *Hex* | *Character* | *Octal* | *Hex* |
|---|---|---|---|---|---|
| @ | 100 | 40 | ` | 140 | 60 |
| A | 101 | 41 | a | 141 | 61 |
| B | 102 | 42 | b | 142 | 62 |
| C | 103 | 43 | c | 143 | 63 |
| D | 104 | 44 | d | 144 | 64 |
| E | 105 | 45 | e | 145 | 65 |
| F | 106 | 46 | f | 146 | 66 |
| G | 107 | 47 | g | 147 | 67 |
| H | 110 | 48 | h | 150 | 68 |
| I | 111 | 49 | i | 151 | 69 |
| J | 112 | 4A | j | 152 | 6A |
| K | 113 | 4B | k | 153 | 6B |
| L | 114 | 4C | l | 154 | 6C |
| M | 115 | 4D | m | 155 | 6D |
| N | 116 | 4E | n | 156 | 6E |
| O | 117 | 4F | o | 157 | 6F |
| P | 120 | 50 | p | 160 | 70 |
| Q | 121 | 51 | q | 161 | 71 |
| R | 122 | 52 | r | 162 | 72 |
| S | 123 | 53 | s | 163 | 73 |
| T | 124 | 54 | t | 164 | 74 |
| U | 125 | 55 | u | 165 | 75 |
| V | 126 | 56 | v | 166 | 76 |
| W | 127 | 57 | w | 167 | 77 |
| X | 130 | 58 | x | 170 | 78 |
| Y | 131 | 59 | y | 171 | 79 |
| Z | 132 | 5A | z | 172 | 7A |
| [ | 133 | 5B | { | 173 | 7B |
| \ | 134 | 5C | \| | 174 | 7C |
| ] | 135 | 5D | } | 175 | 7D |
| ^ | 136 | 5E | ~ | 176 | 7E |
| _ | 137 | 5F | DEL | 177 | 7F |

## *Control Characters and Display Characters*

Let's conclude this chapter with a few words about control characters and display characters. Suppose this text file is displayed on your screen:

```
Type this:    85
Then wait.
```

Now here's a question: Assuming that you pressed the TAB key before typing *85* and you pressed the RETURN key at the end of each line, how many characters are there in this file?

- If you are completely new to computers, you will probably say 20.
- If you know a little about computers, you may say 22.
- The correct answer is 25. What?

Explanation: There are only 20 **visible** characters. But there are also two blank spaces (which bring the total to 22), and there are three control characters, one TAB character and two *newline* characters (which bring the total to 25). The TAB character, also known as CTRL-I, is HT (octal code 011); the newline character, also known as CTRL-J, is NL (octal code 012). (Note that this newline convention is unique to UNIX. The usual ASCII convention for beginning a new line is to use CTRL-M (CR), followed by CTRL-J (LF).)

This is how this file looks to UNIX in octal representation (split into two lines here only to accommodate the width of a printed page):

```
124 171 160 145 040 164 150 151 163 072 011 070 065 010
124 150 145 156 040 167 141 151 164 056 010
```

Translated:

```
T  y  p  e  [sp]  t  h  i  s  :  HT  8  5  NL
T  h  e  n  [sp]  w  a  i  t  .  NL
```

From our point of view, display characters appear on the screen and control characters do not. But to UNIX they are all just characters. It's something like the characters who bring you a television show. There are the characters you see on your screen (the actors) and the others you never see (those who take care of the cameras, costumes, make-up, props, and so on).

## *Other Methods of Terminal Control*

Control characters are not the only means of controlling a terminal. Many of the newer terminals are controlled by sequences of characters that begin with the **ESC** (escape) character (octal 033)—known as **escape sequences.** ESC L and ESC ] 12 are examples of escape sequences. In an effort to increase the number of control characters available, some terminal manufacturers are enlarging the basic character set from 128 characters (7-bit ASCII) to 256 (8-bit coding). The result is the emergence of brand new control characters.

# Summary of Chapter 5

In this chapter you have learned about communication: first communicating with other users on your own system, then communicating with other UNIX systems.

## *Communicating with Other Users*

**Sending mail.** To send electronic mail to another user on your system, use the **mail** command, followed by the desired user identifier(s). Type your message, then type CTRL-D by itself (or a period followed immediately by RETURN) on the line following the last line of your message.

**Receiving mail.** If another user has sent you a message via electronic mail, you will see the message *You have mail* the next time you log on. To find out exactly what you have received, use the **mail** command by itself, then press RETURN to look at each individual message. You can also type *d* to delete the current message or *p* to repeat it.

**Reminding yourself of something.** To remind yourself of something, you can either mail an electronic message to yourself with **mail** or post messages after dates in a special reminder file called *calendar*, which will be automatically checked by the system.

**Writing directly to another user.** To send a message directly to another user's terminal, use the **write** command followed by your message starting on the next line and then CTRL-D to exit the **write** command.

## *Communicating Outside Your System*

**Calling outside your UNIX system.** To dial up another UNIX system or to a non-UNIX system, use the **cu** (call up) command, including the telephone number of the other party and the speed at which both of you are sending data to each other. Once you have established a connection, you can type messages to each other at the keyboard and send files back and forth.

**UNIX-to-UNIX copying.** To copy files from one UNIX system in a network to another, use the **uucp** (UNIX-to-UNIX copy) command, including the names of the two UNIX systems with the filename(s). To execute UNIX commands on another system in the network, use the **uux** (UNIX-to-UNIX execute) command, receiving the commands via a pipeline. All of this assumes, of course, that someone has already set up such a network in which to use these commands.

**Encrypting information**. To encrypt a file, use the **crypt** command with a key, redirecting input from the original file and redirecting output to the encrypted file. To view (or print) the original text at a later time, use the **crypt** command again with the same key, redirecting input from the encrypted file.

To ensure the security of your encrypted files, select a long, complex key. Don't store this key anywhere in the UNIX system.

**Basics of communication.** Computers communicate with other computers and other equipment through wires (sometimes with the help of modems), using one of several timing methods, speeds, protocols, and duplex modes. Micromputers communicate (both internally and externally) with ASCII codes.

# II

# *Text Editing with* ***ed***

# 6

# *Introduction to the Line Editor* **ed**

In Chapters 1-5, we took a brief tour of the UNIX operating system to sample some of its features. In the chapters that follow we'll focus on the text editors that come with UNIX. You can use one of these (or some other UNIX editor) to enter and modify documents, command files, programs, and data records. Software vendors are beginning to offer text editors and word processing systems for the UNIX operating system.

Here are the editors we'll be discussing in this book:

*Part II*

- **ed**, a primitive interactive editor, originally designed for Teletype machines, that performs most of its functions on entire lines

*Part III*

- **vi**, a full-screen visual editor that allows you to display text on the entire screen and move the cursor around to make changes

- **ex**, an extended editor based on **ed**, that allows you to perform operations on a text file line by line

Chapters 6 and 7 provide an introduction to **ed**, with more detailed discussions following in Chapters 8-10. Because the visual editor **vi** is much easier and more convenient to use, you may want to use that instead of **ed**. However, if you don't have anything but **ed** or if you don't have an intelligent terminal with cursor-addressing, then you may be forced to use **ed**. If you have **vi** on your system, then you automatically have **ex**, **vi**'s line-oriented counterpart (actually, **vi** is a special mode of **ex**).

# Getting Acquainted With **ed**

## *Starting with a New Directory*

As you learned earlier in this book, one way to take full advantage of the UNIX file system is to organize your home directory into subdirectories to contain different kinds of files. Let's start this chapter by creating a new subdirectory in your home directory to contain your **ed** files, then move to this directory for the exercises in this chapter.

1. Create a new subdirectory:

   a. Create a directory called *text_files* with the **mkdir** command:

   ```
   $ mkdir text_files
   $ _
   ```

   b. The directory has been created, but you are still in your home directory.

2. Move from your home directory to *text_files*:

   a. Move to subdirectory *text_files* with the **cd** command:

   ```
   $ cd text_files
   $ _
   ```

   b. Confirm that you have moved to *text_files*:

   ```
   $ pwd
   /usr/robin/text_files
   $ _
   ```

   c. Now *text_files* is your working directory; any files you create will be stored in this directory.

In this book, we'll be using names like *text_files* and *c_progs* for subdirectories. These names are fine for learning the system; however, once you've started using UNIX, you should use names that describe the contents of the files in your subdirectories (for example, *atc.acctg*, *atc.invoices*).

## *A Short Session*

Let's go through a short session with **ed** to learn a few basics: Starting a session, entering text, and ending a session.

1. Start an editing session:

   a. Type *ed* (not *ED*) in the space following the UNIX shell prompt, and press RETURN. Now your screen should look like this:

```
$ ed        or       % ed
_                    _
```

b. This time there is no UNIX shell prompt in front of the cursor. That is **ed**'s way of telling you that you have entered the editor and that **ed** is waiting for you to enter a command.

2. Try entering some **ed** commands:

   a. First try a command **ed** doesn't know; type *z* and press RETURN:

```
z
?

_
```

   b. The question mark is **ed**'s only reply. It means, "I've never heard of that command. Please try something else."

   c. Now try a real **ed** command; type *a* (not *A*) and press RETURN:

```
a

_
```

   d. There is no question mark this time, which means you've just entered a valid **ed** command. In this case, it also means, "You have just requested 'append to text,' which **ed** is ready to accept."

3. Enter a few lines of text:

   a. Starting in the space below "a", type the following, pressing RETURN at the end of each line:

```
If you're tired of getting
scalped by someone else,
```

   b. Now the screen should look like this:

```
If you're tired of getting
scalped by someone else,

_
```

4. Tell **ed** that you don't have any more to type:

   a. It won't do any good to type, "That's all I have to say, **ed**." Just type a period (.) on a line by itself and press RETURN:

```
.
_
```

b. Nothing happens. Just to be sure that **ed** realizes that you don't have anything more to add, type another period by itself on the next line and press RETURN again:

```
.
.
scalped by someone else,
_
```

c. This time **ed** responds by repeating the last line you typed. This is **ed**'s way of telling you, "I'm ready for your next command now."

5. Save the text in a file called *barbershop*:

a. Right below the second period (.), type *w barbershop* and press RETURN:

```
w barbershop
52
_
```

b. The *w* stands for "write," as in "Write this text to a file called 'barbershop'." This time **ed** answers you with a number (52). This is **ed**'s way of saying, "I just stored 52 characters for you in a file called 'barbershop'."

6. End the session with **ed**:

a. It's time to say good-bye to **ed** for now. Type *q* (for "quit") and press RETURN:

```
q
$ _
```

b. The UNIX shell prompt has now returned to the screen. That's how UNIX tells you that you have left **ed** and returned to the shell.

That concludes your first session with **ed**. Here's a summary of what you've learned (remember, always press RETURN after each line you type):

| | |
|---|---|
| `$ ed` | Start a session with **ed** |
| `z` | Let's try a little "z" |
| `?` | What do you mean, "z"? |
| `a` | Start adding new text here |
| `If you're tired of getting` | |
| `scalped by someone else,` | |

| | |
|---|---|
| . | Stop adding text here |
| . | Ask **ed** to verify end of text |
| scalped by someone else, | **ed** verifies end of text |
| w barbershop | Write the text to a file called *barbershop* (52 characters in all) |
| 52 | |
| q | Quit this session with **ed** |
| $ _ | Now you're back to the UNIX shell prompt again |

## *Typing Another Document*

You've just had a chance to go through a complete editing session with **ed**. Now you can practice typing some more text, using the procedures you just learned.

In the first example, we invoked **ed** by typing just two letters (*ed*). Then, after typing the text, we gave the name of the file in the w command (*w_ barbershop*). Beginning with this example, we'll start right off by naming the file after the **ed** command, which is probably a better way to work. When **ed** replies with a question mark in front of the filename, that means the file does not yet exist.

1. Prepare to enter text for a file named *rates*:

   a. Type *ed rates* after the UNIX shell prompt and press RETURN:

   ```
   $ ed rates
   ?rates                [ed doesn't recognize this name]
   _
   ```

   b. Type *a* to begin adding text:

   ```
   a
   _
   ```

2. Enter the text:

   a. Type the lines shown, using the TAB key for spacing, and end each line with a RETURN:

   ```
           Rates             [One tab before Rates]
   Self service    $5        [One tab before $5]
   Full service    $10       [One tab before $10]
   _
   ```

   b. Type a period (.) and press RETURN to end the text.

   ```
   .
   _
   ```

c. Type another period (.) and press RETURN again to verify:

```
[.]
Full service    $10

_
```

3. Save the text by writing it to *rates*:

a. Type *w* and press RETURN:

```
[w]
40

_
```

b. **ed** will respond with a total (40 characters).

4. Return to the UNIX shell:

a. Type *q* and press RETURN:

```
[q]
$ _
```

b. The UNIX shell prompt will return to the screen, indicating that you have left **ed**.

## *Typing a Third Document*

You've had a chance to go through two complete editing sessions with **ed**. Now you can practice typing some more text using the same procedures again. Once again, we'll name the new file right after the **ed** command.

1. Prepare to enter text for a file named *hours*:

a. Type *ed hours* after the UNIX shell prompt and press RETURN:

```
$ [ed hours]
?hours            [ed doesn't recognize this name]

_
```

b. Type *a* to begin adding text:

```
[a]

_
```

2. Enter the text:

a. Leave one blank line, then type the lines shown, using the TAB key for spacing and ending each line with a RETURN:

```
        Hours             [Blank line here]
                          [One tab before Hours]
Monday-Friday 10-6        [One tab before 10-6]
_
```

b. Type a period (.) and press RETURN to end the text:

```
.
_
```

c. Type another period (.) and press RETURN again to verify:

```
.
Monday-Friday 10-6
_
```

3. Save the text by writing it to *hours*:

a. Type *w* and press RETURN:

```
w
27
_
```

b. **ed** will respond with a total (27 characters).

4. Return to the UNIX shell:

a. Type *q* and press RETURN:

```
q
$ _
```

b. The UNIX shell prompt will return to the screen, indicating that you have left **ed**.

# Displaying Text

## *Using an Existing File*

In a moment, we'll display some text on the screen. Before we can do that, we have to have some text to display.

1. Start another editing session with the file *barbershop*:

a. Type *ed barbershop* and press RETURN:

```
$ ed barbershop
52
_
```

b. **ed** will respond with the number of characters (52) read from the file *barbershop*.

2. Add a few more lines of text to *barbershop*:

a. Type *a* and press RETURN to add text:

```
a
_
```

b. Type two more lines of text, followed by a blank line:

```
come to the Scissor's Edge
and do it yourself.

_
```

[Leave a blank line here]

c. Type a period (.) to end the addition:

```
.
_
```

## Using the "Print" Command

**p**

The process of displaying text on your screen is referred to as *printing* in UNIX. Why? Because UNIX was designed for Teletype terminals, which didn't have video monitors. Input and output were both printed on paper, not displayed on a screen. Unfortunately, UNIX users are still stuck with the word "printing," even though no printing takes place if you have a video monitor.

1. Display a few lines of text:

a. Display lines 1 and 2 by typing *1,2p* (with a comma between one and two) and pressing RETURN:

```
1,2p
If you're tired of getting
scalped by someone else,

_
```

b. Display lines 3 and 4 by typing *3,4p* and pressing RETURN:

```
3,4p
come to the Scissor's Edge
and do it yourself.

_
```

2. Display lines of text with the "last line" symbol:

   a. Display from line 3 to the last line of text by typing *3,$p* and pressing RETURN:

```
3,$p                              [Display from line 3 to the end]
come to the Scissor's Edge
and do it yourself.

_
```

   b. Display the entire text by typing *1,$p* and pressing RETURN:

```
1,$p
If you're tired of getting
scalped by someone else,
come to the Scissor's Edge
and do it yourself.

_
```

3. Display single lines of text:

   a. Display line 3 by typing *3p* and pressing RETURN:

```
3p
come to the Scissor's Edge

_
```

   b. Display the last line by typing *$p* and pressing RETURN:

```
$p

_
```

4. Save the text and end the editing session:

   a. Save this text by writing it back to *barbershop*:

```
w barbershop
100

_
```

   b. Type *q* and press RETURN to end the session:

```
q
$ _
```

   c. The UNIX shell prompt returns to the screen, indicating that you have left **ed**.

# Reading Existing Files

**r**

## *Reading One File*

You can **read** the contents of any existing text file into the work area (or editing buffer) at any time with the **r** command. This text will then be added to the current contents of the work area.

1. Start another editing session with the file *barbershop*:

   a. Type *ed barbershop* and press RETURN:

   ```
   $ ed barbershop
   100
   _
   ```

   b. **ed** will respond with the number of characters (100) read from *barbershop*.

2. Read *rates* into the work area and look at the results:

   a. Read *rates* by typing *r rates* and pressing RETURN:

   ```
   r rates
   40
   _
   ```

   b. Now display (print) the entire buffer to see what it contains:

   ```
   1,$p
   If you're tired of getting
   scalped by someone else,
   come to the Scissor's Edge
   and do it yourself.

       Rates                        [rates has been added here.]
   Self service    $5
   Full service    $10
   _
   ```

## *Reading Another File*

We've just read one file into the work area. Why not read another?

1. Read *hours* into the work area and look at the results:

   a. Read *hours* by typing *r hours* and pressing RETURN:

   ```
   r hours              [You: "ed, read hours"]
   27                   [ed: "I've just read 27 characters"]
   _
   ```

b. Now display the last seven lines of the work area:

```
6,$p                         [Display from line 6 to the end]
    Rates
Self service    $5
Full service    $10

    Hours                    [hours has been added here.]
Monday-Friday   10-6

_
```

Instead of **7,$p** you could also use **$-6,$p** to display the last seven lines of the work area. *$-6,$p* means, "Display the work area starting at the sixth line from the last line and ending with the last line."

2. Store the work area again:

a. Use the **w** command to write the work area to *barbershop*:

```
w barbershop
167

_
```

b. Again, **ed** responds with the number of characters stored (167).

In the language of computers, the previous contents of *barbershop* have now been **overwritten** by new text. In everyday life, if you take a sheet of paper with a message written on it and write a new message on it, you now see one message written on top of another, with garbled results. In UNIX (and other operating systems), text written to a file replaces whatever was previously stored in that file.

## Line Numbers

### *The Current Line*

As you learned earlier in this chapter, you can display the third line of text in the editing buffer by typing

```
3p
Come to the Scissor's Edge

_
```

When you do this, **ed** makes a note of this number (3), which identifies the line most recently referred to (that is, **the current line**). Any time you execute a command that uses line numbers, you can refer to the current line by using the dot (.), or period. Here are some examples with the **p** and **d** commands:

1. Display various lines of text:

   a. Display the third line again by typing *.p* and pressing RETURN:

   ```
   .p
   Come to the Scissor's Edge
   _
   ```

   b. Display the fourth line by typing *.+1p* (move to the line after the current line and display it) and pressing RETURN:

   ```
   .+1p
   and do it yourself.
   _
   ```

   c. Display the third line again by typing *.−1p* (move to the line before the current line and display it) and pressing RETURN:

   ```
   .-1p
   Come to the Scissor's Edge
   _
   ```

After you displayed the fourth line, dot (.) became 4; after you displayed the third line the second time, dot (.) became 3 again.

## *Using Line Numbers with Other Commands*

So far you have used line numbers with only the **p** (**print**) command. But you can also use line numbers with the **a** (**append**), **r** (**read**), and **w** (**write**) commands.

Use a single line number in front of the **a** (**append**) command to add text **after** the line indicated:

1. Type new text after the current text and show the results:

   a. Add text to the end of the existing text by typing *$a* and pressing RETURN:

   ```
   $a
   _
   ```

   b. Type the line, using the TAB key for spacing and a period to show end the text:

   ```
   $a
   Weekends	10-4
   .
   _
   ```

   [One tab before *10-4*]

c. Show the results with *$-2,$p*:

```
$-2,$p
          Hours
Monday-Friday     10-6
Weekends          10-4

_
```

Use a pair of line numbers in front of **w** (**write**) to write only part of the work area to a file.

2. Write the last four lines of the work area back to *hours* and the entire work area back to *barbershop*:

   a. You can write the last four lines by typing *$-3,$w hours* and pressing RETURN (count back three from the last line):

```
$-3,$w hours
41                          [41 characters written]

_
```

   b. Write the entire work area by using **w** without line numbers:

```
w barbershop
181                         [181 characters written]

_
```

   c. Now read *hours* back into the work area, overwriting the current text, with the **e** command:

```
e hours
41

_
```

   d. Verify that there are now just four lines of text in the work area:

```
1,$p

          Hours
Monday-Friday     10-6
Weekends          10-4

_
```

Use a single line number in front of the **r** (**read**) command to read a file and insert it after the line indicated before **r**.

3. Insert *rates* between lines 1 and 2 and show the results:

   a. Display line 1 to set dot (.) to 1:

```
1p
                            [Blank line displayed]

_
```

b. Read *rates* by typing *.r rates* and pressing RETURN:

```
.r rates
40

_
```

c. Check the results with *1,$ p*:

```
1,$ p

    Rates
Self service     $5
Full service     $10
    Hours
Monday-Friday    10-6
Weekends         10-4

_
```

4. End this editing session:

   a. Leave **ed** by typing *q* and pressing RETURN twice in succession.

   b. Now the UNIX shell prompt will return to the screen.

## Summary of Chapter 6

In this chapter you learned the basic operations of the interactive line editor **ed**: starting an editing session, entering text, writing text to a file, ending a session, editing an existing file, printing (displaying) text, reading an existing file, and using line numbers. You also learned that **ed** uses line numbers and one-letter commands.

**Starting a session.** At the UNIX shell prompt ($), type *ed* and press RETURN. If you plan to work with a file that you have already stored in a previous session, you can type the name of that file after *ed*.

**Characters to avoid.** Avoid using any of the following characters in the name of a file:

\ . * [ ] $ &

These characters will be discussed in detail in Chapter 8.

**Entering text.** Type *a* (**append**) and press RETURN, type the text desired with a RETURN at the end of each line, then follow the last line with a period (.) on a line by itself and another RETURN.

**Writing text to a file.** To save the text you have typed, type *w* (**write**), a space, the name of a file, and press RETURN. If you typed the file's name when you first called up **ed**, then you won't have to type it again here.

**Displaying text.** To print text from the current editing buffer (that is, to display it on the screen), type either a single line number or a pair of line numbers, *p* **(print)**, and press RETURN. If you type one line number, then one line will be printed (displayed); if you type two line numbers separated by a comma, then all lines between and including the lines with the two numbers will be printed (displayed).

**Reading a file.** To read the contents of a file into the editing buffer (and add it to any text already in the buffer), type *r* **(read)**, a space, and the name of the file. You can also type a line number in front of *r* to indicate the line the file is to follow.

**Using line numbers.** Using either actual numbers, a dollar sign ($) to indicate the last line of text, or a dot (.) to indicate the current line of text, you can type line numbers in front of **ed** commands. The **a (append)** and **r (read)** commands allow only single numbers; the **p (print)**, **w (write)**, and **e (edit)** commands allow either single numbers or pairs of numbers separated by commas.

You can also form expressions like this: .+1 (the next line); $-1 (the line before the last)

**Spaces in commands. ed** allows you to type spaces between characters in a command, which means, for example, that any of the following would be equivalent:

```
1,5p
1,5 p
1, 5 p
```

# 7

# Handling Entire Lines with **ed**

In Chapter 6, you learned some of the basics of using **ed**: starting and ending an editing session, entering text, displaying text on the screen, reading an existing file, and using line numbers. In this chapter, we'll discuss methods for inserting, deleting, changing, and moving text, along with methods for undoing an **ed** command, retrieving an existing file, and displaying text with invisible control characters.

## MAKING CHANGES IN TEXT

### *Returning to the Right Directory*

In case you've changed to another directory since Chapter 6, here's how to return to the subdirectory we're using for our **ed** files. (If you're still in your home directory, use the shorter command on the left.)

```
$ cd text_files          or       $ cd /usr/robin/text_files
$ _                               $ _
```

Now *text_files* is your current directory. You can use **ls** to display the files you've already stored in this directory like this:

```
$ ls | sp
barbershop     hours     rates
$ _
```

### *Inserting Text* **i**

You have used the **a** (append) command a number of times: Sometimes to add text to an empty text buffer, sometimes to append new text to existing text. The command for inserting text, **i** (insert), is very similar to the **a** command. The main difference is that **i** inserts the new text **in front of** the line indicated, while **a** inserts the new text **after** the line indicated. Let's enter some text to see how it works.

1. Start a new file called *sections* and enter the eight lines of text shown. Use the TAB key (not the space bar) to position the columns of text. (These are the names of the sections in the **UNIX User's Manual**, with the number of pages shown in the right-hand column.)

```
$ ed sections
?sections                          [ed doesn't recognize this name yet]
a
1 Commands                         [five tabs here]            182
2 System Calls                                                 58
3 Subroutines                                                  62
4 Special Files                                                22
5 File Formats and Conventions                                 26
6 Games                                                        18
7 Macro Packages and Language Conventions                      14
8 Maintenance                                                  12
.
w
204
_
```

2. Insert a new line of text between lines 4 and 5 (sometimes it's handy to have each line begin with its own line number):

   a. Type *5i* to request an insertion in front of the fifth line:

   ```
   5i
   _
   ```

   b. Enter the line shown (six asterisks, each at a different tab):

   ```
   [tab]   *   *   *   *   *   *
   _
   ```

   c. Type a period (.) to end entry of the new text:

   ```
   .
   _
   ```

   d. Type *1,$p* and press RETURN to display the results:

   ```
   1,$p
   1 Commands                                              182
   ```

```
2 System Calls                                  58
3 Subroutines                                   62
4 Special Files                                 22
  *      *      *      *      *      *
5 File Formats and Conventions                  26
6 Games                                         18
7 Macro Packages and Language Conventions       14
8 Maintenance                                   12

_
```

e. **ed** has inserted the new line into the existing text.

3. For practice, enter the following four lines between items 6 and 7 (because of the inserted line, these are now lines 7 and 8):

   a. Carry out the **insert** command:

```
8 i
  Games: arithmetic, backgammon, banner, bcd/ppt,
  bj (blackjack), checkers, chess, ching, fortune,
  maze, moo, quiz, reversi (Othello), tic-tac-toe,
  cubic tic-tac-toe, hangman, words, and wump
.
_
```

   b. Display the results:

```
6,$p
5 File Formats and Conventions                          26
6 Games                                                 18
  Games: arithmetic, backgammon, banner, bcd/ppt,
  bj (blackjack), checkers, chess, ching, fortune,
  maze, moo, quiz, reversi (Othello), tic-tac-toe,
  cubic tic-tac-toe, hangman, words, and wump
7 Macro Packages and Language Conventions               14
8 Maintenance                                           12

_
```

## *Deleting Text* d

Deleting text is a little easier than inserting it. Use the **d** command to delete either a single line or selected lines, using line numbers for **d** just as you would for **p**.

1. Delete the four lines you just inserted between items 6 and 7 (lines 8, 9, 10, and 11):

   a. First type *8,11 p* and press RETURN to display the lines (and make sure that you're deleting the correct lines):

```
8,11 p
          Games: arithmetic, backgammon, banner, bcd/ppt,
          bj (blackjack), checkers, chess, ching, fortune,
          maze, moo, quiz, reversi (Othello), tic-tac-toe,
          cubic tic-tac-toe, hangman, words, and wump

_
```

b. Type *8,11 d* and press RETURN to delete the lines:

```
8,11 d

_
```

c. Display the results:

```
$-3,$ p
5 File Formats and Conventions                  26
6 Games                                         18
7 Macro Packages and Language Conventions       14
8 Maintenance                                   12

_
```

Since the **d** command itself shows you nothing on the screen (and since there's no way to recover the lines deleted), always take the three steps shown above: Display the line(s), delete the line(s), and display the results.

2. Delete the line of asterisks you inserted earlier:

   a. First use *4,5p* to display the line (plus the previous line as a point of reference):

```
4,5p
4    Special Files                              22
*      *      *      *      *      *
```

   b. Use *5d* to delete the line:

```
5 d

_
```

   c. Display the results:

```
4,5p
4 Special Files                                 22
5 File Formats and Conventions                  26

_
```

   d. Now the text is back to its original form.

The command you used to delete the line (*5d*) contained the actual line number (5). Since you don't always know the exact number of a particular line, this is not very convenient. A little later in the book you will learn how to identify lines by their contents.

## *Changing Text* c

**ed** allows you to replace an entire line of text (or a group of consecutive lines) with another line (or group of lines). The command that allows you to do this, the **c** (change) command, works very much like the **i** (insert) command.

1. Change line 6 to two lines of asterisks:

   a. Type *6 c* and press RETURN to request a change:

   ```
   6 c
   _
   ```

   b. Enter the two lines of asterisks, using the TAB key to indent them, followed by a period (.) on the next line:

   ```
   *       *       *       *       *       *
   *       *       *       *       *       *
   .
   _
   ```

   c. Now display the results:

   ```
   5,$p
   5 File Formats and Conventions                  26
           *       *       *       *       *       *
           *       *       *       *       *       *
   7 Macro Packages and Language Conventions        14
   8 Maintenance                                   12

   _
   ```

   d. As expected, you have replaced line 6 (*Games*) with two lines of asterisks.

2. Replace the two lines of asterisks (lines 6 and 7) with line 6:

   a. Type *6,7 c*, press RETURN, and enter the original line, followed by a period (.) and RETURN on the next line:

   ```
   6,7 c
   6 Games                                         18
   .
   _
   ```

   b. Display the results:

   ```
   5,$p
   5 File Formats and Conventions                  26
   ```

c

```
6 Games                                       18
7 Macro Packages and Language Conventions     14
8 Maintenance                                 12

_
```

You have now restored the original text. The **c** (change) command is very flexible. You can use it to replace one line with two lines, two lines with one line, three lines with five lines, or one of many other combinations. Note that typing a **c** command, followed by a period (.) without typing any text will result in a deletion.

## *Moving Text* **m**

If you need to move a line (or a group of lines) from one location in the work area to another, use the **m** (move) command. We'll continue with the same sample text.

1. Move lines 1 and 2 to the end of the work area:

   a. First type *1,2 p* and press RETURN to display the lines:

```
1,2 p
1 Commands                                    182
2 System Calls                                58

_
```

   b. Next type *1,2 m $* and press RETURN to move the lines:

```
1,2 m $                  [Move lines 1 and 2 to the end ($)]

_
```

   c. Type *1,$p* to display the results:

```
1,$p
3 Subroutines                                 62
4 Special Files                               22
5 File Formats and Conventions                26
6 Games                                       18
7 Macro Packages and Language Conventions     14
8 Maintenance                                 12
1 Commands                                    182
2 System Calls                                58

_
```

2. Move the two lines back to the beginning again:

   a. Use *7,8 p* to display the lines:

```
7,8 p
1 Commands                                    182
```

```
2 System Calls                          58

_
```

b. Since lines are moved with the **m** command to the line that **follows** the target line, we have to use zero (0) as the target line number:

```
7,8 m 0

_
```

c. Use *1,3p* to display the results:

```
1,3p
1 Commands                              182
2 System Calls                           58
3 Subroutines                            62

_
```

3. Store the text and end this session with **ed**:

a. Type *w* and press RETURN to write the text to *sections*:

```
w
204

_
```

b. Type *q* and press RETURN to end this editing session and return to the UNIX shell prompt:

```
q
$ _
```

## *Copying Text*

**t**

If you need to copy a line (or a group of lines) from one location in the work area to another, use the **t** (transfer) command, which is similar to the **m** (move) command. The difference is that the **t** command leaves the original text in place, while the **m** command does not. Let's begin by returning to the file *sections*:

1. Start another editing session with *sections*:

a. After the UNIX shell prompt, type *ed sections* and press RETURN:

```
$ ed sections
204

_
```

b. Display the first half of the work area with *1,4p*:

```
1,4p
1 Commands                                          182
2 System Call                                       58
3 Subroutines                                       62
4 Special Files                                     22
_
```

2. Copy lines 1 and 2 to the lines following item 4:

a. Type *1,2 t 4* and press RETURN to copy the lines:

```
1,2 t 4
_
```

b. Type *1,6p* to display the results:

```
1,6p
1 Commands                                          182
2 System Calls                                      58
3 Subroutines                                       62
4 Special Files                                     22
1 Commands                                          182
2 System Calls                                      58
_
```

## *Marking Lines* **k**

Use the **k** command, followed by a lowercase letter (a-z), to mark a line of text. Then use this name in front of either the **m** (move) command or the **t** (transfer) command to have that line either moved or copied. To move or copy a block of text, rather than just one line, you can "bracket" the block by marking the first and last lines. Then type the two names, separated by a comma in front of one of the commands (**m** or **t**). Let's take a look at some examples. First we'll copy lines 4, 5, and 6 to the end of the text.

1. Mark line 4:

a. Display line 4:

```
4p
4 Special Files                                     22
_
```

b. With line 4 now the current line, mark it:

```
ka                                        [Call line 4 a]
_
```

2. Mark line 6:

   a. Display line 6:

```
6p
2 System Calls                                              58
_
```

   b. With line 6 now the current line, mark it:

```
kb                                                [Call line 6 b]
_
```

With a pair of lines now marked (*a* and *b*), you are ready to form a t (transfer) command to copy the three lines to the end of the text. In the t command, you have to precede each name with an apostrophe like this: *'a, 'b*. This distinguishes them from **ed** commands.

3. Copy lines 4, 5, and 6 to the end of the text:

   a. Type *'a, 'b t $* and press RETURN:

```
'a,'b t $                  [Copy lines a through b to the end ($)]
_
```

   b. Display the text with *9,$p* to see the results:

```
9,$p
7 Macro Packages and Language Conventions      14
8 Maintenance                                  12
4 Special Files                                22
1 Commands                                     182
2 System Calls                                 58
_
```

Now you have copied the three lines to the end of the work area. You could also select a block of text and **move** it to a new location using the same method. The only difference is that you would use the **m** command instead of the **t** command. Try moving a block for practice.

4. Abandon the text in the work area:

   a. Type *q* and press RETURN to abandon the text:

```
q
?                            [ed won't accept this the first time]
_
```

k

b. Type *q* and press RETURN again to abandon the text:

```
q
$ _
```

## Displaying Text with Control Characters

You have already learned how to display text on the screen with the **p** command. Another **ed** command, called **l** (list), displays not only text on the screen, but also the locations of tab stops, backspaces, form feeds, and other control characters. We'll use the text you've been working with.

1. List the first six lines of text in the editing buffer:

   a. Start another editing session with the file *sections*:

   ```
   $ ed sections
   204

   _
   ```

   b. Type *1,$ l* (one comma dollar el) and press RETURN:

   ```
   1,$ l
   1>Commands>>>>>182
   2>System Calls>>>>>58
   3>Subroutines>>>>>62
   4>Special Files>>>>>22
   5>File Formats and Conventions>>>26
   6>Games>>>>>>18
   7>Macro Packages and Language Conventions>>14
   8>Maintenance>>>>>12

   _
   ```

   b. Here **ed** indicates the location of each tab stop with a >, with all the spaces left out. (If you have a Teletype machine, you will see —> instead of >.)

2. Now add some control characters after the last line of text:

   a. Type *a* and press RETURN to add text:

   ```
   a

   _
   ```

   b. Do the following five times: Press the TAB key, then, while holding down the CTRL key with one finger, press *G* with another (that is, press CTRL G). Then press RETURN.

   ```
   _
   ```

c. The line you just typed will be invisible. You may hear a beep from your terminal each time you press CTRL-G.

d. Now type a period (.) and press RETURN to indicate the end of your addition to the text:

```
.
_
```

3. To see the invisible control characters you typed on this line, use the **l** command:

a. Type *$-1,$ l* (dollar minus one comma dollar el) and press RETURN to display the last two lines of text:

```
$-1,$ l
8>Maintenance>>>>>12
>\07>\07>\07>\07>\07
_
```

b. Once again, each > represents one tab stop.

c. Each *\07* represents one CTRL-G (the seventh control character).

4. Prepare to resume the editing session:

a. Store the text:

```
w sections
215
_
```

b. This editing session will be continued momentarily.

Control codes, which do not usually appear on the screen when typed, are used to cause such functions as cursor motion, screen attributes, and blanking on terminals (as well as such functions as paper positioning, spacing, and overstriking on printers). A complete list of these codes may be found in a special table of codes called an ASCII table. (See Table 5-1.)

With the **l** (list) command, each control character except tab is represented by a reverse slash (\) followed by a two-digit number. In the example above, *\07* stands for CTRL-G, also known as BEL (ASCII code 07), the code used to sound the terminal's beeper. (For a complete list of the control codes used by UNIX, display the file */usr/pub/ascii* with the **cat** command—at the conclusion of this editing session.)

Why would it ever be useful to see codes like these displayed? Because **ed** and UNIX see these just like any other characters you type, even though they don't appear on the screen, as explained in Chapter 5. If you accidentally type one of these control characters in the middle of a command stored in a file, the system won't be able to recognize the command. Therefore, the command won't be executed, and (without the **l** command) you won't know why.

## *Editing an Existing File* **e**

In Chapter 6, you learned how to use the **r** (read) command to read text from a file into the editing buffer and append it to the existing text. Another command, the **e** (edit) command, performs a similar function. If you are working on several different files in succession, you can store the text for one file and then call a second file into the editing buffer without leaving **ed**. As an example, let's use a file you have already stored.

1. Retrieve *barbershop*:

   a. Type *e barbershop* and press RETURN:

   ```
   e barbershop
   181

   _
   ```

   b. All you see after *181* is the cursor on the next line. This is **ed**'s way of telling you that it has retrieved *barbershop* (all 181 characters) and is ready for you to start editing.

2. Insert a few lines of text into *barbershop* and store them:

   a. Type *1 i* and press RETURN to tell **ed** that you're going to **insert** some lines above the first line of text:

   ```
   1 i                    [Insert text in front of line 1]

   _
   ```

   b. Nothing happens. That means it's all right with **ed**, so go ahead and start typing, following each line with RETURN and following the last line with a period (.) and RETURN:

   ```
   ------------------------        [Type 24 hyphens]
           Notice                  [One tab before Notice]
   ------------------------        [Type 24 hyphens]
   .
   _
   ```

   c. Save this text by writing it back to *barbershop*:

   ```
   w
   239

   _
   ```

   d. **ed**'s response means, "239 characters in 'barbershop'."

3. Now, with *barbershop* stored, retrieve *sections* again:

   a. Type *e sections* and press RETURN:

```
e sections                         [Start editing sections]
215

_
```

   b. Now *sections* is back in the editing buffer and *barbershop* is gone. To see this, type *1,3 l* (one comma three el) and press RETURN:

```
1,3 l
1>Commands>>>>>182
2>System Calls>>>>>58
3>Subroutines>>>>>62

_
```

4. Leave **ed** and end this editing session:

   a. Type *q* and press RETURN to quit:

```
q
$ _
```

   b. The UNIX shell prompt appears, indicating that you have left **ed**.

The **e** (edit) command allows you to work on one file, store it, and then retrieve another file without having to leave **ed**. (If you fail to store the first file, **ed** will not retrieve the second, thereby protecting the text in your work area.) In a later chapter you will learn how to do some other things without having to leave **ed**.

## Summary of Chapter 7

In this chapter you learned how to work with whole lines in **ed**: Inserting text, deleting text, changing text, moving text, copying text, displaying text with invisible control characters, and editing an existing file.

**Inserting text**. To insert text in front of a line of existing text, type a line number and *i*, press RETURN, type the text to be inserted, then follow the last line with a period (.) on a line by itself and another RETURN.

**Deleting text**. To delete text from the editing buffer, type either a single line number or a pair of line numbers, **d (delete)**, and press RETURN. If you type one line number, then one line will be deleted; if you type two line numbers, then all lines between and including the two numbers will be deleted.

**Changing text.** To replace text with different text, type a line number (or a pair of line numbers separated by commas), **c**, press RETURN, type the text, then follow the last line with a period (.) on a line by itself and another RETURN:

**Moving text.** To move text from one location to another, type a line number (or a pair of line numbers separated by commas), **m**, the target line number, and press RETURN.

**Copying text.** To copy text from one location to another, type a line number (or a pair of line numbers separated by commas), **t**, the target line number, and press RETURN.

**Marking lines.** To mark a line to be moved or copied, display the line (to make it the current line), then type *kx*, where *x* may be any lowercase letter of the alphabet. To refer to that line in an **m** (move) or **t** (transfer) command, type *'x*.

**Displaying text with invisible characters.** To list text from the current editing buffer (that is, to display it on the screen along with tab stops, backspaces, and other control characters), type either a single line number or a pair of line numbers, *l* (**list**), and press RETURN. If you type one line number, then one line will be listed (displayed); if you type two line numbers, then all lines between and including the two numbers will be listed (displayed).

**Editing a file.** To retrieve an existing file (and overwrite any text currently in the editing buffer), type *e* (**edit**), a space, the name of the file desired, and press RETURN.

# 8

# Making Changes within a Line Using **ed**

In Chapters 6 and 7, you learned how to use **ed** to change, insert, copy, and move whole lines of text. In this chapter we'll discuss searches and replacements, which allow you to make changes **within** a line.

In case you've changed to another directory since Chapter 7, here's how to return to the subdirectory we're using for our **ed** files. (If you're still in your home directory, you can use the shorter command on the left.)

```
$ cd text_files           or         $ cd /usr/robin/text_files
$ _                                  $ _
```

Now *text_files* is your current directory. You can use **ls** to display the files you've already stored in this directory:

```
$ ls | sp
barbershop         hours          rates          sections
$ _
```

## Searches and Simple Replacements

### Searching for Text

Let's use a file you've already created (*barbershop*) to illustrate how to search for text with an **ed** command:

1. Open the file:

   a. From the shell prompt, type *ed barbershop* and press RETURN:

```
$ ed barbershop
239

_
```

b. **ed** will respond with the size of the file in characters (239).

2. Search line 4 for the word *you're*, change it to *you are*, and display the changed line on the screen:

   a. Display the line as it is now with *4p*:

```
4p
If you're tired of getting
_
```

[underlining added for emphasis]

   b. Type *.s/you're/you are/p* and press RETURN:

```
.s/you're/you are/p
If you are tired of getting

_
```

[dot es slash . . . ]

Taking a close look at this command, we are asking **ed**

| | |
|---|---|
| `.s` | to search the current line (line 4) of the text |
| `/you're/` | for one sequence of characters (*you're*) |
| `you are/` | replace it with another (*you are*) |
| `p` | and then display line 4 with the replacement |

The period, or dot (.), in front of the s (substitute) command to indicate the current line is not required. From now on we'll leave it out.

3. Similarly, change *someone else* in line 5 to *a professional*:

   a. First display the line:

```
5p
scalped by someone else,
```

   b. Then make the change:

```
s/someone else/a professional/p
scalped by a professional,

_
```

## *Deleting Text*

You can also use the s command to delete text within a line. Type the text to be deleted between the first pair of slashes; then type nothing between the second pair (that is, type the slashes next to each other).

1. Let's delete the words *by a* from line 5:

   a. First display the line:

```
5p
scalped by a professional,
```

   b. Then type *s/by a //p* and press RETURN:

```
s/by a //p                    [You need a space after a]
scalped professional,
_
```

2. Let's also delete *the* from line 6:

   a. First display the line:

```
+p                            [Dot (.) omitted here, too]
come to the Scissor's Edge
_
```

   b. Delete the word *the*:

```
s/the //p                     [You need a space after the]
come to Scissor's Edge
_
```

The **p** (print) command that we've been using at the end of command lines is required in some instances, but not in others. However, to avoid confusion, we'll continue using it in all our examples.

3. Think of a way to change *professional* in line 5 to *professionally*:

   a. First display the line:

```
5p
scalped professional,
_
```

   b. Type *s/nal/nally/p* and press RETURN:

```
s/nal/nally/p
scalped professionally,
_
```

4. Now think of a way to restore *the* to line 6:

   a. First display the line:

```
+p                   [This plus sign is equivalent to +1]
come to Scissor's Edge
_
```

b. Insert the word *the*:

```
s/to/to the/
come to the Scissor's Edge
_
```

## *Context Searching*

So far you have used either absolute numbers (1, 3) or relative expressions (+2, -2) to locate lines. **ed** offers a third way: Using text surrounded by slashes. For example, since line 6 contains the word *Edge*, we can use this word to locate line 6 in a search. Once having located the desired line, we are then free to look for any text the line may contain.

1. As a simple example, let's change *come to* in line 6 to *enter*:

   a. First display the line number with an equal sign (=):

```
/Edge/=
6
_
```

[This is a handy way to determine the line number of any line]

   b. Display the text:

```
/Edge/p
come to the Scissor's Edge
_
```

   c. Type *s/come to/enter/* and press RETURN:

```
s/come to/enter/p
enter the Scissor's Edge
_
```

Taking a close look at this **substitute** command, we are asking **ed**

| | |
|---|---|
| `s` | to search the current line |
| `/come to/` | for one sequence of characters (*come to*) |
| `enter/` | replace it with another (*enter*) |
| `p` | and then display the line with the replacement |

In this example, */Edge/* is just another way of saying *6*, since this string of characters (*Edge*) is found in the sixth line.

2. Use a similar command to change *do* to *try* in line 7:

   a. First display the line number with an equal sign (=):

```
/and/=
7
_
```

b. Then display the text:

```
/and/p
and do it yourself.
_
```

c. This time type *s/do/try/p* and press RETURN:

```
s/do/try/p
and try it yourself.
_
```

In this example, we use *and* like a line number to locate the line. The substitution within the line can then be carried out (search for *do*, then replace *do* with *try*). Once again, */and/* is used here instead of 7. Since we may not know the exact number of the line we are looking for, something like */and/* is generally easier to use.

## More Context Searching

In the example you just tried, you used one word (*and*) to find the line; then you searched that line for another word (*do*). It would also be possible to substitute for the same word that you used to find the line. For example, suppose you wanted to change *and* to *then*. You could just type */and/s/and/then/* , but **ed** gives you a shorter way.

1. Change *and* to *then* in line 7:

   a. Move back to an earlier line (any line will do):

   ```
   4p
   If you are tired of getting
   _
   ```

   b. Type */and/s//then/p* and press RETURN:

   ```
   /and/s//then/p
   then try it yourself.
   _
   ```

Taking a close look at this command, we are asking **ed**

| | |
|---|---|
| `/and/s` | to search the first line that contains *and* |
| `//` | for the same sequence of characters (*and*) |
| `then/` | replace it with another (*then*) |
| `p` | and then display the line with the replacement |

In this example, the absence of a sequence of characters after the slash that follows *s* tells **ed** to search for the same string that was used to locate the line (*and*). This is what is known as the *remembered pattern.*

Haven't you seen this technique before—typing slashes back-to-back with nothing between them? Yes, you saw it earlier in this chapter, but it had a different meaning. Let's review that now.

2. Delete *professionally* from line 5:

   a. Display the line:

```
/scalped/p
scalped professionally,
_
```

   b. Type */ professionally/s///p* (with a space before *professionally* and three slashes after *s*) and press RETURN:

```
/ professionally/s///p
scalped,
_
```

[If you don't type a space in front of *professionally*, you will get a space between *scalped* and the comma.]

Taking a close look at this command, we are asking **ed**

| | |
|---|---|
| `/ professionally/s` | to search the first line that contains this string |
| `//` | for the same string of characters (*professionally*) |
| `/` | replace it with another ( )—no characters |
| `p` | and then display the line with the replacement |

In this example, adjacent slashes were used with two different meanings. With the first pair of adjacent slashes after *s*, you were telling **ed**, "Use the 'remembered pattern.'" With the second pair of adjacent slashes, you were telling **ed**, "Replace these characters with the characters I am typing between these slashes (no characters)."

3. Using the same techniques, delete *yourself* from line 7:

   a. Display the line number:

```
/try/=
7
_
```

   b. Display the text in the line:

```
/try/p
then try it yourself.
_
```

c. Type *s/ yourself//p* (with a space after *s/*) and press RETURN:

```
s/ yourself//p
then try it.
_
```

This concludes our discussion of single substitutions. Next we'll talk about multiple substitutions. But first, let's abandon the editing buffer so that we can start over with the original text in the file *barbershop*. Just type *q* and press RETURN twice in succession (on separate lines), and the UNIX shell prompt will return to the screen, with *barbershop* untouched by the changes we've made so far in this chapter.

# Multiple Substitutions

## *Making More Than One Substitution*

Until now, you have made only single substitutions with the **s** command. However, **ed** also allows you to make multiple substitutions. To illustrate how this works, we'll use something different this time.

1. Re-enter **ed** and start a new editing session with the file *multiple*:

   a. At the shell prompt, type *ed* and press RETURN:

   ```
   $ ed multiple
   ?multiple
   _
   ```

   b. Using **a** to begin the text and . to end it, type the following:

   ```
   a
   Down the trail they rode, one by one, one by one,
   through the canyon, one by one, one by one,
   into the clearing, one by one, one by one,
   across the desert, one by one, one by one.
   .
   _
   ```

   c. Save the text:

   ```
   w
   128
   _
   ```

This text may not say very much, but it contains many instances of the same word in a few lines, which is just what we need to illustrate multiple substitutions. (Any character, word, or phrase for which you are searching or which you are replacing is called a **string**—not just in UNIX, but in computer usage in general.)

2. Start by making a single substitution in the first line:

   a. First display the line:

```
1p
Down the trail they rode, one by one, one by one,
_
```

   b. Replace *one* with *two* once:

```
s/one/two/p
Down the trail they rode, two by one, one by one,
_
```

   c. **ed** will replace the first instance of *one* in the first line.

In this form, the command replaces only the first instance of a string in the first line in which it is found. The next step is to use a command that will replace a sequence as many times as it occurs in a line. This involves adding a **g** (global) command **to the end of** the command line.

3. Make multiple substitutions in the first line:

   a. Display the first line again:

```
1p
Down the trail they rode, two by one, one by one,
_
```

   b. Use the **global** modifier this time:

```
s/one/two/gp
Down the trail they rode, two by two, two by two,
_
```

   c. Now type *1,$* to display all the lines together:

```
1,$p
Down the trail they rode, two by two, two by two,
through the canyon, one by one, one by one,
into the clearing, one by one, one by one,
across the desert, one by one, one by one.
_
```

**ed** changes every instance of *one* to *two* in the first line, but not in any of the other lines. Added **to the end of** a command line for a substitution, the **g** (global) command produces multiple substitutions on a single line. The word *global* means "applicable anywhere in the text."

*"He's just returned from a global search."*

Now you've learned how to make multiple replacements in the horizontal direction (within a line). The next step is to make multiple replacements in the vertical direction (within the entire work area). This involves placing line numbers **in front of** the substitute command string.

4. Make substitutions in all lines:

   a. Display the first line again:

```
1p
Down the trail they rode, two by two, two by two,
_
```

   b. Make the substitution and display the first six lines:

```
1,$s/one/two/
1,$p
Down the trail they rode, two by two, two by two,
through the canyon, two by one, one by one,
into the clearing, two by one, one by one,
across the desert, two by one, one by one.
_
```

This time **ed** changes the first instance of *one* to *two* in each line of text. Added **to the beginning of** a command line for a substitution, line numbers produce substitutions on all lines, but only for the first instance on each line. This provides multiple substitutions in the vertical direction (down through a work area).

Now that you've learned how to make multiple substitutions in either the horizontal direction or the vertical direction, the next step is to make multiple substitutions in both directions (that is, to make substitutions for all instances on all lines). This involves placing line numbers **in front of** the command line and **g at the end of** the command line.

5. Make substitutions in all lines:

   a. Display the first line again:

```
1p
Down the trail they rode, two by two, two by two,
_
```

   b. Make the substitution and display the first six lines:

```
1,$s/one/two/g
1,$p
Down the trail they rode, two by two, two by two,
through the canyon, two by two, two by two,
into the clearing, two by two, two by two,
across the desert, two by two, two by two.
_
```

c. This time **ed** changes all remaining instance of *one* to *two* in each line.

With line numbers **in front of** the command line and another **g at the end**, you can have **ed** make replacements everywhere in the work area.

## *Repeated Searches* **//p**

A context search does not always bring you the line you are looking for on the first try. Sometimes you have to continue the search several more times. Let's use the text you've been editing to see how this works.

1. Return to the first line of text:

   a. Use *1p* to display the first line:

   ```
   1p
   Down the trail they rode, two by two, two by two,

   _
   ```

   b. With the first line displayed on the screen, the current line (.) is now 1.

2. Begin a search for a string that occurs more than once:

   a. Use a context search to locate the next line that contains *two*: **//p**

   ```
   /two/p
   through the canyon, two by two, two by two,

   _
   ```

   b. Suppose this isn't the line you are looking for.

3. Continue the search:

   a. Use // to indicate the *remembered pattern* (*two*):

   ```
   //p
   into the clearing, two by two, two by two,

   _
   ```

   b. Now you have found another line with *two*.

4. Continue the search again:

   a. Use // to indicate the "remembered pattern" (*two*):

   ```
   //p
   across the desert, two by two, two by two.

   _
   ```

b. Now you have found yet another line with *two*.

If necessary, you could continue to use the *remembered pattern* many more times to carry on an extensive search through a long editing buffer.

Stop the editing session and abandon the text by typing *q* and pressing RETURN twice in succession (on separate lines).

# Other Aids in Searching

## *Beginning of a Line* ^

A caret (^) is used in **ed** and other UNIX programs to indicate the beginning of a line of text.

1. Begin another editing session:

   a. Start an **ed** session with *barbershop*:

```
$ ed barbershop
239

_
```

   b. Again, **ed** responds with the number of characters read (239).

2. Use the caret (^) to insert spaces in front of line 1:

   a. First display the line:

```
1p
          ______________________

_
```

   b. Then use ^ to insert five spaces in front of the line:

```
s/^/     /p                [Replace beginning of line with     ]
          ______________________
```

3. Take advantage of the spaces to select line 3:

   a. Display lines 1-3 to see the difference:

```
1,3p
          ______________________
                    Notice
     ______________________

_
```

   b. Display line 1 again to make line 1 the current line:

```
1p
          ______________________

_
```

c. Use ^ to select line 3 instead of line 1 to make a change (only line 3 **begins with** a hyphen):

```
/^-/s/-----/+++++/   [Five minus signs and five plus signs]
+++++-------------------

_
```

d. Display the results with *1,3p*:

```
1,3p
        ------------------------
               Notice
+++++--------------------
```

**ed** bypasses line 1 and selects line 3 instead because the minus sign is the very first character on line 3. The caret (^) tells **ed** to select a line only if the minus sign is found **at the beginning** of the line. Line 1 also contains many minus signs, but not at the beginning of the line.

## *End of a Line* $

When used in front of an **ed** command as a line number, the dollar sign ($) indicates the last line of the editing buffer. But when used between slashes in a search string, the dollar sign ($) takes on another meaning—a meaning at least similar to its other meaning—*end of line.* The dollar sign ($) is used very much the way the caret (^ ) is used. For example, you could use *$* to add a missing word to the end of a line. ^ $

1. Add more characters to the end of line 3:

   a. Display the line:

```
3p
+++++------------------

_
```

   b. Use *$* to add +++++ (five plus signs) to the end of the line:

```
s/$/+++++/p
+++++--------------------+++++

_
```

You could also use *$* in conjunction with a string to make a distinction between two strings that are otherwise identical. For example, in line 3, we have two sequences of plus signs, one at the beginning of the line and one at the end. With the dollar sign ($), we can direct **ed**'s attention to the string of plus signs on the right (that is, at the end of the line).

In UNIX terminology, the caret (^) and the dollar sign ($) are said to **anchor** the text.

*"Captain, which one of these anchors should I use?"*

2. Replace the plus signs at the end of line 3 with equal signs:

   a. Display the line:

```
3p
+++++-------------------+++++
_
```

b. Replace the plus signs at the end of the line with equal signs:

```
s/+++++$/=====/p
```
[Note the dollar sign ($)]

```
+++++--------------------=====

_
```

If we had left the *end of line* character ($) out of the command, **ed** would have replaced the plus signs on the left, and we would have ended up with this:

```
s/+++++/=====/p
```

```
=====--------------------+++++

_
```

Since +++++ occurs first at the beginning of the line, /+++++/ is equivalent to /^+++++/ in this instance.

## Beginning and End of a Line ^ $

By combining the beginning of line (^) and end of line ($) characters within the same pair of slashes, you can single out a string that appears by itself on a line. For example, if you wanted to locate a line that contained no characters (that is, a blank line), you could use /^$/ as a search string. Let's use this to replace the two blank lines in the editing buffer: ^ $

1. Prepare to replace the blank lines:

   a. Display lines 8-15 of the editing buffer:

```
8,15p
```

```
          Rates
Self service      $5
Full service      $10

          Hours
Monday-Friday    10-6
Weekends         10-4

_
```

   b. Make line 8 the current line:

```
8p
```

```

_
```

2. Replace the blank lines with lines that contain plus signs:

   a. Make the replacement (8 spaces, then 3 plus signs):

```
g/^$/s//        + + +/
_
```

   b. Display the results:

```
8,15p
        + + +
        Rates
Self service      $5
Full service      $10
        + + +
        Hours
Monday-Friday    10-6
Weekends         10-4
_
```

## *Repeat the Search String* &

There is a special character (&) that allows you to make insertions into a line without unnecessary typing. The ampersand (&) tells **ed** to repeat the search string in the replacement string. For example, you could use */word/s//&s/p* to change *word* to *words* (that is, to make it plural). Here are some more examples:

1. Insert a word into the middle of a line:

   a. First display line 4:

```
4p
If you're tired of getting
_
```

   b. Use *&* to insert *really* in front of *tired*:

```
s/tired/really &/p
If you're really tired of getting
_
```

In this example, & represents *tired* repeated in the replacement string. But it could also be used to repeat something longer, as the next example shows.

2. Surround *Notice* with characters:

a. First display line 2:

```
2p
          Notice

_
```

b. Then use the *repeat* symbol & to surround *Notice* with plus signs (and spaces):

```
s/Notice/+ & +/p
        + Notice +

_
```

This calls for an instant replay:

| | |
|---|---|
| `s` | Search the current line (line 2) |
| `/Notice/` | for *Notice* |
| `+ & +/` | place one plus sign before and one after *Notice* |
| `p` | and then display the line as modified. |

Now abandon the text in the editing buffer by typing *q* and pressing RETURN twice in succession (on separate lines).

## *Turning Off Special Meaning* \

As you have learned, the following characters are used for special purposes in **ed**. They cannot ordinarily be used in context searches and substitution commands.

/ ^ $ & . * [ ]

One character (\) can be used to turn off the meaning of any special character in an **s** (substitute) command, thereby making it possible to search for one of these characters in its literal meaning. Note, however, that \ cannot be used in an **a** (append), **i** (insert), or **c** (change) command. Let's return to *barbershop* to see how this works.

1. Start an editing session:

   a. Execute **ed** with *barbershop*:

```
$ ed barbershop
239

_
```

   b. Display lines 10 and 11:

```
10,11p
Self service       $5
Full service      $10

_
```

We would like to replace *$5* with *$7* and *$10* with *$15*, but there's a problem: The dollar sign means *end of line* in **ed**. However, there's a way to get around this. If we type a backslash (\) in front of the dollar sign ($), **ed** will ignore the dollar sign's special meaning and treat it literally.

2. Change the dollar amounts:

   a. Use a backslash to **quote** the dollar sign:

```
/\$5/s//$7/p
Self service      $7
_
```

   Here's an instant replay:

| | |
|---|---|
| `/\$5/s` | Search the line that contains *$5* (you need a backslash here) |
| `//` | for *$5* |
| `$7/` | and replace it with *$7* (no backslash—you're not searching) |
| p | then display the line with the correction. |

   b. Make a similar substitution in line 11:

```
/\$10/s//$15/p
Full service      $15
_
```

In each case, we need a backslash in the search string, but not in the replacement string. Since no searching is taking place, the replacement string can be typed literally.

## *Match a Character*

When placed in front of an **ed** command like **s** or **i**, the period (.) stands for the current line. But in a search string, it can be used to match any character you are searching for. For example, you could use *A.E* in a search string to find *ABE*, *ACE*, *APE*, *ATE*, and so on. This can be useful in searching for other special characters and control characters.

To show how this works, let's add a few lines of text. The first line of new text will contain three CTRL-G characters (sometimes abbreviated as *^G*). These characters will not appear on the screen; they are shown below so that you will know where to type them.

1. Type an extra line with control characters embedded:

   a. Use *$a* to make the addition:

```
$a
```

```
Th^Gis i^Gs the pl^Gace.
.
_
```

This line (line 16 of the editing buffer) contains a CTRL-G (^G) in the middle of three different words.

b. Save the text and note the character count:

```
w
261
_
```

2. Display line 16, then remove the embedded control characters:

a. Display line 16 with the **p** (print) command:

```
16 p
This is the place.              [You may hear three beeps]
_
```

b. Now display line 16 with the **l** (list) command:

```
16 l                            [sixteen el]
Th\07is i\07s the pl\07ace.[No beeps this time]
_
```

c. We'll need a separate **s** command for each correction:

```
s/Th.is/This/l
This i\07s the pl\07ace.       [Change Th\07is to This]
s/i.s/is/l
This is the pl\07ace.          [Change i\07s to is]
s/pl.ace/place/l
This is the place.             [Change pl\07ace to place]
_
```

The period (.) in each search string was able to locate a control character so that it could be removed from the text.

## *Repeat a Character*

Use the asterisk (*) in a search string to mean "any number of repetitions of the previous character." For example, you could use *s/a*/B/* to change *a*, *aaa*, *aaaaa*, and so on, to *B*. Here is an example from line 1 of *barbershop*:

1. Display line 1, then delete the minus signs:

   a. Display line 1 with the **p** command:

```
1p
-----------------------
_
```

   b. Use the s command to make the replacement:

```
s/-*/No more hyphens/p
No more hyphens                    [The hyphens are gone.]
_
```

In this command, -* means "any number of consecutive hyphens." This can be a handy device, because it means you don't have to know the exact number of characters you are looking for.

The expression .*, combining the period (.) and the asterisk (*), has a very broad meaning: *Any number of any combination of characters.* For example, you could use *s/.*//* to delete any string of any length. Or you could use *s/.*:/*______*/* to replace all text that precedes a colon with five blank spaces. Let's try .* with our text in file *barbershop.*

2. Display line 5, then delete all text after *scalped*:

   a. Display line 5 with the **p** command:

```
5p
scalped by someone else,
_
```

   b. Use s and .* to delete the words after *scalped*:

```
s/ped.*/ped,/p
scalped,
_
```

   Here's an instant replay:

| | |
|---|---|
| `s` | Search the current line (line 5) |
| `/ped.*` | for *by someone else,* |
| `ped,/` | replace that with a comma |
| `p` | then display the corrected line. |

   The period in *ped.** means *any character.*

Note that the asterisk's interpretation of "any number of characters" includes "no characters." For example, **ed** could take *n** to mean any of the following: *nnnnnnnnnn* (10), *nnnnn* (5), *nn* (2), *n* (1), or (0). (However, if there is any choice, the longest leftmost string that can be matched is selected.)

To make sure that **ed** will interpret the search string as meaning "at least one character," type the character **twice** in front of the asterisk (for example, nn* to match *n*). In some instances, when you want to be sure there are at least **two** characters, you will even have to type the character **three times** in front of the asterisk (for example, *nnn** to match *nn*).

## *Match One of a Set* [ ]

If *any character* is too broad a set to have to match, you can narrow the selection to a specific set of characters by enclosing them within square brackets. For example, you could use either of the following to search for any single digit and replace it with a number sign (#).

```
/[0123456789]/s//#/p
```

or

```
/[0-9]/s//#/p
```

You can either enumerate all choices between the brackets or indicate a range of characters, using a hyphen between the two extreme values. Here are three more examples:

| | |
|---|---|
| `[A-Z]` | All uppercase letters |
| `[a-z]` | All lowercase letters |
| `[A-Za-z]` | All letters of the alphabet |

To illustrate the use of these methods, let's start by looking at the lines under *Hours* in *barbershop.* [ ]

1. Look at the two lines under *Hours*:

   a. Use */Hours/,/Hours+2/p* (or *13,15p*) to display the lines:

   ```
   /Hours/,/Hours/+2p
             Hours
   Self service   10-6
   Full service   10-4

   _
   ```

   b. Notice how the last two lines contain some letters and some numbers.

2. Change each set of times to *Closed*:

   a. Display the *Hours* line again (to move the current line back):

   ```
   13 p
             Hours

   _
   ```

   b. Change the hours:

   ```
   14,15s/1[0-9]-[0-9]$/ Closed/
   14,15 p
   Self service   Closed
   Full service   Closed

   _
   ```

Here's an instant replay:

| | |
|---|---|
| `14,15s` | Search lines 14 and 15 |
| `/1[0-9]-[0-9]$/` | for the pattern 1n-m at the end of the line (where *n* and *m* are both digits) |
| `Closed/` | replace it with *Closed* |

You can also ask **ed** to search for "any characters **except** those listed." To do this, start the list with a caret (^) immediately after the left bracket. For example, you could use *./[^ijklmn]/s//real/p* or *./[^i-n]/s//real/p* to search for any characters **except** i, j, k, l, m, or n.

End this session by typing *q* and pressing RETURN twice in succession.

## Summary of Chapter 8

In this chapter you learned how to search the buffer for a given sequence of characters (or **string**), delete a string, substitute one string for another, use a string to locate a line (context searching), search in reverse, make multiple substitutions, and repeat a search. You also learned how to use the characters that perform special functions in a search or in an **s** (substitute) command: Beginning of a line (^), end of a line ($), repeat a search string (&), turn off special meaning ( \ ), match a character (.), repeat a character (*), and match one of a set ([ ]). These are sometimes called **metacharacters.**

### *Searches and Simple Replacements*

**Searching and replacing.** To search a line of text for a string and replace this string with another, enter a command line that contains the line number, the **s** command, and the two strings between slashes. You can also add **p** at the end of the command to have the resulting line displayed on the screen.

**Deleting a string.** To delete a string from a line of text, enter a command line for a substitution, but leave the replacement string empty.

**Searching by context.** If you don't know the exact number of a line that contains a string, you can use the string itself (or another string) to search for the line, then enter the rest of the command line.

**Using the search string as the old string.** If the search string is also the string you intend to replace, **ed** allows you to leave the latter empty, thereby abbreviating the command.

**Using another separator.** If necessary, you can use another character, such as a colon (:), in place of the slash (/) to separate items in an **s** command.

## *Multiple Substitutions*

**Making more than one replacement on a line.** To replace all instances of a string, rather than just the first on a line, add **g** to the end of the command string.

**Making replacements on all lines.** To replace the first instance of a string on all lines, rather than on only the first matching line, type line numbers in front of the command line.

**Making all replacements.** To replace all instances of a string on all lines, type line numbers in front of the command line **g** at the end.

**Repeating a search.** To repeat a search, you can just type a pair of slashes (//) for a forward search instead of having to type the entire search command again.

## *Other Searching Aids*

**Beginning of line.** To indicate the beginning of a line of text, type a caret (∧) at the beginning of a search string (not within brackets).

**End of line.** To indicate the end of a line of text, type a dollar sign ($) at the end of a search string.

**Repeat search string.** To repeat the entire search string, use an ampersand (&) in a substitution string.

**Turning off special meaning.** To turn off the special meaning of a character to **ed** (that is, to have it entered as an ordinary text character), type a backslash ( \ ) in front of any special character.

**Match a character.** To have **ed** search for any single character, type a period (.) in a search string.

**Repeat a character.** To have **ed** search for any number of the characters (including none), type an asterisk (*) immediately after a character. The combination .* in a search string means *anything*.

**Match one of a set.** By placing characters between a pair of square brackets, you can enumerate the characters for which **ed** is to search.

Enter a caret (∧) as the first character after the left bracket to indicate negation (that is, to have **ed** search for all characters **except** those listed).

# 9

# Editing Techniques Using ed

In Chapter 8 you learned how to use special characters in searches and replacements. In this chapter you will learn how to use these characters to perform a variety of editing techniques: Splitting a line, joining lines, rearranging a line, and using an editing script.

## Operations on Lines

### Splitting a Line

In Chapter 8 you used the backslash ( \ ) in front of a special character to remove its special meaning. By using this same backslash just before pressing the RETURN key, you can split a single line of text into two lines. First we'll need a new file and some text to work with:

1. Start an editing session:

   a. Move to directory *text_files* if necessary:

   ```
   $ cd text_files
   $ _
   ```

   b. Start editing with *pfl.deal*:

   ```
   $ ed pfl.deal
   ?pfl.deal

   _
   ```

   c. Add some text (leave a blank space at the end of each line, don't type the line numbers, and use the TAB key for spacing information in the columns):

```
    a
1   Dear Mr. Madison:
2   The purpose of this letter is
3   to confirm Monday's agreement.
4   Tupelo gets "Porkchop" Peterson,
5   you get "Earthquake" Emerson,
6   and we get "Rotunda" Robinson.
7   Here are the players' names, heights, weights, and new teams:
8   Emerson, Ezekiel R.     6'5"   273 Rochester
9   Robinson, Charles F.    6'3"   287 Des Moines
10  Peterson, Paul N.       5'9"   178 Tupelo
11  You will be getting one of the finest players in the People's Football League.
12  Your Friend and Mine, Chuck

    .
    w
    467
    _
```

2. Split line 11 into two lines:

   a. First display the line:

```
11p
You will be getting one of the finest players in the People's
Football League. [This will appear as one line.]

_
```

   b. Use the backslash (\) just before a RETURN to split the line after *finest* (using *est*):

```
s/est /est \    [Press RETURN right after typing the backslash]
/               [Type the closing slash on this line]
11,12p          [Display the two lines]
You will be getting one of the finest
players in the People's Football League.

_
```

Here's an instant replay:

```
s        Search the current line (line 11)
/est /   for the string est (with a space following the t)
est \    and replace it with "est ", followed by a RETURN.
/
11,12p   Then display the line with the modification.
```

Pressing the RETURN key after the backslash (\) told **ed** that you wanted a RETURN placed at that location in the text (that is, that you wanted a new line of text to begin at that location).

## *Joining Lines* j

You can join separate lines together to form a single line by using the **j** (join) command. If used by itself (that is, without a pair of line numbers in front of it), **j** joins the current line with the line that follows, and is equivalent to *.,.+1j*. For any other case, you must supply the line numbers, using either actual numbers or context strings. For our first example, let's join lines 4 and 5 of the editing buffer.

1. Join lines 4 and 5 to form a single line:

   a. Display the lines to be joined:

```
4,5p
Tupelo gets "Porkchop" Peterson,
you get "Earthquake" Emerson,
_
```

   b. Join them together with the **j** command:

```
4,5jp
Tupelo gets "Porkchop" Peterson, you get "Earthquake" Emerson,
_
```

2. Join lines 2 and 3 into a single line:

   a. Display the lines to be joined:

```
2,3p
The purpose of this letter is
to confirm Monday's agreement.
_
```

   b. Use *j* to join the lines:

```
2,3jp
The purpose of this letter is to confirm Monday's agreement.
_
```

The success of this operation rests on the assumption that there is a blank space after *is* in line 2. If you forgot the blank space, then the line will look like this:

The purpose of this letter **isto** confirm Monday's agreement.

j

You can insert the space now with a command like this: *s/__ is/& /p.*

If necessary, you can also use the **j** (join) command to combine three or more lines into a single line. Just place a pair of line numbers in front of *j* to indicate the first and last line to be included.

## *Rearranging Lines*

\\( \\)

If you need to rearrange a group of lines according to a fixed format, you can bracket substrings of each line with the symbols \\( and \\) in a search string. You can then call these substrings by numbers in the replacement string to accomplish the rearrangement. For example, suppose you have a list of names in this format (last name first):

| | | | |
|---|---|---|---|
| Emerson, Ezekiel R. | 6'5" | 273 | Rochester |
| Robinson, Charles F. | 6'3" | 287 | Des Moines |
| Peterson, Paul N. | 5'9" | 178 | Tupelo |

and you would prefer to have them in this format (first name first):

| | | | |
|---|---|---|---|
| Ezekiel R. Emerson | 6'5" | 273 | Rochester |
| Charles F. Robinson | 6'3" | 287 | Des Moines |
| Paul N. Peterson | 5'9" | 178 | Tupelo |

In other words, you would like to delete the commas and move the first names and middle initials in front of the surnames. To do this, we group the contents of each line into substrings: (1) surname and (2) first name and middle initial, plus (3) height, (4) weight, and (5) team. In the exercise that follows, we'll be dealing with substrings 1 and 2, leaving substrings 3, 4, and 5 unchanged.

Here's the way it works: We can designate substrings in the search string of an s (substitute) command by surrounding them with "quoted parentheses." These "quoted parentheses" look like this:

\\( substring 1 \\)    \\( substring 2 \\)    \\( substring 3 \\)    etc.

Make no mistake about it. These things are not easy to read. You already have enough backslashes and other assortments of characters floating around in your search string. These "quoted parentheses" (also known as **tags**) don't make it any easier to read.

Anyway, once we have these substrings (also known as **tagged regular expressions**) designated **in the search string**, we can then call them by number **in the substitution string**, using notation like this:

\\1    \\2    \\3    etc.

These are very much like the ampersand (&), which you can use to repeat the **entire** search string. The difference is that you can use each substring symbol to repeat **part** of the search string. Once again, **ed** simply numbers substrings from left to right in the search string.

1. Rearrange the three lines according to this plan:

   a. First display the three lines as they appear now:

```
$ 6,8p
Emerson, Ezekiel R.      6'5"    273    Rochester
Robinson, Charles F.     6'3"    287    Des Moines
Peterson, Paul N.        5'9"    178    Tupelo

_
```

   b. Construct a command to carry out the plan:

```
6,8s/^\([^,]*\), *\([^\.]*\.\)/\2 \1/
6,8p
Ezekiel R. Emerson       6'5"    273    Rochester
Charles F. Robinson      6'3"    287    Des Moines
Paul N. Peterson         5'9"    178    Tupelo
_
```

   c. Study the instant replay:

```
6,8s/^ \( [^,]* \), *\( [^\.]* \. \) /\2 \1/
```

| | |
|---|---|
| `6,8s` | Search lines 6, 7, and 8 and substitute in all |
| `/` | Start the search string here |
| `^` | Search at the beginning of each line for . . . |
| `\(` | (the first substring starts here) |
| `[^,]*` | any number of non-commas (everything up to, but not including, the comma that follows the last name) |
| `\)` | (the first substring ends here) |
| `, *` | Then search for a comma, followed by some spaces |
| `\(` | (the second substring starts here) |
| `[^\.]*` | Search for any number of non-periods (everything up to, but not including, the period), |
| `\.` | then the period that follows the middle initial |
| `\)` | (the second substring ends here) |
| `/` | End the search string; start the replacement string |
| `\2` | The second substring goes first on the new line |
| `\1` | followed by a space and then the first substring |
| `/` | End the replacement string |
| `6,8p` | Print the lines that have been changed |

This command took advantage of the fact that a comma separated first names from last names and that each name ended with a period (after the middle initial). For the sake of simplicity, the remaining three items (height, weight, and team) were ignored in the substitution string. To move them around also, we could refer to them as *\3*, *\4*, and *\5*.)

2. Continue to ponder the instant replay of this **strange** command:

   a. Think what it means to be able to execute commands like this.

   b. See if you can think up other commands like this one.

c. Abandon the text and end this editing session:

```
q
$ _
```

# Using an Editing Script

## *Setting Up the Files*

Suppose you have a long sequence of **ed** commands, and suppose you need to use these commands on more than one file. You could call in the first file for editing, type all the commands and execute them, call in the second file, type the commands again, and so on. **ed** provides an easier way to do all this: just enter the commands once into a separate file, then name that file each time you need to process another text file. The file that contains nothing but commands is called a **command file**, or **editing script**. In the following example, you will enter some commands into an editing script, then call on the editing script to process several text files.

1. Start an editing session and enter commands as text:

   a. Start an editing session with *switch*:

   ```
   $ ed switch
   ? switch
   _
   ```

   b. Enter the "re-arrangement command" you learned earlier in this chapter (with line numbers *1,$*), plus three additional **ed** commands (**1,$p**, **w**, and **q**):

   ```
   a
   1,$s/^\([^,]*\), *\([^\.]*\.\)/\2 \1/
   1,$p
   w
   q        [Make sure you have these three lines]
   .
   _
   ```

   c. Save this text and end the editing session:

   ```
   w
   47
   q
   $ _
   ```

2. Begin another editing session and write out the players' names:

   a. Start an editing session with *pfl.deal* and display the lines with the players' names:

```
$ ed pfl.deal
467
8,10 p
Emerson, Ezekiel R.     6'5"    273    Rochester
Robinson, Charles F.    6'3"    287    Des Moines
Peterson, Paul N.       5'9"    178    Tupelo

_
```

   b. Write these lines to a new file called *players.in*:

```
8,10 w players.in
113
$ _
```

   c. Abandon the text and end the editing session:

```
q
$ _
```

3. Begin another editing session and enter some new names:

   a. Start an editing session with *owners.in* and enter five lines:

```
$ ed owners.in
?owners.in
a
Williams, Kenneth L.
Emerson, Patrick R.
Lanier, Benjamin G.
Barton, Rudolph W.
Peterson, Michael E.
.
_
```

   b. Save this text and end the editing session:

```
w
101
q
$ _
```

At this point you have a set of commands stored in one file (*switch*) and some lists stored in two other files (*players.in* and *owners.in*). Now you are ready to issue a command to process each of the text files, using the commands in the **command file**, or **editing script**. (Since processing by **ed** will change the input files, we'll work with **copies** of the original files.)

4. First make copies of the files:

   a. Copy *players.in* to *players.out*:

```
$ cp players.in players.out
$ _
```

   b. Copy *owners.in* to *owners.out*:

```
$ cp owners.in owners.out
$ _
```

5. Process each text file with the command file:

   a. Switch the names in *players.out*, using *switch* as the input:

```
$ ed players.out < switch
113                                       [113 characters input]
Ezekiel R. Emerson     6'5"    273    Rochester
Charles F. Robinson    6'3"    287    Des Moines
Paul N. Peterson       5'9"    178    Tupelo
110                                       [110 characters output]
$ _
```

   b. Switch the names in *owners.out*, using *switch* as the input:

```
$ ed owners.out < switch
101       [101 characters input]
Kenneth L. Williams
Patrick R. Emerson
Benjamin G. Lanier
Rudolph. W. Barton
Michael E. Peterson
96        [96 characters output]
$ _
```

What has happened? In each case, you typed an ordinary **ed** command line, with one additional item added at the end (< *switch*). This told **ed** to accept input from a file named *switch*, instead of from the standard input (the keyboard). **ed** then sent the results to the standard output (displayed them on the screen). Since the arrow is pointing **away** from the name *switch*, this means that information is coming from this file (that is, you are redirecting **input**).

## Alphabetizing a List

**sort**

Suppose that, in addition to switching surnames with initials, you would also like to alphabetize each of these lists. Although **ed** doesn't have a feature to take care of this, UNIX does—the **sort** command. Let's use the **sort** command here to alphabetize these lists, and also to introduce another feature of UNIX.

1. Since a list must be alphabetized before switching, begin with the **sort** command, then proceed with **ed**:

   a. Sort *owners.in*, placing the results in a file called *temp*:

   ```
   $ sort owners.in >temp
   $ _
   ```

   b. Display the contents of *temp*:

   ```
   $ cat temp
   Barton, Rudolph. W.
   Emerson, Patrick R.
   Lanier, Benjamin G.
   Peterson, Michael E.
   Williams, Kenneth L.
   $ _
   ```

   **sort**

   c. Switch the names, placing the results in *owners.sort*:

   ```
   $ ed temp < switch > owners.sort
   $ _
   ```

   d. Display the contents of *owners.sort*:

   ```
   $ cat owners.sort
   101
   Rudolph. W. Barton
   Patrick R. Emerson
   Benjamin G. Lanier
   Michael E. Peterson
   Kenneth L. Williams
   96
   $ _
   ```

   e. Remove the first and last lines (101 and 96):

   ```
   $ ed owners.sort
   103
   1d                        [Delete the first line]
   $d                        [Delete the last line]
   1,$p
   ```

```
Rudolph. W. Barton
Patrick R. Emerson
Benjamin G. Lanier
Michael E. Peterson
Kenneth L. Williams
w
96
q
$ _
```

f. Remove the temporary file *temp*:

```
$ rm temp
$ _
```

## Summary of Chapter 9

In this chapter you learned how to split a line, how to join lines, how to rearrange a line, how to move text from one file to another, and how to use editing scripts.

### *Operations on Lines*

**Splitting a line.** Use a backslash (\) followed by a RETURN in the replacement string of an **s** (substitution) command to split a line.

**Joining lines.** Use the **j** command, preceded by a pair of line numbers (indicating the first and last line to be joined), to join several lines together.

**Rearranging a line.** Use the symbols \( and \) to bracket substrings of each line in the search string of an **s** command, then use numbers in the replacement string to rearrange these substrings.

### *Using an Editing Script*

Enter the desired command(s) in a special file; then when you enter your **ed** command, redirect input from that special file, using the < symbol in front of the file's name.

# 10

# Executing UNIX Commands Using **ed**

## Staying in an Editing Session

Suppose you're in the middle of an editing session with **ed** (or another editor) and you need to execute a UNIX command. For example, you may want to run **date** to find out what time it is or you may want to run **wc** to check the length of a file. Ordinarily, you would have to end your editing session, run the UNIX command from the shell prompt, then return to your editing session. UNIX has a feature that allows you to **escape** temporarily without having to end your editing session: just precede the UNIX command with an exclamation mark (!). The command will be handed over to the shell to be executed, and you won't have to leave **ed**. This is known as "**escaping**" to the shell."

### *Checking the Time*

For example, suppose you're in the middle of an editing session and you'd like to check the time. Let's try this:

1. Start an editing session with a new file:

   a. Start **ed** with *spaces*:

```
$ ed spaces
?spaces
_
```

   b. Type the text with blank lines between:

```
a
```

*"We'd like to escape to the shell."*

```
This is line 1

This is line 2


This is line 3
.
_
```

[Two blank lines]

[Three blank lines]

2. Now check the time:

   a. Type an exclamation mark (!) in front of the **date** command:

```
!date
Tue Mar 23 11:36:43 PST 1985
!

_
```

   b. Now you are free to resume editing (or to execute another UNIX command).

### *Checking the Length of a File*

As another example, you could use an escape (!) to determine how long a file is. Continuing the steps just given above, use the **wc** (word count) command like this:

1. Display the statistics on *barbershop*:

```
!wc barbershop
16 37 265 barbershop
!

_
```

This tells you that *barbershop* contains 16 lines, 37 words, and 259 characters.

2. Store the text and return to the UNIX shell prompt:

```
w
50
q
$ _
```

## Executing a C Program

### *Compiling as an Example*

In the previous section you learned how to execute a UNIX command without leaving **ed**. In this section we'll combine that concept with a very brief discussion of C programming. We'll enter a C program and then compile the program. This book is not about C programming, so we will use only simple C programs in this chapter. The main point of this chapter is not how to write a C program, but how to execute a UNIX command during an editing session with **ed**. Some of the UNIX commands we'll be using here will be the C compiler **cc**, **chmod**, **ls**, and **sort**.

## Starting with a New Directory

Once again, let's start this chapter by creating a new subdirectory in your home directory to contain your C programs, then move to this directory for the exercises in this chapter.

1. Create a new directory:

   a. From your home directory, create a directory called *c_progs* with the **mkdir** command:

   ```
   $ mkdir c_progs
   $ _
   ```

   b. The directory has been created, but you are still in your home directory.

2. Move from your home directory to *c_progs*:

   a. Move to subdirectory *c_progs* with the **cd** command:

   ```
   $ cd c_progs
   $ _
   ```

   b. *c_progs* is now your working directory; any files you create will be stored in this directory.

## Entering the First Program

In this section you will use **ed** to enter a short C program, compile the program, make corrections with **ed**, compile again, and then run the program. To run the C compiler **cc** during an editing session, precede the command with an exclamation point (!). Once compilation is completed, another exclamation point will appear and control will return to **ed**.

The C program you enter next will convert gallons to liters for six specified amounts (10, 12, 14, 16, 18, and 20 gallons). You can also make adjustments in the variables to convert other amounts if you like. Before you begin with step 1, make sure you are still in subdirectory *c_progs*. If you aren't sure, use the **pwd** command to find out the name of your working directory.

## Entering the Program

Since you now have a directory for storing your two C programs, enter the first program and store it in this directory.

1. Start a new editing session:

a. Type *ed* and the name of the file and press RETURN to start:

```
$ ed metric.c
_
```

b. Enter this C program (not including the line numbers):

```
a
/* Print a list of conversions from gallons to liters */
main()
{
  int low, high, incr;
  float gals, ltrs;

  low = 10;   /* starting value in gallons */
  high = 20;  /* ending value in gallons */
  incr = 2;   /* increment for each step */

  gals = low;
  while (gals <= high)
  {
    ltrs = (gals * 3.785)                          [Error on this line]
    printf("%4.0f %6.2f\n", gals, ltrs);
    gals = gals + incr;
  }
}
.
w
370
_
```

2. Compile the program without leaving **ed**:

a. Type *!cc metric.c* and press RETURN:

```
!cc metric.c
_
```

b. The C compiler will respond with these messages:

```
!cc metric.c
metric.c:15: Expression syntax
metric.c:15: Unknown character
metric.c:17: f undefined
metric.c:17: n undefined
!
_
```

## Making Corrections

Once again, your job is to correct the error reported by the C compiler, recompile the program, and try running it. Although there are four error messages this time, there is only one error (a missing semicolon).

1. Return to **ed** to correct the error:

   a. Type *14 p* to display the line with the error:

```
14 p
ltrs = (gals * 3.785)

_
```

   b. Type *s/$/;/p* to add the missing semicolon and display the corrected line:

```
14 p
ltrs = (gals * 3.785)
s/$/;/p
ltrs = (gals * 3.785);

_
```

   c. Save the correction:

```
w
371

_
```

This time, instead of allowing **cc** to send the output to the standard output file *a.out*, we're going to redirect the output to another file.

2. Recompile the program without leaving **ed**:

   a. Use the **-o** iption to redirect the output to a file named *metric* and press RETURN:

```
!cc -o metric metric.c
!
_
```

   b. The C compiler will respond with another exclamation point, which tells you that the program has compiled successfully.

3. Now you are ready to run the program:

   a. Type *!metric* and press RETURN:

```
!metric
10    37.85
12    45.42
14    52.99
16    60.56
```

```
18    68.13
20    65.70
!
```

b. The program works.

## Modifying the Program

As mentioned earlier, you can modify the metric conversion program *metric.c* to obtain different results. One way to do this is to change the initializations on lines 7, 8, and 9. For example, by changing *low* to 11, *high* to 25, and *incr* to 1, you can obtain conversions for 11, 12, 13, . . . , 25 gallons:

```
low = 11
high = 25
incr = 1
```

## Entering Another C Program

1. Start a new editing session with **ed**:

   a. Start an editing session with a new file called *compact.c*:

   ```
   $ ed compact.c
   ?compact.c

   _
   ```

   b. Enter and save the following program (but **not** the line numbers).

| Program | Comment |
|---|---|
| `a` | |
| `/* Remove newlines */` | [Descriptive comment line] |
| `#include <stdio.h>` | [This is the standard I/O file] |
| `main()` | [Start of program] |
| `{` | [Start of first block] |
| `int c, nnl=0;` | [Declare *c* as an integer; delcare *nnl* as an integer and set it to zero] |
| `  while ((c=getchar()) != EOF)` | [Read a character; stop if it's an end-of-file character ( ∧D )] |
| `  {` | [Start of second block] |
| `    if (c=='\n')` | [Is the character newline?] |
| `      nnl++` | [If so, add to the counter] |
| `    else` | [If not, . . . |
| `      nnl=0;` | reset the counter to zero] |

```
12        if (nnl<=2)          [Are there fewer than two
                                 newlines?]
13          putchar(c);        [If so, output this character]
14        }                    [End of second block]
15    }                        [End of first block]
   .
   w
   178                         [Don't type q; stay in ed]
   _
```

Before proceeding, we should include a short discussion of this program. It takes characters from the keyboard and counts the number of consecutive newlines encountered. Any time there are at least two, the program ignores all but the first two and goes on to the next character, thereby compacting the file. Line 9, as you have entered it, contains an error: A semicolon (;) is missing. Because of this, an error message will result when the program is compiled, and this error message will provide a few useful lessons. You will get a chance to correct the error in line 9 shortly.

2. Compile the program without leaving **ed**:

   a. Use the temporary exit symbol (!) in front of *cc* to have **cc** compile *compact.c*:

   ```
   !cc compact.c
   _
   ```

   b. The C compiler **cc** will respond with a message something like this (the exact wording may vary from system to system):

   ```
   !cc compact.c
   compact.c:10: Expression syntax
   !
   _
   ```

An error message resulted on line 10 when **cc** attempted to compile *compact.c*. Because of the missing semicolon back on line 9, **cc** has run into trouble on line 10, and compilation of *compact.c* is unsuccessful. The solution is to add the missing semicolon and try **cc** again.

## Making Corrections to the Program

Now that you have entered the program and attempted a first compilation, you are ready to correct the error reported by the compiler and try a second compilation:

1. Return to your editing session and add the missing semicolon:

a. Type *9p* and press RETURN to display line 8:

```
9p
 nnl++

_
```

b. Type *s/$/;/p* to add the missing semicolon and display the corrected line:

```
s/$/;/p
nnl++;

_
```

c. Store the corrected text:

```
w
179

_
```

2. Recompile the program without leaving **ed**:

a. Use the temporary escape (!) in front of **cc** again:

```
!cc -o compact compact.c
```
[Place the output in *compact*]

```
_
```

b. After **cc** has run, **ed** will respond with another exclamation point:

```
!cc -o compact compact.c
!
```
[Place the output in *compact*]

```
_
```

This time the compilation is successful; there are no error messages. Again, unless you specify another file, **cc** places the output of any compilation in a file named *a.out*. This is the standard output for **cc**. However, we have directed output to *compact* by using the **-o** option with **cc**.

## Running the Program

With *compact.c* successfully compiled, you are now ready to run the program. Note that *compact* is an executable file, which means that all you have to do to run your program is type *compact* after the UNIX shell prompt. However, since you are still in an editing session with **ed**, you won't see the shell prompt this time.

1. Run the program:

a. Copy file *spaces* from *text_files* to *c_progs*:

```
!cp ../text_files/spaces spaces

_
```

b. Use the temporary escape symbol (!) again to run **compact**:

```
!compact < spaces
_
```

c. The output will appear on the screen:

```
This is line 1

This is line 2

This is line 3
!                              [Conclusion of the program's
                               output]

_
```

This program illustrates one method for eliminating extra blank lines from a file. You could also do this with an s (substitution) command.

2. End the editing session by typing *q*.

## More on C Programming

In this chapter you worked briefly with C, the language in which most of UNIX is written. If you would like to know more about C, you will need another book. It won't be possible to say much more about C in this book, so here are a few titles:

*C Programming Guide* by Jack Purdum, Que Corporation, Indianapolis, Indiana 46250 (1983)

*Learning to Program in C* by Thomas Plum, Plum Hall, Cardiff, New Jersey 08232 (1983)

*Programming in C* by Stephen G. Kochan, Hayden Book Company, Inc., Hasbrouck Heights, New Jersey 07604 (1983)

*The C Programming Language* by Brian W. Kernighan and Dennis M. Ritchie, Prentice-Hall, Inc., Englewood Cliffs, New Jersey 07632 (1978)

*The UNIX Programming Environment* by Brian W. Kernighan and Rob Pike, Prentice-Hall, Inc., Englewood Cliffs, New Jersey 07632 (1984)

## Other Programming Languages

Although C and UNIX have been closely related from the beginning, some of the other languages popular with microcomputers, such as FORTRAN and Pascal, have also become available with UNIX. The standard FORTRAN compiler, called **f77**, compiles source programs in files that end in *.f*. One widely-used Pascal compiler from the University of California, called **pc**, compiles source programs in files that end in *.p*. Both compilers, like C, place the executable program produced by compilation in *a.out* if no other output file is named. All three compilers (C, FORTRAN, and Pascal) have an **-o** option that allows you to direct the output to another file.

Finally, there is another language closely associated with UNIX that is covered later in this book. You have been dealing with the UNIX **shell** almost since you started reading this book. The shell is the command processor that takes each command you enter, makes sure that the command is executed and then returns the results to you. However, the shell also offers a language that you can use to write programs called **shell procedures**. This aspect of the shell is discussed in Chapters 21-27.

For some jobs you may prefer using shell procedures because they don't require compilation and storing an extra file. For other jobs you may prefer using C programs because they can better handle character processing. For still other jobs you may prefer to use FORTRAN, Pascal, or some other language available on your system.

## Summary of Chapter 10

In this chapter you have learned how to execute UNIX commands without leaving **ed**. As examples of executing UNIX commands, you entered, compiled, corrected, recompiled, and ran two C programs.

### *Interrupting editing*

To interrupt editing with **ed** to execute another UNIX command, type an exclamation point (*!*), the name of the command, and press RETURN. After the other UNIX command has been executed, you will be able to return to **ed**, which will remain in the same state unchanged.

### *Producing a C program*

To produce a C program ready to run, you have to follow these steps:

**Enter the source code.** Call up **ed** (or another text editor), enter the code, and store it in a file (which must have a *.c* suffix).

**Compile the program.** Use the **cc** compiler, sending the object code either to the standard output file *a.out*:

```
!cc file.c
```

or to a file of your choice:

```
!cc -o ex.file file.c
```

**Make corrections.** Since you are still in **ed**, you can easily make corrections to any errors reported by **cc** using the **s** (substitution) command.

**Run the program.** To run your program, just type the name of the output file produced by **cc**.

## *Other Programming Languages*

FORTRAN is a standard language, while Pascal and other languages are also available on many UNIX systems. The FORTRAN compiler (**f77**) compiles source code stored in files that end in *.f*; one Pascal compiler (**pc**) compiles source code stored in files that end in *.p*. Both of these, like C, allow you to direct output to another file with the **-o** option.

# III

# *Text Editing with **vi** and **ex***

# 11

# Introduction to the Visual Editor vi

**vi** and **ex** are two different names for an enhanced version of **ed**. This program acts like a screen-oriented editor when invoked as **vi**, but acts like a line-oriented editor when invoked as **ex**. **vi** (vee-eye, the "visual interpreter), developed at the University of California by William Joy, may or may not be included in your UNIX system.

Since **vi** uses the entire screen, like some popular word processing programs, you will find it very convenient to work with. However, you can't just invoke the program and start using it, as you did with **ed**. You first have to make sure that UNIX has detailed information about your terminal. (This corresponds to the **installation** procedure for some word-processing programs).

To determine whether or not your UNIX system has been prepared for your terminal, proceed to the next section and try invoking **vi**. If the correct display appears on your screen as described, you can complete the rest of this chapter right now. However, if the display is distorted or doesn't appear at all, turn to Appendix H ("Initializing a Terminal for **vi**) for the information you will need. Then return to this chapter and continue.

# Typing a Letter

Once someone has identified your terminal to the UNIX shell, as described in Appendix H, you can call up **vi** and start typing a letter.

## *Starting with a New Directory*

As you learned earlier, one way to take full advantage of the UNIX file system is to organize your home directory into subdirectories for different kinds of files. In case you skipped the chapters on **ed**, let's start this chapter by creating a new subdirectory in your home directory to contain your **vi** files, then move to this directory for the exercises in this chapter.

1. Create a new subdirectory (only if you skipped Part II):

   a. Create a directory called *text_files* with the **mkdir** command:

   ```
   $ mkdir text_files
   $ _
   ```

   b. The directory has been created, but you are still in your home directory.

2. Move from your home directory to *text_files*:

   a. Move to subdirectory *text_files* with the **cd** command:

   ```
   $ cd text_files
   $ _
   ```

   b. Now *text_files* is your working directory (verify this with the **pwd** (print working directory) command. Any files you create will be stored in this directory.

3. Call up the visual editor **vi**:

   a. After the UNIX shell prompt, type *vi letter* and press RETURN:

   ```
   $ vi letter
   ```

   b. After a few moments, the screen will clear and the following display will appear:

```
_
~
~
~
~
~
~
~
~
~
~
~
~
"letter" [New file]
```

In earlier versions of **vi**, the last line (the **status line**) will look like this:

```
"letter" No such file or directory
```

The number of lines that appear in the **display window** varies from terminal to terminal.

## *Typing the First Draft*

With **vi** running and a file named, you are ready to start entering the text of your letter:

1. Select **appending**:
   a. Type *a* (without RETURN) to append text in **text entry mode.**
   b. The *a* will **not** appear on the screen, but once you have typed it, you can begin entering text.
2. Type a few lines of text:
   a. Type the following, pressing RETURN at the end of each line:

```
Dear Mr. Fenton: RETURN
RETURN
We can't do the job you asked for. RETURN
We don't know what we're doing. RETURN
RETURN
```

b. The text will appear on the screen as you type it, with each new line replacing one of the tildes in the left-hand column.

3. Return to **vi command mode**:

   a. Press the **ESC (Escape)** key to leave **text entry mode.**

   b. The screen display will not change, but you will return to **vi command mode,** from which you can enter more commands.

4. Try the **repeat command**:

   a. Type a period (.) (without RETURN) to repeat the insertion you just made.

   b. Now the screen will look like this:

```
Dear Mr. Fenton:

We can't do the job you asked for.
We don't know what we're doing.

Dear Mr. Fenton:

We can't do the job you asked for.
We don't know what we're doing.

_
~
~
~
```

Once you typed the period (.), **vi** repeated the insertion of five lines of text (including two blank lines)—beginning at the cursor's location on the screen. The unused lines below the text still begin with tildes.

5. Try the **undo command**:

   a. Type **u** to undo the insertion you just inserted.

   b. Now the screen will look like this again:

```
Dear Mr. Fenton:

We can't do the job you asked for.
We don't know what we're doing.

_
~
~
~
```

   c. Type **u** again to restore the insertion.

   d. Type **u** once more to remove the insertion.

You can use the **undo command** to recover from an error. It will undo the results of the most recent change performed, no matter how extensive. Note that when used twice in succession, the **u** command undoes the action of the previous **undo command**.

6. Write the text to the file:

   a. Now type *:w* and press RETURN to write this text to "letter".

   b. First you will see :w at the bottom of the screen; then you will see this display on the status line:

   ```
   "letter" [New file] 6 lines, 88 characters
   ```

A colon (:) always means a temporary change to **ex command mode**, from which you can use an **ex** command—in this case, the **w** (write) command.

## *Inserting the Date*

Now we'll begin adding things to the letter, starting with the date. To do this, we'll have to move the cursor to the top of the screen and make room for another line of text.

1. Move the cursor to the top of the screen:

   a. Hold down the SHIFT key and type capital *H* (not *h*) to move the cursor to the upper left hand corner of the screen.

   b. The display should look like this:

```
Dear Mr. Fenton:

We can't do the job you asked for.
We don't know what we're doing.

~
~
~
```

2. Open a new line above:

   a. Hold down the SHIFT key and type capital *O* (not *o*) to open a new line above the first line.

   b. Now there will be a blank line above the first line, with the cursor resting in the leftmost column.

3. Type the date:

   a. Type the date as shown on the blank line and press RETURN.

   b. Now the display should look like this:

```
March 17, 1985

Dear Mr. Fenton:

We can't do the job you asked for.
We don't know what we're doing.

~
~
~
```

4. Return to **vi command mode**:

   a. Press the **ESC** key to leave "line-opening" and return to **text entry mode**.

   b. You have to do this every time you finish typing new text. Otherwise, **vi** will interpret your next keystroke as another character of text instead of a command.

## *Inserting a New Paragraph*

Having inserted the date and selected **vi command mode** again, you are now ready to insert a new paragraph. This involves moving the cursor down and selecting **insert mode**.

1. Move the cursor down:

   a. Type *j* (unshifted) twice to move the cursor down to the blank line after the salutation.

   b. If your terminal has arrow keys (and your *termcap* entry permits), you can use the "down arrow" key (↓) instead of *j*.

2. Prepare to insert a new paragraph:

   a. Type *i* to select inserting in **text entry mode**.

   b. You won't see *i* on the screen and the display won't change:

```
March 17, 1985

Dear Mr. Fenton:

We can't do the job you asked for.
We don't know what we're doing.

~
~
~
```

3. Insert a new paragraph:

   a. Press RETURN to leave a blank line after the salutation, type the following, and press RETURN after each line:

   ```
   Thank you for your recent letter. RETURN
   It is always a delight to read RETURN
   your ideas. RETURN
   ```

   b. Your display should look like this:

```
March 17, 1985

Dear Mr. Fenton:

Thank you for your recent letter.
It is always a delight to read
your ideas.

We can't do the job you asked for.
We don't know what we're doing.

~
~
~
```

4. Return to **vi command mode**:

   a. Press the **ESC** key to leave **text entry mode.**

   b. Don't forget to return to **vi command mode** after completing text entry.

5. Repeat the paragraph:

   a. For practice, type a period (.) to repeat the paragraph you just typed.

   b. Your display will look like this:

```
March 17, 1985

Dear Mr. Fenton:

Thank you for your recent letter.
It is always a delight to read
your ideas.

Thank you for your recent letter.
It is always a delight to read
your ideas.

We can't do the job you asked for.
We don't know what we're doing.

~
~
~
```

6. Since that paragraph isn't worth repeating, delete the second copy of it:

   a. Type *u* (not *U*) to undo the last command.

   b. The repeated paragraph will now disappear.

## *Adding a Closing*

This letter needs a suitable closing. This involves moving the cursor down and adding more text.

1. Move the cursor to the last line of the display:
   a. Hold down the SHIFT key and type *L* to move the cursor to the blank line below the second paragraph.
   b. The cursor should now be in the lower left hand corner of the display window.
2. Select appending in **text entry mode** again:
   a. Type *a* to append more text.
   b. Nothing will happen, but **vi** is now ready to receive more text.
3. Type the closing:
   a. Type the following, pressing RETURN after each line of text:

```
Your most humble, obedient servant, RETURN
RETURN
Frank Failsquick (''Mr. Macho'') RETURN
```

b. Your display should look like this:

```
March 17, 1985

Dear Mr. Fenton:

Thank you for your recent letter.
It is always a delight to read
your ideas.

We can't do the job you asked for.
We don't know what we're doing.

Your most humble, obedient servant,

Frank Failsquick (''Mr. Macho'')

_
~
~
~
```

4. Return to **vi command mode**:
   a. Press the **ESC** key to leave **text entry mode**.

   b. Don't forget to return to **vi command mode** after completing entry of text.

5. Write the text to the file:

   a. Type *:w* and press RETURN to write this text to *letter.*

   b. You will see :w, then this display at the bottom of the screen:

   ```
   "letter" [Modified] 15 lines, 255 characters
   ```

# Making Changes to the Letter

Now that we have a complete letter, let's make some changes to it. This will help us try various features of **vi**.

## *Changing the Date*

Let's start with the date at the top of the letter. We'll start by moving the cursor, then make a change.

1. Move the cursor up to the first line:

   a. Hold down the SHIFT key and type *H* to move the cursor to the top of the display.

   b. The cursor should now be positioned over the *M* in *March.*

2. Change *March* to *September*:

   a. Type *cw* to change a word. The display will look like this:

   ```
   Marc$ 17, 1985
   ```

   b. Without pressing the space bar, type *September* and press **Esc.**

   c. The first line should now look like this:

   ```
   September 17, 1985
   ```

The **c** (change) command can be used either alone or in conjunction with another character (in this case, **w** for *word*). The character that follows **c** specifies exactly how much text is to be changed. You'll learn how to use **c** and other commands with characters like **w** in the chapters that follow.

## *Changing a Name*

Next we'll change the name on the salutation line. This involves moving the cursor into position and making a double change.

1. Move the cursor to the start of the name on the salutation line:

   a. Type a slash (/) to request a search, followed immediately by *Mr.* At the bottom of the screen, you will see

   ```
   /Mr_
   ```

   b. Now press RETURN to begin the search.

   c. The cursor will jump to the *M* in *Mr.* on the third line.

2. Change *Mr. Fenton* to *Mrs. Benson*:

   a. Type *2cW* to change two words. The line will look like this:

   ```
   Dear Mr. Fenton$
   ```

   b. Without pressing the space bar, type *Mrs. Benson* immediately after *2cW*, then press the **Esc** key.

   c. The salutation line will now look like this:

   ```
   Dear Mrs. Benson:
   ```

## *Running a UNIX Command*

Sometimes you work so hard at your terminal that you lose track of the time. However, **vi** lets you take a look at the clock (using the **date** command) without having to interrupt your editing session. You can also run any other UNIX command from **vi**.

1. Find out what time it is:

   a. Type *:!date* and press RETURN to find out the date and time.

   b. You should see a display like this appear:

   ```
   :!date
   [No write since last change]
   Mon Apr 3 13:52:27 PST 1985
   [Hit return to continue]_
   ```

   c. As the prompt says, press RETURN to return to **vi**.

2. Find out who else is on the system:

   a. Type *:!who* and press RETURN to obtain a list of active users.

   b. You should see a display like this appear:

```
:!who
john     tty07   Apr 3 08:43
janice   tty16   Apr 3 09:17
billy    tty03   Apr 3 08:24
[Hit return to continue]_
```

You can type any shell command in this way. The main thing to remember is that you can run any UNIX command from within **vi** by preceding the command line by the two characters *:!*. The colon gives you **ex**; the exclamation mark gives you the shell. (For an extensive session with the shell, you can also use *:sh*, execute your commands, then type *CTRL-D* to return to vi.)

## *Getting Information*

Before making any more changes, let's ask **vi** for some information.

1. Move to a specific line:

   a. Type *7G* to have the cursor "go to line 7."

   b. Now hold down the CTRL key and press *G* (unshifted )to ask **vi** for status information.

   c. You will see a display like this at the bottom of the screen:

   ```
   "letter" [Modified] line 7 of 15 --46%--
   ```

This line tells you the name of your file (*letter*), the line number where the cursor is resting (*7*), the total number of lines (*15*), how far the cursor is from the beginning of the file (*46%* of the file), and whether you have made changes to the file (*[Modified]*) that haven't been written.

2. Move to the first and last lines:

   a. Type *L* to move the cursor to the last line on the screen, and type CTRL-G again. At the bottom of the screen you will see

   ```
   "letter" [Modified] line 15 of 15 --100%--
   ```

b. Now type *H* to move back to the first line and type CTRL-G a third time. At the bottom of the screen you will see

```
"letter" [Modified] line 1 of 15 --6%--
```

Each time you type *CTRL-G*, **vi** gives you status information based on the cursor's location in the text.

## Deleting Words

Now we'll delete a couple of words just to show you how different **vi** commands have many things in common.

1. Move the cursor to *most* in the twelfth line:

   a. Type */most* and press RETURN.

   b. Now the cursor is resting on the *m* of *most* in *most humble.*

2. Delete the words *most humble* (along with the comma):

   a. Type *d2W* to delete these two words (and the comma).

   b. the line should look like this:

   ```
   Your obedient servant,
   ```

3. Undo the deletion:

   a. Since the closing is no longer ridiculous enough, let's restore the original closing by typing *u*.

   b. Now the closing is back the way it was before:

   ```
   Your most humble, obedient servant,
   ```

## Capitalizing Words

Before concluding this brief sampling of **vi** commands, let's try one more thing: Capitalizing a word. Any word will do; let's pick *letter* in line 5. Since the cursor is currently resting on line 12, this involves a "backwards search" (unless you have selected the "wrapscan" feature—see Appendix D).

1. Move the cursor into position:

   a. Type *?letter* and press RETURN to move the cursor up to line 5.

   b. The cursor should now be resting on the *l* of *letter.*

2. Capitalize the word:

   a. Type the tilde (~) to make the change.

   b. Line 5 should now look like this:

   ```
   Thank you for your recent Letter.
   ```

   c. Since it doesn't make any sense to have this word capitalized, restore it by typing the "undo" command **u**.

## Ending the Session

Now it's time to write the updated text to disk file *letter* and return to the UNIX shell.

1. Write the text to file *letter*:

   a. Type *:w* and press RETURN to write to the file.

   b. You will see a display like this at the bottom of the screen:

   "letter" [Modified] 15 lines, 241 characters

2. End this session with **vi**:

   a. Type *:q* and press RETURN to end the session.

   b. The following display will appear, indicating that you have left **vi** and returned to the UNIX shell:

   ```
   :q
   $ _
   ```

Note that **vi** also allows you to combine the write and quit commands into a single command, like this:

```
:wq        or        :x        or        ZZ
$ _                  $ _                 $ _
```

## Summary of Chapter 11

In this chapter you learned the preliminary setup procedures, along with a number of common **vi** procedures, such as beginning a session, entering text, inserting new text, making changes, and ending a session.

**Getting set up**. Before you can use **vi**, you have to make sure that two things have been done:

- Someone has placed an entry for your terminal in the file */etc/termcap*.
- You have assigned one of the names for your terminal to the shell

variable TERM and exported TERM to the environment (two steps in the Bourne shell, one step in the C shell):

| Bourne shell | C shell |
|---|---|
| `$ TERM=adm3; export TERM` | `% setenv TERM adm3` |

**Calling up *vi*.** Call up **vi** by typing *vi*, a space, and the name of a file. For a new file, the screen will be cleared, the cursor will move to the upper left hand corner of the screen, and **vi command mode** will be in effect. For an existing file, its contents will be displayed on the screen.

**Inserting text.** To insert text, type *a* (append), *i* (insert), or one of several other letters without pressing RETURN, enter the text, then press **Esc** to return to **vi command mode**.

**Repeating and undoing.** Two of the most useful commands in **vi** are the **repeat command** (.), which repeats the most recent command, and the **undo command** (**u**), which undoes the most recent change performed.

**Opening a new line.** To open a new blank line for inserting new text, use either the **o** command (to open **below**) or the **O** command (to open **above** the current line). Again, enter the text, then press **Esc** to return to **vi command mode.**

**Inserting text.** To insert new text, use either **i** (to insert in front of the cursor) or **I** (to begin inserting in the first column of the current line). Enter the text, then press **Esc** to return to **vi command mode**.

**Changing text.** To change a word, move the cursor to the first letter of the word, then type *cw* or *cW* (change word), followed by the new word (without a space) and **Esc**. To change two words, use *2cw* or *2cW*; to change three, use *3cw* or *3cW*.

**Searching.** To search for a string, type either / (to search forward) or ? (to search backwards), followed immediately by the desired string, and press RETURN.

**Running a UNIX command.** To execute a UNIX command without having to end your session with **vi**, type *:!*, followed immediately by the name of the command, and press RETURN. (Use *:sh* to spawn a subshell.)

**Finding out where you are.** To determine your relative position in the text, press CTRL-G to see a display like this:

```
"letter" [Modified] line 15 of 60 --25%--
```

**Deleting text.** To delete a word, move the cursor to the first letter of the word, then type *dw* or *dW* (delete word). To delete two words, use *d2w* or *d2W*; to delete three, use *d3w* or *d3W*.

**Changing the case of a letter.** To change a lowercase letter to uppercase or an uppercase letter to lowercase, position the cursor over the letter in **vi command mode** and type the tilde ( ~ ). Non-alphabetic characters are not affected.

**Ending a session.** To end a session with **vi**, type *:w* to write the text to the file, then type *:q* to end the session (quit) and return to the UNIX shell. You can also combine these two in a single command, like this:

```
:wq        or        :x        or        ZZ
$ _                  $ _                 $ _
```

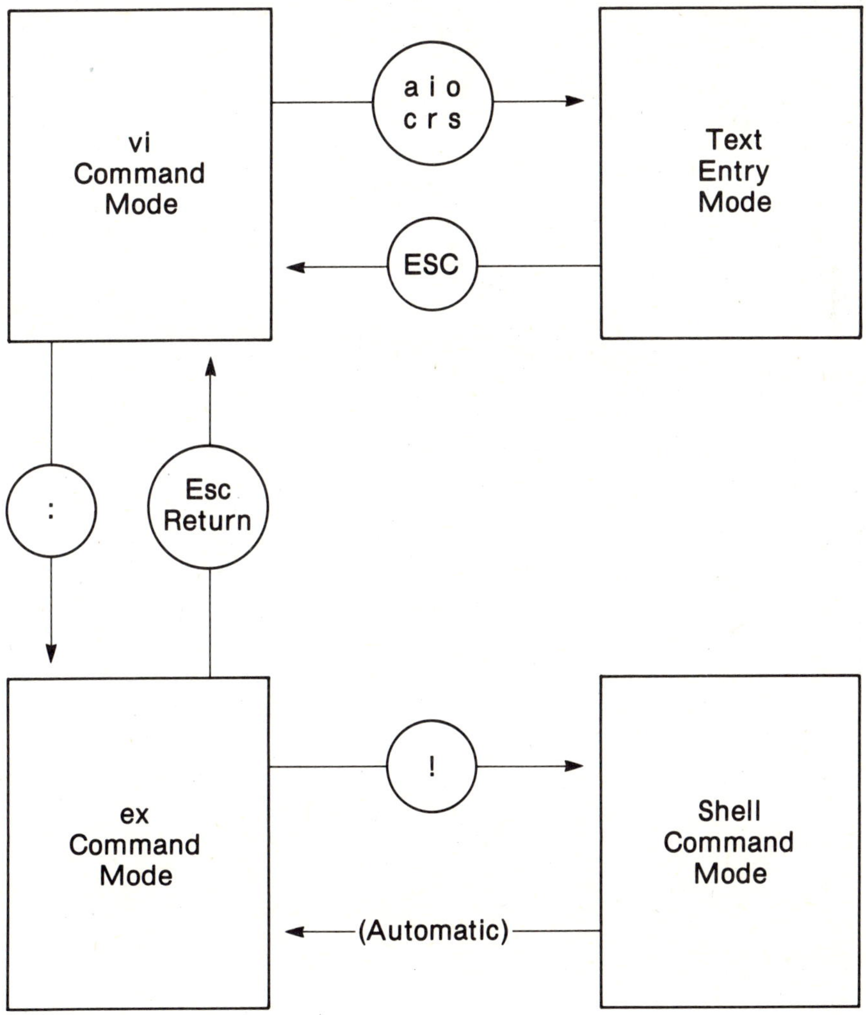


Automatic

# 12

# Making Changes Using vi

Now that you've had a chance to sample some of the most common features of **vi**, let's examine some of those features in more detail. In this chapter we'll look at ways to insert, change, and delete text. Let's start by beginning a new session and getting acquainted with the various ways of moving the cursor around the display window.

## Beginning a New Session

Things may have changed a little since you completed the previous chapter on **vi**. If so, here are a few words about returning to **vi** with the same file you were working with in that chapter:

1. If necessary, move from your home directory to *text__files*:

   a. Use the **cd** (change directory) command like this:

```
$ cd text_files
$ _
```

b. Use the **pwd** (print working directory) command to verify:

```
$ pwd
/usr/robin/text_files
$ _
```

2. Call up **vi** with the same file (*letter*):

a. At the UNIX shell prompt, type *vi letter* and press RETURN:

```
$ vi letter
```

b. After a few moments, the screen will clear, and the text of your letter will appear on the screen, with the cursor at the beginning of the first line.

```
September 17, 1985

Dear Mrs. Benson:

Thank you for your recent letter.
It is always a delight to read
your ideas.

We can't do the job you asked for.
We don't know what we're doing.

Your most humble, obedient servant,

Frank Failsquick ("Mr. Macho")
~
~
~
"letter" 15 lines, 255 characters
```

## Moving the Cursor

To use **vi** effectively, the first thing you must learn is how to move the cursor from one location to another. This will not only enable you to move the cursor to where you need it; it will also help you see how **vi** works. Many functions in **vi** begin working at the position of the cursor. In this section, you will learn how to use certain characters to position the cursor on the screen. Later in this chapter you will learn to use many of these same characters with **vi**'s operators to perform a variety of functions.

## Moving a Character at a Time

Your keyboard may have a separate cursor pad with arrow keys like this:

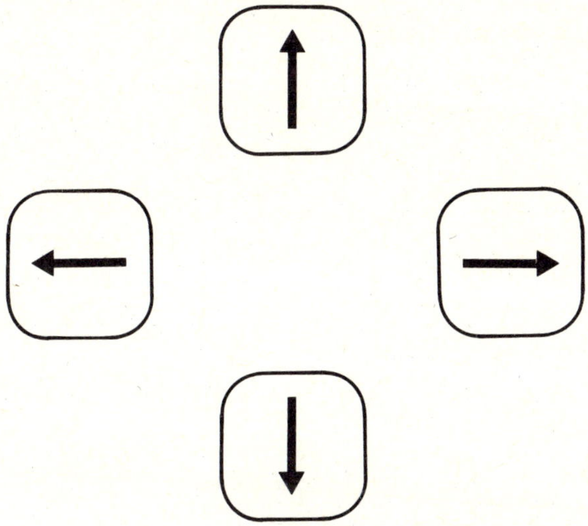

Fig. 12-1.

If so, then you may want to use these keys to move the cursor one space at a time. If not, you will have to use the keys **h, j, k,** and **l.** Some people prefer to use these keys, even when arrow keys are available, like this:

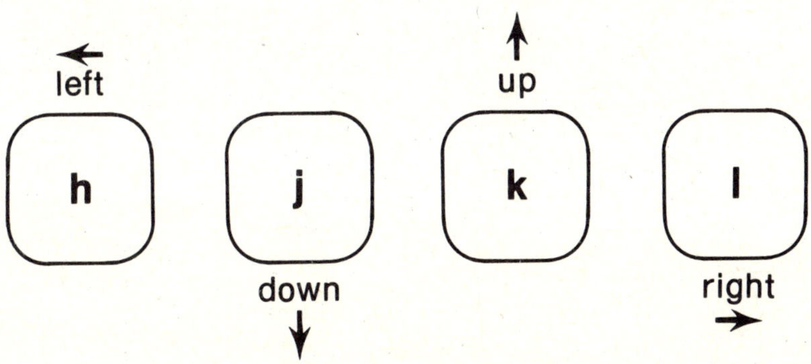


Fig. 12-2.

Press the **character down** key (↓ or j) five times to move the cursor to the sixth line (*It is always . . .* ). Now try all four keys to become familiar with them. When you are finished practicing, leave the cursor at the beginning of the fifth line (*Thank you . . .* ).

Yet another set of keys, which will work for any version of **vi**, is the following (don't worry—the space bar won't erase your text):

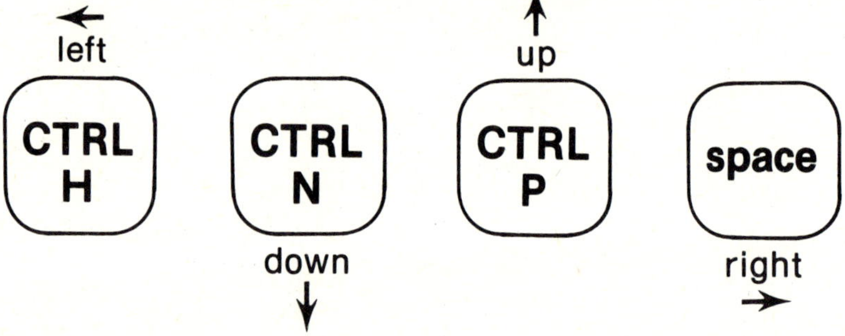


Fig. 12-3.

## *Moving a Word at a Time*

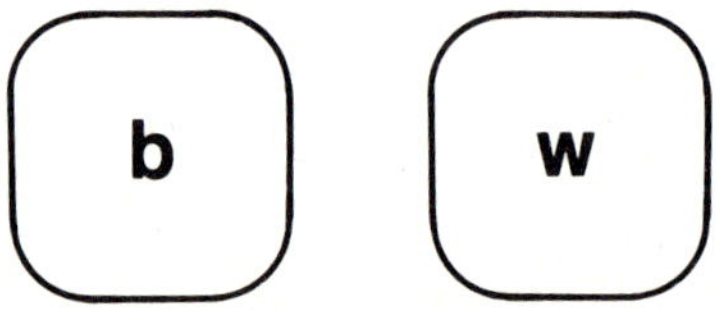


You also have keys for moving the cursor either forward (**w**) or back (**b**) one entire word at a time. Press *w* about ten times to move forward; press *b* a few times to move back again. As you can see, motion continues from the end of one line to the beginning of the next, and vice versa. When capitalized (shifted), these two keys perform nearly the same functions. However, **W** and **B** disregard punctuation. If you use either **w** or **b**, the cursor will stop on punctuation marks. Two related commands, **e** and **E**, move the cursor to the **last** character of a word rather than the **first**.

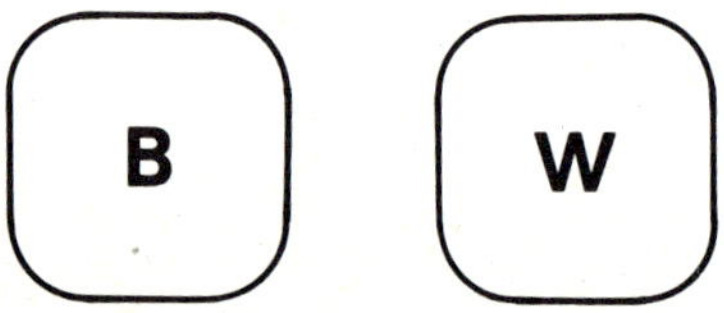


Note that you can type a **multiplier** in front of the letter to multiply the number of jumps, as in *2w*, *3b*, and so on. Try commands like these also.

## *Moving a Sentence at a Time*

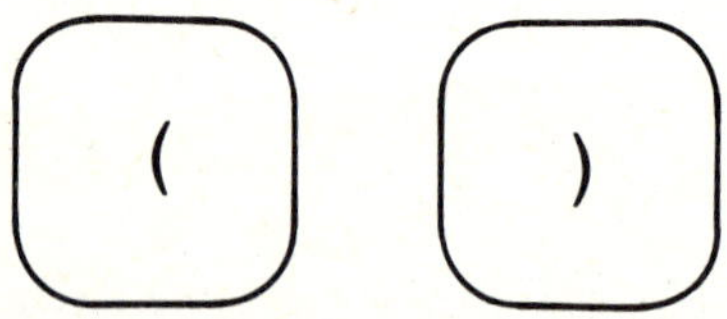


The left and right parenthesis keys (shifted 9 and 0) provide cursor motion to either the beginning (**(**) or the end (**)**) of the current sentence. (Note that **vi** expects a period, followed by two spaces—or a blank line—to mark the end of a sentence.) Try these two keys a few times.

Once again, you can use **multipliers**: *3(*, *4)*, and so on.

## Moving a Paragraph at a Time

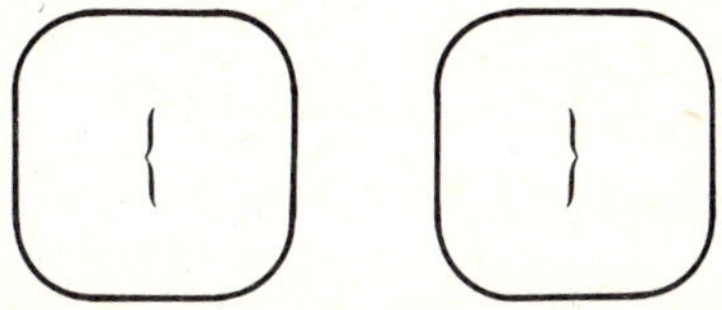


The left and right brace keys provide cursor motion to either the beginning ({) or the end (}) of the current paragraph. (Ordinarily, **vi** regards blank lines as separators of paragraphs. However, if you are writing programs in C, you can change the separators to braces, which delimit blocks of code. For details, see Chapter 17, Customizing **vi**.) Try these two keys a few times. Again, you can also use **multipliers**: *3*{, *5*}, and so on.

## Moving to Either End of a Line

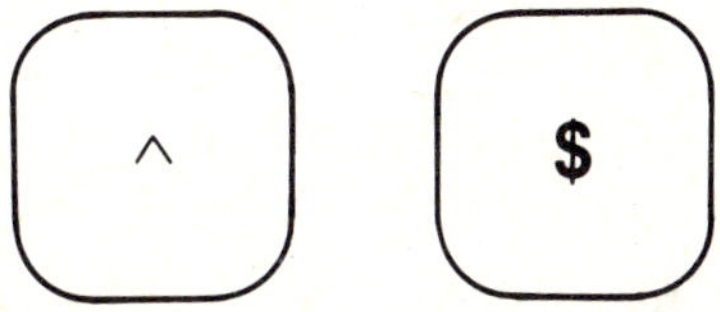


You have a pair of keys for moving the cursor either to the beginning ( ∧ ) or the end (**$**) of the current line (the same two symbols used by **ed**). The character (**0**) is similar to ∧ . It also moves the cursor to the beginning of the line. However, **0** always moves the cursor all the way to the left-hand margin, whereas ∧ moves the cursor only to the first **visible** character. Try a few jumps with these keys.

## Moving to the Top and Bottom of the Screen

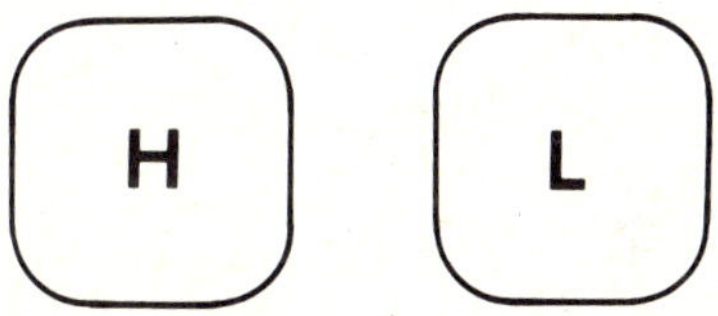


The **H** and **L** keys allow you to move the cursor either to the top (**H**) or the bottom (**L**) of the screen. You can remember the letters as "home" and "lower left". Try your hand with these keys a few times.

## Moving to the Middle of the Screen

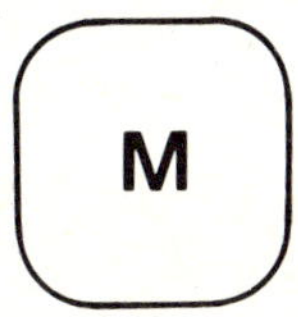


The **M** key allows you to move the cursor to the middle (**M**) of the screen. *M,* of course, stands for *middle.* Try this one in conjunction with the **H** and **L** commands.

## Moving to a Given Line

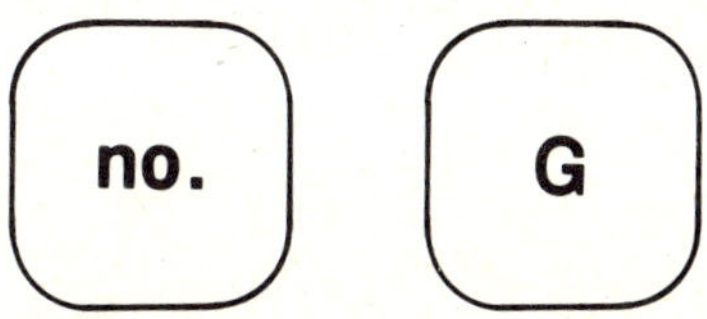


The letter **G** (from "Go to") provides cursor motion to any line in the editing buffer, regardless whether the line is currently displayed on the screen. By this convention, *2G* would take you to the second line; *5G* would take you to the fifth line; and so on. One limitation of this key is that you usually have to know the number of the desired line. (If you would like to have **vi** display line numbers on the screen, there is a way to do this. For details, see Chapter 17, Customizing **vi**.)

Note that **G** alone designates the last line of the file and that CTRL-G answers the question, "What is the number of the current line?" Try all these different variations.

## Moving to the Matching Bracket

%

If the cursor is currently resting on any of the general bracketing symbols, namely

- parentheses ( )
- square brackets [ ]
- braces { }

you can use the percent sign (%) to move the cursor to the matching symbol. To see how this command works, move the cursor to the last line of text (*H*, then cursor up), and experiment with % on the parenthetical expression ("Mr. Macho").

## Moving the Cursor to a Character

**T or t**

To move the cursor to a character on the current line, use the **T** command to move to the left or the **t** command to move to the right. Just position the cursor on the line, type *Tx* or *tx* (where *x* is the character you are looking for), and the cursor will jump to the space next to the first occurrence of the character. Let's look at an example on the last line of *letter*:

1. Move the cursor to *Mr.*:
   a. With the cursor now resting at the beginning of the last line of *letter* (on the *F* of *Frank*), type *tM*.
   b. You will see the cursor jump to the space in front of *Mr.*:

   ```
   Frank Failsquick (_"Mr. Macho")
   ```
2. Move the cursor to *Macho*:
   a. Type *tM* to repeat the motion.
   b. The cursor will now jump to the space in front of *Macho*:

   ```
   Frank Failsquick ("Mr._Macho")
   ```

3. Move the cursor back to *Failsquick*:

   a. This time, type *TF*.

   b. You will see the cursor jump back to *a* in *Failsquick*:

   ```
   Frank Failsquick ("Mr. Macho")
   ```

4. Move the cursor back to *Frank*:

   a. Once again, type *TF* to continue the movement.

   b. You will see the cursor jump back to the *r* in *Frank*:

   ```
   Frank Failsquick ("Mr. Macho")
   ```

### A Note on Cursor Motion Keys

You must be in **vi command mode** to use any of the cursor motion keys just described. (Press **ESC** to return to **vi command mode**. If you hear a beep, your terminal is already in this mode.) None of the cursor motion keys will work after you have entered one of the text insertion modes.

## Using Markers

### Marking a Place

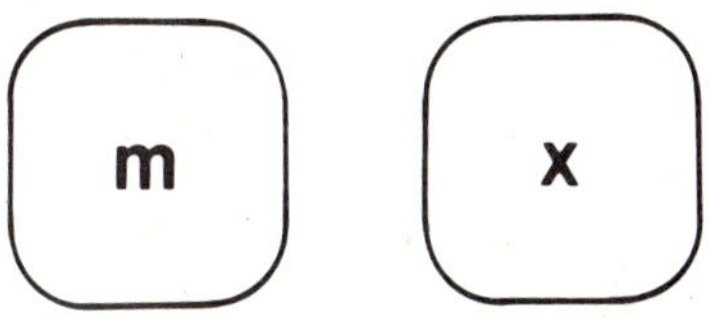


T or t

You can set a place marker anywhere in the work area with the **m** command. Just move the cursor to the desired location and type *m*, followed by any lowercase letter of the alphabet. The letter then becomes the name of the place marker.

### Moving to a Marker

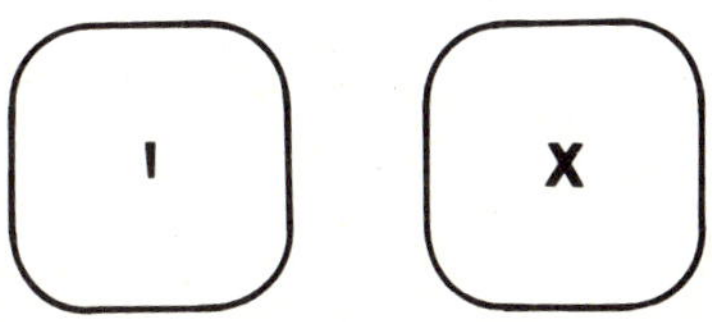


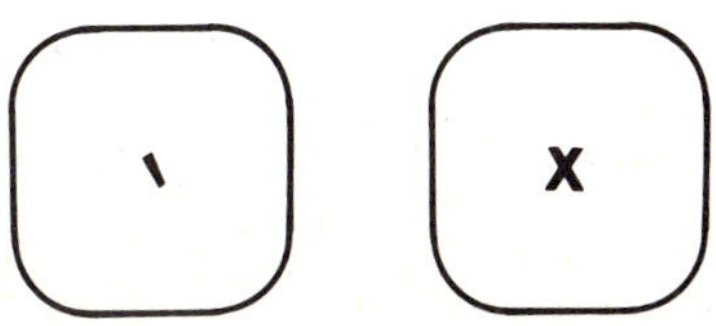


Once a place marker has been set in the work area with the **m** command, you can move the cursor to the marker with either of the two types of single quotation mark. Type the back quotation mark (or grave accent) ‘, followed by the letter name of the mark, to move the cursor to the exact location of the mark. Type an ordinary quotation mark ’, followed by the letter, to move the cursor to the beginning of the line that contains the mark.

# Controlling the Screen Display

## *Scrolling*

You have a pair of keys that produce either a scroll up (**CTRL-U**) or a scroll down (**CTRL-D**). If the cursor is near the top of the screen, a scroll up may push the cursor down; if the cursor is near the bottom of the screen, a scroll down may push the cursor up.

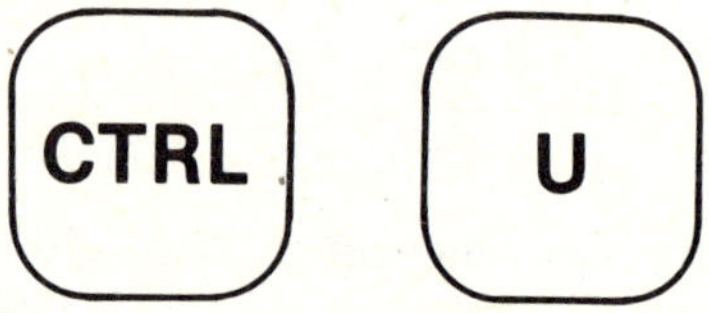


To practice scrolling, move the cursor to the last line (*L*), type **a** to enter more text, press RETURN about 12 times, then press **ESC**. Now you can try CTRL-U and CTRL-D.

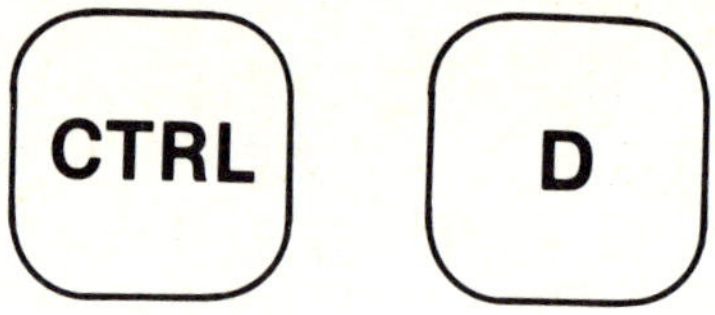


## *Paging*

**vi** also provides one key for paging back (**CTRL-B**) and one for paging forward (**CTRL-F**). ("Paging" means advancing the text one screenful at a time.) Later on, when you are working with long documents, you will find these features very handy.

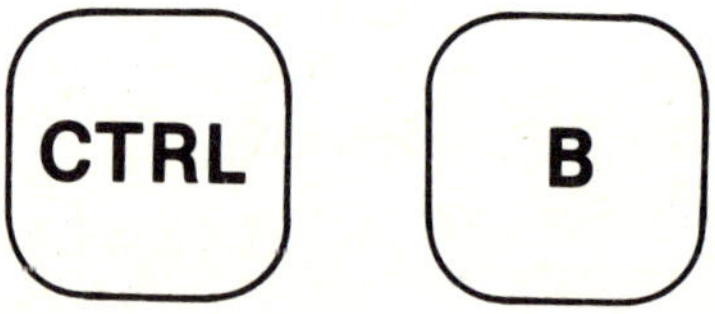


After practicing with these keys, you can remove the extra blank lines by abandoning the text (*:q!*) then starting again (**vi letter**).

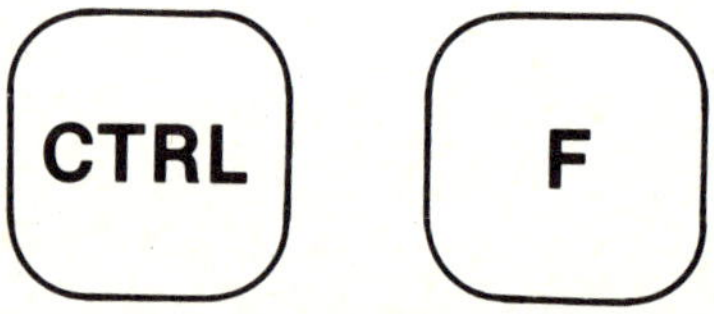

### *Repositioning the Current Line*

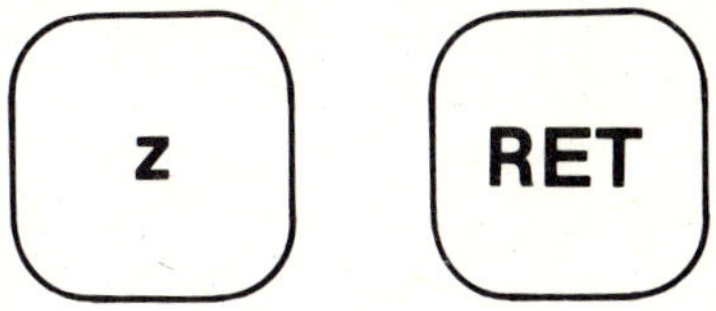


You have a command that you can use to reposition the current line in the display window—**z**, the "zero screen" command. To place the current line at the **top** of the screen, type *z* and press RETURN; to place the current line in the **middle** of the screen, type *z.*; to place the current line at the bottom of the screen, type *z-*.

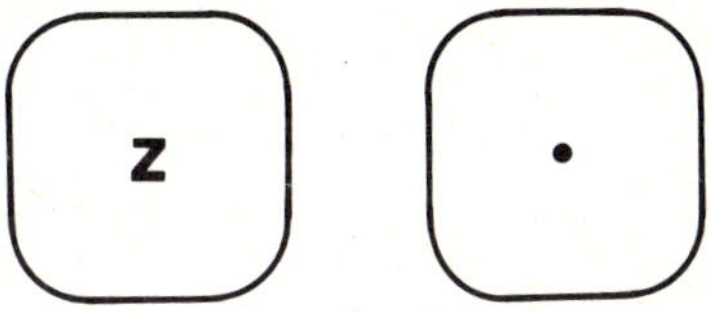


This command also has several variations: If you type a line number **in front of** *z*, that line will be placed at the top of the screen; if you type a number **after** *z*, your display window will be reduced (or increased) to that many lines. For example, type *15z* to place line 15 at the top of the screen. Type *z12* to reduce your display window to 12 lines.

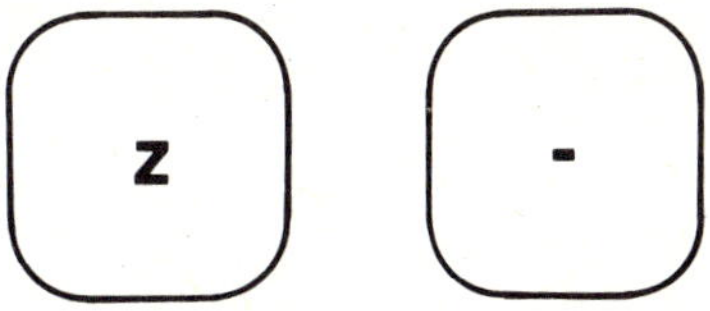


### *Clearing System Messages*

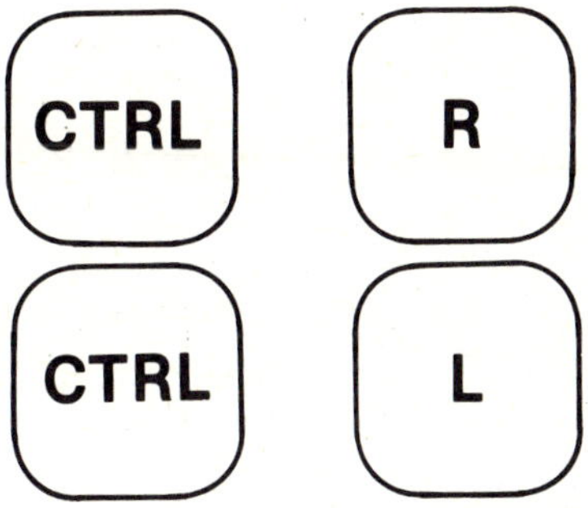


You have two related commands for clearing system messages from your screen—**CTRL R** and **CTRL L**. Either one of them will clear system messages from your screen, but leave the text in your work area unchanged.

a and A

## Adding New Text

a and A

As you saw in Chapter 11, you have three choices when you want to add new text in **vi** without altering existing text:

- You can **append** text after existing text
- You can **insert** text in front of existing text
- You can **open** up space for a new line of text

In this chapter we'll explore each of these in greater detail.

### *Appending Text*

To append text after existing text on the screen, you can use one of two commands: One that lets you add the new text immediately after the cursor (**a**) or one that lets you add the next text at the end of the current line (**A**). Let's take a look at each of them, using the second line of the first paragraph (line 6) of *letter.*

1. Move the cursor into position:

   a. In **vi command mode,** type *6G* to place the cursor on line 6.

   b. Type *3w* to move the cursor across the line to *a.*

   c. The line should now look like this:

   ```
   It is always a delight to read
   ```

2. Append *special* (with a preceding space) after *a*:

   a. In **vi command mode,** type *a* to append text after the cursor.

   b. Type *special* and press **ESC** to return to **vi command mode.**

3. Append *and enjoy* (with a preceding space) to the end of the line:

   a. In **vi command mode,** type *A* to append text at the end of the line.

   b. Type *and enjoy* and press **ESC** to return to **vi command mode.**

   c. Now the line should look like this:

   ```
   It is always a special delight to read and enjoy
   ```

As you can see from these examples, **vi** commands have one meaning in lowercase (**a**) and another in uppercase (**A**).

## *Inserting Text*

**i and I**

To insert text in front of existing text on the screen, you can use one of two commands: One that lets you add the new text immediately before the cursor (**i**) or one that lets you add the new text at the beginning of the current line (**I**). (If the text is indented, you will want to use **0i** or **0I.**) Let's take a look at **i** and **I** using line 5 of *letter.*

1. Move the cursor into position:

   a. In **vi command mode,** type *k* (or ↑) to move the cursor to line 5.

   b. Type *b* four times to move the cursor back to the *f* in *for.*

   c. The line should now look like this:

   ```
   Thank you for your recent letter.
   ```

2. Insert *profusely* (with a trailing space) in front of *for*:

   a. In **vi command mode,** type *i* to insert text before the cursor.

   b. Type *profusely* and press **ESC** to return to **vi command mode.**

3. Insert *I wish to* (with a trailing space) to the beginning of the line:

   a. In **vi command mode**, type *I* to insert text at the beginning of the line.

   b. Type *I wish to*  and press **ESC** to return to **vi command mode.**

4. Uncapitalize the *T* in *Thank you*:

   a. Type *W* to move the cursor to the *T*.

   b. Type ~ to change the *T* to a *t*.

   c. Now the line should look like this:

```
I wish to thank you profusely for your recent letter.
```

## Opening a New Line

**o and O**

You can open space for a new line either **below** the current line (**o**) or **above** the current line (**O**). Once again, we'll try one example of each, using the last line of text in *letter.*

1. Move the cursor into position:

   a. Type *G* then *k* to move the cursor to the last line of text.

   b. The cursor will be at the beginning of the line (but it doesn't really matter where on the line the cursor is for these commands):

**i and I**
**o and O**

```
Frank Failsquick ("Mr. Macho")
```

2. Add *Chief Consulting Officer* on a new line to follow:

   a. Type *o* to open a new line below the current line.

   b. Type *Chief Consulting Officer* and press **ESC** to return to **vi command mode.**

3. Add *The Man for the Job:* on a new line above:

   a. Type *k* to return to the *Frank Failsquick* line.

   b. Type capital *O* to open a new line above the current line.

   c. Type *The Man for the Job:* and press **ESC** to return to **vi command mode.**

   d. The final three lines should now look like this:

```
The Man for the Job:
Frank Failsquick ("Mr. Macho")
Chief Consulting Officer
```

This session will be continued in Chapter 15.

## Summary of Chapter 12

In this chapter you learned how to move the cursor and add new text.

### *Moving the Cursor*

**Moving a space at a time.** You can move the cursor one space at a time with either a set of arrow keys in a cursor pad or the typewriter keys **h, j, k, l** like these:

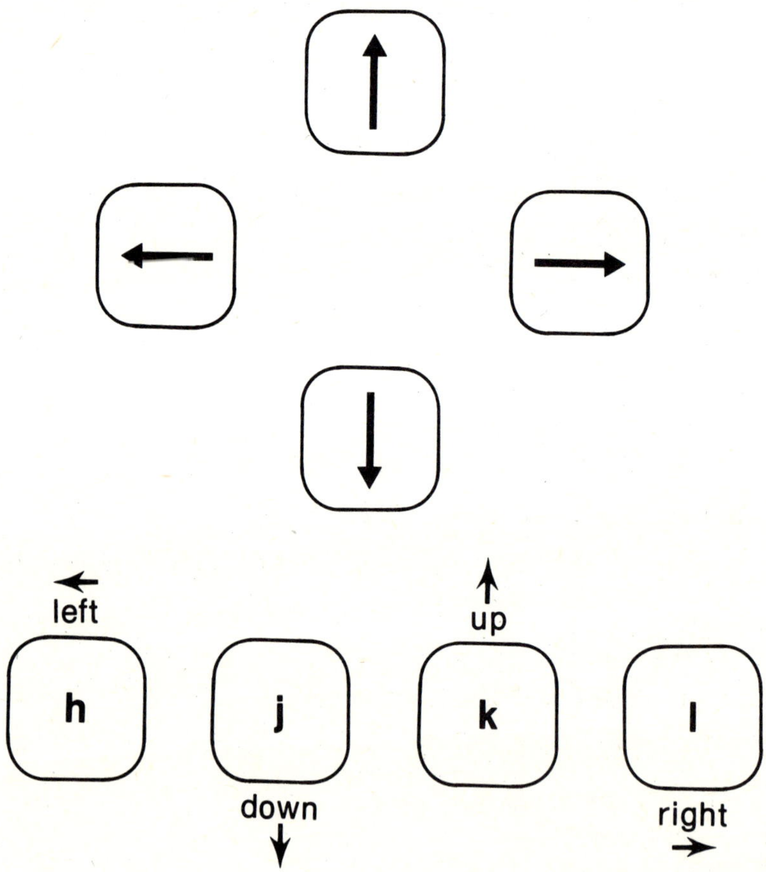

Another set of keys, which will work for any version of **vi**, is the following:

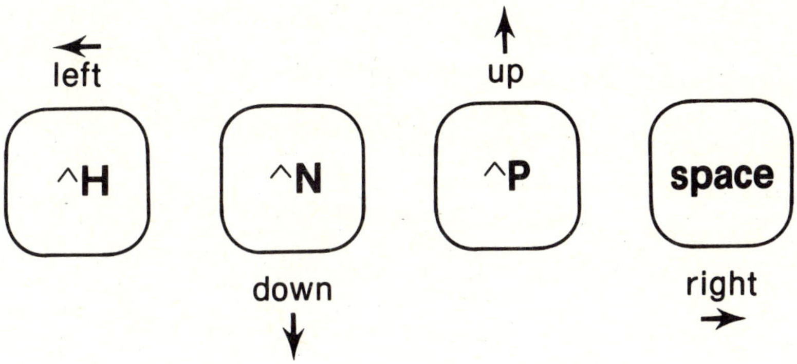


**Moving other amounts**

| | | | |
|---|---|---|---|
| Previous word: | **b** | Next word: | **w** |
| | **B** | **W** | |
| End of a word: | **e** | | |
| | **E** | | |
| Previous sentence: | **(** | Next sentence: | **)** |
| Previous paragraph: | **{** | Next paragraph: | **}** |
| Beginning of a line: | **∧** | End of a Line: | **$** |
| Top of screen: | **H** | Bottom of screen: | **L** |
| Middle of screen: | **M** | | |
| Line n: | **nG** | Matching bracket: | **%** |
| End of text: | **G** | | |

**Moving to a character (*x*)**

| | | | |
|---|---|---|---|
| Left | **Tx** | Right | **tx** |

**Multipliers.** Many of these commands can be multiplied:
**2b, 2B, 3w, 3W, 4(, 4), 5{, 5}**

## *Controlling the Screen Display*

**Scrolling**

| | |
|---|---|
| Up: | **CTRL-U (∧U)** |
| Down: | **CTRL-D (∧D)** |

**Paging**

| | |
|---|---|
| Back: | **CTRL-B (∧B)** |
| Forward: | **CTRL-F (∧F)** |

**Placing current line**

| | |
|---|---|
| Top: | **z RETURN** |
| Middle: | **z.** |
| Bottom: | **z-** |

**Clearing messages**

**CTRL-R** or **CTRL-L**

**Adding New Text**

**Appending text**

| | | | |
|---|---|---|---|
| *After cursor:* | **a** | *At end of line:* | **A** |

**Inserting text**

| | | | |
|---|---|---|---|
| *Before cursor:* | **i** | *At beginning of line:* | **I** |

**Opening a new line**

| | | | |
|---|---|---|---|
| *Below current line:* | **o** | *Above current line:* | **O** |

# 13

# *Changing and Deleting Text Using vi*

**cw or cW**

In Chapter 12 you learned how to move the cursor and adjust the display in **vi**. You then learned how to add new text. In this chapter you will learn how to change and delete text. These two functions are very similar in **vi**.

## Changing Text **cw or cW**

So far we have only added new text to existing text. We can also make changes to existing text, using the cursor motion characters in conjunction with the change command (**c**) to produce a number of variations. Later in this section we'll talk about shifting text in either direction.

### *Changing a Word*

The change command (**c**) can be used by itself to change a single letter. But we'll save another command for that, and go on to the next possibility: changing a word. To show how this works, let's move to the first line of the second paragraph.

1. Move the cursor into position:

   a. In **vi command mode**, type *?can't* and press RETURN.

   (Since the line we are moving to is above our starting location, we used *?* in place of */* to search backwards.)

   b. The cursor should now be be over the *c* in line 9:

   ```
   We can't do the job you asked for.
   ```

2. Change *can't* to *cannot*:

   a. In **vi command mode**, type *cW* to change a word.

   b. A dollar sign will appear in place of the *t*:

   ```
   We can'$ do the job you asked for.
   ```

   c. Type *cannot* and press **ESC** to return to **vi command mode**.

   d. The line should now look like this:

   ```
   We cannot do the job you asked for.
   ```

We used **cW** in this exercise instead of **cw** because *can't* has an apostrophe in the middle of it. With **cw**, this would have happened:

```
We ca$'t do the job you asked for.
```

## *Cursor Motion and vi Commands*

The previous example looks very simple, but let's review what happened anyway. The example illustrates some things that you will be seeing again and again in **vi**. You may recall from Chapter 12 that **W** by itself makes the cursor jump to the next word (ignoring punctuation), like this:

```
We can't do the job you asked for.
                                                    W
We can't do the job you asked for.
```

When you combine **W** with **c**, you are telling **vi** to change (**c**) the text (not counting the blank space) that **W** would make the cursor jump over:

```
   Change text from here
   ↓
We can't do the job you asked for.
                                                    cW
```

```
We can't do the job you asked for.
         ↑
```

to here.

In the examples that follow, we'll be using different characters, but the rule is always the same: the change starts where the cursor is now and stops just before the place where the cursor would land after a jump.

## *Changing More Than One Word* **cnw or cnW**

Changing more than one word is similar to changing one word. The only difference is that you place a number in front of **w** to tell **vi** how many words to change. Let's use the same line of text to illustrate this.

1. Move the cursor into position:

   a. In **vi command mode**, type *b* to move the cursor back to the *c* in *cannot.*

   b. The line should now look like this:

   ```
   We cannot do the job you asked for.
   ```

2. Change *cannot do* to *are unable to complete in a timely manner*:

   a. Type *c2w* to change two words.

   b. You will see a dollar sign appear in front of *this*:

   ```
   We cannot d$ the job you asked for.
   ```

   **cnw or cnW**
   **c∧**

   c. Type *are unable to complete in a timely manner* and press **ESC** to return to **vi command mode.**

   d. The line should now look like this:

   ```
   We are unable to complete in a timely manner the job you asked for.
   ```

As you can see, the rule for cursor motion applied here: the change started at the cursor's original position and stopped before the *t* in *this* (which is where 2w by itself would have moved the cursor).

## *Changing to the Beginning of the Line* **c∧**

To change text from somewhere in the middle of a line to the beginning of the line, use **c** followed by ∧, the command to move the cursor to the beginning of a line. To illustrate this, we'll use the third line of the first paragraph.

1. Move the cursor into position:

    a. In **vi command mode**, type *?ideas* and press RETURN.

    b. The cursor will now be on the *i* in *ideas*:

    ```
    your ideas.
    ```

2. Change *your* to three words:

    a. Type *c∧* to request a change from the beginning of the line to the cursor's current position:

    ```
    your$ideas.
    ```

    b. Immediately type *all your extraordinary* (with a space following *y*) immediately after *c∧* and press **ESC** to return to **vi command mode.**

    c. The line should now look like this:

    ```
    all your extraordinary ideas.
    ```

## *Changing to the End of the Line* **c$**

To change text from anywhere in a line to the end of the line, use **c** followed by **$**, the command to move the cursor to the end of a line. To illustrate this, we'll use the first line of the same paragraph.

1. Move the cursor into position:

    a. In **vi command mode**, type *?recent* and press RETURN.

    b. Now the cursor will be on the *r* in *recent*:

    ```
    I wish to thank you profusely for your recent letter.
    ```

2. Change *recent letter.* to several words:

    a. Type *c$* to request a change from the cursor's position to the end of the line:

    ```
    I wish to thank you profusely for your recent letter$
    ```

    b. Type *letter of March 2.* immediately after *c$* and press **ESC** to return to **vi command mode**.

    c. The line should now look like this:

    ```
    I wish to thank you profusely for your letter of March 2.
    ```

## *Changing an Entire Line* **cc**

One of the rules of **vi** for most commands is this: To make a command apply to an entire line, type the command twice in succession. Using this rule, the command to change an entire line is **cc**. To illustrate this, we'll use the next to last line of text.

1. Move the cursor into position:

   a. In **vi command mode**, type */Frank* and press RETURN.

   b. The cursor will now be on the *F* in *Frank*:

   ```
   Frank Failsquick ("Mr. Macho")
   ```

2. Change *Frank Failsquick ("Mr. Macho")* to *Franklin F. Failsquick, Jr.*:

   a. Type *cc* to request a change to the entire line. (The line will vanish.)

   b. Type *Franklin F. Failsquick, Jr.* immediately after *cc* and press **ESC** to return to **vi command mode**.

   c. The line should now look like this:

   ```
   Franklin F. Failsquick, Jr.
   ```

   After all these changes, the entire letter should look like this:

**c$**
**cc**

```
September 17, 1985

Dear Mrs. Benson:

I wish to thank you profusely for your letter of March 2.
It is always a special delight to read and enjoy
all your extraordinary ideas.

We are unable to complete in a timely manner the job you asked for.
We don't know what we're doing.

Your most humble, obedient servant,

The Man for the Job:
Franklin F. Failsquick, Jr.
Chief Consulting Officer
```

```
~
~
~
~
```

## *Changing to the Beginning of the Sentence* **c(**

Changing text from anywhere in a sentence to the beginning is just like changing to the beginning of a line, described above. The only difference is that you use *c(* instead of *c0*. To illustrate this, let's use the third line of the second paragraph (*We don't know . . .*).

1. Move the cursor into position:

   a. In **vi command mode**, type *?what* and press RETURN.

   b. Now the cursor will be on the *w* in *what.*:

   ```
   We don't know what we're doing.
   ```

2. Change the first half of the sentence:

   a. Type *c(* to request a change from the beginning of the line to the cursor's position:

   ```
   We don't know$what we're doing.
   ```

   b. Immediately type *We have no notion* (with a space following) and press **ESC** to return to **vi command mode.**

   c. The line should look now like this:

   ```
   We have no notion what we're doing.
   ```

3. Undo the change:

   a. Type *u* (undo) to restore the sentence.

   b. The sentence should now look like this again:

   ```
   We don't know what we're doing.
   ```

## *Changing to the End of the Sentence* **c)**

Changing text from anywhere in a sentence to the end is just like changing to the end of a line, described above. The only difference is that you use *c)* instead of *c$*. To illustrate this, let's use the same line.

1. Change the second half of the sentence:

   a. Advance the cursor to the *w* in *what* with *3W*.

   b. With the cursor resting on the *w* in *what*, type *c)* to request a change from the cursor's position to the end of the line:

   ```
   We don't know what we're doing$
   ```

   c. Immediately type *what's going on.* and press **ESC** to return to **vi command mode.**

   d. The line should now look like this:

   ```
   We don't know what's going on.
   ```

2. Undo the change:

   a. Type *u* to restore the sentence.

   b. The sentence should now look like this again:

   ```
   We don't know what we're doing.
   ```

## *Changing to the Beginning of the Paragraph* c{

Changing text from anywhere in a paragraph to the beginning is just like changing to the beginning of a line. The only difference is that you use *c{* instead of *c(*. To illustrate this, let's use the same paragraph. **c( c) c{**

1. Move the cursor into position:

   a. In **vi command mode**, type *?this* and press RETURN.

   b. The cursor will now be on the *t* in *the*:

```
We are unable to complete in a timely manner the job you asked for.
We don't know what we're doing.
```

2. Change the first part of the paragraph:

   a. Type *c{* to request a change from the beginning of the paragraph to the cursor's position:

   ```
   We are unable to complete in a timely manner$the job
   you asked for. [This should appear as a single line.]
   We don't know what we're doing.
   ```

   b. Immediately type *We are incapable of completing* (with a space following) and press **ESC** to return to **vi command mode**.

c. Now the paragraph should look like this:

```
We are incapable of completing the job you asked for.
We don't know what we're doing.
```

## *Changing to the End of the Paragraph* c}

Changing text from anywhere in a paragraph to the end is just like changing to the end of a line, described above. The only difference is that you use *c}* instead of *c$*. To illustrate this, let's use the same line.

1. Change the last part of the paragraph:

   a. With the cursor resting on the *t* in *this*, type *c}* to request a change from the cursor's position to the end of the paragraph (the text will vanish from the screen):

   ```
   We are incapable of completing _
   ```

   b. Immediately complete the paragraph as shown, then press **ESC** to return to **vi command mode.**

   ```
   We are incapable of completing anything we attempt. <RETURN>
   We just don't know what we're doing at all._
   ```

2. Undo the change:

   a. Type *u* to restore the paragraph.

   b. It should now look like this again:

   ```
   We are incapable of completing the job you asked for.
   We don't know what we're doing.
   ```

## *Shifting a Line* <<**and**>>

If you ever need to "push" text to a different location on a line, **vi** provides one command for shifting a line to the left (<<) and one for shifting to the right (>>). Just move the cursor to the desired line and type either << or >>. (The exact amount of the shift will be eight spaces by default. However, you can change this amount by changing the "shiftwidth" variable—see Chapter 17, Customizing **vi**.) To see how shifting works, we'll use the line with the date.

1. Move the cursor into position:

   a. In **vi command mode**, type *?17* and press RETURN.

b. The cursor will now be on *17*:

```
September 17, 1985
```

2. Shift the date back and forth across the line:

a. Type >>, then the period (.) a few times to push the date to the right.

```
                                September 17, 1985
```

b. Type <<, then the period (.) to push the date back to the lefthand margin.

```
September 17, 1985
```

## *Shifting More Than One Line* **n<<and n>>**

To shift more than one line, use a multiplier in front of << or >>. To see how this works, we'll indent the lines in the closing.

1. Move the cursor into position:

a. In **vi command mode**, type */Man* and press RETURN.

b. Now the cursor will be on the *M* in *Man*:

```
The Man for the Job:
Franklin F. Failsquick, Jr.
Chief Consulting Officer
```

2. Shift the three lines back and forth across the line: **c}**

**<<and>>**

a. Type *3*>> then the period (.) several times to push the lines across the screen: **n<<and n>>**

```
               The Man for the Job:
               Franklin F. Failsquick, Jr.
               Chief Consulting Officer
```

b. Now type *3*<< then the period (.) to push the lines back to the lefthand margin:

```
The Man for the Job:
Franklin F. Failsquick, Jr.
Chief Consulting Officer
```

# Deleting Text

To **delete** text, use the cursor motion characters in conjunction with the delete command (**d**) to produce variations like those for **changing** text. Since we'll be making a lot of deletions, we'll have to undo most of them with the **u** (undo) command; otherwise, we'll run out of text to delete.

## Deleting a Character **x**

The command for deleting a single character (**x**) doesn't follow the pattern for deleting other segments of text. To delete a character, move the cursor to the character and type *x* (not *d*).

## Deleting More Than One Character **nx**

To delete more than one character (say four characters), place a multiplier (4) in front of the **x** command. Let's try this now.

1. Move the cursor into position:

   a. In **vi command mode**, type */ankl* and press RETURN.

   b. Now the cursor will by on the *a* in *Franklin*:

   ```
   Franklin F. Failsquick, Jr.
   ```

2. Change *Franklin* to *Frin* by deleting four characters:

   a. Type *4x* to make the deletion.

   b. The line should look like this:

   ```
   Frin F. Failsquick, Jr.
   ```

   c. Undo the deletion with **u**:

   ```
   Franklin F. Failsquick, Jr.
   ```

## Deleting a Word (or Words) **dw**

To delete a word, move the cursor to the first letter of the word and type *dw*. This works just like *cw*, except that you don't have to enter any replacement text with *dw*. Let's try deleting several words in the text.

1. Move the cursor into position:

   a. Type *?in a timely* and press RETURN.

   b. The cursor will move up to the *i* in *in* in the second paragraph:

```
We are unable to complete in a timely manner the job you asked for
```

2. Delete one word:

   a. Type *dw* to delete *in*:

   b. The line should now look like this:

```
We are unable to complete a timely manner the job you asked for.
```

3. Delete several words:

   a. Type *3dw* (or *d3w*) to delete *a timely manner*:

   b. The line should now look like this:

```
We are unable to complete the job you asked for.
```

If the word (or words) you are deleting are next to punctuation or contain punctuation (*isn't, won't, $5.67*), use *W* instead of *w*). Here's an example:

4. Drop the cursor down to the following line:

   a. Type */we're* and press RETURN.

   b. The cursor will move to the *w* in *we're*:

```
We don't know what we're doing.
```

5. Delete two words along with punctuation:

   a. Type *2dW* (or *d2W*).

   b. The line should now look like this:

```
We don't know what_
```

   c. Undo the deletion with **u**:

```
We don't know what we're doing.
```

**x**
**nx**
**dw**
**d∧**

To delete **part** of a word, move the cursor to the first letter to be deleted and follow the same procedure. For example, to delete *ment* from *establishment*, move the cursor to the *m* and type *dw*.

## *Deleting to the Beginning of a Line* **d∧**

To delete text from anywhere in a line to the beginning of the line, use *d∧*, which is analogous to *c∧*. Move the cursor to the first character to be retained and type *d∧*. All text on the line to the left of the cursor will be deleted. Without moving the cursor, type *d∧* on the current line. All text to the left of the cursor will vanish:

```
we're doing.
```

Undo this deletion with **u**:

```
We don't know what we're doing.
```

## *Deleting to the End of a Line* d$

To delete text from anywhere in a line to the end of the line, use *d$*, which is analogous to *c$*. Move the cursor to the first character to be deleted and type *d$*. All text on the line to the right of the cursor will be deleted. Let's try this.

1. Move the cursor up to the first paragraph:
   a. Type *?and* and press RETURN.
   b. The cursor will land on the *d* in *and*:

   ```
   It is always a special delight to read and enjoy
   ```

2. Delete the rest of the line to the right:
   a. Type *d$* to make the deletion.
   b. The line should now look like this:

   ```
   It is always a special delight to read_
   ```

   c. Undo the deletion with **u**:

   ```
   It is always a special delight to read and enjoy
   ```

## *Deleting an Entire Line* dd

To delete an entire line, use the "double rule" (*dd*). Move the cursor to any location on the line and press *dd*. For this example, leave the cursor where it is and type *dd*. The line will vanish, leaving the cursor on the following line like this:

```
I wish to thank you profusely for your recent letter.
all your extraordinary ideas.
```

To restore the deleted line, use **u**:

```
I wish to thank you profusely for your recent letter.
It is always a special delight to read and enjoy
```

Note that you can precede the command with a multiplier to delete more than one line. For example, to delete four lines of text (the current line and the next three), type *4dd*. Let's try that now. Four lines will vanish and the screen will look like this:

```
I wish to thank you profusely for your recent letter.
We don't know what we're doing.
```

Restore the missing text with **u**:

```
It is always a special delight to read and enjoy
all your extraordinary ideas.

We are incapable of completing the job you asked for.
We don't know what we're doing.
```

## *Deleting to the Beginning of a Sentence* d(

To delete text from anywhere in a sentence to the beginning of the sentence, use *d(*, which is analogous to *c(*. Move the cursor to the first character to be retained and type *d(*. All text in the sentence that precedes the cursor will be deleted. Let's try this.

1. Drop the cursor down to the next line:

   a. Type */extra* and press RETURN.

   b. The cursor will land on the *e* in *extraordinary*:

   ```
   It is always a special delight to read and enjoy
   all your extraordinary ideas.
   ```

2. Delete the first part of the sentence:

   a. Type *d(* to delete all words in front of the cursor.

   b. The display should now look like this:

   ```
   I wish to thank you profusely for your recent letter.
   extraordinary ideas.
   ```

   c. Restore the deleted words with **u**:

   ```
   It is always a special delight to read and enjoy
   all your extraordinary ideas.
   ```

**d$**
**dd**
**d(**
**d)**

## *Deleting to the End of a Sentence* d)

To delete text from anywhere in a sentence to the end of the sentence, use *d)*, which is analogous to *c)*. Move the cursor to the last character to be retained and type *d)*. All text in the sentence that follows the cursor will be deleted.

1. Move the cursor across the line to *to*:

   a. Type *6w* to advance the cursor.

   b. The cursor will land on the *t* in *to*:

```
It is always a special delight to read and enjoy
all your extraordinary ideas.
```

2. Delete the last part of the sentence:

   a. Type *d)* to delete all words that follow the cursor.

   b. The display should now look like this:

```
It is always a special delight_
```

   c. Restore the deleted words with **u**:

```
It is always a special delight to read and enjoy
all your extraordinary ideas.
```

To delete an entire sentence, simply move the cursor to the beginning of the sentence and type *d)*. To delete several sentences, precede the command with a multiplier and follow the same procedure.

## Deleting to the Beginning of a Paragraph **d{**

To delete text from anywhere in a paragraph to the beginning of the paragraph, use *d{*, which is analogous to *c{*. Move the cursor to the first character to be retained and type *d{*. All text in the paragraph that precedes the cursor will be deleted. Without moving the cursor, try this from your present location in the first paragraph. After you type *d{*, the display will look like this:

```
Dear Mrs. Benson:
to read and enjoy
all your extraordinary ideas.
```

Restore the missing words with **u**:

```
Dear Mrs. Benson:

I wish to thank you profusely for your letter of March 2.
It is always a special delight to read and enjoy
all your extraordinary ideas.
```

## Deleting to the End of a Paragraph **d}**

To delete text from anywhere in a paragraph to the end of the paragraph, use *d}*, which is analogous to *c}*. Move the cursor to the last character to be retained and type *d*}. All text in the paragraph that follows the cursor will be deleted. Let's move the cursor and try this.

1. Move the cursor into position:

   a. Type */for* and press RETURN to advance the cursor.

   b. The cursor will land on the *f* in *for*:

   ```
   I wish to thank you profusely for your letter of March 2.
   It is always a special delight to read and enjoy
   all your extraordinary ideas.
   ```

2. Delete the rest of the paragraph:

   a. Type *d*} to delete the rest of the paragraph:

   b. Now the display will look like this:

   ```
   I wish to thank you profusely_
   ```

   c. Now restore the paragraph with **u**:

   ```
   Dear Mrs. Benson:

   I wish to thank you profusely for your letter of March 2.
   It is always a special delight to read and enjoy
   all your extraordinary ideas.
   ```

To delete an entire paragraph, simply move the cursor to the beginning of the paragraph and type *d*}. To delete several paragraphs, precede the command with a multiplier and follow the same procedure. **d{** **d}**

## Ending the Session

Now it's time to write the updated text to *letter* and return to the UNIX shell.

1. Write the text to file *letter*:

   a. Type *:w* and press RETURN to write to the file.

   b. You will see a display like this at the bottom of the screen:

   ```
   "letter" [Modified] 17 lines, 391 characters
   ```

2. End this session with **vi**:

   a. Type *:q* and press RETURN to end the session.

b. The following display will appear, indicating that you have left **vi** and returned to the UNIX shell:

```
:q
$ _
```

Note that **vi** also allows you to combine the write and quit commands into a single command, like this:

```
:wq
$ _
"letter" 17 lines, 377 characters
```

## Summary of Chapter 13

In this chapter you learned how to change and delete text.

| **Changing Text** | **Commands** | |
|---|---|---|
| Changing a word | **cw** or **cW** | |
| Changing several words | **c2w**, **c2W**, **c3w**, **c3W**, and so on | |
| Changing to | *beginning of line:* **c0** | *end of line:* **c$** |
| Changing entire line | **cc** | |
| Changing several lines | **2cc**, **3cc**, **4cc**, and so on | |
| Changing to | *start of sentence:* **c(** | *end of sentence:* **c)** |
| Changing several sentences | **c2)**, **c3)**, **c4)**, and so on | |
| Changing to | *start of paragraph:* **c{** | *end of paragraph:* **c}** |
| Changing several paragraphs | **c2}**, **c3}**, **c4}**, and so on | |
| Shifting a line | *to the left:* << | *to the right:* >> |
| Shifting several lines | *to the left:* **n**<< | *to the right:* **n**>> |

| Deleting Text | Commands | |
|---|---|---|
| Deleting a word | **dw** or **dW** | |
| Deleting several words | **d2w, d2W, d3w, d3W,** and so on | |
| Deleting to | *beginning of line:* **d0** | *end of line:* **d$** |
| Deleting entire line | **dd** | |
| Deleting several lines | **2dd, 3dd, 4dd,** and so on | |
| Deleting to | *start of sentence:* **d(** | *end of sentence:* **d)** |
| Deleting several sentences | **d2), d3), d4),** and so on | |
| Deleting to | *start of paragraph:* **d{** | *end of paragraph:* **d}** |
| Deleting several paragraphs | **d2}, d3}, d4},** and so on | |

# 14

# Finding and Replacing Text Using **vi**

In Chapter 13 you learned a number of different ways to change or delete text with vi. In this chapter you will learn various ways to search for text and make replacements.

## Beginning a New Session

Here is another brief reminder about how to get started with this session of **vi**: If necessary, move from your home directory to *text files*, then start an editing session with the same file (*letter*):

```
$ cd text_files
$ pwd
/usr/robin/text_files
$ vi letter
$ _
```

Now you should see something like this:

```
September 17, 1985

Dear Mrs. Benson:

I wish to thank you profusely for your letter of March 2.
It is always a special delight to read and enjoy
all your extraordinary ideas.

We are incapable of completing the job you asked for.
We don't know what we're doing.

Your most humble, obedient servant,

The Man for the Job:
Franklin F. Failsquick, Jr.
Chief Consulting Officer
~
~
~
"letter" 17 lines, 377 characters
```

## Searching on a Line

**fx**

There are two **vi** commands that allow you to search in either direction for a character on the current line and make changes.

### *Searching to the Right*

To search from left to right for a single character on the current line, use the **fx** command (where *x* represents the character you are looking for). Then, if you need to continue searching for the same character, you can use one of two commands to repeat:

; to repeat the search in the **same** direction

, to repeat the search in the **opposite** direction

For example, suppose you want to search for *r* on the first line of the first paragraph.

1. Move the cursor into position:

   a. Move the cursor to the beginning of the line (*5G* or */I*).

   b. The line should look like this:

```
I wish to thank you profusely for your letter of March 2.
```

2. Move to the first *r*:

   a. Type *fr.*

   b. Now the cursor will jump to the *r* in *profusely*:

```
I wish to thank you profusely for your letter of March 2.
```

3. Move to the next *r*:

   a. Press *;* to continue the search forward.

   b. The cursor will jump to the *r* in *for*:

```
I wish to thank you profusely for your letter of March 2.
```

4. Move to the next *r*:

   a. Type *;* to continue the search again.

   b. The cursor will jump to the *r* in *your*:

**fx**

```
I wish to thank you profusely for your letter of March 2.
```

**Fx**

You can type *;* two more times to jump to the next two r's. You can then type *,* to jump back to each successive *r* in the other direction.

## *Searching to the Left* **Fx**

To search from right to left for a single character on the current line, use the **Fx** command (where *x* represents the character you are looking for). Again, if you need to continue searching for the same character, you can use one of two commands to repeat:

; to repeat the search in the **same** direction

, to repeat the search in the **opposite** direction

As an example, let's search for *r* on the first line **from the other direction.**

1. Move the cursor into position:

   a. Move the cursor to the end of the line (*$*).

   b. The line will look like this:

```
I wish to thank you profusely for your letter of March 2.
```

2. Move to the first *r*:

   a. Type *Fr* to begin a search to the left.

   b. Now the cursor will jump to the *r* in *March*:

```
I wish to thank you profusely for your letter of March 2.
```

3. Move to the next *r* to the left:

   a. Type *;* to continue the search to the left.

   b. The cursor will jump to the *r* in *letter*:

```
I wish to thank you profusely for your letter of March 2.
```

4. Move to the following *r*:

   a. Type *;* to continue the search again.

   b. The cursor will jump to the *r* in *your*:

```
I wish to thank you profusely for your letter of March 2.
```

You can type *;* two more times to jump to the next two *r*'s. Then you can type *,* to jump back to each successive *r* in the other direction.

## Searching in a File *Istring*

To help you search for a string anywhere in the work area, **vi** provides a pair of commands analogous to **f** and **F**: one for searching forward and one for searching backwards in the editing buffer.

### *Searching Forward*

To search forward for a string in a file, type */string* and press RETURN. If you need to continue searching for the string, you can use one of two keys:

**n** Repeat the search in the same direction (forward)

**N** Repeat the search in the opposite direction (backwards)

As an example, suppose you need to search for *you* in the letter.

1. Move the cursor into position:

   a. Position the cursor at the beginning of the file (*1G*).

   b. The first line should look like this:

   ```
   September 17, 1985
   ```

2. Begin the search:

   a. Type */you* and press RETURN.

   b. The cursor will jump to the *y* in *you* in line 5:

   ```
   I wish to thank you profusely for your letter of March 2.
   ```

3. Continue the search:

   a. Type *n* to continue the search forward.

   b. The cursor will jump to the *your* in the same line:

   ```
   I wish to thank you profusely for your letter of March 2.
   ```

4. Continue the search again:

   a. Type *n* again. ***/string*** ***?string***

   b. The cursor will move to *your* in line 7:

   ```
   all your extraordinary ideas.
   ```

You can type *n* again to continue searching forward or *N* to search back toward the beginning of the letter. If you don't want the cursor to stop at *your*, *yourself*, or other words that contain *you*, leave a space after the *u* when you begin the search, like this: */you* .

## *Searching Backward* ***?string***

To search backwards for a string in a file, type *?string* and press RETURN. Again, if you need to continue searching for the string, use one of these two keys:

**n** to repeat the search in the same direction (backwards)

**N** to repeat the search in the opposite direction (forward)

For example, suppose you need to search for *you* from the end of the letter.

1. Move the cursor into position:

   a. Position the cursor at the end of the file (*G*).

   b. The line should look like this:

   ```
   Chief Consulting Officer
   _
   ```

2. Begin the search:

   a. Type *?you* and press RETURN to begin searching in reverse.

   b. The cursor will jump to the *y* in *you* in line 9:

   ```
   We are incapable of completing the job you asked for.
   ```

3. Continue the search:

   a. Type *n* to continue searching in reverse.

   b. The cursor will jump to the *your* in line 7:

   ```
   all your extraordinary ideas.
   ```

4. Continue the search again:

   a. Type *n* again to continue searching in reverse.

   b. The cursor will move to *your* in line 5:

   ```
   I wish to thank you profusely for your letter of March 2.
   ```

Type *n* again to continue searching backwards or *N* to search forward. Again, if you don't want the cursor to stop at *your, yourself,* or other words that contain *you,* leave a space after *you* when you begin the search, like this: *?you* . Since all searches wrap from one end of the editing buffer to the other, the command for searching forward (/***string***) is sufficient by itself.)

## Making Replacements

Each time the cursor stops during a search, you can replace text (or append or insert text, for that matter). Since appending and inserting text have already been discussed in detail, we'll concentrate on replacements here. To replace text in a file, **vi** offers the following basic commands (in addition to the change command discussed in the previous chapter): one that replaces a single character with another, one that replaces a sequence of characters one at a time, one that replaces a single character with more than one, and one that replaces an entire line.

## *Replacing One Character with Another* r

To replace one character with another, **vi** provides a simple command—**r**. Move the cursor to the character, type *r*, and then type the new character. For example, suppose you want to change the date on the current line from *March 2* to *March 9.*

1. Move the cursor into position:

   a. Type *f2* to move the cursor to the *2.*

   b. Now the line should look like this:

   ```
   I wish to thank you profusely for your letter of March 2.
   ```

2. Make the change:

   a. Type *r9* **without** RETURN or **ESC** to change *2* to *9.*

   b. Now the line should look like this:

   ```
   I wish to thank you profusely for your letter of March 9.
   ```

r
R

## *Replacing Characters One at a Time* R

To replace several consecutive characters one at a time, use the **R** command. Move the cursor to the first of the characters, type *R*, and then type the new characters, followed by RETURN. For example, suppose you want to change the date a second time from *March 9* to *April 9.*

1. Move the cursor into position:

   a. Type *b* to move the cursor to the *M* in *March.*

   b. Now the line should look like this:

   ```
   I wish to thank you profusely for your letter of March 9.
   ```

2. Make the change:

   a. Type *R*, then *April* without a space, followed by **ESC**, to replace *March* with *April.*

b. Now the line should look like this:

```
I wish to thank you profusely for your letter of April 9.
```

**Caution:** If the replacement text is longer than the text being replaced, the **R** command won't stop you from typing beyond the original text.

## *Replacing One Character with Several* **s**

To replace one character with any number of characters, **vi** provides the **s** command. Move the cursor to the character, type *s*, and then type the new characters. For example, suppose you wanted to change the date on the current line from *April 9* to *April 12.*

1. Move the cursor into position:

   a. Type *w* to advance the cursor to the *9.*

   b. Now the line should look like this:

   ```
   I wish to thank you profusely for your letter of April 9.
   ```

2. Make the change:

   a. Type *s12*, followed by **ESC**, to change *9* to *12.*

   b. Now the line should look like this:

   ```
   I wish to thank you profusely for your letter of April 12.
   ```

## *Replacing an Entire Line* **S**

To replace an entire line of text, use the **S** command (which is equivalent to **cc**). Move the cursor to any location on the line, type *S*, and then type the new line (or lines), followed by RETURN. For example, suppose you want to change the *title line* from *Chief Consulting Officer* to *Supreme Supervisor.*

1. Move the cursor into position:

   a. Type */Chief* to move the cursor to the last line of text.

   b. The line should look like this:

   ```
   Chief Consulting Officer
   ```

2. Make the change:

   a. Type *S* to request a change to the line (which will vanish).

   b. Without leaving a space, type *Supreme Supervisor*, followed by **ESC**, to type the new line.

   c. The new line should look like this:

   ```
   Supreme Supervisor
   ```

   d. Type *U* to undo the change.

**Note:** If **vi** were 100 percent consistent, the **S** command would be equivalent to the **c$** command, not the **cc** command.

### *Ending the Session*

Now it's time to write the updated text to disk file *letter* and return to the UNIX shell. Type *:wq* and press RETURN to write the buffer and quit **vi**.

## Making Substitutions

In Chapter 8 you learned about the substitution command **s** provided by **ed**. It may not be surprising to find that **ex** has a substitution command called **s** that is very similar to **ed**'s. (Recall that **vi** is the visual mode of a more general text editor called **ex**, which is an enhanced version of **ed**.)

### *Copying Files from Another Directory*

Before proceeding with the **s** command in **vi**, let's copy a file you may already have worked with (*metric.c* in directory *c_progs*) into your current directory (*text_files*). To help you with this, here is how your main directory and subdirectories look now:

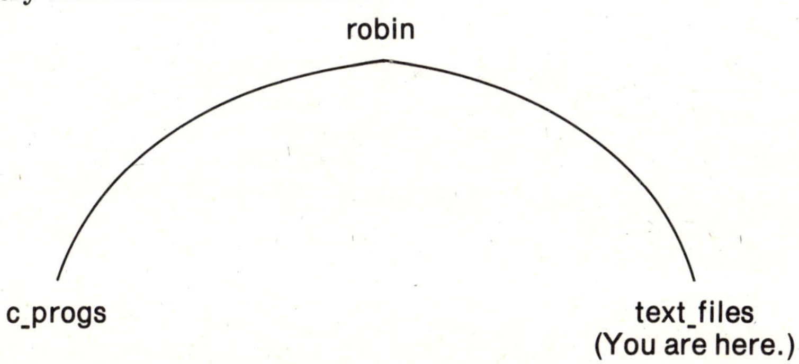


Fig. 14-1. Your subdirectories.

1. Check your directories:

   a. Check your current directory:

```
$ pwd
/usr/robin/text_files
$ _
```

   b. Now check the subdirectories in your home directory:

```
$ ls .. | sp
.profile     ed_files     c_progs     vi_files
```

2. Copy file *metric.c* to your current directory:

   a. Make the copy:

```
$ cp ../c_progs/metric.c vi_files
$ _
```

   b. Check your directory to verify that the copy was successful:

```
$ ls | sp
barbershop hours rates letter compact.c metric.c
```

You found copies of files *display.c* and *metric.c* there. Now we can proceed with substitutions. (In the event that you skipped Part II of this book, you won't have this file entered yet. You will have to type it now.)

## Starting a New Session with vi

Now that you have a copy of *metric.c* in your *text__files* directory, we can edit this file with vi.

```
$ vi metric.c
$ _
```

The screen should look something like this:

```
/* List conversions from gallons to liters*/
main()
}
    int low, high, incr;
    float gals, ltrs;

    low = 10;  /* starting value in gallons */
    high = 20; /* ending value in gallons */
```

```
    incr = 2;  /* increment for each step */

    gals = low;
    while (gals <= high)
    {

        ltrs = (gals * 3.785);
        printf("%4.0f %6.2f\n", gals, ltrs);
        gals = gals + incr;
    }
}
~
~
~
"metric.c" 18 lines, 319 characters
```

## *Changing Some Settings*

Since this is a program, not a letter, let's makes some changes to the basic settings in **vi**. To make this simple, we'll change only two of these:

- number (nu) — the option that produces line numbering
- shift-width (sw) — the option that determines how far across the screen lines will be shifted by the **shift** commands << and >>

1. Turn on line numbering:
   a. Type *:set nu* and press RETURN.
   b. Before you press RETURN, you will see *:set nu* at the bottom of the screen.
   c. After you press RETURN, you will see line numbers appear at the lefthand margins, with the text indented.
2. Set the shift-width to 5:
   a. Type *:set sw=5* and press RETURN.
   b. Before you press RETURN, you will see *:set sw=5* at the bottom of the screen.
   c. The width for all shifts will be changed from 8 (the default) to 5.

At this point you have **vi** active with file *metric.c* and you have line numbering turned on and option *shift-width* set to 5 columns. Now you are ready to begin trying out some substitutions.

## Making Substitutions

**:s**

One reason for selecting this file to make substitutions is that it contains so many repetitions of the same words. For example, the variable *gals* occurs seven different times in this short program. You could probably make seven replacements manually without much bother, but the substitution command (**s**) makes these changes automatically. In a long program, this would be an enormous convenience.

1. Change *gals* to *gallons*:

   a. Type *:1,$s* to request a substitution for all lines in the file (line 1 to the last line ($)).

   b. Without leaving a space, type */gals/gallons/g* to request a substitution of *gallons* in place of *gal* for all occurrences on each line (g).

   c. If the display at the bottom of the screen looks like this, press RETURN to begin the substitution:

   ```
   :1,$s/gals/gallons/g
   ```

   d. If you see mistakes, back up the cursor and correct them before you press RETURN.

2. Change *ltrs* to *liters*:

   a. Type *:1,$s* to request a substitution for all lines in the file (line 1 to the last line ($)).

   b. Without leaving a space, type */ltrs/liters/g* to request a substitution of *liters* in place of *ltrs* for all occurrences on each line (g).

   c. If the display at the bottom of the screen looks like this, press RETURN to begin the substitution:

   ```
   :1,$s/ltrs/liters/g
   ```

   d. If you see mistakes, back up the cursor and correct them before you press RETURN.

If you should ever make mistakes and then press RETURN by accident, you can always undo the results with the **u** (undo) command.

3. Look at the results on the screen:

```
/* List conversions from gallons to liters */
main()
{
  int low, high, incr;
  float gallons, liters;

  low = 10;  /* starting value in gallons */
  high = 20; /* ending value in gallons */
  incr = 2;  /* increment for each step */

  gallons = low;
  while (gallons <= high)
  {
    liters = (gallons * 3.785);
    printf(''%4.0f %6.2f\n'', gallons, liters);
    gallons = gallons + incr;
  }
}
~
~
~
3 substitutions on 3 lines
```

**:s**

As you can see, the substitution works about the same way in **vi** as it does in **ed**. Here are a few words about using **s** in **vi** (which is very similar to **s** in **ed**):

- The **s** command always begins with a colon (:) to escape to **ex**, followed by a range of line numbers.
- The line numbers may be actual integers, search strings, or symbols, as illustrated here:

| | |
|---|---|
| `:1,20` | Line 1 to line 20 |
| `:15,/place/` | Line 15 to the first line that contains *place* |
| `:5,.` | Line 5 to the current line |
| `:.,$` | The current line to the last line of the file |

`:.-20,?end?` Twenty lines ahead of the current line to the first line that contains *end*

`:?WPP?,$-2` The first line that contains *WPP* (above the current line) to two lines before the last line of the file

- Use slashes to search forward and question marks to search backwards
- Use the **g** command at the end of the command line to substitute all occurrences in each line, rather than just the first occurrence.

## *Shifting Lines*

**<<or>>**

Try out the new setting for shift width by moving the cursor to different lines and typing << or >>. Each shift will be five columns now instead of eight.

## *Shifting Paragraphs*

**<}or>}**

Try shifting paragraphs (in this case, groups of lines separated by blank lines) with the <} and >} operators.

1. Shift lines 4 and 5:

   a. Type *4G* to move the cursor to line 4.

   b. Type >} to shift the two lines (a paragraph to vi) to the right:

   ```
             int low, high, incr;
             float gallons, liters;
   ```

   c. Type <} to shift the lines back again:

   ```
   int low, high, incr;
   float gallons, liters;
   ```

2. Shift lines 7, 8, and 9:

   a. Type *7G* to move the cursor to line 7.

   b. Type >} to shift the three lines to the right:

   ```
     low = 10;    /* starting value in gallons */
     high = 20;   /* ending value in gallons */
     incr = 2;    /* increment for each step */
   ```

c. Type <} to shift the lines back again:

```
low = 10;        /* starting value in gallons */
high = 20;       /* ending value in gallons */
incr = 2;        /* increment for each step */
```

3. Shift lines 11-17:

   a. Type *11G* to move the cursor to line 11.

   b. Type >} to shift the lines to the right:

```
    gallons = low;
    while (gallons <= high)
    {
          liters = (gallons * 3.785);
          printf("%4.0f %6.2f\n", gallons, liters);
          gallons = gallons + incr;
    }
  }
```

   c. Type <} to shift the lines back again:

```
    gallons = low;
    while (gallons <= high)
    {
      liters = (gallons * 3.785);
      printf("%4.0f %6.2f\n", gallons, liters);
      gallons = gallons + incr;
    }
  }
```

<<or>>
<}or>}

You can also shift sentences with vi. The commands to use are *<)* and *>)*. Now end this session with vi by typing *:wq* and pressing RETURN.

## Summary of Chapter 14

In this chapter you learned how to search for text on a line and in a file and how to make replacements.

### *Searching for a Character on the Current Line*

Searching to the left **Fx**

Searching to the right **fx**

## Searching for a String in the Editing Buffer

| | |
|---|---|
| Searching forward | **/string** |
| Searching backward | **?string** |

No matter which direction you search in, the search will cover the entire editing buffer, all the way back to your starting location.

## Making Replacements

| | |
|---|---|
| Replacing one character with another | **r** |
| Replacing any number of characters | **R** |
| Replacing one character with any number of characters | **s** |
| Replacing an entire line | **S** |

**Making substitutions.** To substitute each instance of one string with another from line **n** to line **N**, enter an **ex** command of the form

| | |
|---|---|
| :n,Ns/old string/new string/g | (forward search) |
| :n,Ns?old string?new string?g | (backward search) |

The line numbers **n** and **N** may be integers, search strings, or symbols for line numbers (as is customary with the **s** in **ed**).

**The g** indicates that every instance of the string on a given line is to be substituted, not just the first instance on that line.

# 15

# Making Changes within a File Using **vi**

In Chapter 14 you learned how to search for text and how to make replacements. You also copied another file into your *text_files* directory. In this chapter you will learn different methods for moving and copying text within a file. But first, here are a few words about ways to exit from **vi**.

## Exiting vi

So far you have used only the **w** (write) and **q** (quit) commands to exit a **vi** file. This includes the combined command *wq*:

```
:wq <RETURN>
```

### *Conditional Writing*

To perform a write before quitting **only** if you have made changes (that is, to request a **conditional write**), you can use

```
:x <RETURN>
```
(which in turn is equivalent to ZZ)

### Abandoning a File

To abandon a file (and not save any changes you might have made to it), use the **forced quit**, like this:

```
:q! <RETURN>
```

## Moving Text Within a File

In Chapter 14 you learned how to use the change (**c**) and delete (**d**) commands, which operate in similar ways. In this chapter you will learn two new commands called "yank" (**y**) and "put" (**p** or **P**). You will learn that delete and yank are also similar, and that you can use either one of them with "put" to make text disappear, reappear, or multiply.

If you think of yourself as a magician and the words, sentences, and paragraphs you work with as handkerchiefs, rabbits, and assistants, then you won't have any trouble seeing how **delete**, **yank**, and **put** work. Using **delete** is like putting a rabbit into a hat and then showing the audience an empty hat. Using **yank** is like putting a handkerchief into your pocket while still keeping another in your hand. Using **delete** and **put** in succession is like having your assistant step into a wooden box, and then reappear at the other end of the stage. Using **yank** and **put** in succession is like having your assistant step into a wooden box, and then emerge from one box while a twin emerges from another.

### Creating a New File

Before discussing how to move text from one location to another, let's create a new file in directory *text__files* called *disks*. Use **vi** to edit a file named *disks*:

```
$ vi disks
```

and enter the following text (leaving a blank space and pressing RETURN at the end of each line, and pressing **ESC** at the conclusion of the text):

```
              Advertisement                 [One tab]
                                            [Blank line]
* * * * * * * * * * * * * * * * * *         [18 asterisks]
                                            [Blank line]
Spinrite diskettes have a lifetime
guarantee. That's right, every
```

```
Spinrite diskette is guaranteed
for life. Not two years, not three
years, not five years, but life.
                                          [Blank line]
Advanced technology makes it possible.
Sophisticated marketing makes it
incredible. Superior distribution
makes it available. And state-of-
the-art manufacturing makes it.
                                          [Blank line]
No matter what you've read, no matter
what you've heard, no matter what
you've thought, our warranty stands:
Every Spinrite diskette will last
until it wears out. That's quality,
and that's our guarantee.
                                          [Blank line]
Don't settle for anything less.
Don't waste your time with the
amateurs. Step up to the pro-
fessionals. Step up to Spinrite.          ESC
```

Now write the text to file *disks* (*:w*).

## *Moving a Character* **xp**

To move text from one location to another, you can make it disappear from one location (with **delete**), then reappear in another (with **put**). **xp**

After writing to *disks*, move the cursor to the *o* in *thought* on line 19 (*?ought*). Now, with the cursor resting on the *o*, type *xp* (no RETURN is necessary). The word will now be spelled *thuoght*—the *o* and the *u* have been switched. This is the simplest kind of move.

Now type *h* (cursor left), followed by *xp* again, to undo the switch, and try it again. Here's what happens in slow motion:

1. The cursor is on the *o* (keep your eye on the cursor):

   ```
   you've thought, our warranty stands:
   ```

2. Now delete the *o* with the **x** command:

   ```
   you've thught, our warranty stands:
   ```

3. Then "put" the *o* back with the **p** command:

   ```
   you've thuoght, our warranty stands:
   ```

4. Undo the change by typing *U* (not *u*)—U is for the entire line.

Did you keep your eye on the cursor? As soon as the *o* vanishes, the cursor moves forward to the *u*. Since the **p** command always puts the text **ahead** of the cursor, the *o* ends up on the other side of the *u*. (Remember, the command to delete a single character is **x**, not **d**.)

## Moving a Word

**dw and P**
**dw and p**

Moving a word is like moving a character. The main difference is that the command to delete a word is **dw** (or **dW**), not **x**. We plan to move the cursor to a word, delete the word, then move to the new location and "put" the word there. As an example, let's move *every* from line 6 to line 8.

1. Move the cursor into position:

   a. Type *?every* and press RETURN to move the cursor to *every*.

   b. The display should now look like this:

   ```
   Spinrite diskettes have a lifetime
   guarantee. That's right, every
   Spinrite diskette is guaranteed
   for life. Not two years, not three
   years, not five years, but life.
   ```

2. Delete the word at its current location:

   a. Type *dw* to delete *every*.

   b. The line should now look like this:

   ```
   guarantee. That's right,_
   ```

3. Move the cursor to the new location:

   a. Type */life* and press RETURN to move the cursor to *life* in line 8.

   b. The line should now look like this:

   ```
   for life. Not two years, not three
   ```

4. "Put" the word at the new location:

   a. Type capital *P* (not *p*) to put *every* in front of *life*.

   b. The paragraph should now look like this:

   ```
   Spinrite diskettes have a lifetime
   guarantee. That's right,
   Spinrite diskette is guaranteed
   for everylife. Not two years, not three
   years, not five years, but life.
   ```

c. To insert a space between *every* and *life*, type *a*, press the space bar, and press **ESC**. (This won't be necessary if you originally typed a space after *every*.)

In this example, you used a capital **P** instead of **p** because capital **P** puts text **before** the cursor (**above** the current line in a line operation). Use **p** when you want to put text **after** the cursor (or **below** the current line).

## Moving a Sentence

**d) and P**
**d) and p**

Moving a sentence is like moving a word. The main difference is that the command to delete a sentence is **d)**, not **dw**. We plan to move the cursor to the beginning of a sentence, delete the sentence, then move to the new location and "put" the sentence there. As an example, let's move the second sentence of the first paragraph to the end of the paragraph.

1. Move the cursor into position:

   a. Type *?That* and press RETURN to move the cursor to *That's*.

   b. The display should now look like this:

```
Spinrite diskettes have a lifetime
guarantee. That's right,
Spinrite diskette is guaranteed
for every life. Not two years, not three
years, not five years, but life.
```

**dw and P**
**dw and p**
**d) and P**
**d) and p**

2. Delete the sentence at its current location:

   a. Type *d)* to delete the entire second sentence.

   b. The paragraph should now look like this:

```
Spinrite diskettes have a lifetime
guarantee. Not two years, not three
years, not five years, but life.
```

3. Move the cursor to the new location:

   a. Type */life* and press RETURN to move the cursor to *life* in line 8.

   b. Advance the cursor to the end of the line with *$*.

   c. The line should now look like this:

```
years, not five years, but life.  _
```

4. "Put" the sentence at the new location:

   a. Type lowercase *p* to put the second sentence after the third.

   b. The paragraph should now look like this:

```
Spinrite diskettes have a lifetime
guarantee. Not two years, not three
years, not five years, but life.That's right,
Spinrite diskette is guaranteed
for every life.
```

   c. To insert two spaces between the period and *That's,* type *i,* press the space bar twice, and press **ESC**.

## Moving a Paragraph

**d} and P**
**d} and p**

Moving a paragraph is like moving a sentence. The main difference is that the command to delete a paragraph is **d}**, not **d)**. We plan to move the cursor to the start of a paragraph, delete the paragraph, then move to the new location and "put" the paragraph there. As an example, let's move the second paragraph to where the third paragraph is now (switch paragraphs).

1. Move the cursor into position:

   a. Type } to advance the cursor to the beginning of the second paragraph.

   b. The display should now look like this:

```
Spinrite diskette is guaranteed
for every life.

Advanced technology makes it possible.
Sophisticated marketing makes it
```

2. Delete the paragraph at its current location:

   a. Type *d}* to delete the entire second paragraph.

   b. The display should now look like this:

```
Spinrite diskette is guaranteed
for every life.

No matter what you've read, no matter
what you've heard, no matter what
```

3. Move the cursor to the new location:

   a. Type } to advance the cursor to the beginning of the next paragraph.

   b. The display should now look like this:

```
until it wears out. That's quality,
and that's our guarantee.

Don't settle for anything less.
Don't waste your time with the
```

4. "Put" the paragraph at the new location:

   a. Type capital *P* (not *p*) to "put" the second paragraph above the fourth.

   b. The display should now look like this:

```
                 Advertisement

* * * * * * * * * * * * * * * * * *

Spinrite diskettes have a lifetime
guarantee. Not two years, not three
years, not five years, but life. That's right,
Spinrite diskette is guaranteed
for every life.

No matter what you've read, no matter
what you've heard, no matter what
you've thought, our warranty stands:
Every Spinrite diskette will last
until it wears out. That's quality,
and that's our guarantee.

Advanced technology makes it possible.
Sophisticated marketing makes it
incredible. Superior distribution
makes it available. And state-of-
the-art manufacturing makes it.
```

[This paragraph has been moved—switched with the paragraph above]

**d} and P**
**d} and p**

```
Don't settle for anything less.
Don't waste your time with the
amateurs. Step up to the pro-
fessionals. Step up to Spinrite.
```

## *Moving a Line*

**dd and P**
**dd and p**

Moving a line is like moving a word. The main difference is that the command to delete a line is **dd**, not **dw**. We plan to move the cursor to a line, delete the line, then move to the new location and "put" the line there. As an example, let's move the second line of the first paragraph to where the fourth line is now.

1. Move the cursor into position:

   a. Type *?two* and press RETURN to move the cursor to *two* (line 6).

   b. The display should now look like this:

   ```
   Spinrite diskettes have a lifetime
   guarantee. Not two years, not three
   years, not five years, but life. That's right,
   Spinrite diskette is guaranteed
   for every life.
   ```

2. Delete the line at its current location:

   a. Type *dd* to delete the entire second line.

   b. The paragraph should now look like this:

   ```
   Spinrite diskettes have a lifetime
   years, not five years, but life. That's right,
   Spinrite diskette is guaranteed
   for every life.
   ```

3. Move the cursor to the new location:

   a. Type *j* to move the cursor to *Spinrite* in the next line.

   b. The paragraph should now look like this:

   ```
   Spinrite diskettes have a lifetime
   years, not five years, but life. That's right,
   ```

```
Spinrite diskette is guaranteed
for every life.
```

4. "Put" the line at the new location:

   a. Type lowercase *p* to "put" the second line **below** the current line.

   b. The paragraph should now look like this:

```
Spinrite diskettes have a lifetime
years, not five years, but life. That's right,
Spinrite diskette is guaranteed
guarantee. Not two years, not three
for every life.
```

## *Other Possible Moves*

In the examples you just tried, you moved one entire item (character, word, sentence, paragraph, or line) from one location to another. However, it is also possible to move part of an item (assuming the cursor is somewhere in the middle of it), or several items. Here are some suggestions:

| | |
|---|---|
| **db** and **p** (or **P**) | Move the left-hand side of a word. |
| **d(** and **p** (or **P**) | Move the beginning of a sentence. |
| **d{** and **p** (or **P**) | Move the beginning of a paragraph. |
| **d∧** and **p** (or **P**) | Move the left-hand side of a line. |
| **dw** and **p** (or **P**) | Move the right-hand side of a word. |
| **d)** and **p** (or **P**) | Move the ending of a sentence. |
| **d}** and **p** (or **P**) | Move the ending of a paragraph. |
| **d$** and **p** (or **P**) | Move the right-hand side of a line. |
| **x3** and **p** (or **P**) | Move three characters. |
| **d3w** and **p** (or **P**) | Move three words. |
| **d3)** and **p** (or **P**) | Move three sentences. |
| **d3}** and **p** (or **P**) | Move three paragraphs. |
| **3dd** and **p** (or **P**) | Move three lines. |

**dd and P**
**dd and p**

Once again, **p** puts the item **after** the cursor, while **P** puts the item **before** the cursor. (In line operations, **p** puts the item **above** the current line, while **P** puts the item **below** the current line.)

## *Abandoning the File*

Before going on to **copying** text within the editing buffer, let's abandon the changes we've made to the text in our work area. Then we can start all over again with *disks.* Type *:q!* and press RETURN to abandon the work area, then type *vi_ disks* to begin a new session with the original text.

## Copying Text Within a File

Copying text from one location to another with **vi** is similar to moving text. The only difference is that you use the "yank" command (**y**) instead of the **delete** command (**d**). "Yanking" leaves a copy of the text in its original location. Everything else is about the same. Let's begin by starting a new session:

```
$ vi disks
```

### *Copying a Word*

**yw and P**
**yw and p**

We'll dispense with the subject of copying a character, and move right on to copying a word. **Copying** a word is like **moving** a word. The main difference is that you will "yank" the word, rather than delete it. We plan to move the cursor to a word, "yank" the word, then move to the new location and "put" the word there. As an example, let's copy *Spinrite* from line 5 to several other places.

1. Move the cursor into position:

   a. Type */Spinrite* and press RETURN to move the cursor to *Spinrite.*

   b. The display should now look like this:

   ```
   Spinrite diskettes have a lifetime
   guarantee. That's right, every
   Spinrite diskette is guaranteed
   for life. Not two years, not three
   years, not five years, but life.
   ```

2. "Yank" the word at its current location:

   a. Type *yw* to "yank" *Spinrite.*

   b. The line should now look like this (the same):

   ```
   Spinrite diskettes have a lifetime
   ```

3. Move the cursor to a new location:

   a. Type */years* and press RETURN to move the cursor to *years* in line 8.

b. The line should now look like this:

```
for life. Not two years, not three
```

4. "Put" the word at the new location:

   a. Type capital *P* to put *Spinrite* in front of *years.*

   b. The paragraph should now look like this:

```
Spinrite diskettes have a lifetime
guarantee. That's right, every
Spinrite diskette is guaranteed
for life. Not two Spinrite_years, not three
years, not five years, but life.
```

Typing *n* twice, then repeating step 4 (that's *n n P*), insert copies of *Spinrite* between *three* and *years* and *five* and *years.* After you have done this, the paragraph should now look like this:

```
Spinrite diskettes have a lifetime
guarantee. That's right, every
Spinrite diskette is guaranteed
for life. Not two Spinrite years, not three
Spinrite years, not five Spinrite_years, but life.
```

## Copying a Sentence

**y) and P**
**y) and p**

**yw and P**
**yw and p**
**y) and P**
**y) and p**

Copying a sentence is like copying a word. The main difference is that the command to "yank" a sentence is y), not yw. We plan to move the cursor to the beginning of a sentence, "yank" the sentence, then move to the new location and "put" the sentence there. As an example, let's copy the second sentence of the first paragraph to the end of the paragraph.

1. Move the cursor into position:

   a. Type *?That* and press RETURN to move the cursor to *That's.*

   b. The display should now look like this:

```
Spinrite diskettes have a lifetime
guarantee. That's right, every
Spinrite diskette is guaranteed
for life. Not two Spinrite years, not three
Spinrite years, not five Spinrite years, but life.
```

2. "Yank" the sentence at its current location:

   a. Type *y)* to "yank" the entire second sentence.

   b. The paragraph should now look like this (the same):

```
Spinrite diskettes have a lifetime
guarantee. That's right, every
Spinrite diskette is guaranteed
for life. Not two Spinrite years, not three
Spinrite years, not five Spinrite years, but life.
```

3. Move the cursor to the new location:

   a. Type */five* and press RETURN to move the cursor to *five* in line 8.

   b. Drop the cursor to the blank line by typing *j*.

   c. The display should now look like this:

```
Spinrite years, not five Spinrite years, but life.

Advanced technology makes it possible.
```

4. "Put" the sentence at the new location:

   a. Type a lowercase *p* to put the second sentence after the third.

   b. The paragraph should now look like this:

```
Spinrite diskettes have a lifetime
guarantee. That's right, every
Spinrite diskette is guaranteed
for life. Not two Spinrite years, not three
Spinrite years, not five Spinrite years, but life.
That's right, every
Spinrite diskette is guaranteed
for life.
Advanced technology makes it possible.
```

   c. To restore the blank line between paragraphs, type *j* twice to drop the cursor to *for*, type *o* to open a new line below, and press ESC.

## *Copying a Paragraph*

**y} and P**
**y} and p**

Copying a paragraph is like copying a sentence. The main difference is that the command to "yank" a paragraph is **y}**, not **y)**. We plan to move the cursor to the start of a paragraph, "yank" the paragraph, then move to the new location and "put" the paragraph there. As an example, let's copy the second paragraph after the third paragraph. This is how the display should look now:

```
Spinrite diskette is guaranteed
for life.

Advanced technology makes it possible.
Sophisticated marketing makes it
```

1. "Yank" the paragraph at its current location:

   a. Type *y}* to "yank" the entire second paragraph.

   b. The display should now look like this:

   ```
   Spinrite diskette is guaranteed
   for life.

   Advanced technology makes it possible.
   Sophisticated marketing makes it
   ```

2. Move the cursor to the new location:

   a. Type } twice to advance the cursor to the beginning of the following paragraph.

   b. Type *k* to move the cursor up one line to the *a* in *and*.

   c. The display should now look like this:

   ```
   until it wears out. That's quality,
   and that's our guarantee.

   Don't settle for anything less.
   Don't waste your time with the
   ```

**y} and P**
**y} and p**

3. "Put" the paragraph at the new location:

   a. Type a lowercase *p* to "put" the second paragraph **after** the third.

   b. The display should now look like this:

```
        Advertisement

* * * * * * * * * * * * * * * * * *

Spinrite diskettes have a lifetime
guarantee. That's right, every
Spinrite diskette is guaranteed
for life. Not two Spinrite years, not three
Spinrite years, not five Spinrite years, but life.
That's right, every
Spinrite diskette is guaranteed
for life.

Advanced technology makes it possible.
Sophisticated marketing makes it
incredible. Superior distribution
makes it available. And state-of-
the-art manufacturing makes it.
```

[This paragraph has been copied below.]

```
No matter what you've read, no matter
what you've heard, no matter what
you've thought, our warranty stands:
Every Spinrite diskette will last
until it wears out. That's quality,
and that's our guarantee.

Advanced technology makes it possible.
Sophisticated marketing makes it
incredible. Superior distribution
makes it available. And state-of-
the-art manufacturing makes it.
```

[This paragraph has been copied from above.]

```
Don't settle for anything less.
Don't waste your time with the
amateurs. Step up to the pro-
fessionals. Step up to Spinrite.
```

## Copying a Line

**yy and P**
**yy and p**

Copying a line is like copying a word. The main difference is that the command to "yank" a line is **yy**, not **yw**. We plan to move the cursor to a line, "yank" the line, then move to the new location and "put" the line there. As an example, let's copy the first line of the last paragraph to several other places.

1. Move the cursor into position:

   a. Type */settle* and press RETURN to move the cursor to *settle* (first line of last paragraph).

   b. The display should now look like this:

   ```
   Don't settle for anything less.
   Don't waste your time with the
   amateurs. Step up to the pro-
   fessionals. Step up to Spinrite.
   ```

2. "Yank" the line at its current location:

   a. Type *yy* to "yank" the entire second line.

   b. The paragraph should now look like this (it's the same):

   ```
   Don't settle for anything less.
   Don't waste your time with the
   amateurs. Step up to the pro-
   fessionals. Step up to Spinrite.
   ```

**yy and P**
**yy and p**

3. Move the cursor to the new location:

   a. Type *?No matter* and press RETURN to move the cursor to *No matter* in the previous paragraph.

   b. The line should now look like this:

   ```
   No matter what you've read, no matter
   ```

4. "Put" the line at the new location:

   a. Type a capital *P* (not *p*) to "put" the line above the current line.

   b. The beginning of the paragraph should now look like this:

   ```
   Don't settle for anything less.
   No matter what you've read, no matter
   what you've heard, no matter what
   you've thought, our warranty stands:
   ```

## Other Possible Copying

In the examples you just tried, you copied one entire item (word, sentence, paragraph, or line) from one location to another. However, it would also be possible to copy part of an item (assuming the cursor is somewhere in the middle of it), or several items. Here are some suggestions:

| | |
|---|---|
| **yb** and **p** (or **P**) | Copy the left-hand side of a word. |
| **y(** and **p** (or **P**) | Copy the beginning of a sentence. |
| **y{** and **p** (or **P**) | Copy the beginning of a paragraph. |
| **y^** and **p** (or **P**) | Copy the left-hand side of a line. |
| **yw** and **p** (or **P**) | Copy the right-hand side of a word. |
| **y)** and **p** (or **P**) | Copy the ending of a sentence. |
| **y** and **p** (or **P**) | Copy the ending of a paragraph. |
| **y$** and **p** (or **P**) | Copy the right-hand side of a line. |
| **y3w** and **p** (or **P**) | Copy three words. |
| **y3)** and **p** (or **P**) | Copy three sentences. |
| **y3}** and **p** (or **P**) | Copy three paragraphs. |
| **3yy** and **p** (or **P**) | Copy three lines. |

Once again, **p** puts the item **after** the cursor, while **P** puts the item **before** the cursor. (In line operations, **p** puts the item **below** the current line, while **P** puts the item **above** the current line.)

## Abandoning the File

Before leaving this chapter, let's abandon the text in our work area. Then we can start all over again with the original version of *disks* in the next chapter. Type *:q!* to abandon the work area.

# Summary of Chapter 15

In this chapter you learned different ways to exit **vi** and the methods to move and copy text within a file.

## Exiting vi

**Write and quit.** To write the text in the work area to a file and end the session, type *:wq* <RETURN>

**Conditional write.** To write the text only if there have been changes and quit, type *:x* <RETURN> or *ZZ*.

**Abandon the text in the work area.** To abandon the text in the work area (thereby retaining the text in the file), type *:q!* <RETURN>.

## Moving Text within a File

**Moving a character.** To move a character from one location to another, move the cursor to the character's current location, type *x*, move the cursor to the new location, and type lowercase *p*. If you omit the move between *x* and *p*, you can transpose two adjacent characters.

**Moving a word.** The procedure is the same. This time use *dw* (or *dW* and *p* (or *P*).

**Moving a sentence.** Use *d)* and *p* (or *P*).

**Moving a paragraph.** Use *d* and *p* (or *P*).

**Moving a line.** Use *dd* and *p* (or *P*).

**Other moves.** Using the rules of **vi**, you can also perform a number of other moves by varying the expression typed after **d**.

In each case, **p** puts the item **after** the cursor, while **P** puts the item **before** the cursor. (In line operations, **p** puts the item **below** the current line, while **P** puts the item **above** the current line.)

## Copying Text Within a File

**Copying a word.** Use *dw* (or *dW* and *p* (or *P*).

**Copying a sentence.** Use *d)* and *p* (or *P*).

**Copying a paragraph.** Use *d}* and *p* (or *P*).

**Copying a line.** Use *dd* and *p* (or *P*).

**Other copies.** Using the rules of **vi**, you can also perform a number of other copies by varying the expression typed after **d**.

In each case, **p** puts the item **after** the cursor, while **P** puts the item **before** the cursor. (In line operations, **p** puts the item **below** the current line, while **P** puts the item **above** the current line.)

## Moving and Copying in General

**Moving text.** In general, the procedure for moving any segment of text defined in **vi** is to position the cursor at the beginning of the text to be moved and type

```
dtext
```

then position the cursor at the new location and type

`P` to place the text either `before` the cursor or `above` the current line

or

`p` to place the text either `after` the cursor or `below` the current line

**Copying text.** In general, the procedure for copying any segment of text defined in **vi** is to position the cursor at the beginning of the text to be copied and type

`y`<u>`text`</u>

then position the cursor at the new location and type

`P` to place the text either `before` the cursor or `above` the current line

or

`p` to place the text either `after` the cursor or `below` the current line

**Segments of text.** In either of the general statements above, *text* can be any of the characters for cursor motion that you have learned: w, W, e, E, ), }. (For moving a **character**, use **x** alone—this is the only exception.)

**Multiple functions.** In these chapters we have used multipliers mainly **between** the two characters (as in *d2W*). Note, however, that **vi** also allows a multiplier **in front of** the characters (as in *2dW*) and even one multiplier in each location (as in *3d2W*), which would indicate a deletion of 6 words—with punctuation ignored.

# 16

# *Working with More Than One File Using* **vi**

In Chapter 15 you learned how to move and copy text from one location in a file to another. In this chapter you will learn how to move and copy text from one file to another, which involves editing a second file without leaving **vi**. You will also learn how to tag a file and how to begin an editing session with various options. **:e**

## Editing Another File

In **vi**, as in **ed**, it is possible to begin editing a new file without having to leave your editor and return to the shell. There are several commands you can use, depending on how you want to save your current file.

### *Save and Edit* **:e**

If you have already saved your current file (*:w*), you can begin editing another file without leaving **vi** using the *:e* (edit) command. The sequence is as follows:

| | |
|---|---|
| `:w old file RETURN`<br>`:e new file RETURN` | Save the old file<br>Begin editing a new file |

## Abandon and Edit

`:e!`

If you don't want to save your current file, you can begin editing another file immediately with the *:e!* (edit!) command. The sequence is as follows:

| | |
|---|---|
| `:e! new file RETURN` | Abandon the old file and begin editing a new file |

## Auto-Edit

`:n`

If you want to have your current file saved automatically whenever you begin work on another file, you have to have the **auto-write** option set with the **:set** command (as described in Chapter 17, Customizing **vi**). Once that has been done, you can then use the *:n* command to begin editing a new file. The sequence is as follows:

| | |
|---|---|
| `:n new file RETURN` | Begin editing a new file (the old file is automatically saved) |

There's another variation of the **:n** command that you can use during an editing session with more than one file. Suppose you have invoked **vi** by naming three files to be edited, like this:

```
$ vi file.1 file.2 file.3
```

This editing session will begin with *file.1.* At the conclusion of your work with *file.*, you can type *:n* by itself without a filename. If you have the **auto-write** feature set, the text in the editing buffer will automatically be written to *file.1* and *file.2* will be read into the editing buffer. After you're finished with *file.2*, type *:n* again to write to *file.2* and call in *file.3*.

Let's try this feature right now.

1. Prepare for auto-editing:

   a. Begin an editing session with three different files:

   ```
   $ vi letter metric.c disks
   3 files to edit
   "letter" 17 lines, 377 characters
   ```

   b. When the text of *letter* appears on the screen, set **auto-write** mode:

   ```
   :set aw
   ```

2. Perform auto-editing:

   a. Without making any changes to *letter*, proceed to the next file (*metric.c*):

```
:n
"metric.c" 19 lines, 332 characters
```

   b. Without making any changes to *metric.c*, proceed to the next file (*disks*):

```
:n
"disks" 27 lines, 733 characters
```

3. End this short session:

```
:q!
```

So here you have a very handy editing tool that allows you to call up a number of files at the same time and move from one to another. If you try to move a third time in this example, you will see this: *No more files to edit.*

## Moving Text Between Files

Moving text from one file to another is similar to moving text within a file. There are only two differences:

**:e!**
**:n**
**"xd) and "xP**
**"xd) and "xp**

- You must leave the text in a temporary storage area (a **buffer**) with a one-letter name
- You have to call up the new file without leaving **vi**, using one of the commands you learned earlier in this chapter:

| | |
|---|---|
| `:e file RETURN` | Edit after save (the save is required) |
| `:e! file RETURN` | Abandon text and edit |
| `:n_file RETURN` | Edit with automatic save |

### *Beginning a New Session*

Before moving any text, let's begin a new session of vi with *disks*. Type *vi_ disks* and press RETURN:

```
$ vi disks  RETURN
```

**"xd) and "xP**
**"xd) and "xp**

### *Moving a Sentence*

Moving a sentence to another file is like moving a sentence within a file. We plan to move the cursor to a sentence, delete the sentence to a

**buffer**, then move to the location in the new file and "put" the sentence there **from the same buffer**. As an example, let's move a sentence from *disks* to the end of *letter*.

1. Move the cursor into position:

   a. Type */That* and press RETURN to move the cursor to *That's*.

   b. The display should now look like this:

```
Spinrite diskettes have a lifetime
guarantee. That's right, every
Spinrite diskette is guaranteed
for life. Not two years, not three
years, not five years, but life.
```

2. Delete the sentence at its current location:

   a. Type *"ad)* to delete the entire second sentence to buffer "a".

   b. The paragraph should look like this:

```
Spinrite diskettes have a lifetime
guarantee. Not two years, not three
years, not five years, but life.
```

3. Call up *letter* and move the cursor to the new location:

   a. Type *:n letter* and press RETURN to save *disks* automatically and bring in *letter* for editing.

   b. When the text appears on the screen, type *G* to move the cursor to the end of the file.

   c. The display should look like this:

```
The Man for the Job:
Franklin F. Failsquick, Jr.
Chief Consulting Officer

_
```

4. "Put" the sentence at the new location from buffer "a":

   a. Type *"ap* to take the sentence from buffer "a" and "put" it after the end of the letter.

   b. The display should now look like this:

```
The Man for the Job:
Franklin F. Failsquick, Jr.
Chief Consulting Officer
That's right, every                    [No blank line here]
Spinrite diskette is guaranteed
for life.
```

## *Moving a Paragraph*

**"xd} and "xp**
**"xd} and "xP**

Moving a paragraph is like moving a sentence. The main difference is that the command to delete a paragraph is **d}**, not **d)**. We plan to move the cursor to the start of a paragraph, delete the paragraph **to a buffer**, then move to the new location and "put" the paragraph there **from the same buffer**. As an example, let's move a paragraph from *letter* to *disks*.

1. Move the cursor into position:

   a. Type *?I wish* to move the cursor to the beginning of the first paragraph of "letters."

   b. Type *k* to move the cursor up to the previous blank line.

   c. The display should now look like this:

```
I wish to thank you profusely for your letter of March 2.
It is always a special delight to read and enjoy
all your extraordinary ideas.
```

2. Delete the paragraph from here and place it in buffer "b".

   a. Type *"bd}* to delete the entire second paragraph to buffer "b".

   b. The display should look like this:

```
Dear Mrs. Benson:

We are incapable of completing the job you asked for.
We don't know what we're doing.
```

**"xd} and "xp**
**"xd} and "xP**

3. Begin editing *disks* and move the cursor to the new location:

   a. Type *:e! disks* to abandon the text from *letter* and bring in *disks*.

   b. When the text appears, type */No matter* to advance the cursor to the beginning of the third paragraph.

   c. Type *k* to move the cursor up to the previous blank line.

   d. The display should look like this:

```
No matter what you've read, no matter
what you've heard, no matter what
you've thought, our warranty stands:
```

4. "Put" the paragraph at the new location from buffer "b":

   a. Type *"bP* to "put" the paragraph **above** the current line.

   b. The display should now look like this:

```
Advanced technology makes it possible.
Sophisticated marketing makes it
incredible. Superior distribution
makes it available. And state-of-
the-art manufacturing makes it.

I wish to thank you profusely for your letter of March 2.
It is always a special delight to read and enjoy
all your extraordinary ideas.

No matter what you've read, no matter
what you've heard, no matter what
you've thought, our warranty stands:
Every Spinrite diskette will last
until it wears out. That's quality,
and that's our guarantee.
```

### *Abandoning the Text*

Before going on to **copying** text to another file, let's abandon the text in our work area. Then we can start all over again with *letter* and *disks*. Type *:q!* to abandon the work area, then type

```
$ vi disks RETURN
```

to begin a new session with the original text.

## Copying Text To Another File

**Copying** text from one file to another in **vi** is similar to **moving** text. The only difference is that you use the "yank" command (**y**) instead of the delete command (**d**).

### *Copying a Sentence*

**"xy) and "xp**
**"xy) and "xP**

**Copying** a sentence is like **moving** a sentence. We plan to move the cursor to a sentence, "yank" the sentence **to a buffer**, then move to the new location and "put" the sentence there **from the same buffer**. As an example, let's copy a sentence from *disks* to *letter*.

1. Move the cursor into position:

   a. Move the cursor to the *S* in *Superior*:

```
/Superior RETURN
```

b. The display should now look like this:

```
Advanced technology makes it possible.
Sophisticated marketing makes it
incredible. Superior distribution
makes it available. And state-of-
the-art manufacturing makes it.
```

2. "Yank" the sentence at its current location into buffer "c".

   a. Type *"cy)* to "yank" the entire second sentence.

   b. The paragraph should look like this (the same):

```
Advanced technology makes it possible.
Sophisticated marketing makes it
incredible. Superior distribution
makes it available. And state-of-
the-art manufacturing makes it.
```

3. Begin editing *letter* and move the cursor to the new location:

   a. Type *:e!_ letter* and press RETURN to abandon *disks* and call up *letter.*

   b. When the display appears, type */Your* and press RETURN to move the cursor to the line that says, *Your . . . servant.*

   **"xy) and "xp**
   **"xy) and "xP**
   **"xy} and "xp**
   **"xy} and "xP**

   c. The display should look like this:

```
We don't know what we're doing.
Your most humble, obedient servant
```

4. "Put" the sentence at the new location from buffer "c".

   a. Type *"cP* to put the sentence above the current line.

   b. The display should now look like this:

```
We are incapable of completing the job you asked for.
We don't know what we're doing.
Superior distribution
makes it available. Your most humble, obedient servant
```

## *Copying a Paragraph*

**"xy} and "xp**
**"xy} and "xP**

Copying a paragraph is like moving a sentence. We plan to move the cursor to the start of a paragraph, "yank" the paragraph to a buffer, then move to the new location and "put" the paragraph there from the same buffer. As an example, let's copy a paragraph from *letter* to *disks*.

1. Move the cursor into position:

   a. Type { twice to move the cursor to the beginning of the previous paragraph.

   b. The display should now look like this:

```
We are incapable of completing the job you asked for.
We don't know what we're doing.
Superior distribution
makes it available. Your most humble, obedient servant
```

2. "Yank" the sentence at its current location to buffer "d":

   a. Type *"dy* to "yank" the entire second paragraph to buffer "d".

   b. The display should look like this (the same):

```
We are incapable of completing the job you asked for.
We don't know what we're doing.

Superior distribution
makes it available. Your most humble, obedient servant
```

3. Call up *disks* and move the cursor to the new location:

   a. Type *:e! disks* to abandon the text from *letter* and bring in *disks.*

   b. Type */Don't* to advance the cursor to the beginning of the last paragraph, then type *k* to move the cursor up to the blank line.

   c. The display should look like this:

```
Don't settle for anything less.
Don't waste your time with the
amateurs. Step up to the pro-
fessionals. Step up to Spinrite.
```

4. "Put" the paragraph at the new location from buffer "d":

   a. Type *"dP* to "put" the paragraph above the current line from buffer "d."

b. The display should now look like this:

```
Every Spinrite diskette will last
until it wears out. That's quality,
and that's our guarantee.

We are incapable of completing the job you asked for.
We don't know what we're doing.          [Inserted text]

Don't settle for anything less.
Don't waste your time with the
amateurs. Step up to the pro-
fessionals. Step up to Spinrite.
```

### *Abandoning the Text*

Before leaving this discussion of copying text, let's abandon the text in our work area. Then we can start all over again with the original version of *disks* in the next chapter. Type *:q!* to abandon the work area.

## Invoking vi

So far you have always invoked **vi** with the simplest form of the command line, which places the cursor at the beginning of the file with no options:

```
$ vi letter
```

However, there are a number of options available when you begin an editing session. **+line**

### *Specifying a Starting Line* **+line**

To begin with, you can specify the line number on which you wish to begin editing. Simply type a plus sign followed by the desired line number after **vi**. To see how this works (assuming you are in directory *text_files*), try calling up *metric.c* with the cursor positioned at the beginning of the main routine of the program (line 14). Here is the command:

```
$ vi +14 metric.c
```

The opening display should look like this:

```
    gallons = low;
    while (gallons <= high)
    {
        liters = (gallons * 3.785);
        printf("%4.0f %6.2f\n", gallons, liters);
        gallons = gallons + incr;
    }
}
~
~
~
"metric.c" 18 lines, 404 characters
```

A simple variation of this is to use a search pattern in place of an actual number. To see how this works, type *:q* and press RETURN to leave vi, then re-enter the file at the first line that contains *float*:

$ `vi +/float/ metric.c`   [You can also type +/*float* here]

The opening display should look like this:

```
/* List conversions from gallons to liters    */
main()
{
    int low, high, incr;
    float gallons, liters;

    low = 10;     /* starting value in gallons */
    high = 20;    /* ending value in gallons */
    incr = 2;     /* increment for each step */
~
~
~
"metric.c" 18 lines, 404 characters
```

Another variation is to use a plus sign by itself to position the cursor on the last line of the file. (This would be handy if you wanted to add new text to the end.) To see how this works, type *:q* and press RETURN to leave **vi**, then re-enter the file on the last line:

```
$ vi + metric.c
```

The opening display should look like this:

```
        low = 10;     /* starting value in gallons */
        high = 20;    /* ending value in gallons */
        incr = 2;     /* increment for each step */
        gallons = low;
        while (gallons <= high)
        {
            liters = (gallons * 3.785);
            printf("%4.0f %6.2f\n", gallons, liters);
            gallons = gallons + incr;
        }
}
~
~
~
"metric.c" 18 lines, 404 characters
```

Now you can type *:q* and press RETURN again to leave **vi** and return to the UNIX shell prompt. -option

## *Selecting an Option* **– option**

While a plus sign introduces a starting line number, a minus sign indicates one of four possible options for invoking **vi**. Each option is selected by typing a single letter after the minus sign:

- **-r** **Recover the file**. Use this option after a system or program crash (UNIX or **vi**) to retrieve the most recently-saved version of the file. If you omit the filename, the names of the files that can be recovered will be printed. (Note that a system or program crash is usually not catastrophic. You just have to get things restarted.)
- **-R** **Read-only**. Use this option to edit a file in read-only mode, meaning that the file can be viewed, but not modified.
- **-t** **Locate Tag**. Use this option to call up the file that contains the

tag named and begin editing at the location of the tag's definition. (This option will be explained in the section that follows.)

**-x** **Decrypted Read.** Use this option to view the cleartext of an encrypted file. (The file itself is not actually decrypted.)

Here are a few examples to illustrate the use of these options:

| | |
|---|---|
| `$ vi -r letter` | Recover *letter* after a crash. |
| `$ vi -R metric.c` | Edit *metric.c* as if it were a read-only file. |
| `$ vi -t tag` | Begin editing the file that contains the tag named, and position the cursor at its location. |
| `$ vi -x remark.crypt` | Edit an encrypted file named *remark.crypt*. |

## *Using Tags for Text Files*

You just learned how to have **vi** open a file and move the cursor immediately to a specified line ("Specifying a Starting Line" above). A **tag** is an extension of this same concept. **vi** allows you to set aside a file that contains a list of starting points (or "tags") for a text file that you are working with. The name of the file that contains the tags must be *tags*; no other name can be used.

For example, suppose you are using *disks* so extensively that you would like to be able to retrieve the file very quickly. And suppose you would like to be able to mark the beginning of each paragraph, so that you could begin editing at any one of those lines right away. Here is how you could do this:

1. Set up your tags in a separate **tags file**:

   a. Create a new file called *tags*:

   ```
   $ vi tags
   ```

   b. Press *a* to request text entry mode and enter the following four lines, with columns set at tab stops:

   ```
   par.1  disks  5
   par.2  disks  /Advanced/
   par.3  disks  17
   par.4  disks  /settle/
   ESC
   ```

   c. Now store the text and return to the UNIX shell prompt with *:wq:*

   ```
   :wq
   ''tags'' 5 lines, 74 characters
   $ _
   ```

Each line in a tag file contains three things, separated by tabs:

Name of the tag    Name of the file    Location of the tag

The location of the tag is indicated by either a line number or a search command, as described above under *Specifying a Starting Line.* In a tag file, however, no plus sign is used in front of the information. Two of the entries above contain line numbers and two contain search commands. For the third entry, *par.3* (paragraph 3) is the **name** of the tag, *disks* is the name of the **file** that contains the tag, and *17* indicates the **location** of the tag (line 17, the line number of the beginning of the third paragraph).

2. Use this new tag file to start a new editing session:

   a. Use the **-t** option in a **vi** command to start editing right at the beginning of the third paragraph (tag *par.3*):

   ```
   $ vi -t par.3
   ```
   [You don't even need the name of the file]

   b. File *disks* will be displayed, with the cursor at the first line of the third paragraph:

   ```
   Advanced technology makes it possible.
   Sophisticated marketing makes it
   incredible. Superior distribution
   makes it available. And state-of-
   the-art manufacturing makes it.

   No matter what you've read, no matter
   what you've heard, no matter what
   you've thought, our warranty stands:
   Every Spinrite diskette will last
   until it wears out. That's quality,
   and that's our guarantee.
   ```
   [Here is the cursor]

You aren't restricted to using tags when beginning an editing session; you can also use tags in the middle of editing another file. Just use the **:tag** command from **vi command mode**, indicating the name of the tag. For example, suppose you are in the middle of a session with *letter.* If you have stored the text since your most recent changes, you can type a command like this in **vi command mode**:

```
:tag par.3
```

One final note: In our example above, we used only tags from a single file. However, your *tags* file can contain entries for many different files, provided that you have them in alphabetical order. (The **sort** command will take care of this for you.) Since line numbers can change with revisions, it is best to use search commands to indicate the location of a tag.

## Using Tags in Programs

For programs written in C, FORTRAN, or Pascal, you can use the UNIX **ctags** program to have a tag file created automatically. The **ctags** program will insert one entry for each function in your program. For example, suppose you wanted a tag file for a program called *list.c*, which contained three functions:

```
main()
split(x)
unite(y)
```

If you execute the command line

```
$ ctags list.c
$ _
```

the **ctags** program will create a three-line tags file called *tags*, which you can then look at with **cat**:

```
$ cat tags
Mlist list.c ?^main()$?
split list.c ?^split(x)$?
unit  list.c ?^unite(y)$?
$ _
```

The first tag name used by **ctags** will always be the name of the source file (with *M* added in front of the name and *.c* deleted from the end). To avoid tagging a comment line that names one of the functions, **ctags** selects only those function names that appear on separate lines by themselves.

**Caution**

The **ctags** program will wipe out your current *tags* file, overwriting it with its own entries.

Since the **ctags** program tags only functions and since it doesn't spare your current tags, it has serious flaws. Use it only if you can tolerate its limitations.

## Summary of Chapter 16

In this chapter you learned how to begin editing a different file without leaving **vi**. You also learned two different methods for moving (or copying) text from one file to another. Finally, you learned about the options available when you begin a new editing session, and tried using tags.

## *Editing Another File*

**Save and edit.** To save the text from your current file before calling up another, use **:w** to write to the old file, **:e** to read the new one.

**Abandon and edit.** To abandon the text from your current file and begin editing another immediately, use **:e!**.

**Auto-edit.** To have your current file saved automatically before you call up another, first make sure you have the **auto-write** option set. Then use **:n**.

## *Moving Text to Another File*

**Moving a sentence.** Use **"xd)** and **"xp** (or **"xP**), where "x" is any of 26 buffers named after lowercase letters of the alphabet.

**Moving a paragraph.** Use **"xd}** and **"xp** (or **"xP**).

**Other moves.** Using the rules of **vi**, you can also perform a number of other moves by varying the expression typed after *"xd* (w, e, ), and so on).

Once again, **p** puts the item **after** the cursor, while **P** puts the item **before** the cursor. (In line operations, **p** puts the item **below** the current line, while **P** puts the item **above** the current line.)

## *Copying Text to Another File*

**Copying a sentence.** Use **"xd)** and **p** (or **P**).

**Copying a paragraph.** Use **"xd}** and **p** (or **P**).

**Other copies.** Using the rules of **vi**, you can also perform a number of other copies by varying the expression typed after **"xd** (w, e, ), and so on).

Once again, **p** puts the item **after** the cursor, while **P** puts the item **before** the cursor. (In line operations, **p** puts the item **below** the current line, while **P** puts the item **above** the current line.)

## *Moving and Copying in General*

**Moving text.** In general, the procedure for moving any segment of text defined in **vi** to another file is to position the cursor at the beginning of the text to be moved and type

```
"xdtext
```

then move the cursor to the new location and type

`P` to place the text either **before** the cursor or **above** the current line

or

`p` to place the text either **after** the cursor or **below** the current line

**Copying text.** In general, the procedure for copying any segment of text defined in **vi** to another file is to move the cursor to the beginning of the text to be copied and type

`"xytext`

then move the cursor to the new location and type

`P` to place the text either `before` the cursor or `above` the current line

or

`p` to place the text either `after` the cursor or `below` the current line

**Buffer names.** You can use any lowercase letter of the alphabet to name a buffer ($x$).

**Segments of text.** In either of the general statements above, *text* can be any of the cursor motion characters that you have learned: w, W, e, E, ), or }. (For moving a **character**, use **x** alone—this is the only exception.)

## Options for Beginning a New Editing Session

**Specifying a starting line.** To specify a starting line when you begin a session with **vi**, type *vi*, a space, a plus sign, a line number, another space, and the name of the file. The "line number" may be any of the following: a number, a search string, a blank space.

**Selecting an option.** To select one of four special options when you begin a session with **vi**, type *vi*, a space, a minus sign, a letter, another space, and the name of the file. The options are **-r** (recover the file), **-R** (read-only), **-t** (locate the tag), and **-x** (decrypted read).

**Using tags.** You can set up a **tag file** to list starting-points for an editing session with **vi**, then begin editing at one of these points by using either the **-t** option in a **vi** command line or the **tag** command during an editing session in progress.

# 17

# Customizing vi

In the previous chapters you learned how to use vi in its standard operating modes. In this chapter you will learn how to modify the options of vi to change its many user-definable features. You will also learn how to use abbreviations and define keys. **set**

## Setting Options

In Chapter 16 you used the :set command to set two of vi's options, line-numbering and shift width:

**:set nu** Set line-numbering.

**:set sw=5** Set shift width to 5 columns.

You may already have noticed a few things about these options. First of all, most have abbreviations, such as **nu** (for **number**) and **sw** (for **shift width**). The majority of options are set as "toggles," which means that the feature is either on (**nu**) or off (**nonu**). The other options require specific assigned values, which may be either numbers or strings of characters.

In this chapter we'll discuss only a few of the most commonly-used options. For a complete list of all the options for **vi**, see Appendix D, where they are described in detail by type: toggled, number-valued, and string valued.

## *Making Temporary Changes*

To set an option for the duration of an editing session, all you have to do is to type a **:set** command in **vi command mode** and press RETURN. The option you set will be in effect only until you exit **vi** and return to the UNIX shell. This is the best way to try out the different settings. Here are three examples of commands:

| | |
|---|---|
| **:set aw** | Set **auto-write** (force automatic write before calling up a new file or executing an UNIX shell command). |
| **:set report=3** | Set **report** to *3* (request a message after any operation involving at least three repetitions, such as three lines deleted, three lines appended, and so on—but no message for fewer than three). |
| **:set wm=6** | Set your wrap margin to 6. |

## *Changing the Width of Each Shift*

To see what happens when you change the setting of an option, let's use a file to do some experimenting.

1. Begin a new session with a new file:

   a. At the UNIX shell prompt, type *vi custom* and press RETURN to begin a new session with file *custom.*

   b. Type the following, with a RETURN at the end of each line (and **ESC** at the end to return to **vi command mode**):

```
Settings for vi

Here are a few lines of text
to demonstrate how we can
change the way the editor
works. ESC
```

2. Try shifting text with the current setting:

   a. Type *?Here* to move the cursor up to the *H* in *Here,* then type *>)* to shift the sentence to the right:

```
Settings for vi

        Here are a few lines of text
```

```
to demonstrate how we can
change the way the editor
works.
```

b. As you can see, each shift moves the text 8 columns to the right.

3. Change the **shift width** option:

a. Type *:set sw?* (with a question mark) and press RETURN to check the current value of **shift width**:

```
:set sw?
```

b. You will see the response on the status line at the bottom of the screen, telling you that each shift will currently move 8 columns:

```
shiftwidth=8
```

c. Type *:set sw=5* and press return to change the value to *5*:

```
:set sw=5
```

d. Type *<(* to shift the sentence back to the left.

```
Settings for vi
  Here are a few lines of text
  to demonstrate how we can
  change the way the editor
  works.
```

As you can see, each shift moves the text 5 columns now, instead of 8. Try a few more shifts, then restore the text to its original appearance.

## Wrapping Words Near the Margin

Another option changes **vi**'s handling of words that are entered as the cursor approaches the right-hand margin of the screen. With the standard default setting, if you type a word into the margin, it just keeps going right past the edge of the screen. (Your terminal, not **vi**, may wrap the words to the beginning of the next line.) With the **wrap-margin** option, however, you can have **vi** "wrap" a word to the next line—a common feature of word processing systems. Just set it to any positive number.

1. Try entering some text with the standard default setting:

a. Move the cursor to the last line (*L*).

b. Press RETURN and type *a* to append text and type the following, **without** pressing RETURN at the end of the line:

```
We're going to type a very long line of text to see
what happens when we get close to the side of the screen.
```

c. Type **ESC** at the end to return to **vi command mode.**

The word *close* should be split at the edge of the screen (assuming you have an 80-column screen), like this: clo/se. But this is the work of your terminal, not of **vi.**

2. Change the **wrap-margin** option:

   a. Type *:set wm?* (with a question mark) and press RETURN to check the current setting of **wrap-margin**:

```
:set wm?
```

   b. You will see the response at the bottom of the screen, telling you that there is no wrapping of words:

```
wrapmargin=0
```

   c. Type *:set wm=10* and press RETURN to change the value to *10*:

```
:set wm=10
```

3. Now enter the same text to try out the new setting:

   a. Move the cursor to the last line (*L*), type *a*, and type the following a second time—again **without** pressing RETURN at the end of the line:

```
This time we're going to type a very long line of text to see what happens
when we get close to the side of the screen.
```

   b. Type **ESC** at the end to return to **vi command mode.**

Because you had **wrap-margin** set to 10, **vi** wraps the word *when* to the next line (assuming you have an 80-column screen). The *10* tells **vi** to wrap any word that comes within 10 columns of the right-hand side of the screen.

## *Making Other Changes*

You may want to change a few more options to suit the kind of work you plan to be doing. Here are a few of the most commonly-used:

**:set ai** Set **auto-indent** (RETURN moves the cursor to the next line, but at the same indentation as for the previous line).

**:set list** Set **list** (shows tab stop and new line symbols on the screen, as is customary with the **ed** list command).

**:set nu** Set **number** (displays line numbers).

To see a list of the current values for all **vi** options, use the **:set all** command:

```
:set all
```

to produce a display like this (see Appendix D for details):

```
noautoindent    open                          noslowopen
autoprint       nooptimize                    tabstop=8
noautowrite     paragraphs=IPLPPPQPP LIpplpipbp taglength=0
nobeautify      prompt                        tags=tags /usr/lib/tags
directory=/tmp  noreadonly                    term=adm3
noedcompatible  redraw                        noterse
noerrorbells    remap                         timeout
hardtabs=8      report=5                      ttytype=adm3
noignorecase    scroll=11                     warn
nolisp          sections=NHSHH HUnhsh         window=23
nolist          shell=/bin/sh                 wrapscan
magic           shiftwidth=5                  wrapmargin=10
nonumber        noshowmatch                   nowriteany
[Hit return to continue]_
```

## *Making Changes Permanent*

Once you've decided which options you would like to have in effect every time you use **vi**, you can store the commands to set them in a separate file. This file, called **.exrc** (ex read command), is read at the beginning of every **vi** session. For example, suppose you would like to have automatic indentation, automatic writing, and word wrapping 6 columns from the side of the screen. End this session with **vi**, go to your home directory, create a file named *.exrc*, and enter the following lines (without colons):

```
set autoindent          set ai
set autowrite     or    set aw     or    set ai aw wm=6
set wrapmargin=6        set wm=6
```

Save the text (*:wq*) and return to *text files* (*cd text files*). The next time you begin a new session with **vi**, these options will take effect automatically. You won't have to type any **:set** commands.

# Assigning Abbreviations **ab**

If you ever have to type a long name or other string repeatedly, it is convenient to be able to enter a shortened form of it quickly. The **vi** editor provides a command that allows you to assign a long string to a shorter abbreviation. Then, once you've made the assignment, any time you type the abbreviation, **vi** will replace it with the longer text.

## *Making Temporary Assignments*

To have an abbreviation assigned for the duration of the current session, type the command *:ab*, a space, the abbreviation, another space, the full, unabbreviated string, and then press RETURN. For example, using file *custom* again, here's the procedure:

1. Call up **vi** (if necessary) and move to the end of the work area:

   a. If **vi** is not active, type *vi + custom* to begin a new session with *custom* with the cursor at the end of the file.

   b. If **vi** is active and the text of *custom* is already on the screen, type *L* to move the cursor to the end of the text.

2. Assign three abbreviations:

   a. Type *:ab xen XENIX operating system* and press RETURN to assign *XENIX operating system* to *xen.*

   b. Type *:ab unx UNIX operating system* and press RETURN to assign *UNIX operating system* to *unx.*

   c. Type *:ab btl Bell Telephone Laboratories* and press RETURN to assign *Bell Telephone Laboratories* to *btl.*

3. Type a sentence using the three abbreviations:

   a. Type *a* and enter the following sentence, followed by ESC:

```
The xen was derived from the unx, which originated at btl in
1969. ESC
```

   b. This is how the text should now look on the screen:

```
The XENIX operating system was derived from the UNIX operating
system, which originated at Bell Telephone Laboratories in
1969.
```

This brief example should convince you of the value of this feature (often referred to in the word-processing industry as a "glossary" feature).

### *Making Assignments Permanent*

Any abbreviations that you plan to use frequently can be added to your **.exrc** file, along with your **set** commands. For example, to have the three abbreviations you just tried available to you every time you use **vi**, include them in **.exrc**, like this:

```
set autoindent
set autowrite
set wrapmargin=6
ab xen XENIX operating system
ab unx UNIX operating system
ab btl Bell Telephone Laboratories
```

In these examples, we've deliberately used three-character abbreviations. You can use shorter abbreviations if you want to, but you run the risk of typing your abbreviation as part of another word, thereby substituting in the longer text by accident. For example, suppose we had selected *un* as our second abbreviation. Then, if we attempted to type *run*, we would get *rUNIX operating system* instead.

## Defining Keys

**map**

**ab**
**map**

There's another kind of abbreviation you can perform with **vi**. It involves assigning a sequence of commands (or keystrokes) to a key on your keyboard (sometimes referred to as "mapping"). Once you've made such an assignment, then you can press that key to invoke the commands. This is another time-saving device that can mean pressing one key instead of a dozen. However, there is one slight catch to it: you have to select a key that you don't plan to use for any other purpose. Otherwise, you could trigger your command sequence unexpectedly. Your best bets are either the function keys or one of the following: **K V g q v k ; _** = (which are not used by **vi**).

### *Making a Temporary Assignment*

To set up a mapping for the duration of an editing session, all you have to do is type a **:map** command in **vi command mode** and press RETURN. The mapping will remain in effect only until you end the editing session.

The first thing you have to do is to find a key that doesn't have another function already assigned to it. To do this, just press a key in **vi command mode**. If your terminal beeps, then the key is unassigned. For example, try the asterisk (*). There's a beep, so it's available.

Now that we have an available key, we need a useful command sequence to assign to it. Suppose we want to be able to indent an entire paragraph to the next tab stop with one keystroke (*), assuming that we begin with the cursor somewhere in that paragraph. Let's go through the commands we'd have to enter to accomplish this manually:

- Move the cursor to the beginning of the paragraph {
- Indent the entire paragraph to the next tab stop >}

With an available key and a sequence of commands to assign to it, we're ready to construct our command (with the characters spread out for easier viewing):

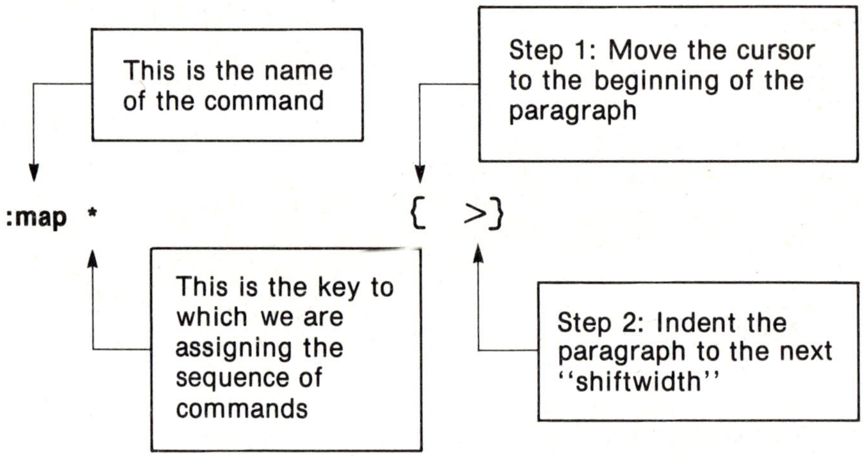


Figure 17-1. A simple mapping command.

Here's how you actually type it (without spaces):

```
:map * {>} RETURN
```

Now, with the key assigned, you are ready to try it out. So let's bring in a file you've worked with before.

1. Store the text of *custom* and start editing with *disks*:

   a. Type *:w* to store the text in *custom*.

   b. Type *:e +/Sophist/ disks* and press RETURN to call up *disks* with the cursor in the middle of the second paragraph.

   c. The display should now look like this:

```
Advanced technology makes it possible.
Sophisticated marketing makes it
incredible. Superior distribution
makes it available. And state-of-
the-art manufacturing makes it.
```

2. Try out your new key:

   a. Type * to invoke the sequence of commands.

   b. You should see the cursor move to the *A* in *Advanced* and the entire paragraph shift to the right.

## *Making Another Temporary Assignment*

That was a simple sequence of commands—just three keystrokes and two commands. Let's try another example that's a little more involved. This time, we'll pick a key (=), and assign to it the sequence that will insert the following two words in front of the current sentence:

```
Note this:
```

This is how you would accomplish this manually:

| | |
|---|---|
| • Move the cursor to the beginning of the sentence | `(` |
| • Request an insertion | `i` |
| • Type the text to be inserted | `Note this:` |
| • Terminate insertion of text | ESC |

This is similar to the previous example, but it involves more keystrokes and one additional problem: How do we let **vi** know that we've typed an **ESC** key at the end of the text? (If we just press the **ESC** key, **vi** will read that as "End of text entry.") **vi** provides a command to take care of this, as you'll see in a moment. Now that we have a key available (=) and a sequence of commands, we're ready to construct a command (with the characters spread out again for clarity, as shown in Fig. 17-2). Here's how you actually type it (without spaces):

```
:map @ (iNote this: ^[ RETURN
```

To enter **ESC** as a text character, first type CTRL-V, then **ESC**. When you do this, you will see ∧*[* appear on the screen. CTRL-V is what you type in **vi** any time you want to enter a control character **as a text character**. For example, to enter RETURN as a character (as in terminating an **ex** command), type CTRL-V, then press the RETURN key. On the screen you will see ∧*M*.

With the = key assigned to a command sequence, you are now ready to try the key out.

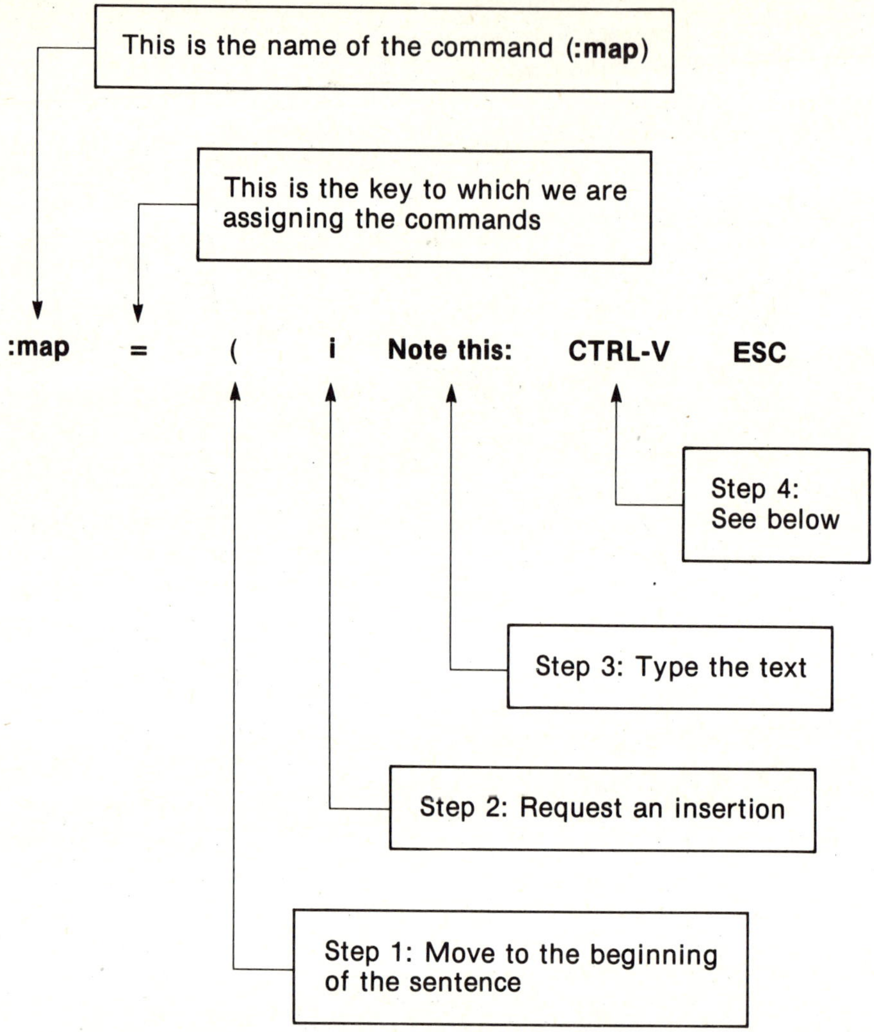


Figure 17-2. A more involved mapping command.

1. Find a suitable location to start from:

   a. Move the cursor near the end of the third paragraph.

   b. The display should look like this:

   ```
   No matter what you've read, no matter
   what you've heard, no matter what
   you've thought, our warranty stands:
   Every Spinrite diskette will last
   until it wears out. That's quality,
   and that's our guarantee.
   ```

2. Try out your new key:

   a. Type = to invoke the sequence of commands.

   b. You should see the cursor move to the *N* in *No matter* and the text inserted:

```
Note this:_No matter what you've read, no matter
what you've heard, no matter what
you've thought, our warranty stands:
Every Spinrite diskette will last
until it wears out. That's quality,
and that's our guarantee.
```

### *Making Assignments Permanent*

Once again, any abbreviations you plan to use all the time can be added to your **.exrc** file, along with your **set** and **ab** commands. For example, to have the two key assignments you just tried available to you every time you use **vi**, just include them in **.exrc** (without colons, of course):

```
set autoindent
set autowrite
set wrapmargin=6
ab xen XENIX operating system
ab unx UNIX operating system
ab btl Bell Telephone Laboratories
map * {>}
map = (iNote this: ^[
```

Now the * and = keys will have these command sequences assigned to them every time you begin a new session with **vi**.

## Summary of Chapter 17

In this chapter you learned how to change **vi**'s options, how to abbreviate a long segment of text, and how to assign a sequence of commands to a key on the keyboard.

**Setting options.** To set a **vi** option for the duration of the current session, use the **set** command, as shown in these examples:

```
:set aw
:set report=3
:set wm=6
```

**Assigning abbreviations.** To assign a longer segment of text to an abbreviation for the duration of the current session, use the **ab** command, as shown in these examples:

```
:ab xen XENIX operating system
:ab unx UNIX operating system
:ab btl Bell Telephone Laboratories
```

**Assigning Command sequences to keys.** To assign a sequence of commands to a key on the keyboard for the duration of the current session, use the **map** command, as shown in these examples:

```
:map * {>}
:map = (iNote this: ^]
```

**Making permanent changes.** To activate any of these modifications in **vi** each time you begin a new session, place these commands in the file *.exrc* (without colons), as illustrated here:

```
set autowrite report=3 wrapmargin=6
ab xen XENIX operating system
ab unx UNIX operating system
ab btl Bell Telephone Laboratories
map * {>}
map @ (iNote this: ^[
```

# IV

# Text Processing and Formatting

# 18

# Processing Text and Numbers

Now that you have learned how to create and edit text files, we can talk in greater detail about processing the text already stored in a file that you have created. In this chapter we'll discuss the UNIX programs that allow you to search for text in a file, sort lines of text, and program text output. In Chapters 19 and 20 we'll discuss the programs that allow you to format text for printing.

## Searching for Text **grep**

You are already familiar with the search facilities that are built into the UNIX text editors **ed**, **vi**, and **ex**. These same search facilities have also been incorporated into another UNIX command called **grep** ("globally find and replace regular expressions and print"), to which you were briefly introduced in Part I. The acronym doesn't quite match, but the features for searching, which have been enhanced in **grep**, enable you to match what you're looking for very nicely.

To get some practice in searching with **grep**, let's create three new files called *dawson.farms*, *jenkins.farms*, and *parker.farms*. These names represent three suppliers for a maker of juices, jams, jellies, and canned fruit called *Fruit-of-the-Tree*. Each file contains a short list of the fruits supplied and the prices. Let's move to subdirectory *text_files* and create these files, using the TAB key to position the prices and identifiers: **grep**

```
$ cat > dawson.farms
Bing cherries           0.51   D
Concord grapes          0.48   D
D'Anjou pears           0.13   D
Comice pears            0.51   D
                                  [CTRL-D to terminate text]
$ _
```

```
$ cat > jenkins.farms
Concord grapes          0.51  J
Bartlett pears          0.12  J
Navel oranges           0.26  J
                                 [CTRL-D to terminate text]
$ _

$ cat > parker.farms
Bing cherries           0.48  P
Thompson grapes         0.35  P
Valencia oranges        0.29  P
                                 [CTRL-D to terminate text]
$ _
```

## Conducting Simple Searches

With three new files in *text_files* containing information about various fruits, we can now begin making some simple searches with **grep**. In each instance, **grep** will output every line that contains the string we are looking for.

1. Does Parker supply grapes?

   a. Check file *parker.farms* for *grapes*:

   ```
   $ grep grapes parker.farms
   Thompson grapes         0.35 P
   $ _
   ```

   b. Answer: Yes, Parker supplies Thompson grapes.

2. Does Dawson supply oranges?

   a. Check file *dawson.farms* for *oranges*:

   ```
   $ grep oranges dawson.farms
   $ _
   ```

   b. Answer: No. (There was no output.)

3. Does Jenkins supply Bartlett pears?

   a. Check file *jenkins.farms* for *Bartlett pears*:

   ```
   $ grep "Bartlett pears" jenkins.farms
   Bartlett pears 0.12 J
   $ _
   ```

   b. Answer: Yes, Jenkins supplies Bartlett pears.

Because we were searching for two words separated by a space, quotation marks were required for this search.

4. Who supplies Bing cherries?

   a. Check all three files for *Bing cherries*:

```
$ grep "Bing cherries" *farms
dawson.farms: Bing cherries      0.51   D
parker.farms: Bing cherries      0.48   P
$ _
```

   b. Answer: Dawson and Parker.

We used the wild-card symbol (*) here to abbreviate *dawson.farms jenkins.farms parker.farms*. This example illustrates one of the enhanced features of **grep**: its ability to search several different files for a given string. As the output shows, **grep** supplies the name of each file that contains the string.

## *Using Aids in Searching*

Like other UNIX programs that provide searching, **grep** allows you to use the special characters, or **metacharacters**, that make it easier to match patterns. The expressions formed from these characters are called **regular expressions** (the **re** in **grep**). Here is a quick review of these characters:

^ beginning of line
. any single character
[ ] any of the characters enclosed
$ end of line
* repeat any number of times
\ turn off special meaning

Here are some examples of regular expressions formed from these characters, with a few strings they would match if used in a **grep** command line:

| **Regular Expression** | **Some of the Strings Matched** |
|---|---|
| "^3." | 30 31 3a 3b 3+ 3) (at the beginning of a line) |
| "t..$" | too two ten t36 t\|T t+5 (at the end of a line) |
| "[Ff]arm" | Farm farm |
| "\$[0-9]\.[0-9][0-9]" | $4.67 $8.32 $1.99 $3.71 |
| "[abc]\[i\]" | a[i] b[i] c[i] |
| "^$" | (A blank line) |

Here are a couple of simple searches with regular expressions:

1. Does Dawson supply D'Anjou pears?

a. Check file *dawson.farms* for *D'Anjou pears*:

```
$ grep "D.Anjou pears" dawson.farms
D'Anjou pears                        0.13    D
$ _
```

b. Answer: Yes, Dawson supplies D'Anjou pears.

A period was used in the search string because an apostrophe (') would have been interpreted as a single quotation mark ('), and an error would have resulted. (Both are the same on the keyboard.)

2. Are anyone's prices over $0.50?

   a. Check all three files for all amounts over $0.50:

```
$ grep "[0-9]\.[5-9][0-9]" *farms
dawson.farms.Bing cherries           0.51    D
jenkins.farms.Concord grapes         0.51    J
dawsonfarms.Comice pears             0.51    D
$ _
```

   b. Answer: Yes, Dawson's Bing cherries and Jenkins' Comice pears and Concord grapes.

## Using Options to Modify the Output

The **grep** command has many options that you can use to vary the output. Here are the most commonly-used options:

| Option | Effect |
|---|---|
| -c | Show how many times the string was found, but not the text. |
| -l | Show the name(s) of the file(s) in which the string was found, but not the text. |
| -n | Show line numbers along with the text. |
| -y | For alphabetic characters, match either upper- or lowercase. |
| -v | Invert the search (that is, show those lines in which the string was **not** found). |

You can use more than one of these options in a single **grep** command, but you can't bundle them (combine more than one behind a single minus sign). Here are some examples of **grep** commands with these options:

1. How many varieties of pear does each farm supply?

   a. Check all three files for *pear*, but show counts only:

```
$ grep -c pear *farms
```

```
dawson.farms: 2
jenkins.farms: 1
parker.farms: 0
$ _
```

b. Answer: Dawson supplies two varieties, Jenkins supplies one, and Parker does not supply any.

2. Which farms supply Thompson grapes?

   a. Check all three files for *Thompson grapes*, but show names only:

```
$ grep -l "Thompson grapes" *farms
parker.farms
$ _
```

   b. Answer: Parker only.

## *Sending the Output to a File*

As with most UNIX programs, you can redirect the output of **grep** to a file instead of just displaying the results on the screen. Use the redirection symbol (>). Here are two examples, both employing the **-v** (invert) option to delete lines of text. In both examples, the plan is to make a temporary copy of the file, then do the processing from the temporary copy back to the original file (see Figure 18-1).

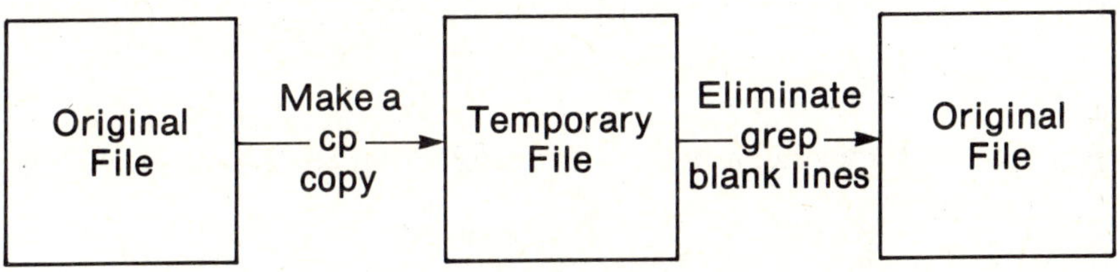


Figure 18-1. Processing from a temporary file.

1. Clear all the blank lines out of *jenkins.farms*:

   a. First make a temporary copy of *jenkins.farms*:

```
$ cp jenkins.farms jenkins.temp
$ _
```

   b. Eliminate all blank lines (that is, send only non-blank lines from the temporary file to *jenkins.farms*):

```
$ grep -v "^$" jenkins.temp > jenkins.farms
$ _
```

The file *jenkins.farms* will be overwritten by the output from this **grep** command. (Since the original *jenkins.farms* didn't contain any blank lines, the file won't really be changed in this instance. In actual practice, however, this could be a handy procedure.)

2. Update your records to show that Dawson has dropped all varieties of pear:

   a. Make a temporary copy of *dawson.farms*:

```
$ cp dawson.farms dawson.temp
$ _
```

   b. Eliminate all lines that refer to pears (that is, send only non-pear lines from the temporary file to *dawson.farms*):

```
$ grep -v pear dawson.temp > dawson.farms
$ _
```

   c. Verify the update:

```
$ cat dawson.farms
Bing cherries            0.51    D
Concord grapes           0.48    D
$ _
```

## Using Related Search Programs

Here are two programs in the **grep** family that you may be interested in:

- **fgrep** (fast **grep**), a scaled down version of **grep** that allows all the options, but no metacharacters for constructing regular expressions.
- **egrep** (extended **grep**), an enhanced version of **grep** that allows you to search for repeated strings and alternate strings.

Here are two brief examples:

1. Does Jenkins supply Bartlett pears?

   a. Check file *jenkins.farms* for *Bartlett pears*:

```
$ fgrep "Bartlett pears" jenkins.farms
Bartlett pears              0.12    J
$ _
```

   b. Answer: Yes, Jenkins supplies Bartlett pears.

This is identical to an earlier example, with **fgrep** substituted for **grep**. With **fgrep**, it should run a little faster.

2. Who supplies either Concord grapes or Thompson grapes?

   a. Check all three files for either Concord grapes or Thompson:

```
$ egrep "(Concord|Thompson) grapes" *.farms
dawson.farms: Concord grapes             0.48    D
jenkins.farms: Concord grapes            0.51    J
parker.farms: Thompson grapes            0.35    P
$ _
```

   b. Answer: Dawson and Jenkins supply Concord grapes, while Parker supplies Thompson.

## Sorting Files

**sort**

You had a brief introduction to the **sort** command in Chapter 4. Now we'll discuss it in greater detail. The **sort** command arranges the lines of a file in either alphabetical or numerical order, depending on whether the lines contain letters or numbers. As you will learn in this chapter, **sort** can be focused on specific items of text within each line of a file. We'll use the three *farms* files to illustrate this. But before we start, let's add a few more lines of text to *dawson.farms*:

```
$ cat >> dawson.farms
Navel oranges     0.26 D
Kadota figs       0.42 D
Valencia oranges 0.29 D
Smyrna figs       0.48 D
                                [CTRL-D to terminate text]
$ _
```

### *Selecting a Field (or Fields)*

If we take a look at *dawson.farms* after displaying its contents with a **cat** command, we see three columns of text: a list of varieties of fruits, a list of prices, and an identifier. However, **sort** sees the contents as **four** columns (or **fields**) of text, as shown on the right:

**sort**

```
$ cat dawson.farms
Bing cherries     0.51  D
Concord grapes    0.48  D
Navel oranges     0.26  D
Kadota figs       0.42  D
Valencia oranges 0.29  D
Smyrna figs       0.48  D
$ _
```

| Field 1 | Field 2 | Field 3 | 4 |
|---|---|---|---|
| Bing | cherries | 0.51 | D |
| Concord | grapes | 0.48 | D |
| Navel | oranges | 0.26 | D |
| Kadota | figs | 0.42 | D |
| Valencia | oranges | 0.29 | D |
| Smyrna | figs | 0.48 | D |

Unless we specify otherwise, **sort** views spaces and tabs as **field separators**, marking boundaries between different fields. So, from the point of view of **sort**, field 1 is variety, field 2 is generic type, field 3 is price, and field 4 is identifier.

If we issue a simple **sort** command without specifying any fields or options, we get this ordering (alphabetical, fields 1-4):

```
$ sort dawson.farms
Bing cherries          0.51   D
Concord grapes         0.48   D
Kadota figs            0.42   D
Navel oranges          0.26   D
Smyrna figs            0.48   D
Valencia oranges       0.29   D
$ _
```

Once we see how **sort** views fields, we can indicate to **sort** which field (or sequence of fields) we wish to be sorted, using numbers to represent the different fields:

- a plus sign (+) in front of a number means "**begin** sorting after this field"
- a minus sign (−) means "**stop** sorting after this field"

Using these conventions, we can use the notation +*1* -*2* to mean, "Begin sorting after field 1 and stop sorting after field 2" (that is, sort field 2 only). Let's try this (see Figure 18-2):

```
$ sort  +1  -2 dawson.farms
Bing cherries              0.51    D
Kadota figs                0.42    D
Smyrna figs                0.48    D
Concord grapes             0.48    D
Navel oranges              0.26    D
Valencia oranges           0.29    D
$ _
```

| Field 1 | Field 2 | Field 3 | Field 4 |
|---|---|---|---|
| Bing | cherries | 0.51 | D |
| Concord | grapes | 0.48 | D |
| Navel | oranges | 0.26 | D |
| Kadota | figs | 0.42 | D |
| Valencia | oranges | 0.29 | D |
| Smyrna | figs | 0.48 | D |
| +1 | | −2 | |
| Begin sorting after field 1 (start with field 2) | | Stop sorting after field 2 (don't include field 3 or field 4 in this sort) | |

Figure 18-2. Notation to sort field 2 only.

In this example, we are sorting only one field. But, as we'll see in a moment, it's possible to sort one field, then another, and so on, to create ordering within a category of items.

## *Using Options to Modify the Output*

The **sort** command has a number of options that you can include in the command line to modify **sort**'s output. Here are some of the most-commonly used options:

| Option | Effect |
|---|---|
| **-b** | Ignore leading blanks (spaces and tabs) when comparing fields—useful if different items in a given field are of varying lengths. |
| **-n** | Sort a numeric field (allow for optional blanks, minus signs, zeroes, or decimal points)—this option includes **-b** automatically. |
| **-r** | Sort in reverse order (Z-A, z-a, 9-0)—usually used to place the highest number in a numeric sort at the top of the list. |
| **-f** | Fold uppercase letters onto lowercase (for example, treat *CASE, Case,* and *case* as identical when sorting). |
| **-u** | Sort uniquely (that is, if two or more lines are identical, discard all but one of them). |
| **-m** | Merge several files: the files are already sorted; just merge them. |
| **-tx** | Make *x* (any character) the field separator—the most logical candidates are colon (:) and vertical bar (\|) (a \| must be typed as \\| to be interpreted correctly). |
| **-o file** | Place the output in *file*—the same as > *file*. |

Note that you can use more than one option in a given **sort** command line, and that options can be bundled.

Let's illustrate the use of some of these options by sorting on price (highest price first). To do this correctly, we need to use the **n** (numeric) and **r** (reverse) options. We could enter the command line this way:

```
$ sort -nr +2  dawson.farms
Bing cherries        0.51    D
Smyrna figs          0.48    D
Concord grapes       0.48    D  [Dawson fruits in order of
Kadota figs          0.42    D  price (highest price first)]
Valencia oranges     0.28    D
Navel oranges        0.26    D
$ _
```

If we type it this way, it means that **n** and **r** apply to **all** fields to be sorted. Since we are sorting on just one field, it doesn't make any difference in this example. But if we sort one field after another, as in the example that follows, we have to bundle **n** and **r** with the price field indicator. **n** and **r** will then apply only to that one field.

```
$ sort +2nr +0 -1  dawson.farms
Bing cherries       0.51  D
Concord grapes      0.48  D
Smyrna figs         0.48  D [Dawson fruits in order by price
Kadota figs         0.42  D and in alphabetical order under
Valencia oranges    0.28  D identical prices]
Navel oranges       0.26  D
$ _
```

If you compare this example to the previous example, you will notice one slight difference: *Concord grapes* moved ahead of *Smyrna figs* on the list (*figs* before *grapes*).

## Sending the Output to a File

As with most UNIX programs, you can redirect the output of **sort** to a file, instead of just displaying the results on the screen. You can use either the redirection symbol (>) or the **-o** option interchangeably. Here are two examples, both involving sorting multiple files:

1. Store a list from all three suppliers sorted **by generic type** in *fruit.sort*:

   a. Perform the sort:

```
$ sort +1 -2 *farms > fruit.sort
$ _
```

   b. Display the results:

```
$ cat fruit.sort
Bing cherries         0.48   P
Bing cherries         0.51   D
Kadota figs           0.42   D
Smyrna figs           0.48   D
Concord grapes        0.48   D
Concord grapes        0.51   J    [Fruits from all
Thompson grapes       0.35   P    suppliers in
Navel oranges         0.26   D    alphabetical
Navel oranges         0.26   J    order by
Valencia oranges      0.29   D    generic type]
```

```
Valencia oranges       0.29   J
Bartlett pears         0.12   J
$ _
```

2. Store a list from all three suppliers sorted by price in *price.sort*:

   a. Perform the sort:

```
$ sort -o price.sort +2nr +1 *farms
$ _
```

   b. Display the results:

```
$ cat price.sort
Bing cherries          0.51   D
Concord grapes         0.51   J
Bing cherries          0.48   P
Smyrna figs            0.48   D
Concord grapes         0.48   D
Kadota figs            0.42   D
Thompson grapes        0.35   P
Valencia oranges       0.29   D
Valencia oranges       0.29   P
Navel oranges          0.26   D
Navel oranges          0.26   J
Bartlett pears         0.12   J
$ _
```

[Fruits from all suppliers in order by price]

In this file (*price.sort*), we have all fruit listed in order of price (highest price first).

## Programming Text Output **awk**

The **awk** program, which processes files that contain either text or numerical data, allows you to rearrange fields, perform arithmetic operations, and retrieve lines selectively, using programming statements that resemble C. You can use it to set up a spreadsheet in UNIX or to generate reports from files already stored in the system. (The name **awk** is derived from the names of its originators: *A*ho, *W*einberger, and *K*ernighan.) **awk**

A full command line for **awk** contains four parts: the name of the command, an optional **pattern** statement, an optional **action** statement, and the name(s) of the file(s). The **pattern** statement, which is used to select lines from a file, and the **action** statement, which is used to decide what to do with the lines selected, may be omitted. The pattern statement precedes the action statement, which must be enclosed within braces, like this:

```
$ awk pattern_statement { action_statement } file(s)
```

Once again, we'll be using the three files in our "farms" series.

## Referring to Fields

Like **sort**, **awk** is oriented to **fields**, and offers a simple method for referring to fields by name. Just type a dollar sign ($) in front of a number to refer to a field. By this convention, *$1* means field 1, *$2* means field 2, *$3* means field 3, and so on. The notation *$0* has a special meaning: all fields (the entire record). With these, we can easily switch fields 1 and 2 (and then place field 3 at a tab stop):

```
$ awk '{ print $2 ", " $1 "TAB" $3 }' jenkins.farms
grapes, Concord          0.51
pears, Bartlett          0.12
oranges, Navel           0.26
$ _
```

The **action** statement is very straightforward: Print, in the following order, field 2 (generic type of fruit), a comma and a space, field 1 (variety of fruit), a TAB, and then field 3 (price). (When you press the TAB key, the cursor will, of course, advance to the next tab stop on the screen, leaving a gap in your command line. Do not become alarmed when this happens.) If there's any possibility that your pattern and action statements may contain special characters, you should enclose them within single quotes.

That's all there is to it. We have switched fields 1 and 2. How do you like this compared to the monstrosity we created in **ed** to do the very same thing. Remember "switch?" How could you forget it?

## Working from an Input File

In the example above, the command line was manageable, but often the command line becomes too long for the line. One way to get around this (and to avoid a lot of repeated typing) is to place your statements in a separate file, then activate this file in the **awk** command line with the **-f** option. Here's an easier way to type the command line for switching fields 1 and 2:

1. Place the **action** statements (without the single quotes) in a file:

   a. Enter the text with **cat**:

```
$ cat > switch.awk
{print $2 ", " $1 " TAB" $3}
                                    [Press CTRL-D to terminate input]
$ _
```

b. Now *switch.awk* contains the command, and we won't have to type it again on the command line.

2. Name this file when you execute **awk**:

a. Use the **-f** option to redirect input from *switch.awk*:

```
$ awk -f switch.awk jenkins.farms
grapes, Concord          0.51
pears, Bartlett          0.12
oranges, Navel           0.26
$ _
```

b. This command line is equivalent to the command line in the previous example.

Any time you have to run the same statements repeatedly, placing them in a file is much easier than having to type them all over again for each command line. Just for practice, switch fields 1 and 2 on each of the other "farms" files.

## *Using Arithmetic Statements*

As mentioned earlier, one of the things you can do with **awk** is to perform arithmetic operations on files that contain numerical data. To try out this feature, **awk** all three *farms* files to determine the average price of all the fruits supplied to "Fruit-of-the-Tree." This will involve using three new things:

- a **variable** of our own called **sum**.
- an **awk** variable called **NR** (*N*umber of *R*ecords, or the number of lines read by **awk**).
- an **awk** statement called **END**.

We'll use our own variable **sum** to add up all the prices as **awk** reads through the records. After we have them totaled, we'll use a variable provided by **awk** called **NR**, which will tell us how many records **awk** has read (and therefore, how many numbers we've added up). Then we'll use a pattern statement provided by **awk** called **END**. The **END** statement tells **awk** to wait until reading all records before carrying out the action that follows (figuring out the average price).

1. Place the **action** statements (without the single quotes) in a file:

a. This time, call the file *av.price*:

```
$ cat > av.price
{sum = sum + $3}
```

```
END {print "Average price: " , sum / NR}
                    [Press CTRL-D to terminate input]
$ _
```

b. This will redirect the standard output from **cat** to a file named *av.price*.

2. Name this file with the **-f** option when you execute **awk**:

   a. Type your command line with *-f av.price* after *awk*:

```
$ awk -f av.price *farms
Average price: 0.370833
$ _
```

   b. Using the **-f** option is equivalent to typing the statements to obtain the average price on the command line.

## *Selecting Lines Conditionally*

Until now, we've concentrated on the **action** statements used in an **awk** command line, and performed our **action** statements on every line in the file(s) named. Now we'll focus our attention on the **pattern** statements—the statements used to select lines. These statements allow you to decide which lines to process and which lines to ignore. When you combine this ability to make selections with the various **action** statements available, you have an amazingly versatile and flexible tool in your hands.

Let's start with a few simple examples. First, let's have **awk** go through each line (or **record**) of each of the three "farms" files, select those that show a price higher than 0.50, and display them. (Since this one is so simple, we won't bother with a separate file.)

1. Which fruits from all suppliers cost more than 0.50?

   a. List all lines showing a price higher than 0.50:

```
$ awk '$3 > 0.50 {print $0}' *farms
Bing cherries              0.51    D
Concord grapes             0.51    J
$ _
```

   b. Answer: There are two, Dawson's Bing cherries and Jenkins' Concord grapes.

So there it is—a list of all the fruits that cost more than 0.50. The **pattern** statement (*$3 > 0.50*) selects these lines, and the **action** statement (*print $0*) displays them. By the way, you could save these two lines in a file by just adding a redirection statement (> *exp.fruits*) to the end of the command line before executing it.

You can also construct compound **pattern** statements, using ~ to mean "match the pattern," slashes to enclose pattern strings, "&&" to mean "and," "||" to mean "or," and "!" to mean "not." Here is an example:

2. Which grapes cost bewteen 0.31 and 0.35 (inclusive)?

   a. Place the statements in an input file:

```
$ cat > grapes.awk
$2~ /grapes/ && $3 >= 0.31 && $3 <= 0.35 {print $0}
                                [Press CTRL-D to terminate input]
$ _
```

   b. List all lines showing grapes at a price between 0.31 and 0.35 (namely, 0.31, 0.32, 0.33, 0.34, or 0.35):

```
$ awk -f grapes.awk *farms
Thompson grapes          0.35    P
$ _
```

   c. Answer: Parker's Thompson grapes.

## An Example

At the end of Chapter 20, you will find an example of text processing that draws on many of the things you have learned in this chapter. Even if you plan to skip the material on formatting, you will probably be interested in this example.

## Summary of Chapter 18

In this chapter you learned how to search for text with **grep**, sort files with **sort**, and program text output with **awk**.

### *Searching for Text*

**Conducting simple searches.** To conduct a simple search for a string in a file (or files), type *grep*, a space, the string, another space, and the name(s) of the file(s) in a command line and press RETURN.

**Aids in searching.** Rather than just type a literal string, you can alternately form a **regular expression** with UNIX **metacharacters:**

```
^ $ . * [ ] \
```

**Using options to modify the output.** By including an option (or combination of options) in the command line, you can modify the output of

**grep** to show how many times the string was found, to show the name(s) of the file(s) in which the string was found, to show line numbers, to match either uppercase or lowercase, to invert the search, and so on.

**Sending the output to a file.** To send the output to a file, redirect the standard output with > and a filename.

**Using related search programs.** For faster searches with only fixed literal strings, use **fgrep**; for enhanced searching with provisions for finding repeated strings and alternate strings, use **egrep** in place of **grep**.

## *Sorting Files with sort*

**Selecting a field (or fields).** To perform a simple sort of entire lines of text, type *sort*, a space, and the name(s) of the file(s) to be sorted in a command line and press RETURN. To perform sorting on a particular field (or fields), use the plus and minus options with field numbers.

**Using options to modify the output.** By including an option (or combination of options) in the command line, you can modify the operation of **sort** to ignore leading blanks, sort a numeric field, sort in reverse order, fold uppercase onto lowercase, sort uniquely, merge files, designate a **field separator**, redirect the output, and so on.

## *Programming Text Output with awk*

**Statements.** An **awk** command line consists of the name of the command ("awk"), a space, an optional pattern statement, a space, an optional action statement, a space, and the name(s) of the file(s).

**Referring to fields.** To refer to fields in an **awk** command, use a dollar sign and a number typed together (for example, $3 to indicate field 3).

**Working from an input file.** Like many other UNIX commands, **awk** allows you to place your statements in a separate file, then activate them from a command line. With **awk**, use **-f** and the name of the file to activate the statements.

**Using arithmetic statements.** You can use field names with a variety of arithmetic operators and built-in variables to perform computations. In this chapter we used **NR** to obtain the number of records and **END** to defer processing until all records had been read.

**Selecting lines conditionally.** By placing a **pattern** statement in front of each **action** statement, you can select lines for processing. Such a **pattern** statement can either specify line numbers or use arithmetic comparisons as a basis for selecting lines for processing.

# 19

# Formatting with **nroff** Using the ms Macro Package

## Introduction to Formatting

### *The UNIX Formatting Tools*

As mentioned earlier, text editing and text formatting are two separate processes in UNIX. You enter text into a file with one of the editors (**ed** or **vi**), then you use another program to format the text for printing. New **word processing** programs, which combine editing and formatting as two different functions of a single program, are becoming available for UNIX every month.

There are two main formatting programs in UNIX, along with some auxiliary programs and pre-processors. The main formatting programs, both derived from an earlier "runoff" program from MIT, are called **nroff** (new runoff, pronounced "en-roff") and **troff** (typesetting runoff, pronounced "tee-roff"). These two programs have many similarities, but the main difference is that **nroff** is intended for ordinary printers, while **troff** is intended for typesetting equipment. Since **troff** is considerably more sophisticated, we'll confine our discussion in this book to **nroff**.

To aid beginners in using **nroff** and to provide standard sets of formats, people have designed various pre-defined formatting tools called **macro packages**. (The term "macro" here refers to larger commands that have been constructed from smaller primitive commands—"micros" if you will.) Some of the most well-known are called **ms**, **me**, and **mm**.

In addition, there are several pre-processors that handle specialized types of text: **tbl** for tables, and **eqn** and **neqn** for mathematical expressions, among others. Finally, there are utilities: **checkeq** to check usage in **eqn** and **neqn** and **deroff** to remove all formatting commands (**nroff, troff, tbl, eqn,** or **neqn**) from a file, among others. In this chapter we'll focus on **ms.**

## *An Example of Formatting*

The **ms** macro package offers you a wide selection of pre-defined features for text formatting that you can activate and de-activate by placing **embedded commands** (or **requests**) in your file. Let's use text from an earlier chapter.

1. Prepare an input text file for formatting:

   a. Move to subdirectory *text_files* and start an editing session with a file called *pfl.deal*:

```
Dear Mr. Madison:

The purpose of this letter is to confirm Monday's agreement.
Tupelo gets "Porkchop" Peterson, you get "Earthquake" Emerson,
and we get "Rotunda" Robinson.
Here are the players' names, heights, weights, and new teams:
Emerson, Ezekiel R.      6'5"     273       Rochester
Robinson, Charles F.     6'3"     287       Des Moines
Peterson, Paul N.        5'9"     178       Tupelo
You will be getting one of the finest players in the People's Football League.
Your Friend and Mine, Chuck
```

   b. Insert the seven embedded commands shown below (but not the descriptions in brackets). (In case you skipped Part II and haven't already typed this letter, type it now as shown here.)

```
.pl 30
.LP                                                [Block paragraph]
Dear Mr. Madison:
.PP                                                [Standard paragraph]
The purpose of this letter is to confirm Monday's agreement.
Tupelo gets "Porkchop" Peterson, you get "Earthquake" Emerson,
and we get "Rotunda" Robinson.
Here are the players' names, heights, weights, and new teams:
.DS                                                [Start of display]
Emerson, Ezekiel R.      6'5"     273       Rochester
Robinson, Charles F.     6'3"     287       Des Moines
Peterson, Paul N.        5'9"     178       Tupelo
.DE                                                [End of display]
.PP                                                [Standard paragraph]
You will be getting one of the finest players in the People's Football League.
.DS C                                              [Centered display]
```

```
Your Friend and Mine, Chuck
.DE
```
[End of display]

c. Store the text and return to the UNIX shell prompt.

2. Format the text on your screen with **nroff**:

   a. Type an **nroff** command that includes the **−ms** option:

```
$ nroff -ms pfl.deal

Dear Mr. Madison:

The purpose of this letter is to confirm Monday's agree-
ment. Tupelo gets "Porkchop" Peterson, you get "Earthquake"
Emerson, and we get "Rotunda" Robinson. Here are the
players' names, heights, weights, and new teams:

          Emerson, Ezekiel R.   6'5"   273    Rochester
          Robinson, Charles F.  6'3"   287    Des Moines
          Peterson, Paul N.     5'9"   178    Tupelo

You will be getting one of the finest players in the
People's Football League.

                        Your Friend and Mine, Chuck


                             September 2, 1985
```

   b. The words of each paragraph have been joined together, the right margin has been **justified** (aligned), the tabular material have been indented, and the closing has been centered.

## *Using the ms Macro Package*

In formatting this letter, which gives you a brief introduction to **nroff** and **ms**, you used one **nroff** command:

**.pl 30** Set the page length to 30 lines (without this **nroff** request, the letter would sail off the top of the screen before you got a chance to look at it).

and five **ms** commands:

| | |
|---|---|
| **.LP** | Block paragraph (left-justified). |
| **.PP** | Standard paragraph (first line indented). |
| **.DS** | Start of display (text is indented, but otherwise left alone). |
| **.DE** | End of display. |
| **.DS C** | Start of display (centered). |

Each embedded **ms** command (or **request**) consists of a period (or dot) in column 1 followed by one or two capital letters (this conveniently distinguishes them from **nroff** commands, which are lowercase). For example, the **ms** command for a normal paragraph is *.PP*. By placing (or **embedding**) this command directly above lines of text, you can have those lines formatted into a paragraph.

Some embedded commands also require additional information. For example, the start of display command *.DS* may be used either by itself or with one or more characters added (in the example above, we added *C* to get *.DS C* for centering).

In the sections that follow, we'll describe these and other formatting commands in greater detail. To save space, we'll use "miniature examples," showing the input text in the left and the printed result on the right. Full-sized examples work the same way—they just take up more room.

# Forming Paragraphs

## *Standard Paragraph* .PP

To make the first line indented five spaces and all lines right-justified, precede the first line with the **.PP** command. This command is used at the beginning of the text file to initialize the file:

| Input | Output |
|---|---|
| `.PP` | |
| `sssssssssssssssssssssssssssss` | `     sssssssssssssssssss` |
| `ssssssssssss` | `ssssssssssssssssssssssss` |
| `sssssssssssssssssssssssss` | `ssssssssssssssssssssssss` |
| `ssssssssssssssss.` | `ssssssssssssss.` |

## *Block Paragraph* .LP

To form a block paragraph, with all lines left-justified and all but the last line right-justified, precede the first line with the **.LP** command:

| | |
|---|---|
| `.LP` | |
| `bbbbbbbbbbbbbbbbbbbbbbbbbbbb` | `bbbbbbbbbbbbbbbbbbbbbbbb` |
| `bbbbbbbbbbbb` | `bbbbbbbbbbbbbbbbbbbbbbbb` |
| `bbbbbbbbbbbbbbbbbbbbbbbbb` | `bbbbbbbbbbbbbbbbbbbbbbbb` |
| `bbbbbbbbbbbbbbbbb.` | `bbbbbbbbbbbbb.` |

## *Quotation Paragraph* .QP

To highlight a quotation (that is, to form a block paragraph that is indented five spaces on the left and on the right, with all lines left-justified and all but the last line right-justified), precede the first line with the **.QP** command:

```
.PP
ssssssssssssssssssssssssssss
ssssssssssss
ssssssssssssssss.
.QP
qqqqqqqqqqqqqqqqqqqqqq
qqqqqqqqqqq
qqqqqqqqqqqqqqq.
```

```
     ssssssssssssssssssss
sssssssssssssssssssssssss
sssssssssssss.

  qqqqqqqqqqqqqqq
  qqqqqqqqqqqqqqq
  qqqqqqqqqqq.
```

## *Indented Paragraph* **.IP**

To form a block paragraph that is indented five spaces on the left, with all lines left-justified and all but the last line right-justified, precede the first line with the **.IP** command:

```
.LP
bbbbbbbbbbbbbbbbbbbbbbbbbbbbb
bbbbbbbbbbbb
bbbbbbbbbbbbbbbb.
.IP
iiiiiiiiiiiiiiiiiiiii
iiiiiiiiiii
iiiiiiiiiiiiiii.
```

```
bbbbbbbbbbbbbbbbbbbbbbbbb
bbbbbbbbbbbbbbbbbbbbbbbbb
bbbbbbbbbbbbb.

     iiiiiiiiiiiiiiiiiii
     iiiiiiiiiiiiiiiiiii
     iiiiiiiiiii.
```

To have a number, letter, bullet, or other short string appear in front of the first line of the indented paragraph, simply leave one blank space after *.IP*, and type the string:

```
.LP
bbbbbbbbbbbbbbbbbbbbbbbbbbbbb
bbbbbbbbbbbb
bbbbbbbbbbbbbbbb.
.IP (1)
iiiiiiiiiiiiiiiiiiiii
iiiiiiiiiii
iiiiiiiiiiiiiii.
.IP (2)
iiiiiiiiiiiiiiiiiiiii
iiiiiiiiiii
iiiiiiiiiiiiiii.
iiiiiiiiiii.
```

```
bbbbbbbbbbbbbbbbbbbbbbbbb
bbbbbbbbbbbbbbbbbbbbbbbbb
bbbbbbbbbbbbb.

(1)  iiiiiiiiiiiiiiiiiii
     iiiiiiiiiiiiiiiiiii
     iiiiiiiiiii.

(2)  iiiiiiiiiiiiiiiiiii
     iiiiiiiiiiiiiiiiiii
     iiiiiiiiii.
```

**.PP**
**.LP**
**.QP**
**.IP**

To have a longer string appear in front of the first line of the indented paragraph, leave one blank space after *.IP*, then type the string, followed by a number (which must be at least one greater than the length of the string) to indicate how many columns to indent the paragraph to make room for the string. If the string contains any spaces, enclose it in quotation marks:

```
.LP
bbbbbbbbbbbbbbbbbbbbbbbbbbbb     bbbbbbbbbbbbbbbbbbbbbbbb
bbbbbbbbbbbb                     bbbbbbbbbbbbbbbbbbbbbbbb
bbbbbbbbbbbbbbbb.                bbbbbbbbbbbb.
.IP "Part 1" 8
iiiiiiiiiiiiiiiiiiiii            Part 1  iiiiiiiiiiiiiiii
iiiiiiiiiii                              iiiiiiiiiiiiiiii
iiiiiiiiiiiiiii.                         iiiiiiiiiii.
.IP "Part 2"
iiiiiiiiiiiiiiiiiiiii            Part 2  iiiiiiiiiiiiiiii
iiiiiiiiiii                              iiiiiiiiiiiiiiii
iiiiiiiiiiiiiii.                         iiiiiiiiiii.
```

Once a number to indicate indentation has been given, that indentation remains in effect until it is changed again.

## *Shifting Paragraphs* .RS .RE

To shift a paragraph five spaces to the right, use the **.RS** command; to shift a subsequent paragraph back five spaces, use the **.RE** command. The **.RS** command is similar to the **.IP** command, except that **.RS** can be used in conjunction with **.RE** to shift paragraphs right and left (as when displaying an outline):

```
.PP
ssssssssssssssssssssssssssss          sssssssssssssssssss
ssssssssssss                     ssssssssssssssssssssssss
ssssssssssssssss.                sssssssssssss.
.RS
rrrrrrrrrrrrr                         rrrrrrrrrrrrrrrrrrr
rrrrrrrrrrr                           rrrrrrrrrrrrrrrrrrr
rrrrrrrrrrrrrrrrrrrrrrr.              rrrrrrrrrrr.
.RS
rrrrrrrrrrrrrrrr                           rrrrrrrrrrrrrr
rrrrrr                                     rrrrrrrrrr
.RE
lllllllllllllllllllll                 lllllllllllllllllll
lllllllllll                           lllllllllllllllllll
lllllllllllllll.                      llllll.
.RE
lllllllllllllllllll              llllllllllllllllllllllll
llllllllll.                      llllllllllllllllll.
```

The **.RS** request also allows a string in front of the first line. Refer to the **.IP** request above for details.

## Displaying Text

### *Standard Display* **.DS .DE**

To display text (that is, to have it indented but left unchanged), precede the first line with the **.DS** command and follow the last line with the **.DE** command. You could use **.DS** and **.DE** to display poetry, where the lines must be left alone. In a standard display, the text is indented five spaces.

```
.PP
ssssssssssssssssssssss
sssssssssss
sssssssssssssssssssssss.
.DS
ddddddddddddddddd,
ddddddddddddddd.
ddddddddddddddddd,
ddddddddddddd.
.DE
```

```
     ssssssssssssssssss
sssssssssssssssssssssss
ssssssssssss.

     ddddddddddddddddd,
     ddddddddddddddd.
     ddddddddddddddddd,
     ddddddddddddd.
```

### *Blocked Display* **.DS B**

Another style is to center the text, with left-justification. To have text indented and left-justified, but centered when displayed, add the **B** option to the **.DS** command:

```
.PP
ssssssssssssssssssssssssss
sssssssssss
ssssssssssssssssssss.
.DS B
ddddddddddddddddd,
ddddddddddddddd.
ddddddddddddddddd,
ddddddddddddd.
.DE
```

```
     ssssssssssssssssss
sssssssssssssssssssssss
ssssssssssss.

   ddddddddddddddddd,
   ddddddddddddddd.
   ddddddddddddddddd,
   ddddddddddddd.
```

**.RS**
**.RE**
**.DS**
**.DE**
**.DS B**
**.DS C**

### *Centered Display* **.DS C**

Sometimes it's attractive to show a group of lines centered horizontally, as in a title or a beautiful verse. To have each individual line of text centered when displayed, add the **C** option to the **.DS** command.

```
.PP
sssssssssssssssssssssssss                          sssssssssssssssssss
ssssssssssss                                  ssssssssssssssssssssssss
sssssssssssssssssss.                          sssssssssssss.
.DS C
dddddddddddddddddddd,                           dddddddddddddddddddd,
dddddddddddddddd.                                 dddddddddddddddd.
dddddddddddddddddd,                              dddddddddddddddddd,
ddddddddddd.                                        ddddddddddd.
.DE
```

## Keeping Lines of Text Together

### *Standard Keep* **.KS .KE**

Ordinarily, it doesn't make too much difference where the page breaks occur in your text. There are certain lines of text, however, that you want kept together on the same page, and you want to guarantee that they will not be split up by a page break. With **ms**, you can simply bracket the text between a pair of "keep" requests (**.KS** and **.KE**), and **nroff** will keep them together. In the following pair of examples, we have a paragraph with five lines to be printed, but only three available lines for it at the bottom of page 5. (The dashed line used below represents a page break, while *5* and *6* represent the page numbers.)

*Without a "Keep":*

```
.PP
.PP
sssssssssssssssssssssssss          sssssssssssssssssss
ssssssssssss                  ssssssssssssssssssssssss
sssssssssssssssssss.          sssssssssssss. ssssssss   5
ssssssssssssssss            ------------------------------
sssssssssssssssssssss         ssssssssssssssssssssssss  6
ssssssssssss.                 sssssssssssssssssss.
```

*With a "Keep":*

```
bbbbbbbbbbbbbbbbbbbbbb.    bbbbbbbbbbbbbbbbbbbbbbbb
.KS                        bbbbbbbbbbb.
.PP
sssssssssssssssssssssssss
ssssssssssss                                       5
```

```
sssssssssssssssssss.
ssssssssssssssss
sssssssssssssssssssss
ssssssssssss.
.KE
```

```
-----------------------------
        sssssssssssssssssss  6
sssssssssssssssssssssssss
sssssssssssss.  ssssssss
ssssssssssssssssssssssss
sssssssssssssssssss.
```

## *Floating Keep* .KF .KE

A standard "keep" performs a valuable service, but some people object to the blank space it sometimes leaves at the bottom of a page. One way to avoid this is to use a "floating keep." The "kept" text is still moved intact to the following page, as with a standard "keep." However, **nroff** will use the text that follows the "kept" lines to fill the blank lines at the bottom of the previous page, as in this example:

```
.PP
sssssssssssssssssssssssss
ssssssssssss
ssssssss.
.KF
.QP
qqqqqqqqqqqqq
qqqqqqqqqqq
qqqqqqqqqqqqqqqqqqqqq.
.KE
.LP
bbbbbbbbbbbbbbbbbbbbbbbbb
bbbbbbbbbbbbbbbbbbb
bbbbbbbbbbbbbbbbbbbbbbb
bbbbbbbbbbbbbbbbbbbb.
```

```
     sssssssssssssssssss
sssssssssssssssssssssssss.

bbbbbbbbbbbbbbbbbbbbbbbb
bbbbbbbbbbbbbbbbbbbbbbbb  7
----------------------------
                          8
      qqqqqqqqqqqqqq
      qqqqqqqqqqqqqq
      qqqqqqqqqqq.

bbbbbbbbbbbbbbbbbbbbbbbb
bbbbbbbbbbbb.
```

Since page 7 doesn't have room for the three lines of the quotation, the quotation is moved to page 8, leaving two blank lines on page 7. Two lines of the block paragraph are then moved ahead of the quotation to the bottom of page 7. With two lines of the block paragraph moved to page 7, this leaves two more lines to follow the quotation on page 8. Note that you never have to "keep" a **display**, because a display is "kept" automatically.

.KS
.KE
.KF
.KE
.FS
.FE

# Using Footnotes

## *Setting up a Footnote* .FS .FE

If you're typing a document that requires footnotes, **nroff** and **ms** can save you a lot of work. All you have to do is type the footnote right after the location of the reference to it (surrounded by the footnote commands **.FS** and **.FE**), and **ms** will take care of making room for the note at the bottom of the page, and will also print a separator between the footnote and the last line of main text at the bottom of the page. Here is an example:

```
.QP
"I'm not a crook."*
.FS
* Richard M. Nixon, 1974
.FE
.PP
In an interview this afternoon,
three members of the House
Judiciary Committe told . . . .
```

```
     "I'm not a crook."*

     In an interview this
afternoon, three  members
of  the  House  Judiciary
Committee told  reporters

---------------
* Richard M. Nixon, 1974
```

## *Using Numbers with Footnotes*

If you are planning to refer to your footnotes by number, you can use numbers in place of asterisks. If your printer is not capable of half-line spacing, you can use numbers enclosed in brackets like this: [1], [2], [3], and so on. If your printer is capable of half-line spacing, you can have the numbers printed as superscripts by surrounding them with the "up" (\u) and "down" (\d) commands. Here is an example of superscript references:

```
.PP
sssssssssssssss
sssssss.[7]
.FS
.IP " 7."
fffffffffffffffffff
.FE
sssssssssssssssssss
sssssssssss
sssssssssssss.[8]
.FS
.IP " 8."
ggggggggggggggggggg
.FE
.PP
sssssssssssssssssssss
sssssssssssss
sssssssssssssssssss.
```

```
    sssssssssssssssssss
sss.[7]  ssssssssssss
sssssssssssssssssssss
sssssssssssss.[8]

    sssssssssssssssssss
sssssssssssssssssssss
sssssssssss.

---------------
  7. fffffffffff
     fffffff.
  8. ggggggggggg
     ggggggg.
```

This example also illustrates the use of an indented paragraph within a footnote to separate the number from the note.

## Using Headings

In this section you will learn how to use both unnumbered and numbered section headings.

### *Unnumbered Headings* **.SH**

To produce a plain, unnumbered heading of less than one full line, precede it with the **.SH** (section heading) command and follow it with either **.PP** or **.LP** to begin the text that follows. The heading will be underscored, left-justified, and separated from ordinary text above and below by blank lines. Here is an example:

```
.PP
sssssssssssssssssssssssss        sssssssssssssssssss
ssssssssssss                  ssssssssssssssssssssss
sssssssssssssssssss.          sssssssssssss.
.SH
Conclusion                    Conclusion
.PP                           ----------
sssssssssssssssssss              sssssssssssssssssss
ssssssssssss                  ssssssssssssssssssssss
ssssssssssssss.               ssss.
```

If you want to leave more than a single blank line above the heading, insert extra **.LP** or **.PP** commands between the end of the preceding paragraph and the **.SH** command. **.SH**

```
.PP
sssssssssssssssssssssssss        sssssssssssssssssss
ssssssssssss                  ssssssssssssssssssssss
sssssssssssssssssss.          sssssssssssss.
.PP
.PP
.SH
Conclusion                    Conclusion
.PP                           ----------
sssssssssssssssssss              sssssssssssssssssss
ssssssssssss                  ssssssssssssssssssssss
ssssssssssssss.               ssss.
```

### Numbered Headings .NH

Numbered headings work like unnumbered headings, except that each heading is preceded by a section number. When you use the **.NH** (numbered heading) command, leave a space after *.NH* and type a number to indicate the level of subordination (up to five levels). (On a first-order heading, you can omit the number.) You can leave it up to **ms** to assign the next available number at any given level, but **ms** cannot generate a table of contents from your headings automatically, as some programs can do.

| Input | Output |
|---|---|
| `.NH`<br>`The Main Thing` | 1. The Main Thing |
| `.NH 2`<br>`Where to Start` | 1.1. Where to Start |
| `.NH 2`<br>`When to Start` | 1.2. When to Start |
| `.NH 3`<br>`The Best Time` | 1.2.1. The Best Time |
| `.NH 3`<br>`The Worst Time` | 1.2.2. The Worst Time |
| `.NH`<br>`Other Things to Consider`<br>`.LP` | 2. Other Things to Consider |

## Emphasizing and De-emphasizing Text

### Emphasizing Text .I

If you would like to emphasize text in a paragraph, underscore it by inserting the **.I** (italic) command. One way to do this is to place ".I" on a separate line, followed by the text to be emphasized. Although this may appear to break up the paragraph, **ms** will fill the paragraph without interruption.

```
.PP
Now we are coming to the
.I most important
item of the agenda.
```

```
     Now we are coming
to the most  important
item of the agenda.
```

Another way to emphasize text is to use **.I** (italic) in conjunction with the **.R** (Roman) command, with *.I* on the line preceding and *.R* on the line following the text to be underscored. Once again, **ms** will reconstruct the paragraph for you automatically.

```
.PP
```

```
Now we are coming to the
.I
most important
.R
item of the agenda.
```

```
        Now we are coming
to the most  important
item of the agenda.
```

### De-emphasizing Text

The best way to de-emphasize text in your document is to leave it out. No formatting command is required.

## Page Layout

### Standard Layout

Ordinarily, **nroff** lays out a page as shown in Figure 19-1. In the standard **ms** page layout, printing appears in a 6 x 9″ area on each 8-1/2 x 11″ page, with the page number centered at the top between hyphens (CH) and today's date centered at the bottom (CF). The 6 x 9″ area includes

- 6 inches of text across (65 columns)
- 9 inches of text down (54 lines) (66 total lines per page)

This section discusses how you can change the standard page layout.

### Changing the Date

**.ND**
**.DA**

If you want to remove the date completely, place the **.ND** (no date) command near the beginning of the text file. If you want to use some date other than today's, enter a **.DA** command, typing the desired date after *.DA,* as shown here:

```
.DA September 15, 1981
```

### Changing the Header

**.ds LH**
**.ds CH**
**.ds RH**

The **header**, an extra line above the body of text at the top of the page, usually remains fixed throughout the document. You can place your own message in any of three locations on this line: the left, the middle, or the right. For each of these locations, **nroff** has a corresponding string variable: LH (left header), CH (center header), and RH (right header). By default, CH contains the page number, while the other two are empty.

To change any of these variables, use the **nroff .ds** (define string) command to assign your own string. For example, you could use the follow-

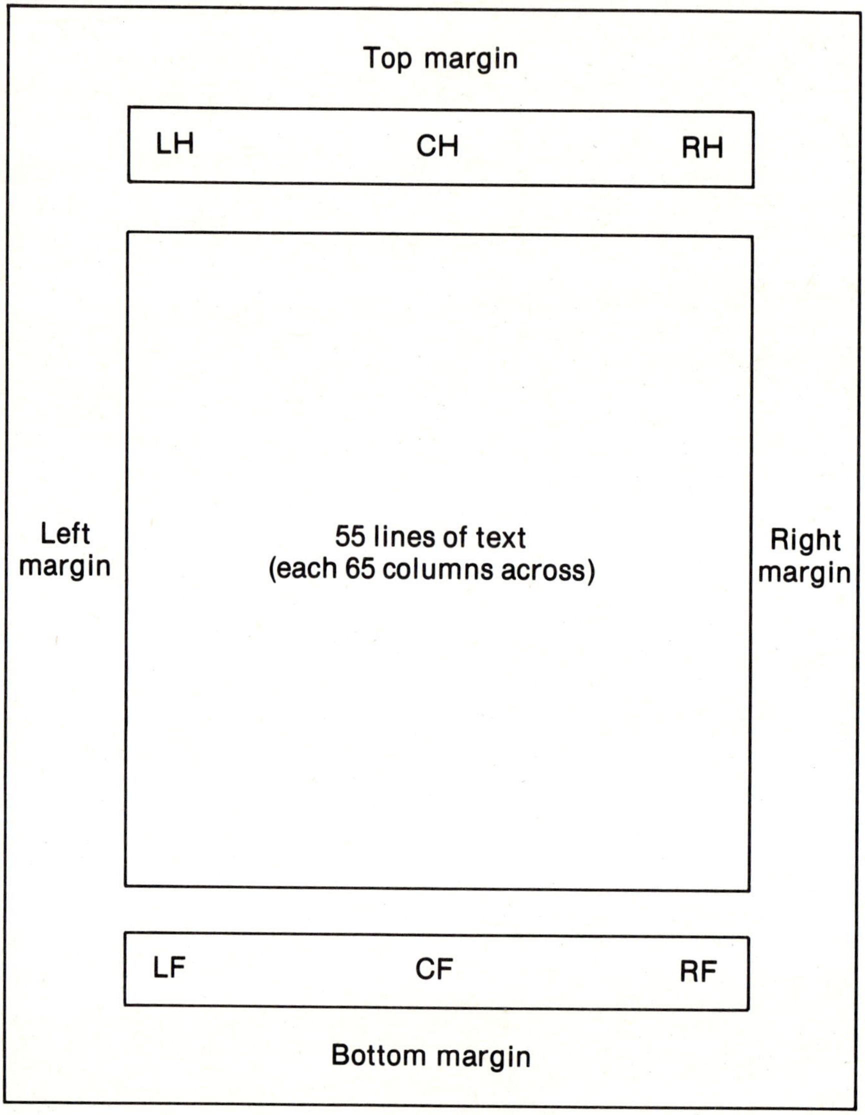


Figure 19-1. Standard ms page layout.

ing commands to place *Draft Copy* on the left and *Revision 3* on the right (leaving the page number in the middle):

```
.PP
.ds LH Draft Copy
.ds RH Revision 3
```

### Changing the Footer

**.ds LF**
**.ds CF**
**.ds RF**

The **footer** is an extra line below the body of text at the bottom of the page. As with the header, you can place your own message in any of three locations on this line: the left (LF), the middle (MF), or the right (RF). By default, CF contains the date and the other two are empty.

To change any of these variables, use the **nroff .ds** (define string) command to assign your own string. For example, you could use the following commands to place *Confidential* at the bottom of every page on the left and *Internal Use Only* on the right (leaving the date in the middle):

```
.PP
.ds LF Confidential
.ds RF Internal Use Only
```

### Moving the Page Number

**%**

Although **nroff** places the page number in the middle of the header by default, you are free to place it somewhere else and in a different format. Use the % (page number) symbol, as in this example, which places the page number on the right side of the footer, preceded by *Page:*

```
.PP
.ds RF Page %
```

## Summary of Chapter 19

In this chapter you learned how to format text with the **nroff** command, focusing primarily on the **ms** macro package.

### Introduction to Formatting

**.ds LF**
**.ds CF**
**.ds RF**
**%**

**The UNIX formatting tools.** The main formatting programs in UNIX are **nroff** (for printing) and **troff** (for typesetting). These are accompanied by **macro packages** (which provide standard, predefined formatting requests) and **preprocessors** (which handle specialized types of text).

Macro packages, such as **ms, me, and mm,** are activated via option switches in an **nroff** command string. Preprocessors, such as **tbl** (for tables), **eqn** and **neqn** (for mathematical expressions), are activated by separate commands that send text to **nroff** via a pipeline.

**The ms macro package.** To use the **ms** macro package, place embedded commands in the text to be formatted, then execute an **nroff** command that includes the **-ms** option and the name of the file to be formatted. To obtain printed results, send the text to the **lpr** print spooler via a pipeline.

**Forming paragraphs.** The **ms** embedded requests for forming paragraphs are as follows. No terminator is required.

| | |
|---|---|
| Standard paragraph | **.PP** |
| Block paragraph | **.LP** |
| Quotation paragraph | **.QP** |
| Indented paragraph | **.IP** |
| Shift right | **.RS** |
| Shift left | **.RE** |

**Displaying text.** The **ms** embedded commands for displaying text are as follows. The text to be displayed must be preceded by one command and followed by a terminating command (**.DE**).

| | | |
|---|---|---|
| Standard Display | **.DS** | (**.DE**) |
| Blocked Display | **.DS B** | (**.DE**) |
| Centered Display | **.DS C** | (**.DE**) |

**Keeping lines of text together.** The **ms** embedded commands for keeping lines of text together are as follows. The text to be "kept" must be preceded by one command and followed by a terminating command (**.KE**).

| | | |
|---|---|---|
| Standard keep | **.KS** | (**.KE**) |
| Floating keep | **.KF** | (**.KE**) |

**Using footnotes.** The **ms** embedded commands for printing footnotes at the bottom of the page are as follows. The text of the footnote must be preceded by the **.FS** command and followed by the **.FE** command.

| | | |
|---|---|---|
| Setting Up a Footnote | **.FS** | (**.FE**) |
| Using Superscripts | **\u** | (**\d**) |

**Using headings.** The **ms** embedded commands for printing headings are as follows. Headings do not require terminators.

| | |
|---|---|
| Unnumbered headings | **.SH** |
| Numbered headings | **.NH** |

**Emphasizing and de-emphasizing text.** The **ms .I** request produces underscoring for emphasis; the **.R** (roman) request can be used to terminate underscoring.

| | | |
|---|---|---|
| Emphasis | **.I** | (**.R**) |
| De-emphasis | (None required) | |

## *Page Layout*

**Standard layout.** The standard page layout for **ms** is a printing area of 6 x 9 inches on an 8-1/2 x 11 page, with the page number centered at the top of the page and the date centered at the bottom of the page. Using the commands that follow, you can make some changes in the layout.

| | |
|---|---|
| Remove the date | **.ND** |
| Change the date | **.DA** |
| Change the header | **.ds LH**<br>**.ds CH**<br>**.ds RH** |
| Change the footer | **.ds LF**<br>**.ds CF**<br>**.ds RF** |
| Move the page number | % |

# 20

# Some Formatting Techniques Using **nroff**

In Chapter 19 you learned how to use the **nroff** program to format text, with a major emphasis on the **ms** macro processor. In this chapter we'll explore different ways to initiate formatting, a few basic **nroff** requests, methods for producing tables and double-column printing, and some of the other programs that relate to formatting.

## Initiating Formatting

In this section we'll look at some of the different ways you can begin formatting, along with some of the options available to you when you format.

### *Executing an nroff Command Line*

In Chapter 19, to get a quick introduction to formatting, we used only the simplest form of the **nroff** command, which sends its output to your screen to be previewed. For **nroff** alone, such a command would look like this:

```
$ nroff text
```

For processing with the **ms** macro package, the command would look like this:

```
$ nroff -ms text
$ _
```

To have the formatted text printed on a line printer, send the output of **nroff** to the **lpr** print spooler via a pipeline:

```
$ nroff text | lpr
$ _
```

If you prefer to have this done in the background, add the background processing symbol & to the end of the command line. The UNIX kernel will then assign a process identifier to the job, like this:

```
$ nroff text | lpr &
1763
$ _
```

If you have a very large file split into smaller files (possibly with the **split** command), you can take advantage of the pattern-recognition features of UNIX and have **nroff** process the smaller files consecutively:

```
$ nroff jumbo.[a-d] | lpr
$ _
```

## *Specifying a Macro Package*

As mentioned above, you can include the **ms** macro package by using the **-ms** option in an **nroff** command line:

```
$ nroff -ms text
$ _
```

Actually, **ms** is just one of a number of macro packages that may be stored in a directory called */usr/lib/tmac.* The full pathname of the file that contains **ms** is */usr/lib/tmac/tmac.s.* Here is a summary of some names of macro packages and pathnames of the files that contain them:

| **Name** | **Option** | **Full Pathname of File** |
|---|---|---|
| ms | -ms | /usr/lib/tmac/tmac.s |
| mm | -mm | /usr/lib/tmac/tmac.m |
| me | -me | /usr/lib/tmac/tmac.e |

## *Requesting a Starting Page Number*

If you have printed the first 10 pages of a document with **nroff,** you may want to continue printing at the next page. To begin formatting at a given page of your document (say 11), you can include an option like **-n11** in your **nroff** command line:

```
$ nroff -n11 text | lpr        [Start printing on page 11]
$ _
```

## *Requesting Specific Pages* **-op**

To format only one page of your document (say 7), you can include an option like **-o7** in your **nroff** command line:

```
$ nroff -o7 text | lpr          [Print page 7 only]
$ _
```

You can also command more than one page at a time, using either commas to list individual page numbers or hyphens to indicate ranges of page numbers:

```
$ nroff -o3,9,18 text | lpr          [Print pages 3, 9, and 18]
$ _
$ nroff -o11-13,22 text | lpr        [Print pages 11 through 13,
                                     then 22]
$ _
$ nroff -o-5 text | lpr              [Print pages 1 through 5]
$ _
$ nroff -o14- text | lpr             [Print from page 14 to the end
$ _                                  of the document]
```

## *Pausing Between Pages* **-sn**

If you are printing on stationery or other paper that has to be fed into the printer one sheet at a time, you can have **nroff** pause between pages with the **-s** (stop) option:

```
$ nroff -s text | lpr          [Stop printing after each page]
$ _
```

If necessary, you can also type a number after "-s" to have **nroff** stop after a given number of pages. For example, to have **nroff** stop after every third page, you can use this:

```
$ nroff -s3 text | lpr          [Stop printing every third page]
$ _
```

## *Specifying a Printer* **-T*name***

The average printer can handle only the most routine printing tasks. It takes a special printer to perform such things as subscripts, superscripts, reverse paper motion, overstriking, and so on. If you have such a printer on your system, you can make this known to **nroff** with the **-T** (type) option. If you don't make this known, the special printing functions won't be performed. For example, if your system has a NEC 5520 Spinwriter, you could use this:

```
$ nroff -T5520 text | lpr        [Print on a NEC 5520 Spinwriter]
$ _
```

or possibly something like this:

```
$ nroff text | spr               [Print on a NEC 5520 Spinwriter]
$ _
```

Since a printer like this can also handle **micro-spacing**, you could also include the **-e** (even) option to command equal spacing of words on a line (also called **proportional spacing**):

```
$ nroff -e -T5520 text | lpr     [Print with equal spacing
$ _                               on a NEC 5520 Spinwriter]
```

Here is a possible alternative:

```
$ nroff -e text | spr            [Print with equal spacing
$ _                               on a NEC 5520 Spinwriter]
```

Here is a partial list of printers that can be named in a **-T** option:

| -T Name | Full Name |
|---|---|
| 37 | Teletype Corporation Model 37 (default) |
| lp | Ordinary line printer |
| tn300 | GE TermiNet 300 (or any terminal lacking half-line capability) |
| 300 | DASI 300 |
| 300S | DASI 300S |
| 450 | DASI 450 |
| 5510 | NEC 5510 Spinwriter |
| 5520 | NEC 5520 Spinwriter |

## Some Basic nroff Requests

In this section we'll take a brief look at some primitive **nroff** embedded commands, or requests ("micros" if you will). These are the basic, atomic instructions used in the operation of **nroff**. Every macro package ever designed to operate with **nroff** is constructed from these.

### *Setting the Length of the Page* .pl

The **.pl** (page length) request sets the length of each page you are printing on in lines (where each line is 1/6 of an inch high). By default, the page length is 66 lines, or 11 inches (see Figure 20-1). If you are

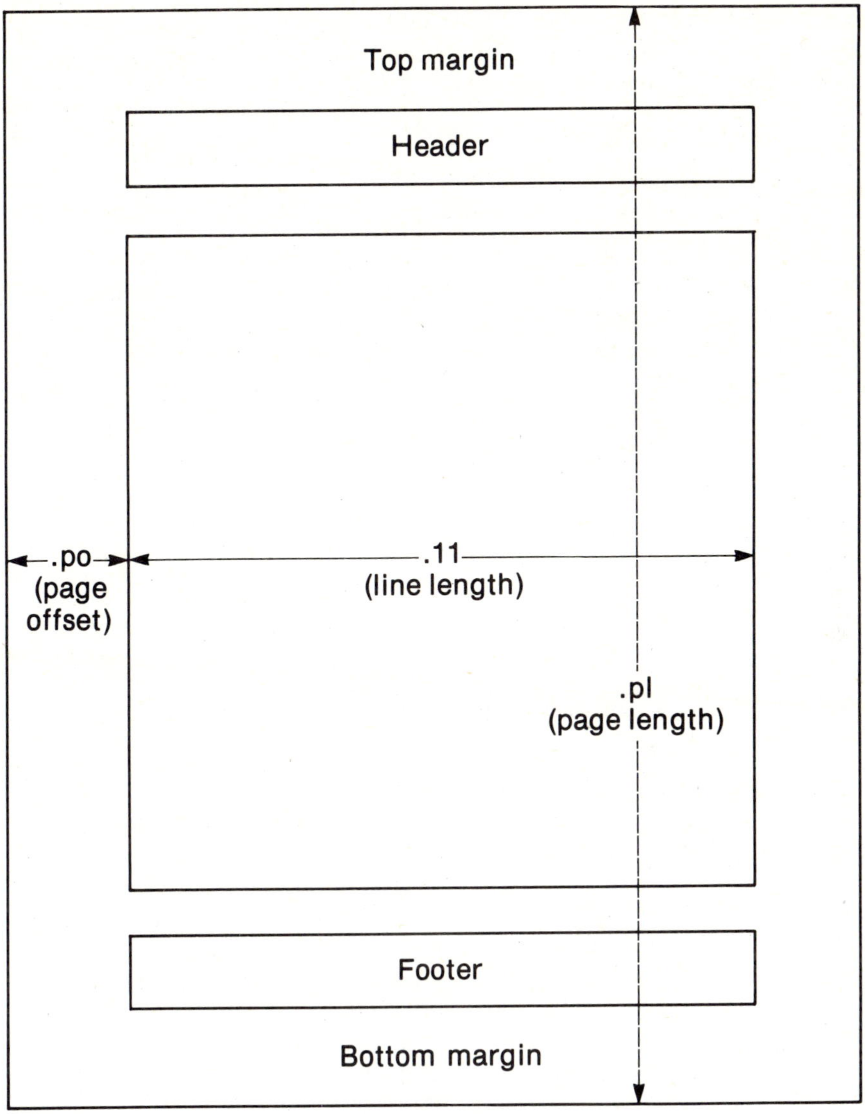


Figure 20-1. Standard nroff page layout.

**.pl**

printing on envelopes or something else that is not 8-1/2 x 11, you will have to reduce the value of **.pl**. For example, suppose you are printing on envelopes that are 4 inches high. You will then have to use this:

```
.pl 24          [Set the page length to 24 lines]
```

You can use either an absolute value (as in the example above) or a relative value, like this:

```
.pl -12         [Reduce the page length by 12 lines]
```

In this case, the new value of **.pl** is understood to be relative to its previous value. To restore the value to the default (66), simply use **.pl** by itself, without any number:

```
.pl                 [Restore the page length to 66 lines]
```

## Setting the Length of the Line **.ll**

The **.ll** (line length) command sets the length of each line in character columns (where each character is 1/10 of an inch wide). By default, the line length is 65 characters, or 6.5 inches (see Figure 20-1). (In **ms**, the default is 60 characters.) If you are printing on wide computer paper or something else that is not 8-1/2 x 11, you will have to increase or reduce the value of **.ll**. For example, suppose you are printing on wide computer paper that is 15 inches wide. You will then have to use this:

```
.ll 132             [Set the line length to 132 characters]
```

You can use either an absolute value (as in the example above) or a relative value, like this:

```
.ll +12             [Increase the line length by 12 characters]
```

In this case, the new value of **.ll** is understood to be relative to its previous value. To restore the value to the default (65), simply use **.ll** by itself, without any number:

```
.ll                 [Restore the line length to 65 characters]
```

## Setting the Offset from the Edge **.po**

The **.po** (page offset) command sets the distance from the left-hand edge of the paper to the first column of printing in character columns, where each character is 1/10 of an inch wide. By default, the page offset is 0 (right on the edge), which you will probably never want to use (see Figure 20-1). A macro package like **ms** usually sets **.po** to about 10, which just about centers the text between the two edges of the paper when the line length is set to 60. To set **.po** to 8, use this:

```
.po 8               [Set the page offset to 8 characters]
```

You can use either an absolute value (as in the example above) or a relative value, like this:

```
.po -2              [Reduce the page offset by 2 characters]
```

In this case, the new value of **.po** is understood to be relative to its previous value. To restore the value before your last change to **.po**, simply use **.po** by itself, without any number:

```
.po                 [Restore the page offset to its previous value]
```

## *Changing the Page Number* .pn

Whenever **nroff** starts formatting a new file, it sets its "page number register" to 1, and then increments this register for each page printed. Ordinarily you would not want to disrupt this scheme. However, suppose you have a larger file broken into two smaller files called *section 1.a* and *section 1.b,* where *section 1.b* is a continuation of *section 1.a.* If *section 1.a* is 26 pages long, then you would want to have this near the beginning of *section 1.b:*

```
.pn 27          [Set the page number to 27]
```

As with the previous commands, you can also use a relative value. For example, to increase the page number by two, you could use this:

```
.pn +2          [Increase the page number by 2]
```

If you use **.pn** by itself, without any number following, **nroff** will ignore the request:

```
.pn             [Ignored by nroff]
```

## *Forcing a Page Break* .bp

Ordinarily it won't make any difference to you where **nroff** ends one page and starts another. But there will be times when you want to be sure that a particular item appears only at the top of a new page. To force a page break at such a point, you can use the **.bp** (break page) command. For example, if you had a major heading in your document, you could precede it with this:

```
.bp             [Start a new page here]
```

This guarantees that **nroff** will print the heading at the top of a new page, no matter how much text appears on the previous page. You can also force a new page number. For example, to start a new page and call that new page "page 21," you could use this:

**.ll**
**.po**
**.pn**
**.bp**

```
.bp 21          [Start a new page and call it "page 21"]
```

You can also use a relative number. For example, suppose the current page is page 15 and you want to make sure that the next page begins on page 17 (which would appear on the front of a two-sided sheet). You could then use this:

```
.bp +2    [Start a new page and increase the page number by 2]
```

### Keeping Lines of Text Together **.ne**

Continuing the reasoning from the previous request (**.bp**), you may have a block of text that you never want to be split. In other words, if it will all fit together on the current page, fine; but if it won't, then you want it all moved to the next page. The **.ne** (need) request, with a number following, allows you to keep a certain number of lines together on the same page. For example, suppose you have a heading followed by five lines of text (a total of seven lines). To ensure that these seven lines never become separated by a page break, precede the heading with this:

```
.ne 7                [Keep the next seven lines together on one page]
```

### Other nroff Commands

There are several **nroff** requests that deal with "adjusting" and "filling" of text, hyphenation, line spacing, centering, underlining, indentation, and title lines. Unfortunately, we won't be able to cover them all right here. We'll move to another subject now, but include the remaining **nroff** requests in the chapter summary.

## Formatting Tables

### Introductory Example

To get a quick glimpse at the basic features of the **tbl** preprocessor for producing tables, let's format the letter we used in Chapter 19 once more. This time we'll use **tbl** instead of **ms** to format the tabular material. This means replacing the two display commands ( *.DS* and *.DE* ) with table commands ( *.TS* and *.TE* ) and adding a few more commands to improve the appearance of the text.

1. Prepare the text for formatting again:

   a. Start another editing session with *pfl.deal.*

   b. Change *.DS* to *.TS* (line 8) and *.DE* to *.TE* (line 12), then add the five extra lines shown below and insert the colons, leaving the rest of the text unchanged:

```
.TS                          [Start of table]
center ;                     [Center the table]
c c c c                      [Center each heading]
l n n l .                    [Allow four columns*]
Name Height Weight Team      [These are the headings,
                             separated by tabs]
```

```
.sp 1                       [Leave a space after the
                            headings]
Emerson, Ezekiel R.    6'5"   273   Rochester
Robinson, Charles F.   6'3"   287   Des Moines
Peterson, Paul N.      5'9"   178   Tupelo
.TE                      [End of table]
```

[ * Columns 1 and 4: left-justified; columns 2 and 3: numeric ]

c. Store the text and return to the UNIX shell prompt.

2. Format the text on your screen with **nroff**:

a. Type a command line that passes the standard output of **tbl** via a pipeline to **nroff** with the **-ms** option:

```
$ tbl pfl.deal | nroff -ms
```

```
Dear Mr. Madison:

 The purpose of this letter is to confirm Monday's agree-
ment. Tupelo gets "Porkchop" Peterson, you get "Earthquake"
Emerson, and we get "Rotunda" Robinson. Here are the
players' names, heights, weights, and new teams:

         Name            Height Weight     Team
Emerson, Ezekiel R.      6'5"    273     Rochester
Robinson, Charles F.     6'3"    287     Des Moines
Peterson, Paul N.        5'9"    178     Tupelo

 You will be getting one of the finest players in
the People's Football League.
           Your Friend and Mine, Chuck


                September 2, 1985
```

b. This time **tbl** has taken over the task of formatting the tabular material in the middle of the letter, with the results shown. **.ne** **tbl**

## *Using the tbl Preprocessor* **tbl**

In the previous example, you used one **nroff** dot command ( *.sp 1* ), two **tbl** dot commands ( *.TS* and *TE* ), and a number of symbols that describe the desired appearance of the table. Here is an instant replay of the commands and symbols you just used in the example:

| | |
|---|---|
| `.TS` | Start of table. |
| `center` | Center the entire table between the side margins. |
| `;` | End of layout for the entire table; start of layout for individual lines. |
| `c c c c` | Center each of four headings over their columns (there could also be two, three, or a larger number of headings). |
| `l n n l` | Position the columns of information as indicated (in this case, left-justified, numeric, numeric, left-justified). |
| `.` | End of layout of individual lines; start of information to appear in the table. |
| | [Column headings within the table, separated by tabs] |
| `.sp 1` | Leave one space (blank line) between the headings and the columns below (**nroff** command). |
| | [Actual contents of the table entered here, separated by tabs] |
| `.TE` | End of table. |

# Using Double-Column Format

## *Setting Up the Text* **.2C**

If you would like to see your text in narrower columns, you can have **ms** print your document in double-column format with the .2C command. Then use the .1C command to revert to single-column format.

```
.2C
.LP
222222222222222222                  222222222     2222222222
2222222222222222                    222222222     2222222222
222222222222222222222222.           222222222     2222222.
.1C
.LP                                 11111111111111111111111
11111111111111111111111             11111111111111111111111
11111111111111111111111.            1111111111.
```

## *Preparing the Output for Your Printer* **col**

Ordinarily, a printer will be able to print a document in more than one column only if the printer is capable of reversing the motion of the paper. Since most printers do **not** have this capability, you usually have to pipe the text from **nroff** to a **filter program** called **col** (columns) and then on to **lpr.** The **col** program rearranges the text in such a way that the printer is not required to reverse the motion of the paper. (This also applies to text that you plan to preview on your screen.)

Any time you use **col**, it is a good idea to specify the type of printer to which you are sending the text. You can do this by including the **-T** (type) option with the **nroff** command. For example, to specify a line printer, type *-t*, followed by *lp* (line printer), or *-Tlp* on the command line. For example, to print a file called *story* in double-column format, you could use this:

```
$ nroff -ms -Tlp story | col | lpr
$ _
```

You must also use **col** whenever you use either the "box" or "allbox" option with **tbl**. (These options go on the same line as the "center" option.)

## *A Two-Column Example*

To see an example of two-column printing very quickly, make a copy of file *disks* called *disks.2C*, then begin an editing session with *disks.2C* and add the six formatting requests shown below. Now the first ten lines of the text will look like this:

```
.PP
.pl 32
.DS C
       Advertisement
* * * * * * * * * * * * * * * * * *
.DE
.2C
.PL
Spinrite diskettes have a lifetime
```

With these formatting requests in place, execute the following command line:

```
$ nroff -ms disks.2C | col
```

**.2C**
**col**

Advertisement

* * * * * * * * * * * * * * * * * * *

Spinrite diskettes have a lifetime guarantee. That's right, every Spinrite diskette is guaranteed for life. Not two years, not three years, not five years, but life.

Advanced technology makes it possible. Sophisticated marketing makes it incredible. Superior distribution makes it available. And state-of-the-art manufacturing makes it.

No matter what you've read, no matter what you've heard, no matter what you've thought, our warranty stands: Every Spinrite diskette will last until it wears out. That's quality, and that's our guarantee.

Don't settle for anything less. Don't waste your time with the amateurs. Step up to the pro- fessionals. Step up to Spinrite.

September 4, 1985

## Other Features

We have been able to offer only a brief sampling of the features of **nroff**. There are also additional commands; additional macro packages; additional preprocessors; and features for switching between files, using different units of length, creating your own macro commands, and changing **nroff**'s default values. Some of the other preprocessors of Version 7 are **refer**, which produces a listing of bibliographic references; **eqn** and **neqn**, which handle mathematical expressions; and **pic**, which handles pictorial representations. For further information, see Volume 2 of the **UNIX Programmer's Manual.**

## Example: Creating an Index

This section allows you to use what you have learned in Part IV, and also provides you with a very useful set of tools. Producing an index for a book or other long document can be quite a tedious and difficult task. Once you have selected the words and phrases to be included in the index, you have to alphabetize them and then combine different references to each item.

UNIX offers some excellent, time-saving tools to make the job easier for you. These tools are not completely automatic, so there will still be some work to do manually—but not nearly as much as if you had to work with a pencil and index cards. Let's suppose that you want an index that looks something like this:

```
antelope  23, 24, 51
bear, grizzly  37, 38
coyote  75
deer  82, 84, 85
```

You can use the UNIX **sort** command to alphabetize the list for you, then apply some of the text-processing commands you have learned. You will still have to enter the original list of items, but you will be relieved of a major chore. One of the options of the **sort** command makes sure that capitalized items (like "Fox") end up next to their non-capitalized counterparts (like "fox").

## *Starting with a New Directory*

Let's start by creating a new subdirectory in your home directory to contain your index, then move to this directory to create the index:

```
$ mkdir index          [Create subdirectory index]
$ cd index             [Move to this subdirectory]
$ pwd                  [Verify that you are now in it]
/usr/robin/index       [You are]
$ _
```

## *Creating the Preliminary List*

In a real-life situation, you would be working with a complete book, which could require hundreds of initial items to be indexed. However, to keep this exercise brief, we'll use another miniature example (a five-page book on wildlife). The basic procedures are the same, no matter how long the book is. We'll show the text-entry with **ed**, but you could also use another editor.

1. Begin editing with a file called *list.prelim:*

```
$ ed list.prelim
?list.prelim

_
```

2. Starting on the first page of the book, enter each word or phrase to be indexed, a colon, a space, then the page number:

```
a
geese: 1
fox: 1
```

```
fox: 2
deer: 2
elk: 3
antelope: 3
Fox, George P.: 4      [Entries of more than one name are fine]
coyote: 4
deer: 4
wolf, grey: 5
coyote: 5
deer: 5
.
_
```

3. Store this list and return to the UNIX shell:

```
w
118
q
$ _
```

The order in which you enter the items doesn't really matter. Entering them in sequential order is probably the most convenient. If you leave out an item while you're on one page and then think of it while you're on a later page, there's no problem. All the items are going to be sorted anyway.

## *Alphabetizing the List*

Now that you have a preliminary list of items to form an index, the next step is to alphabetize the list. To do this, use the UNIX **sort** command. Since your list contains some items in capital letters, you will want to use the **-f** option to merge uppercase and lowercase letters.

1. Alphabetize the list with **sort** and display the results:

```
$ sort -t: +0 -1 +1n -f list.prelim
antelope:  3
coyote:  4
coyote:  5
deer:  2
deer:  4
deer:  5
elk:  3
Fox, George P.:  4
fox:  1
fox:  2
geese:  1
```

```
wolf, grey:  5
$ _
```

Since we really want the results in a file, rather than displayed on the screen, we can use the **-o** option to send the output to another file. (The **-o** option here works just like the redirection symbol for output (>).)

2. Alphabetize the list with **sort** and send the results to a file called *list.final:*

```
$ sort -t: -f +0 -1 +1n -o list.sort list.prelim
$ _
```

Here is a brief explanation of the **sort** command:

| | |
|---|---|
| `-t:` | Use a colon (:) as the tab character, or field separator. For each entry, field 1 will be the subject and field 2 will be the page number (or page numbers). |
| `-f` | Fold uppercase letters onto lowercase. |
| `+0 -1 +1n` | Once the page numbers are in order (**+1n**), sort the subjects (**+0 -1**). This is what allows you to enter the items in any order. |
| `-o list.sort` | Place the output in a file called *list.sort.* |

## *Formatting the List*

Now that you have an alphabetized list of items, you are close to having a final index. But there are still a few things left to be done, such as combining page numbers that refer to the same subject. As a first step in that direction, we'll use **awk** to delete the subject description for all entries after the first in the list. (We'll also have **awk** replace the colons with blank spaces.) Use **cat** to enter the **awk** statements into a file called *combine,* then execute **awk** with the **-f** option to name this file.

1. Enter the **awk** statements:

   a. Type the following with **cat**, using the TAB key for spacing:

```
$ cat > combine
BEGIN       { FS = ":"; subject = " "; n = 0 }
$1=subject  { entry[n] = entry[n] "," $2; break }
            { n++; entry[n] = $1 " " $2; subject = $1 }
END         { for ( i = 1; i <= n; i++ ) print entry[i]}
                                      [CTRL-D]
$ _
```

   b. Here is a brief explanation of the statements:

| | |
|---|---|
| `BEGIN` | This pattern statement, analogous to END, allows you to set things up before any records have been read. |
| `FS = ":"` | Use the colon as a **field separator** to simplify matters; now we can forget about commas and spaces that occur in subject entries (for example, "wolf, grey"); the subject description becomes field 1, and the page number becomes field 2. |
| `subject = " "` | This variable is used to store the subject description for the previous entry on the list. |
| `$1==subject` | Check to see if the current subject description matches the previous one; if it does, execute the two action statements that follow. |
| `entry[n] =`<br>`  entry[n] "," $2` | Insert a comma, then add the new page number ($2) to the current entry. |
| `break` | Skip the action statements that follow. |
| | If the current subject description does **not** match the previous one, execute the following three action statements: |
| `n++` | Increase the entry number by one. |
| `entry[n] =`<br>`  $1 " " $2` | Remove the colon from the new entry; otherwise leave the entry the same. |
| `subject = $1` | Let the new subject become the "previous subject" for the entry that follows. |
| `END` | Execute the following action statement after all records have been read and processed:<br><br>`{ for (i=1; i<=n; i++) print entry[i] }`<br><br>Print all the entries from beginning (i=1) to end (i=n). |

The logic behind this **awk script** is fairly simple:

- if the subject of the current entry is different from the subject of the previous entry, increase the entry count (n) by one and leave the entry alone (except for removing the colon)
- if the subject of the current entry is the same as the subject of the previous entry, add the current page number to the existing list of page numbers, separated by a comma

Then at the end, print all the entries in order. (If you're having trouble following this, don't worry about it. It isn't essential to understand exactly how this **script** works; you can still use it to create an index, and save a lot of time.)

2. Use these statements in an **awk** command line:

   a. The best way to see what these statements do is to try them out on a command line, looking at the results on the screen:

```
$ awk -f combine list.sort
antelope  3
coyote  4, 5
deer  2, 4, 5
elk  3
Fox, George P.  4
fox  1, 2
geese  1
wolf, grey  5
$ _
```

   b. The index is done.

## *Combine the Commands*

Let's consolidate these two commands into one simple command for you to use.

1. Eliminate the intermediate files:

   a. To eliminate the intermediate files, we'll use pipelines to connect all the commands together (they will fit on one line):

```
$ sort -t: -f +0 -1 +1n list.prelim | awk -f combine
antelope  3
coyote  4, 5
deer  2, 4, 5
elk  3
Fox, George P.  4
fox  1, 2
geese  1
wolf, grey  5
$ _
```

   b. There it is in one step. But we can make it even easier still.

2. Give this command line its own name:

   a. Use **cat** to enter the command line into a file called *index:*

```
$ cat > index
sort -t: -f +0 -1 +1n $1 | awk -f combine
                                        [CTRL-D]
$ _
```

b. Use **chmod** to make *index* executable:

```
$ chmod u+x index
$ _
```

You have just created your own **index** command, which you can use to create an index from any list of items entered as described earlier in this section. From now on, this is all you will have to type a command like this:

```
$ index list.prelim                                  [screen output]
```

or this

```
$ index list.prelim > list.final                     [file output]
```

If you would like further explanation of the expression $1 used above, see Part V ("Programming the UNIX Shell").

### Formatting

Finally, to have your index printed in two columns (as is customary), you can place these **ms** requests at the beginning of file "list.final":

```
.PP
.2C
```

You can then print the index in two columns by executing a command like this:

```
$ nroff -ms -Tlp list.final |col| lpr
$ _
```

## Summary of Chapter 20

In this chapter you learned to initiate formatting with **nroff**, using various options with **nroff**, formatting tables with **tbl**, and printing in double-column format with **ms**.

### Initiating Formatting

**Executing an** nroff **command line.** To preview formatting on your screen, simply type a command line with the name of the command ( *nroff* ), a space, and the name of the file to be formatted. For printed results, send the output of **nroff** to the **lpr** print spooler via a pipeline.

**Specifying a macro package.** To use the **ms** macro package, include the **-ms** option between *nroff* and the name of the file. This package is stored in */usr/lib/tmac/tmac.s.* Other macro packages are also stored in the same directory.

| Other options | |
|---|---|
| Starting page number | **-n*p*** |
| Specific pages | **-o*p*** |
| Pausing between pages | **-s*n*** |
| Specifying a printer | **-T*name*** |

## *Some Basic nroff Requests*

**Requests discussed in this chapter:**

| | |
|---|---|
| **.pl** | Page length |
| **.ll** | Line length |
| **.po** | Page offset |
| **.pn** | Page number |
| .bp | Page break |
| .ne | Need (lines together) |

**Other requests:**

| | | |
|---|---|---|
| **.fi** | | Turn on filling |
| **.nf** | | No filling |
| | **l** | flush left |
| | **r** | flush right |
| **.ad** | **c** | Adjust centered |
| | **b** | both* |
| | **n** | normal* |
| | | * flush left and right |
| **.na** | | No adjustment |
| **.hy n** | | Hyphenation |
| **.nh** | | No hyphenation |
| **.br** | | Break to a new line |
| **.ls n** | | Line spacing n |
| **.ce n** | | Center next n lines |
| **.ul** | | Underline |
| **.cu** | | Continuous underline |
| **.in n** | | Indent to n |
| **.ti n** | | Temporary indentation |
| % | | Page number |
| **u** | | Superscript |
| **d** | | Subscript |

**Formatting Tables.** To format a table, place .TS above the headings and information and .TE below, with the appropriate descriptions typed between .TS and the body of the table. Then execute a command like this:

```
$ tbl file | nroff -ms | lpr
```

**Using Double-Column Format.** To print text in two columns side by side, precede the text with .2C. Then execute a command line like this:

```
$ nroff -ms -Tlp file | col | lpr
```

# V

# *Programming the UNIX Shell*

# 21

# Introduction to the Bourne Shell

## Introduction

Until now you have known the UNIX shell as the command interpreter. As the command interpreter, the shell, which itself is not part of the operating system, provides an interface between you and the kernel by executing comands entered at the terminal. The shell also serves as a programming language. As a programming language, the shell allows you to create your own programs called shell programs, or shell files, as you will learn in Chapter 24.

### *The Shell Start-Up File* **.profile**

Your home directory probably contains a file that provides the shell with default values for initialization. This file, which must be called *.profile*, contains information used by the shell to set up your working environment, such as your terminal type, the prompts that will appear on your screen, the names of the UNIX directories that contain the commands you use, the name of the file that contains your electronic mail, the protection that a new file will receive when created, and settings for your terminal.

Whenever you log in, if your home directory has a file named *.profile*, the shell will execute this file before issuing you a prompt. If there is no *.profile* file, the shell will use its own default values for variables. Here are the contents of a typical *.profile* file:

```
TERM=VT100                          [Set the terminal type]
PS1='% '                            [Set the primary prompt]
PS2='> '                            [Set the secondary prompt]
PATH=/bin:/usr/bin:$HOME/bin::      [Set the command search path]
```

**.profile**

| | |
|---|---|
| `MAIL=/usr/spool/mail/`basename $HOME`` | [Set your mail box's path name] |
| `umask Ø22` | [Set file creation mask] |
| `: set tty` <br> `stty erase "^H" -tabs` <br> `stty crØ ffØ` <br> `export MAIL HOME PATH TERM` | [Set information about your terminal: CTRL H to erase; replace tabs with spaces when printing; no delay for carriage return or form feed; export four shell variables—see below] |

## *Shell Variables*

A system administrator usually creates ".profile" when adding a new user's account to the system, and also defines variables such as TERM, PS1, PS2, PATH, HOME, and MAIL. However, you can edit *.profile* with a text editor and redefine any of these variables as needed. You will find a summary of the variables in Table 21-1, with detailed descriptions following.

**Table 21-1. Shell variables.**

| *Variable* | *Description* |
|---|---|
| HOME | *Login Directory*. The login program initializes HOME to the name of the directory that becomes your current directory after you log in. Then any time you execute the **cd** command without an argument, the shell automatically returns you to this directory. |
| MAIL | *Mail File*. When this variable is defined, it tells the shell the name of the file that serves as your mail file and informs you when new mail arrives. |
| PATH | *Command File Search Path*. This variable is used by the shell to search through a sequence of directories for a command whenever you supply a partial pathname. PATH is assigned by entering a list of filenames, separated by colons. Its default value is <br><br> `:/bin:/usr/bin` <br><br> which means, "First look in the current directory, then in /bin in the top directory, then look in */usr/bin*." |
| PS1 | *Primary Prompt*. Use this variable to assign the prompt to be used by the shell when it is ready to accept input. |
| PS2 | *Secondary Prompt*. Use this variable to assign the prompt to be used by a subshell to receive additional input. |

# Setting Variables

## *The Primary Prompt* **PS1**

When the shell is ready to accept a command from your terminal, it issues a prompt. The dollar sign ($) is the default prompt. You can make your own prompt by changing the value of the **PS1** variable:

```
$ PS1='Ready '     [Set the primary prompt to Ready —with a space]
Ready _            [This is your new primary prompt]
```

Note the space that follows *Ready*. This separates the prompt from your command line. From now on until you sign off from the system or reassign the value of PS1, your primary prompt will be *Ready* instead of the dollar sign ($). For the sake of clarity, we will use the dollar sign as the primary prompt throughout this chapter.

## *The Secondary Prompt* **PS2**

The **PS2** variable is used by the shell to inform you that it expects further input. The default value for PS2 is the greater than sign (>). Here is an example:

```
$ (
> cd /bin
> ls -l
> )
$ _
```

The shell interprets *(* as the command grouping symbol. Then the shell creates a subshell, which issues the > prompt to indicate that it is reading and will not execute any commands until you inform the shell that you finished your entry by typing *)*. If you accidentally press the wrong key and get the secondary prompt, the DEL key will get you out, and you will see the primary prompt again. The above example is used to illustrate one of the cases when the shell issues its secondary prompt PS2. Command grouping is discussed in greater detail in Chapter 22. You can change the secondary prompt the same way you change the primary prompt:

```
$ PS2='more please '     [Set the secondary prompt to more please]
$ _
```

Your shell secondary prompt now is set to *more please* .

## *Terminal Type* **TERM**

The terminal variable **TERM** should be set to obtain the proper display on your terminal. The value assigned to TERM should be one of the terminal names given in the file */etc/termcap*. You can set the **TERM**, **PATH**, and **MAIL** variables the same way you set the prompts, as shown here:

```
$ PATH=:/bin:/usr/bin:$HOME/bin
$ TERM=adm3a
$ MAIL=/usr/spool/mail/'basename $HOME'
$ _
```

## *Home Directory* **HOME**

Generally, the **HOME** variable should not be changed. However, in some instances after login, you may want to reinitialize it so you will be put right back into the desired directory without retyping a long pathname, as shown here:

```
$ HOME=/usr/jim/project/planning/report
$ _
```

Recall that the **cd** command without arguments returns you to your home directory (the value of variable HOME). So if you set HOME as shown in the previous example, typing the **cd** command will have the same effect as if you had typed this:

```
$ cd /usr/jim/project/planning/report
$ _
```

## *Exporting Shell Variables*

As shown earlier in this chapter, the TERM, PATH, MAIL, PS1, PS2 variables, along with the **stty** command are defined in *.profile*, making it unnecessary for you to have to set them every time you log in. Normally, these variables should be **exported**, so that any **child processes** can inherit them. (Child processes will be explained later in this chapter.)

Should the exported variable be modified in a child process, these new values will take effect within this child process only, and the previous value will be automatically restored when the child process returns to its parent process. Place the **export** command at the end of your *.profile* file, as shown earlier in this chapter. You can ask the shell to display all the exported variables by typing *export*, as in this example:

```
$ export
MAIL HOME PATH TERM
$ _
```

You can also ask the shell to display the values of shell variables with the **echo** command (**echo** is explained in Chapter 23):

```
$ echo $HOME
/usr/joe
$ _
```

## Commands and Arguments

As the command interpreter, the shell reads command lines entered at your terminal or from a file, interprets the first word as the command name, and any remaining words as arguments. Then, using the command name, the shell searches for the command file, invokes it, and passes all pertinent arguments to it. Arguments that have special meaning to the shell (such as &, |, >>, >, $, *) will not be passed to the command program, but will be retained for interpretation by the shell itself. These special symbols, called **metacharacters**, are discussed later in this chapter. Let's examine the following example:

```
$ mv file1 file2 &
$ _
```

The shell seaches for a command file named *mv*, invokes *mv*, passes *file1* and *file2* to *mv* as arguments, but retains *&* for its own use, interpreting *&* as a request for execution of this command line as a background process. (Background processes are explained in detail later in this section.) Some commands require only one argument, some require more (as in the previous example), and some do not require any arguments, as in this example:

```
$ pwd
/usr/jim/zebra
$ _
```

The **pwd** (print working directory) command displays the full pathname of your current directory. (Refer to the **UNIX User's Manual** for details about each command.) At any rate, even the simplest command requires at least one character, as the case of the *l* command, which lists all filenames in the current directory.

### *How the Shell Invokes Commands*

When you log into UNIX, you are assigned a copy of the shell as the new "parent process." This allows you to use all the resources of the

**TERM**
**HOME**

operating system for which you have permission. From this parent shell process, the shell invokes a command file by creating a new duplicate shell process called a "child process." The parent shell process then waits for this "child process" to complete its execution, provided that the command file is actually a compiled program. On the other hand, if the command file is a shell procedure, the shell will simply read the file and invoke the commands inside it. (Shell procedures are described in Chapter 24.) Figure 21-1 shows the relationship between parent and child processes.

The act of creating a duplicate process is called "forking," and the child process is also called a "forked process." A child process can fork to create another new process, thereby becoming a parent shell process of its own child, while its parent process becomes a "grandparent."

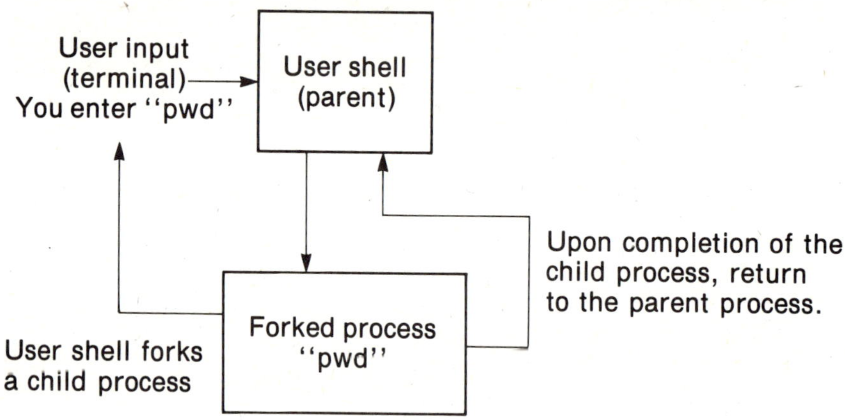


Figure 21-1. An example of forking.

### How the Shell Finds Commands

If you know the exact location of the command file, you can invoke it by giving the full pathname. If you do this, the shell will not search anywhere else to find it. For example, suppose there is a command named *greeting* in directory */usr/jim/print* that displays this message *WELCOME TO UNIX*. You can then identify the location of this command to the shell explicitly:

```
$ /usr/jim/print/greeting
WELCOME TO UNIX
$ _
```

If you don't provide the shell with a full pathname, the shell will use either the value of the **PATH** variable defined in your *.profile* file or its own default value to perform a search for the command. As explained earlier in this chapter, **PATH** may be set with colons (:) separating the directories to be searched, like this:

```
PATH=/bin:/usr/bin::$HOME/bin:
```

If **PATH** in your *.profile* file is set like this, the shell will first attempt to locate *greeting* in the */bin* directory. If the shell doesn't find *greeting* there, it will next search through */usr/bin*. If the shell doesn't find *greeting* there, it will try your current directory (the extra colon). Finally, if the shell doesn't find *greeting* in your current directory, it will try the subdirectory of your home directory (**$HOME**) called */bin*.

For example, if you want to find out who is currently logged on the system, and you are logged in as Jim, type

```
$ who
jim
$ _
```

In this case, the shell found *who* in directory */bin*. By rearranging the names listed after the PATH variable, you can have the shell search from your current directory first by placing the ':' right after the equal sign:

```
PATH=:$HOME/bin:/bin:/usr/bin
```

With this arrangement, you can keep private copies of public commands or custom commands in your directory, even if your commands have the same names as public commands. It is best to keep all of your commands in one directory, so that you don't have to memorize many search paths when you want to invoke one of them. UNIX users usually keep private commands in their *bin* (binary) subdirectory.

The name *bin* is used because most files in this directory are object files, stored in binary form. The top *bin* directory (*/bin*) contains system commands, while the */usr/bin* directory contains user utility commands. Any user can usually use commands in either of these directories. If your PATH is set as shown in the example above, the shell will first search in your current directory, then your subdirectory *bin* before searching through another *bin*.

When setting the **PATH** variable, be careful about the order in which you arrange the directories. If you aren't careful about this, you will cause the system to waste valuable time making inefficient and unnecessary searches. For example, consider a **PATH** setting like this:

```
$ PATH=:/usr/diag/bin:$HOME/bin:/usr/john/bin:/usr/bin:/bin:
```

Every time you enter a command residing in */bin*, the shell is forced to go through these six steps before it can find and execute the command:

(Your current directory)
/usr/diag/bin
$HOME/bin

```
/usr/john/bin
/usr/bin
/bin
```

If your most frequently-used commands reside in */bin* and */usr/bin*, you place an unecessary burden on the system unless you rearrange the setting for **PATH** more efficiently, as in this example:

```
$ PATH=/bin:/usr/bin::$HOME/bin:/usr/john/bin:/usr/diag/bin
```

Now the shell will search for commands in the following order, and the shell can locate your commands faster:

```
/bin
/usr/bin
(Your current directory)
$HOME/bin
/usr/john/bin
/usr/diag/bin
```

## Standard Input, Output, and Diagnostics

Whenever a command begins execution, three files are opened, each associated with a number called a **file descriptor**:

- Standard input (file descriptor 0) from terminal or argument file
- Standard output (file descriptor 1) to terminal or file
- Standard diagnostic output (file descriptor 2) to terminal or file.

In each case, the terminal is the default standard input or output. For example, suppose there is a file named *message* in your current directory that contains *WELCOME TO UNIX*. When you type

```
$ cat message
WELCOME TO UNIX
$ _
```

the **cat** command reads from its standard input (that is, the contents of file *message*), then prints out the contents to its standard output (that is, your terminal).

Any diagnostic output of **cat** is also directed to your terminal. If the file *message* is not in your current directory or you do not have read permission for *message*, an error message will be written to **cat**'s diagnostic output (that is, your terminal), as in this example:

```
$ cat message
cat: can't open message
$ _
```

Furthermore, If you don't provide a file argument for **cat**, **cat** will read what you type as its input, and then display the output on your screen:

```
$ cat
this is a test <cr>     [cat takes this input]
<∧D>                    [end of output]
this is a test          [then displays this output on the screen]
$ _
```

In this example, <cr> is the RETURN key and <∧D> is CTRL-D. You can also use the **cat** command to enter text into a file by directing its output to a file:

```
$ cat > text.file
I am using cat to create my own little file. <cr>
This is the second line of text in my little file. <cr>
<∧D>
$ _
```

Now you have a file called *text.file*, whose contents become whatever you type at the keyboard. (Then CTRL-D terminates the text.)

## Redirection of Input and Output

In the previous section you learned about standard input and output. There will be times when you may want to change the input or output of a command to something other than its standard input or output. You can do this with redirection, using one of these symbols:

< **file** Redirect command input from *file*
> **file** Redirect command output to *file*
>> **file** Append command output to *file*

### *Redirection of Input*

The default standard input of the **mail** command is what you type at your terminal. You can send an existing file instead of keystrokes as your message with the **mail** command by redirecting the input from that file, as in

```
$ mail jim < letter
$ _
```

Now the **mail** command will read file *letter* as its input and send it to Jim.

## Redirection of Output

If you have permission to write to a device or a file, you can use one of them as the output for any command that sends its output to the standard output, as in this example:

```
$ cat message > file_1
$ _
```

In this example, the **cat** command reads the contents of file *message*, and write its output to *file__1*. If *file__1* does not exist, it will be created by the shell; if *file__1* already exists, its contents will be overwritten. If you do not have permission to write to *file__1*, you will see a message like this:

```
$ cat message > file_1
cat: can't create file_1
$ _
```

You can also use **cat** to send a file to the printer, as in this example:

```
$ cat message > /dev/lp
$ _
```

Or you may want to send your file to another output port, as in this example:

```
$ cat message > /dev/tty05
$ _
```

In a shell procedure, you may need to create a empty file. You can do so with the redirection symbol, as shown in this example:

```
$ > empty.file     [Create a file called empty.file]
```

## Redirection of Output with File Descriptors

You can direct standard output or diagnostic output to different files or devices by adding the appropriate file descriptors, as in this example:

```
$ cat message 1>&file.out 2>&file.error
$ _
```

The contents of file *message* will go to *file.out*, while any error message that may arise will be sent to *file.error*. You may want to redirect both standard output and standard error output to the same file in this way:

```
$ cat message 1>&file.all 2>&1
$ _
```

You can append to the end of a file without overwriting its contents by using the double greater than symbol (> >) to add to the end of the file:

```
$ cat message > file.both
$ cat greeting >> file.both
$ _
```

Now *file.both* contains all the contents of file *message* plus all the contents of file *greeting*.

### A Note on Redirection

Only standard input and output of a command can be redirected. For example, the **date** command always consults the system, then displays the current date and time on your screen (that is, its input is not standard, and therefore it cannot be redirected). As another example, the output of the **lpr** command is always directed to the printer port (that is, its output is not standard, and therefore it cannot be redirected). If you are not certain about a particular command, consult the **UNIX User's Manual** before attempting to redirect its input or output.

## Summary of Chapter 18

In this chapter you learned about the UNIX shell. This included discussions of the shell start-up file (*.profile*); shell variables; commands and arguments; standard input, output, and diagnostics; and redirection of input and output.

### Introduction

This chapter begins a discussion of the UNIX shell as a programming language.

**The shell start-up file.** This file (*.profile*), which resides in your home directory, is executed immediately after you log in. Its contents provide UNIX information about your terminal and set your primary prompt, secondary prompt, command search path, the path name of your mail box, file creation mode, and various things that relate to the operation of your terminal.

**Shell variables.** Here are the shell variables commonly defined in **.profile**:

| | |
|---|---|
| **PS1** | Primary prompt |
| **PS2** | Secondary prompt |
| **TERM** | Terminal type |

| | |
|---|---|
| **PATH** | Command file search path |
| **MAIL** | Mail file |
| **HOME** | Login directory |

To obtain the value of a variable, precede its name with a dollar sign ($), as in

```
$ echo $HOME
/usr/robin
```

## *Setting shell variables*

You can execute a command line after the UNIX shell prompt to set the value of any shell variable. This has the same effect as placing the same line in *.profile*. The process of extending the settings of shell variables to all **child processes** executed at your terminal is called **exporting** the variables. This is accomplished with the **export** command.

## *Commands and arguments*

A command line to be processed by the shell must contain a command name, and may contain arguments and special symbols called **metacharacters** that provide the shell with special instructions. For example, in the command line

```
$ mv file.1 file.2 &
```

**mv** is the name of a command file, *file.1* and *file.2* are arguments, and & tells the shell to execute **mv** as a background process.

**How the shell invokes commands.** Whenever you log into UNIX, you are assigned a copy of the shell as the new "parent process." When the shell invokes a compiled program, the shell creates a new process called a "child process" to execute the program. This is called "forking," and the child process is also referred to as a "forked process."

When the shell executes a shell procedure, it simply reads the file and invokes the commands found in the file.

**How the shell finds commands.** If you do not provide the shell with a full pathname, the shell will use the value of the PATH variable to search for the command. The value of PATH is a list of pathnames where commands may be found.

## *Standard input, output, and diagnostics*

Whenever the shell begins to execute a command, the shell opens three files, each associated with a number called a **file descriptor**:

Standard input (0)
Standard output (1)
Standard diagnostic output (2)

**Redirection of input and output.** You can use redirection to change input or output, using one of these symbols:

| | |
|---|---|
| < | Redirect command input from a file |
| > | Redirect command output to a file |
| >> | Append command output to a file |

To redirect selected command output, precede the redirection symbol with a file descriptor, as in this example:

```
$ cat msg 1>&out 2>&error
```

Redirection is not possible with every UNIX command. Some cannot accept input and some do not produce output. Redirection is possible only with standard input or standard output. To be certain, check the **UNIX User's Manual.**

# 22

# Bourne Shell Processes

## Background Commands

To make it possible to run more than one process at your terminal, add an ampersand (&) after the last argument of your command string. This allows you to proceed immediately to another command without having to wait for the first one to be completed. For example:

```
$ cc program.c &
308
$ _
```

calls up the C compiler to compile the source code in file *program.c* in the background. The shell initiates this process, then the kernel assigns it a process number (308 in this example). The number of processes that you can have running at the same time is limited by the system. If you exceed this limit, a warning message will be sent to your terminal. The larger the number of processes running at any given time (foreground or background), the slower the system is able to respond.

Executing a command as a background process does not alter the command's inputs and outputs. So if the standard input of the background process is from your terminal, this input may be disrupted by anything you type for the current foreground process; if the standard output of the background process is to your terminal, this output will disturb the display of the current foreground process. To avoid this, it is best to redirect the input and output of background processes. To change the standard output of the background process, use the **nohup** (no hangup) command, as in this example:

```
$ nohup cmp file1 file2 &
320
Sending output to 'nohup.out'
$ _
```

The output of the **cmp** command will be sent to *nohup.out*. If *nohup.out* does not exist, it will be created by the shell; if it does exist, output will be appended to the end of *nohup.out*. If *nohup.out* in your current directory doesn't have write permission, the shell will direct output to *nohup.out* in your home directory (*$HOME/nohup.out*).

The **nohup** command makes your process immune to hangup and quit signals that could be caused by hanging up on a dial-up line. For this reason, **nohup** is best for keeping a background process running after you log out from a dial-up line.

## *Background Processes*

**ps**

At some point you may want to know if your background processes have completed (or failed). To view the status of background processes, use the **ps** (process status) command. The **ps** command displays information about active processes, with several different options. When **ps** is executed without any options, **ps** displays only active processes associated with the current terminal, as shown in this example:

```
$ cc screen.c &
283
$ ps
PID TTY TIME CMD
283 02 0:02 cc screen.c
037 02 0:11 -sh
290 02 0:01  ps
$ _
```

The number assigned to your background process (*283*) appears in the first display line under the heading *PID* (process identifier), indicating that the background process you just invoked has started. The *TTY* column displays your current log-in port. The *TIME* column displays the cummulative execution time for the process. And, finally, in the *CMD* column you see displayed the commands currently in process. (Here, *−sh* represents the shell.) If you don't find your background process number on the list, it may be completed already.

When invoked with the *a* option, **ps** displays information on all active processes on the system, as shown in this example:

```
$ ps -a
PID  TTY  TIME  CMD
36   co   0:07  -sh
386  02   0:02   ps -a
37   02   0:12  -sh
$ _
```

As you can see, your current port (*02*) has only two processes, *ps −a* and *−sh*. Port *co* (the console) is idle (*−sh*).

To obtain a more detailed display of all active processes, include the *l* option, as shown here:

```
$ ps -al
F S UID PID PPID CPU PRI NICE ADDR SZ WCHAN TTY TIME CMD
1 S   0  36    1   0  28   20   67 16  5a20  co 0:07 -sh
1 S 203  37    1   0  30   20   49 16  6fd4  00 0:13 -sh
1 S   0 367    1   0  28   20   9b 16  193e  01 0:01 - 2
1 S   0 368    1   0  28   20   80 16  1970  02 0:01 - 2
1 S 203 283   37   0  30   20   96 44  703a  00 0:01 cc screen.c
1 R  12 421   37 117  59   20   66 28        00 0:08 ps -al
$ _
```

This gives you detailed information on system processes. In the paragraphs that follow, we discuss only those items that are within the scope of this book. (For other items, refer to the **UNIX Programming Manual**.)

- The *F* column displays the processes flag:

  *01* in core
  *02* indicates that this is the system process
  *04* the process is locked in core
  *10* the process is being swapped
  *20* indicates that the process is being traced by another process.

- The *S* column displays the state of the process:

  *S* indicates that the process is sleeping
  *R* indicates that the process is running
  *W* means that the process is waiting for another process to finish.

- The *UID* column displays the user ID. Your user ID is displayed for all processes invoked at your terminal. In some systems, the user name is displayed instead.

- The *PPID* column displays the process ID of the parent process. As you can see, process ID *37* is the parent of processes *283* and *421*.

- The *PRI* column displays the priority of the process based on the value at NICE. A **higher** number means a **lower** priority.

- The *NICE* column, as mentioned above, displays the value that is used to compute the priority of process. You can increase this value by using the **nice** command, explained in the next section.

- The *SZ* (SIZE) column displays the number of blocks used by the core image of the current process

- The *WCHAN* column, which is related to the *F* column, displays the

ps

event for which the process is sleeping, as indicated by the *S* flag in the *F* column. *WCHAN* is blank if the process is active.

- The *TIME* column displays the cumulative execution time of the process

## Priority of Processes

**nice**

UNIX is a multi-user, multi-tasking system. That is, more than one user can be logged at a given moment and each user can invoke more than one process at a time. Since computer time must be shared among the processes that are active, any process that has a higher priority will receive more computer time. When processes are first invoked, they all begin with the same priority level. However, since this implies that each process receives equal attention from the system's main processor, it can often mean slower operation for the system as a whole. To avoid this, you can use the **nice** command to assign less important processes a lower scheduling priority. Here is an example:

```
$ nice cc screen.c &
212
$ ps -al
F S UID PID PPID CPU PRI NICE ADDR SZ WCHAN TTY TIME CMD
1 S 203  30    1   0  30   20   44 16  6f4c  cc 0:09 -sh
1 S   0  31    1   0  28   20   49 16  190c  00 0:01 - 2
1 S 203 212   30  50  30   30   65 44  6ff6  co 0:01 cc screen.c
1 R  12 217   30 161  62   20   8e 28        co 0:09 ps -al
$ _
```

In the absence of an argument, **nice** increases the priority number of the process by 10 (which decreases its priority). That is why you see *30* in the third display line under *NICE* (the line for *cc screen.c*, with process ID *212*). If you prefer a number other than 10, you can provide any number in the range of 1 to 19 as an argument to the **nice** command. For example, to increase the priority number for *cc program.c* by 12, use this command line:

```
$ nice -12 cc program.c &
$ _
```

This sets the *NICE* value to *32* (20 + 12). Only the super-user can assign to a process a lower **nice** value than 20 (resulting in a higher priority for the process), since the **nice** command allows the super-user to use negative arguments, as shown in this example:

```
$ nice --10 cc screen.c &
285
$ _
```

This assigns to process *285* a priority number of 10 (a higher priority).

## *Terminating Background Processes*

**kill**

If you should ever have to terminate a background process (and you know its process ID), use the **kill** command, followed by the process ID as an argument. As you have learned, the shell displays the process ID at the time you invoke the background process. If you should forget the number, use the **ps** command to display it. Suppose you have a background process whose PID is 283 and you want to terminate it. You can execute this:

```
$ kill 283
$ _
```

You can then use the **ps** command to verify that process 283 is no longer displayed. If it still appears, then it hasn't stopped running. To make sure that a process is terminated, use the 9 option, as shown here:

```
$ kill -9 283
$ _
```

The kill signal generated by **kill −9** cannot be caught or ignored by the process indicated. If you use kill with the 9 option and the argument is either 0 or your login process number, you will log yourself off the system. Unless you have super-user status, you can kill only processes associated with your terminal.

# Connecting Processes

One of the advantages of using UNIX is that you have so many different ways of connecting processes. In this section you will learn three of these methods.

## *Pipelines*

A **pipeline** is a device that allows you to connect two processes by using the output of one as the input of another. The symbol that represents a pipeline on a command line is the vertical bar (|). For example, to count the number of files in the current directory, use this:

```
$ ls -l | wc -l
20
$ _
```

The **ls −l** command lists (in long format) the names of all the files in the current directory, each on a separate line. **wc −l** will count the number of lines in the output of **ls −l**, with the result displayed (20). The

**nice**
**kill**

shell will invoke the *pipe* function to connect the two commands as pictured here:

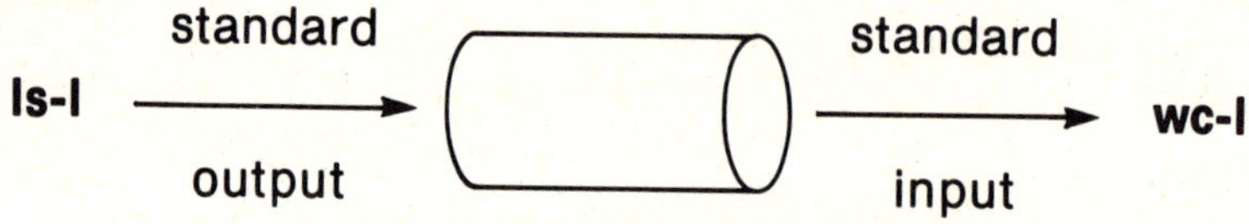


Figure 22-1. A pipeline illustrated.

The output of the **ls −l** command becomes the input of the **wc** command, which is the same as if you typed the following string of commands:

```
$ ls -l > tempfile; wc -l < tempfile; rm tempfile
20
$ _
```

The advantage of using a pipe is that the temporary file *tempfile* becomes unnecessary. You can also connect more than two commands with pipes, as shown here:

```
$ ls -l | grep text | lpr
```

This sequence of piped commands sends the filenames that match the pattern *text* to the printer.

A pipeline can connect only the standard output of the command on the left to the standard input of the command on the right. Just as it would make no sense to try to connect the closed ends of two lead pipes, it would make no sense to try to connect a process with no standard output to a process with no standard input. Some commands, such as **mail** and **lpr**, do not use standard input and output the way other commands do. If you tried to use **lpr** on the left-hand side of a pipeline, there would be no output to pipe.

## *Filter Programs*

Most UNIX commands read from the standard input, and then process data before sending it out to the standard output. These commands, such as **grep, sort, spell,** and **diff,** are called **filter programs** (or just **filters**). As an example of a filter, the **grep** command searches an input file for lines matching a pattern, as illustrated in this example:

```
$ ls -l | grep intro
```

Here **grep** takes the output of **ls −l** and selects only strings containing *intro* to be displayed on the screen. In this sense **grep** filters out strings of text, allowing some through and inhibiting others. Other commands like the following can't be thought of as filters: **ls, kill,** and **mail.**

## *Tees*

The **tee** command allows you to view data as it is being written to a file. If you type,

```
$ ls -l | tee dfile
$ _
```

all the file names in the current directory will be written to **dfile** and also displayed on screen, as illustrated in Figure 22-2.

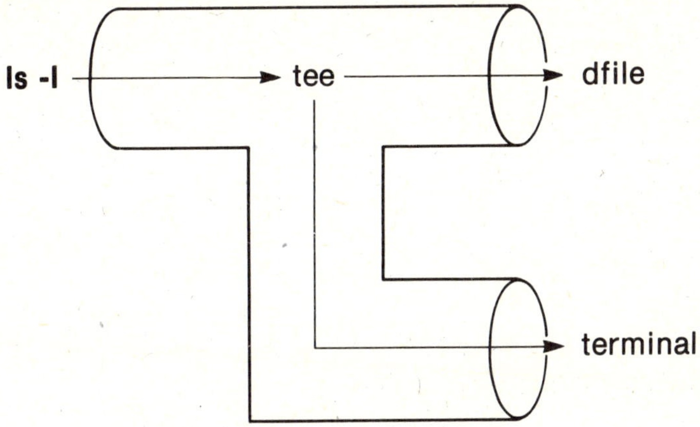


Figure 22-2. A tee illustrated.

Since the data is also sent to the terminal (standard output), you can use a pipeline to process this output, as shown here (see Figure 22-3).

```
$ ls -l | tee dfile | wc -l
20
$ _
```

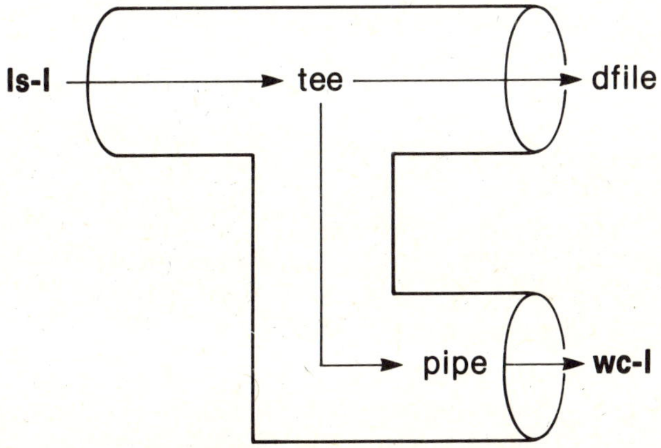


Figure 22-3. A tee with a pipe.

# Giving Directives to the Shell

## Command Grouping

Grouping a list of commands within parentheses causes the shell to create a subshell to read and execute the enclosed commands. This subshell has the ability to run the enclosed command without affecting the values of variables in the current shell. This feature allows the user, for instance, to slip into another directory, run a few commands, and then be automatically returned to the current working directory. Assuming that your current directory is your home directory, you can execute this command line:

```
$ (cd /usr/james/man.spec; nohup nroff doc1 | lpr &)
$ _
```

which is equivalent to

```
$ cd /usr/james/man.spec; nohup nroff doc1 | lpr & ; cd
$ _
```

Parentheses can appear anywhere on the command line. If the shell expects a right parenthesis but doesn't find it at the end of a command line, the shell will prompt with its secondary prompt (PS2) to let you know that it expects further input from you.

Grouping a list of commands within braces causes the shell to read and execute the enclosed commands, which produces the combined output. This method allows you to use the output of several commands as the input to another command, as in this example:

```
$ { nroff -mm text1; nroff -mm text2; } | col | lpr
$ _
```

Unlike parentheses, braces must be separated from the commands they enclose. The exit status of a set of commands grouped by either parentheses or braces is the exit status of the last command executed from the set.

## Conditional Execution

The shell provides a mechanism that allows you to invoke a command list in order with conditional execution. The command list is a sequence of one or more commands separated by semicolons (;), as in this example:

```
$ ls -l; who
-rw-r--r-- 1 john    27832 Jan 12 16:09 file1
-rwxr-xr-x 1 john     5358 Jan 15 14:16 file2
-rwxr-xr-x 1 john    13993 Feb 16 14:04 file3
```

```
john          tty20     Feb 16 11:34
$ _
```

The shell first invokes the **ls −l** command; then, when that has been completed, it invokes the **who** command.

You can have the shell perform additional execution by connecting two commands by either the AND-IF (&&) or the OR-IF (||) symbol. The format of an OR-IF statement is as follows:

```
$ command1 || command2
$ _
```

The shell invokes **command1** and examines its exit status. If **command1** fails, its exit-status will be non-zero and the shell will invoke **command2**. Here is an example:

```
$ mkdir sample                                  [Create directory sample]
$ rmdir sample > /dev/null || echo failure      [Remove directory sample]
$ rmdir sample > /dev/null || echo failure      [Remove directory sample]
failure
$ _
```

The second command line yields no message because the command to remove the directory (**rmdir sample**) is successful. However, the third command line does produce a message. Since the directory has already been removed as a result of the second command line, the shell executes **echo failure** when **rmdir sample** fails (cannot be executed).

The format of an AND-IF statement is

```
$ command1 && command2
$ _
```

This will cause **command2** to be invoked only if the execution of **command1** succeeds. Here is an example:

```
$ test -f .profile && cp .profile backup
$ _
```

The command **test −f .profile** checks to determine whether file *.profile* exists in the current directory. (The **test** command is described in detail in Chapter 24.) If you execute the above command line from your home directory where *.profile* is located, the shell will create a copy of it called *backup*. If you invoke the command line from one of your subdirectories (which doesn't contain *.profile*), nothing will happen.

## Pattern-Matching

The shell provides a means for generating its own list of filenames, based on a pattern-matching expression given as an argument. For example,

```
$ ls -l *.c
```

will cause the shell to generate a list of filenames that end in *.c* to be used as arguments in this command (that is, to be listed). Pattern-matching characters like * are sometimes called **metacharacters**, which are listed here:

```
*      Match any string of any length
?      Match any single character
[ ]    Match any of the characters enclosed
```

For example,

```
$ lpr *
```

matches all filenames in the current directory except those that start with a period (.), such as .profile.

```
$ ls -l [abcd]*
```

matches all names in the current directory that begin with a, b, c, or d.

```
$ ls -l [a-z]*
```

matches all names in the current directory that begin with a lowercase letter of the alphabet.

```
$ ls -l ch??k
```

matches all five-character names in the current directory that begin with *ch* and end with *k*, such as check, chink, ch12k, and so on.

Since the following metacharacters and other characters have special meanings to the shell, they should never be used in a name for any file or directory:

< > >> * ? & |

If you do attempt to use such characters, you may mislead the shell to interpret them rather than read them as arguments. For example, suppose you have a file named *files1*. If you try to change its name to *file?1*, this is what will happen:

```
$ mv files1 file?1
mv: files1 and files1 are identical
$ _
```

Why? Since *?* is a metacharacter, it will match any single character. Now try to change the above file to a different new name,

```
$ mv files1 file&1
148
1: not found
$ _
```

As you can see, the shell interprets the ampersand (&) in its special meaning to invoke a background process to change the name *files1* to *file*, then reports that it can't find the **1** (one) command. (Having interpreted *&* as a request for a background process, the shell now thinks that the *1* that follows is another command.)

# Summary of Chapter 22

In this chapter you learned about the UNIX shell. This included discussions of background commands; connecting processes with pipelines, filters, and tees; command grouping; conditional execution; and pattern-matching.

## *Background commands*

The shell makes it possible for you to run more than one process at your terminal. If you add an ampersand (&) at the end of a command line, the shell will execute the command line as a **background process**, thereby allowing you to proceed immediately to another command without having to wait for the first to be completed. The shell will display the **process identification** number, which you can use to monitor the process.

To make the process immune from hangup and quit signals, begin a command line with the **nohup** (no hangup) command.

**Monitoring background processes.** Use the **ps** (process status) command to monitor background processes. If you execute **ps** without any arguments, the display will give four columns of information with these headings:

| | |
|---|---|
| PID | Process identifier |
| TTY | Terminal number |
| TIME | Cumulative execution time |
| CMD | Name of command |

When you add the −l argument to **ps**, you obtain ten additional columns, some of which are beyond the scope of this book.

**Priority of processes.** One of the 14 columns displayed by **ps** is called *NICE*, which indicates the priority level of each process. You can decrease the priority of a process by beginning the command line with the **nice** command.

**Terminating background processes.** To terminate a background process, use the **kill** command followed by the process identifier.

## Connecting Processes

Here are three ways to connect processes:

**Pipelines.** A **pipeline** allows you to connect the standard output of one process to the standard input of another. The symbol for a pipeline is the vertical bar (|).

**Filters.** Some UNIX commands read from the standard input, and then select some of it to be sent to the standard output. These commands (like **grep**, **sort**, **spell**, and **diff**) are called **filter programs** (or **filters**). They often receive their input through a pipeline.

**Tees.** The **tee** command, which allows you to view data as it is being written to a file, is used in conjunction with a pipeline.

## Giving Directives to the Shell

**Command grouping.** Grouping a list of commands within **parentheses** will cause the shell to create a subshell to read and execute the enclosed commands. With this scheme, you can move to another directory, run some commands, and then have the shell return you to your current directory.

Grouping a list of commands within **braces** will simply cause the shell to read and execute the enclosed commands. With this scheme, you can use the output of several commands as the input to another command.

**Conditional execution.** A command list is a sequence of commands separated by semicolons (;). You can invoke a command list with conditional execution.

An OR-IF construction tells the shell to invoke the second command only if the first fails, like this:

```
$ command 1 || command 2
```

An AND-IF construction tells the shell to invoke the second command only if the first succeeds, like this:

```
$ command 1 && command 2
```

**Pattern-matching.** The shell can use one of the following **metacharacters** to match patterns when selecting a filename:

| | |
|---|---|
| * | Match any string of any length |
| ? | Match any single character |
| [ ] | Match any of the characters enclosed |

# 23

# *Bourne Shell Variables*

In Chapters 21 and 22 you reviewed how the shell interprets commands entered from your terminal. We begin this chapter with a discussion of shell procedures and then go on to command substitution.

## Shell Procedures

A **shell file** (also known as a **shell procedure** or a **shell script**) is a file that contains one or more shell commands to be executed in sequence whenever the file is named as a command. This allows you to create your own commands. For example, here is a shell script that counts the number of characters in a file in the current directory. Just to review, here is how you use **ed** to create a file:

```
$ ed counter
? counter
a
ls | wc -c                [List filenames and pipe them to
.                          the wc -c command]
w
10
q
$ _
```

Now you have a simple command file called *counter* that can be invoked with the **sh** (shell) command, which reads the contents of its argument file *counter*, and then executes these commands:

```
$ sh counter
20                         [Character count of counter]
$ _
```

At this point you have a file that contains a single command line, but you still can't execute it directly. The next step is to change the execution mode of the file with the **chmod** (change mode) command (see Chapter 3):

```
$ chmod u+x counter          [Make file counter executable]
$ _
```

Now, to invoke *counter* as a command in its own right, you no longer need to use the **sh** command. Just type *counter*, the way you would type the name of any standard UNIX command.

The last step is to move *counter* into your **bin** directory, where most of your private commands should reside and add *$HOME/bin* to the value of your variable **PATH**. If you skip this step, you will be able to execute *counter* only when you are in the same directory with it. Otherwise, you must give the full pathname: */usr/john/*newcomd/counter or *$HOME/bin/counter*.

## Preliminary Commands

Before going on to the section on shell variables, let's discuss two commands that you'll be using as examples in that section and the sections that follow: **echo** and **read**.

## The echo Command

**echo**

The **echo** command takes its argument string, which is terminated by a newline (\n), and writes it to the standard output (your terminal). The **echo** command is used mostly by the shell script to display messages on the screen, as in this example:

```
$ echo This is a message
This is a message
$ _
```

The only option for the **echo** command is **−n**, which causes the newline to be omitted from the string displayed. This allows you to append one message to another without a line break between them, as in this example:

```
$ echo -n This is a message
This is a message$ _
```

Note the position of the prompt ($) at the end of the message instead of on the next line. The **−n** option is used often in shell programs to prompt for input from the user. For example, assume that there is a shell file called *getkey* that contains the following two lines:

```
$ cat getkey
echo -n 'Please press any key, then <cr> to continue:'
```

```
read inkey
$ _
```

To create such a file, follow the steps given at the beginning of this chapter (Shell Procedures). Once you have created the file, invoke it as a UNIX command:

```
$ getkey
Please press any key, then <cr> to continue: _
```

The program is now waiting for your input at the keyboard. Any keystrokes you enter will be displayed at the cursor location. As soon as you press RETURN, the program will exit and the prompt will reappear on the next line—the **read** command expects the RETURN key as end of the input string.

## *The read Command*

**read**

The **read** command takes one line from the standard input and assigns the first word to the first name, the second word to the second name, and so on, with any leftover words assigned to the last name. If there is only one name, as in this simple example, **read** assigns the entire input to this name.

In the file *getkey*, the **read** command assigns your keyboard input as the value of the variable *inkey*. If you want to see this input displayed after you've typed it, add another **echo** command to the end of the *getkey* file, like this:

```
$ cat getkey
echo -n 'Please press any key, then <cr> to continue: '
read inkey
echo $inkey                    [Now add this line]
$ _
```

Now when you invoke the *getkey* program (assuming that you enter *KEYBOARD* and then press RETURN after the prompt, you will see this:

```
$ getkey
Please press any key, then <cr> to continue:
                                  [You type KEYBOARD here]
KEYBOARD                          [This time getkey echoes it here]
$ _
```

You will see the **echo** and **read** commands used more in shell files in the next chapter. For now, you are ready to learn about shell variables.

**echo**
**read**

## Shell Variables

A shell variable, which can be assigned either by the shell itself or by a user, provides the shell with basic information. You learned about several shell variables in Chapter 21. The shell usually assigns such variables default settings, which a user can then reassign for different applications. The name of the variable can be any sequence of letters, digits, and underscores, but must always begin with either a letter or an underscore. Use an equal sign (=) with no spaces on either side to assign a value to a shell variable. Additional rules and restrictions will be discussed later in this chapter.

### *Assigning Variables*

The following example shows the value *STRING* being assigned to the variable called *VARIABLE*:

```
$ VARIABLE=STRING
```

To retrieve the value of the variable, precede the variable name with a dollar sign (*$*). The **echo** command provides a simple way to examine the value of variable:

```
$ echo $VARIABLE
STRING
$ _
```

You can assign more than one variable in an assignment statement, as shown in the example below. Note the spaces between assignments:

```
$ a=T b=H c=I d=S        [Assign more than one variable in a
                          statement.]
$ echo $a$b$c$d          [Retrieve the values of the variables
                          assigned.]
THIS
$ _
```

In the following example, variable *b* is assigned the value of variable *a*, so that variables *a* and *b* have the same value:

```
$ a=123                  [Assign 123 to variable a]
$ b=$a                   [Assign variable b the value of variable a]
$ echo $a $b             [Echo both values, separated by a space]
123 123                  [The values of a and b are displayed]
$ _
```

You can combine the two statements above into a single, more complicated statement to obtain the same result:

```
$ z=$y y=123     [Set z equal to the value of variable y (123)]
$ echo $z $y     [Echo both values, with a space between them]
123 123          [Both values are displayed]
$ _
```

Since the shell assigns variables from right to left (not from left to right), you have to be careful in constructing multiple assignment statements, as in the example above. In the example that follows, the shell assigns *z* the previous value of *y* (*123*), not the new value *abc*, as the user expects:

```
$ y=abc z=$y     [The shell assigns 123, not abc, to z]
$ echo $z
123              [Now the shell echoes 123 as the value of z]
$ echo $y
abc              [The shell echoes abc as the value of y, though]
$
```

Variable assignments are used often in shell procedures. However, you can still benefit from these assignments during ordinary interactive use of the shell. For example, you can use variables in place of lengthy command names, arguments, and filenames, thereby avoiding a lot of unnecessary typing. Here, the shell assigns a long pathname to *HERE*:

```
$ HERE=/usr/james/selection/car/camaro
```

Now you can type

```
$ cd $HERE
```

and obtain the same result as if you had typed

```
$ cd /usr/james/selection/car/camaro
```

In the following example we'll use a variable to hold a long command line with many options: *nroff −h −rTl −T450 −mm* <*file*>. Let's assign a variable *form* to this command string (single quotation marks are required here because of the spaces between the individual arguments):

```
$ form='nroff -h -rTl -T450 -mm'
```

So now, intead of typing the entire command every time you want to use it, you only have to type something like this:

```
$ $form file_15
```

which is equivalent to

```
$ nroff -h -rTl -T450 -mm file_15
```

## Using Quotation Marks

So far we have discussed simple variable assignments, without spaces, tabs, semicolons, and newlines. Any time one of these appears in the assigned value string, you have to enclose this assigned value (right-hand side) of the statement in single quotes (') as shown in the following example:

```
$ string='This string has both; semicolon and space'
$ echo $string
This string has both; semicolon and space
$ _
```

If you do not enclose the assigned value above in single quotes, an error message will appear on the screen.

However, if you want to include a variable substitution within an assigned value string, you must use double quotation marks (" "). This will force the shell to scan and substitute the values of the enclosed variables:

```
$ S=space M=semicolon
$ string=" This includes both; $S and $M "
$ echo $string
This includes both; space and semicolon
$ _
```

Besides, the three special characters ( $, ', ") will retain their special meaning when enclosed within double quotes, while the shell will take them literally when they are enclosed within single quotes, like this:

```
$ string=' This string has three; $S,", ' '
$ echo $string
This string has three; $S, ", '  [No substitutions are made ]
$ _
```

## Evaluating a Command String **eval**

You can force the shell to rescan the string using the **eval** command. The **eval** command rescans the command arguments either to perform commands or to substitute variables as specified. Here is an example:

```
$ a=1234                [Assign a the value 1234]
$ b='$a'                [Assign b the value of variable a]
$ eval echo $a $b       [Force the shell to rescan and substitute $b]
1234 1234
$ echo $a $b            [Echo without evaluation]
1234 $a
$ _
```

The advantage of having the shell rescan your command line is that you can have all substitutions made before execution, as shown in here:

```
$ peek=finger               [Assign variable peek the value finger]
$ port=' >/dev/tty01'       [Assign variable port the value in quotes]
$ eval $peek $port          [Evaluate both variables]
finger >/dev/tty01
$ _
```

The **eval** command makes the above statement appear to the shell as if you had typed this:

```
$ finger >/dev/tty01
```

Of course, you could also set the whole command string in one variable, as explained earlier, without the **eval** command, but **eval** gives you a little more flexibility when you need it.

## *Distinguishing a Variable's Name*

As you have already seen, the value that is assigned to a variable can be the value of another variable. You can also use a variable to help define itself, as shown here:

```
$ word=character     [Variable word is assigned the value character]
$ word=meta$word     [Variable word is used in its own definition]
$ echo $word
metacharacter
$ _
```

If you try to append extra characters to the end of a variable's name, as shown here:

```
$ far=tele
$ TV=$farvision
$ echo $TV
$ _
```

the shell will assign a null string to *TV* since it can't find a variable called *farvision*. The solution to this problem is to enclose the variable's name within braces, as shown here:

```
$ TV={$far}vision
$ echo $TV
television
$ _
```

**eval**

For those variables that you may want to be automatically initialized every time you log in, you can have them set in your *.profile* file. To make the variable names easier to read, set them in uppercase.

## Command Substitution

The shell allows you to assign the results of an invoked command string as the value of a variable, by enclosing this command string in grave accents ( ` command string ` ), as illustrated in this example:

```
$ fnames=`ls`          [Assign fnames the results of the ls command]
$ _
```

This will force the shell to invoke the **ls** command, assigning the result as the value of the variable *fnames.* Assume that there are four files in the current directory called *file_1*, *file_2*, *file_3*, *file_4*. Now, using the **echo** command to display the value of *fnames*, you will see the result as follows:

```
$ echo $fnames
file_1 file_2 file_3 file_4
$ _
```

You can use command substitution only with commands that have standard output. Since the **lpr** command gives no standard output, avoid doing this:

```
$ VAL=`lpr file1`          [Not recommended]
$ _
```

The output of **lpr file 1** is sent to the printer, and the shell assigns a null value to the variable *VAL.*

Command substitutions are often useful in shell files, as in the following example:

```
$ CURRENT=`pwd `                 [ Get the current directory ]
$ cd /usr/dennis/plan/goal       [ Move to a different directory ]
$  . . .                         [ Do something in that directory]
$ cd $CURRENT                    [ Return to the previous directory]
```

The variable *CURRENT* is used to hold the pathname of the current directory while the program goes to a different directory to perform some task. The last statement allows you to return to the previous directory without having to remember its name.

### *Evaluating Arithmetic Expressions*

The **expr** command takes its arguments as an expression (logical or arithmetic). The result of this expression is sent to the standard output. These arithmetic operators can be used with the **expr** command:

| | |
|---|---|
| + | addition |
| − | subtraction |
| * | multiplication |
| / | division |
| % | remainder |

Because the **expr** command treats each operator or value as a separate argument, you have to separate operators and values with spaces. To prevent metacharacters like the following from being interpreted by the shell itself

( * & ?^ [ ] (and so on)

You have to **escape** them (release them from their special meanings) either by by enclosing them within single quotes ('*') or double quotes ("*") or by preceding them with backslashes (\). In the fourth example below, the asterisk (*), which could be interpreted by the shell as a wildcard character, is escaped with single quotes.

| | |
|---|---|
| `$ a=2` | [Initialize *a* with value *2*] |
| ``$ a=`expr $a + 7` `` | [Add *7* to the value of *a* and assign to *a*] |
| ``$ b=`expr $a / 3` `` | [Divide *a* by *3* (9 / 3 = 3) and assign to *b*] |
| ``$ c=`expr $a - 1 '*' $b` `` | [Multiply *a−1* by *b* (8 x 3 = 24) and assign to *c*] |
| ``$ d=`expr $c % 5` `` | [Divide *c* by *5* (24 % 5) and assign the remainder to *d*] |
| ``$ e=`expr $d - $b` `` | [Subtract *b* from *d* (4 − 3) and assign to *e*] |

The result is assigned to variable *e*. Let's check all the values:

```
$ echo $a $b $c $d $e
9 3 24 4 1
$ _
```

## Comparing Strings **expr**

The **expr** command also allows you to compare strings with its matching operator (:). The output is the number of characters in the two strings that match. An output of zero (0) indicates failure of the comparison. Here is an example:

| | |
|---|---|
| ``$ R=`expr 'abcdefg' : 'abcd'` `` | [Match the two strings and assign to *R*] |
| `$ echo $R` | [Recall the matching number *R*] |

```
4
$ _
```

**expr**

The string comparator of the **expr** command uses the same scheme used by **ed**. That is, the second string is compared against the first string, starting with the first character. Because of this, even one non-matching character in the second string will cause a failure, resulting in an output of zero (0), as illustrated in the three examples below:

```
$ R=`expr 'abcdefg' : 'abce'`       [Missing d in the second string]
$ T=`expr 'abcdefg' : 'bcde'`       [Missing a in the second string ]
$ V=`expr 'abcd' : 'abcdefg'`       [Second string is longer than
                                     the first]
$ echo $R $T $V
0 0 0                               [All three comparisons fail]
$ _
```

You could perform the same string comparison using variables, as in this example:

```
$ C=`expr $M : $N`
```

By taking advantage of the string-comparison property of the **expr** command and the character-matching that the shell provides, we can also use a string comparison to determine the length of a string. Let's assign to variable *A* a character string, then count the number of characters in this string:

```
$ A='This is an experiment' [Assign a string to variable A]
```

Since **variable** *A* is a character string with spaces in it, A must be enclosed in double quotes in the following example; otherwise, the statement will produce a syntax error. The second argument is enclosed in **single quotes** to preserve the special meaning of the asterisk (*) to the shell:

```
$ count=`expr $A : '.*'`       [Note the asterisk (*) on the right]
$ echo $count                  [This retrieves the value of count]
21                             [String length ]
```

Another feature of the expr command is the ability to extract only a portion of a character string, as in

```
$ B=`expr $A : ' . . . . .\(.*\)'`
```

The five dots in front of the backslash (\) represent the five characters to be skipped (including the space), starting at the beginning of the string. Now, echoing variable *B*, we have

```
$ echo $B
is an experiment          [The first five characters have been omitted]
$ _
```

The **expr** command checks statements for errors before processing. Here are some possible errors:

- A syntax error will occur any time an operator or operand is missing or illegal.
- A *non-numeric argument* message will be displayed any time you try to use an **arithmetic** operation on a character or string.

## Conditional Substitution of Variables

You can test a variable to determine whether or not it has been assigned a value. Then, if it has, you can either use this value in an expression or replace the value with another. This is known as **conditional substitution**. The shell provides four variations of conditional substitution, using four symbols to indicate comparison (–, =, ?, +):

### ${VARIABLE-OTHER}

If *VARIABLE* has been assigned a value, use this value; otherwise, use string *OTHER* instead, leaving *VARIABLE* unassigned. In the example that follows, we assume that variable *VAL* is **not** set, with the result shown:

```
$ echo ${VAL-123}          [Test whether VAL has been set]
123                        [Since it has not, string 123 is used]
```

Here is a similar example with a variable used instead of an actual string on the right as the replacement:

```
$ SUB=456                  [Assign 456 to SUB]
$ echo ${VAL-$SUB}         [Again we assume that VAL is unset]
456                        [So SUB's value is used instead]
```

### ${VARIABLE=OTHER}

If *VARIABLE* has been assigned a value, use this value; otherwise, assign the value *OTHER* to *VARIABLE* before using *VARIABLE*, as shown in the following examples:

```
$ echo ${VAL=xyz}          [VAL has no assigned value]
xyz                        [so xyz becomes the value of VAL]
$ echo $VAL                [Instead of remaining unassigned,
xyz                        VAL now has the value xyz]
```

### *${VARIABLE?EMPTY}*

If *VARIABLE* has an assigned value, use this value; otherwise, display the message *VARIABLE: EMPTY* and abort the procedure. Once again, assume that *VAR* is unassigned:

```
$ error='variable unset, procedure is aborted'
$ echo ${VAR?$error}
VAR: variable unset, procedure is aborted
$ _
```

The default for a missing message on the right side of the question mark is a standard message:

```
$ echo ${VAR?}
VAR: parameter not set
$ _
```

### *${VARIABLE+OTHER}*

If *VARIABLE* has been assigned a value, use the value of *OTHER*. If *VARIABLE* is not set, use a null string as its value, leaving *VARIABLE* unassigned.

```
$ THIS=145               [Assign 145 to THIS]
$ THAT=abc               [Assign abc to THAT]
$ echo ${THIS+$THAT}     [Perform the test]
abc                      [The value of THAT appears]
$ echo $THIS
123                      [THIS retains its value]
$
```

## Positional Parameters

The shell itself sets positional parameters to identify the positions of items (or **arguments**) on the command line. Arguments must be separated by spaces so that the shell can distinguish them from each other. The shell identifies items on a command line with numbers beginning with zero. The first item (the name of a shell procedure) is always denoted by $0; then the first argument is denoted by $1, the second by $2, and so on, up to $9 as illustrated here:

```
  $0    $1    $2   . . .  $9      [ positional parameter]
$ diff file1 file2 . . . file9    [ command line ]
```

## Assigning Positional Parameters

**set**

Before going further into the positional parameter, let's consider the **set** command as it relates to positional parameters. The **set** command is often used to assign a positional parameter to an argument string as in

```
$ set arg1 arg2 arg3 arg4 arg5 arg6 arg7 arg8 arg9
$ _
```

This **set** command forces the shell to assign the first positional parameter *$1* to *arg1*, the second *$2* to *arg2*, the third to *arg3*, and so on. You can verify these assigments by echoing them back:

```
$ echo $1 $3 $4 $2 $4 $5 $6 $7 $8 $9
arg1 arg2 arg3 arg4 arg5 arg6 arg7 arg8 arg9
$ _
```

## Accessing Specific Arguments

When the **set** command is used with command substitution, each element of the output of the command substitution is assigned a positional parameter. In the following example, the **date** command is enclosed within grave accent marks ( \` \` ) to form a command substitution:

```
$ set `date`
$ _
```

The output of the **date** command becomes a sequence of arguments for the **set** command, and no output will show on your screen. However, if you invoke the **date** command by itself, you should see this:

```
$ date
Wed Feb 15 21:49:20 1984
$ _
```

After you invoke **set \` date \`**, each item in this string is assigned a positional parameter $1, $2, $3, $4, $5, as explained in the next section. If you are interested in the time only, select it this way:

```
$ echo $4
21:49:20
$ _
```

You can also rearrange these items in a different format:

```
$ echo 'DATE: $1 $2 $3 $5 TIME: $4'
DATE: Wed Feb 15 1984 TIME: 21:49:20
$ _
```

**set**

## Accessing More Positional Parameters

**shift**

The highest-numbered positional parameter is $9. To access arguments higher then 9, use the **shift** command, which shifts each argument one position to the left. After the **shift** command, positional parameter $4 is moved to position $3, $3 is moved to position $2, $2 is moved to position $1, and $1 is discarded (the command name in position $0 remains unchanged, however). Here is an example:

```
$ echo $1 $2 $3 $4 $5 $6 $7 $8 $9
arg1 arg2 arg3 arg4 arg5 arg6 arg7 arg8 arg9
$ shift                              [Shift arguments to the left]
$ echo $1 $2 $3 $4 $5 $6 $7 $8 $9
arg2 arg3 arg4 arg5 arg6 arg7 arg8 arg9 arg10
$ _
```

After this shift, *arg2* is in the first position and *arg10* is at the end.

## Matching Arguments with a Wildcard

The shell also provides the astrisk (*) as a wildcard to match any positional parameter. You can access all positional parameters by typing

```
$ echo $*
arg2 arg3 arg4 arg5 arg6 arg7 arg8 arg9 arg10 arg11
$ _
```

This **echo** command and the one used in the previous section are not exactly the same. The previous **echo** command displayed nine positions; this one displayed up to the last current positional parameter.

## Passing Arguments to a Command

The shell always assigns arguments to positional parameters before passing them to an invoked command. For example, suppose you have an executable command file named **bounce**, which contains *echo $1 $3 $5 $2 $4 $6*. If you invoke **bounce** with six arguments, this is what happens:

```
$ bounce one two three four five six
one three five two four six
$ _
```

As you can see, the echoed line reflects the order set by the **bounce** file.

# Reserved Variables

The special variables listed here are set by the shell itself, rather than by the user:

\# **Number of Arguments.** The number of positional parameters (not counting $0) that have been used to record arguments. For example, let's see how many arguments were saved by the shell as the result of the **set** command in this example:

```
$ set 'date'
$ echo $#
5                                  [5 positional parameters have been set]
$ _
```

? **Return Code.** The exit status code returned to the shell from the last executed command. In general, successful execution of the command returns a zero; any other execution returns a non-zero value.

```
$ echo $?
0                          [Exit status of the echo command: successful]
$ _
```

$ Process Identification Number of the Current Process. Since this number is unique, it is sometimes used as a temporary filename, as in this example:

```
$ tempfile=file$$                  [Set tempfile variable ]
$ sort file1 -o $tempfile          [Output to variable tempfile]
$ mv $tempfile file1
```

! **Process Identification Number of the Background Process Most Recently Invoked.** This number remains in effect even after the process has been completed.

```
$ echo $!
243                    [The most-recently invoked background process]
```

– **Status of Shell Flags.** This variable identifies all current shell flags that can be turned on or off by the **set** command. To examine the current settings of shell flags, type

```
$ echo $-
s                                 [The s flag is on; all others are off]
$ _
```

These variables can be set only by the shell. If you attempt to assign them any value, an error message will be displayed, as shown here:

```
$ #=256                           [You try to set variable # manually]
#=256: not found                  [This is what happens]
$ _
```

**shift**

## Summary of Chapter 23

In this chapter you learned about shell procedures and shell variables. You learned about assigning shell variables, using quotation marks, naming variables, command substitution, conditional substitution, positional parameters, and pre-defined variables.

**Shell Procedures.** To create a shell procedure, enter the desired shell commands in a file and make the file executable with the **chmod** command.

**Preliminary Commands.** The **echo** command takes its argument string and writes it to the standard output (displays it on your screen). The **read** command takes standard input and assigns it to a variable (or to several variables).

**Shell Variables.** Shell variables, like other variables used in programming, can be assigned values.

To retrieve this value, use the **echo** command, preceding the variable's name with a dollar sign ($).

You can use shell variables to spare yourself extra typing.

**Using quotation marks.** To allow a string to contain spaces, tabs, semicolons, and newlines (but not to allow substitution of variables), use single quotation marks.

To allow a string to contain spaces, tabs, semicolons, and newlines, along with substitution of variables, use double quotation marks.

**Evaluating a command string.** The **eval** command works like the **echo** command, except that **eval** can take an entire command line, evaluate variables, and substitute their assigned values.

**Distinguishing a variable's name.** To distinguish a variable's name from other characters, enclose the name in braces.

**Command Substitution.** To assign to a variable the standard output of an invoked command string, enclose the command string in grave accents.

**Evaluating expressions.** To evaluate arithmetic expressions, use the **expr** command, along with the symbols for addition (+), subtraction (−), multiplication (*), division(/), and remainder (%).

**Comparing strings.** To compare two strings, use the **expr** command with a comparator (:). The result will be the number of matching characters in the two strings.

You can use string comparison to determine the length of a string (compare the string to .*) or to extract a portion of the string (use one dot for each character to be deleted, then enclose .* in substring brackets \( and \)).

**Conditional Substitution of Variables.** To test a variable to determine whether or not it has been assigned a value and then base your next action on the result of the text, use one of the following four types of expressions:

${*var-other*} If *var* has a value, use it; if not, use *other* and leave *var* unassigned.

${*var=other*} If *var* has a value, use it; if not, assign the value of *other* to *var*.

${*var?empty*} If *var* has a value, use it; if not, display the message *var: empty* and abort the process.

${*var+other*} If *var* has a value, use the value of *other* instead; if not, use a null string and leave *var* unassigned.

**Positional Parameters.** The shell sets positional parameters to keep track of a command and its arguments on a command line, using $0 for the command, $1 for the first argument, $2 for the second, and so on.

**Assigning positional parameters.** To assign values to positional parameters, use the **set** command.

**Assigning specific arguments.** To select a specific argument, use the **set** command with a positional parameter.

**Accessing more positional parameters.** To access arguments numbered higher than 9, use the **shift** command.

**Matching arguments with a wildcard.** To match any positional parameter, use the shell wildcard symbol (*) after the dollar sign.

**Rearranging arguments before execution.** You can rearrange the order of the arguments by placing the positional parameters in the desired order, then executing the command.

**Reserved Shell Variables.** The following special variables can be set only by the shell, but can be used by the user:

| | |
|---|---|
| # | Number of arguments in a command line |
| ? | Return code for the command |
| $ | PID of the current process |
| ! | PID of the most recent background process |
| – | Status of shell flags |

# 24

# Bourne Shell Program Control

Within a **shell file**, or **shell procedure**, the shell acts as a programming language. Like other languages, the shell provides features like these:

- Flow control commands (**if . . . then . . . else, while, for,** and so on)
- Interrupt handling (**trap**), variable setting, and parameter passing (refer to Chapter 23)
- Calls to other commands or shell procedures as subroutines

Because a shell procedure is written in a high-level language, it is easy to modify. Also, a shell procedure doesn't need to be compiled. Since there is no object file to recreate, it is easier to maintain your shell program.

The shell also provides devices for debugging a shell procedure. These allow you to watch each step of your program execute, with errors displayed whenever the shell finds illegal expressions.

In this chapter, you will learn about flow-control commands, interrupt handling, and many other features of shell programming. Early examples will be very simple, with more involved examples shown later.

## Constructing Loops

In any kind of programming, it is common to have a segment of a program executed repeatedly, usually with a few changes made just before each repeated execution. Such a segment is called a program **loop**. This section deals with the different ways you can construct a loop when programming the UNIX shell. Before going into looping itself, let's take a look at the **true** and **false** commands, which we'll use to simplify our discussions of the looping commands.

## The true and false Commands

**true**

**false**

When any UNIX command completes execution, it passes a value to its parent process (the calling program) to inform the parent of the outcome. This value, called the **exit status** of the command, is a small integer. A value of zero is agreed to mean "true" (the command ran successfully); a value other than zero is agreed to mean "false" (the command did not run successfully). Furthermore, since there are any number of values that can mean *false,* the particular value often explains **why** the process failed.

To allow you to force one exit status or the other, the shell provides you with a pair of commands called **true** and **false**. The **true** command returns an exit status of *true;* the **false** command returns an exit status of *false.* In a moment we'll use these commands to show clearly how some of the commands used to form loops (**while** and **until**) work. For right now, let's look at the **true** and **false** commands themselves:

```
$ true;A=$?       [Obtain the exit status of the true command ]
$ false;B=$?      [Obtain the exit status of the false command ]
$ echo $A $B
0 1               [The status of each is displayed]
$ _
```

## Looping While True

**while**

The **while** command sets up a loop that continues to be executed as long as the **while** command detects a *true* condition, as shown here:

```
while <command list>
do [execute commands
    between do and done]
done
```

The **while** command examines the exit value of the *command list,* which can be either a single command or a group of commands. Then, based on this return-value, takes appropriate action: if a zero is returned, all commands between **do** and **done** are executed. This process is repeated until the **while** command detects a non-zero return-status (or a **break** command is executed). In the example below, the **while** command nevers see a non-zero value. Since the output of the **true** command is always zero, so this program will loop forever!

```
while true
do echo THIS IS AN ENDLESS LOOP
done
```

To stop this program, press the **DEL** key (shift DEL key).

## Looping While False

**until**

The format of the **until** command and its command execution processes are the same as for the **while** command, except that the looping condition is a non-zero-exit value (false). The following program gives the same result as the one that uses the **while** command in the section above:

```
until false
do echo THIS IS AN ENDLESS LOOP
done
```

The **DEL** key stops this program the same way it stops the **while** loop. The **done** statement closes the loop.

## Nested Loops

It is possible to place one program loop inside another, producing a number of repetitions of the inner loop with each single repetition of the outer loop. This arrangement is called a **nested loop**, and is illustrated in this example:

```
$ cat loop
out=1
in=3
 until out=`expr $out - 1`     ──────────────────────┐
 do echo out loop $out         ──────┐               │
    while in=`expr $in - 1`          │  Inside       │  Outside
    do echo in loop $in              │  loop         │  loop
    done                       ──────┘               │
 done                          ──────────────────────┘
```

Since the variable *out* has been initialized to 1, the expression *$out - 1* decreases the value of *out* to zero (0), which gives the **until** statement a return value of *false.* This causes the **do** statement of the outside loop to be executed.

Since the variable *in* has been initialized to 3, the inside loop will be executed twice—until the expression *$in - 1* reduces the value of *in* to zero (0), which ends the inside loop, and return program control to the outside loop.

This time the expression *$out - 1* at the top of the outside loop reduces the value of *out* to *-1*, a non-zero value that ends the outside loop (and the program). If you execute **loop**, this is what you will see:

```
$ loop
out loop 0
in loop 2
```

**true**
**false**
**while**
**until**

```
in loop 1
$ _
```

## Breaking Out of a Loop

**break**

The **break** command allows you to exit from an enclosing loop involving one of the commands already discussed (**while** and **until**), as well as two commands to be discussed later in this chapter (**for** and **case**). To break from more than one loop level, you must specify the number of levels to break. If you execute the program on the left below, you will see the result displayed on the right. Without **break**, the innermost loop (loop 3) would keep repeating indefinitely. But **break** forces execution back out to the middle loop (loop 2), so that loops 2 and 3 alternate single turns at executing. (This example illustrates how the **echo** command comes in handy when you want to trace the execution of a program.)

```
$ cat multiloop
while true                      ─┐
do echo LOOP 1                   │
   until false            ─┐     │
   do echo LOOP 2          │     │
      while true    ─┐     │     │ loop 1
      do echo LOOP 3 │     │ loop 2
         break       │ loop 3    │
      done          ─┘     │     │
   done                   ─┘     │
done                            ─┘
```

```
$ multiloop
LOOP 1
LOOP 2
LOOP 3
LOOP 2
LOOP 3
LOOP 2
LOOP 3
LOOP 2
LOOP 3
. . .
```

The shell procedure's syntax requires that for every **while**, **for**, or **until** loop command, there must be a matching **done** statement to terminate it. After the *LOOP 3* message is displayed, the innermost loop is broken by the **break** command, and the **until** loop is again executed. This process will repeat endlessly, displaying *LOOP 2* and *LOOP 3* alternately.

Replacing **break** by **break 2** will force the program back to the outermost loop (loop 1), with *LOOP 1*, *LOOP 2*, and *LOOP 3* messages displayed alternately:

```
$ cat multiloop
while true
do echo LOOP 1
   until false
   do echo LOOP 2
      while true
      do echo LOOP 3
         break 2
      done
   done
done
```

(loop 3, loop 2, loop 1)

```
$ multiloop
LOOP 1
LOOP 2
LOOP 3
LOOP 1
LOOP 2
LOOP 3
LOOP 1
LOOP 2
LOOP 3
. . .
```

A *break 3* statement would cause the program to exit all three loops and the program to be terminated.

```
$ cat multiloop
while true
do echo LOOP 1
   until false
   do echo LOOP 2
      while true
      do echo LOOP 3
         break 3
      done
   done
done
```

(loop 3, loop 2, loop 1)

```
$ multiloop
LOOP 1
LOOP 2
LOOP 3
$ _
```

## *Resuming Execution of a Loop* **continue**

The **continue** command resumes program execution at the enclosing **for** or **while** loop, the closest enclosing loop being the default when the command is invoked alone. If the level number is explicitly given, the enclosing **for** or **while** loop at the level specified is where the program resumes execution, as illustrated here:

**break**
**continue**

```
while true
do command list 3
   until false
   do command list 2
      while true
      do command list 1
         continue $level
      done
   done
done
```

If variable *level* has a value of 2, execution will be resumed at the **until** loop. If the value of *level* is 3 the outside **while** loop will be resumed. If variable *level* is not set (or set to 1), the program will remain in the innermost **while** loop.

## Exiting a Loop

**exit**

The **break** and **continue** commands allow your program to leave its current loop. The **exit** command, however, allows your program to abort the entire procedure, not just the current loop. The **exit** command allows you to stop processing in the event of an error. When invoked by itself, **exit** returns an exit status of zero (true) to its parent program. In the following example, *main* is the parent program, which calls procedure *subpro*. By using the name of the procedure as a Boolean variable, this program actually relies on the exit status of the procedure to govern the conditional statement. Then, based on the exit status returned, *main* will display one of two messages.

```
$ cat main
if subpro
   then echo ' Exit status is zero '
   else echo ' Exit status is non-zero '
fi
$ cat subpro
HERE='pwd'
status=0
. . .
exit $status
$ _
```

In procedure *subpro*, variable *status* is initialized to a value of zero (0), which causes the message *Exit status is zero* to be displayed. If the value of *status* were non-zero, the message *Exit status is non-zero* would be displayed.

## Looping on a Variable

**for**

The **for** command sets up a conditional loop using the following format:

```
for variable in list
do [execute command(s) from do to done]
done
```

The **for** command assigns the next word in *list* as a new value of *variable*, then examines this new value. If the variable has a valid value, commands between the **do** and **done** statements are executed; if the variable has a null value (indicating that there are no more words left in the list), the command following the **done** statement is executed. Here is an example:

```
$ cat example
list='word1 word2 word3 word4'
for VAL in $list
   do echo $VAL
   done
echo 'END OF LIST'
$ _
```

```
$ example
word1
word2
word3
word4
END OF LIST
$ _
```

When this shell program is invoked, *word1* is assigned to variable *VAL* first. Then the **for** command examines the value of *VAL*. Since VAL has a valid value (*word1*), *echo $VAL* is executed. The program resumes execution at **for**, this time the next argument (*word2*) is assigned to *VAL*, and the process is repeated. The **for** loop continues through two more iterations (one for *word3* and one for *word4*). Then, in the next iteration after the last argument (*word4*), *VAL* assumes a null value, indicating that the end of the list has been reached. At this point, the **for** loop is broken, and the program by-passes the *do . . . done* list and executes *echo 'END OF LIST'*.

In the shell procedure that follows, variable *VAL* assumes the procedure's arguments, which are passed by the shell as its value:

```
$ cat rebounce
for VAL
do echo $VAL
done
$ _
```

```
$ rebounce one two three
one
two
three
$ _
```

The *rebounce* program is invoked with three arguments, which are passed in the positional variables and assigned one by one as values of variable VAL each time the **for** command is executed. If the *rebounce* program is invoked with the asterisk (*) as its argument, the result is

**exit**
**for**

that the names of files in the current directory are passed in the positional variables to the *rebounce* program. The two shell procedures below produce the same results, as explained below:

```
$ cat rebounce.1
set `ls`
for VAL
   do echo $VAL
   done
$ _
```

```
$ cat rebounce.2
for VAL in *
do echo $VAL
done
$ _
```

In the example on the left (*rebounce.1*), the **set** command assigns positional parameters to the elements of the output of the **ls** command, which form the list of file names and directory names in the current directory. In the example on the right (*rebounce.2*), the shell matches the names of files and directories of the current directory, then assigns them one by one to variable *VAL*.

## The Conditional Statement

**if**

The general format of the **if** command in its simplest form is as follows:

```
if <expression>
   then <command list>
fi
```

The **if** command evaluates the return-value of the expression that follows and then takes action: if the return-value is zero (true), the commands between **then** and **fi** are executed; if the return value is non-zero (false), the command following **fi** is executed. Here is a simple example:

```
$ cat check
if true
   then echo 'TRUE VALUE'
fi
```

```
$ check
TRUE VALUE
$ _
```

The **true** command passes a zero value to **if**, which causes the **echo** command to be invoked. As an experiment, modify the program by replacing *true* with *false*, then invoke the program again.

```
$ cat check
if false
then echo 'TRUE VALUE'
fi
```

```
$ check
$ _
```

No message is displayed this time. Because **false** exits with a non-zero value, the **echo** command is skipped.

## An Alternate Path

**else**

The **else** statement goes with the **if** command to provide an alternate execution path for the program when a condition doesn't satisfy the **if** command. The command format is as follows:

```
if <expression>
  then <command list 1>
  else <command list 2>
fi
```

If the return value of *expression* is zero (true), the commands between **then** and **else** are executed. If the return value is non-zero (false), commands between the **else** and **fi** statements are invoked. Here is an example:

```
$ cat file1
if a=`expr "information" : "$1"`
   then echo " $a characters matched "
   else echo 'No character matched'
fi
$ _
```

The expression *expr "information" : "$1"* compares the argument string "$1" with the string "information". If the expression's return status is zero (indicating that there are some matches between two strings), the statement between **then** and **else** is executed. Otherwise, the statement between **else** and **fi** is executed and then the program exits. Let's invoke program *file1* with arguments and see the results:

```
$ file1 info
4 characters matched
$ file1 format
No character matched
$ _
```

## Combining else and if

**elif**

The **elif** statement is a combination of the **else** and **if** statements, allowing the shell program with nested **if** commands to be written in a shorter form. For example, here is a program *checkname* that attempts to match the argument being passed with strings *Mark*, *John*, and *Dennis*. Here is the program's contents:

**if**
**else**
**elif**

```
$ cat checkname
if expr "$1" : "Mark" >/dev/null
then echo Matching word is Mark
```

```
else if expr "$1" : "John" >/dev/null
     then echo Matching word is John
     else if expr "$1" : "Dennis" >/dev/null
          then echo Matching word is Dennis
          else echo * * * No match * * *
          fi
     fi
fi
$ _
```

This program can be rewritten with the **elif** statement as follows:

```
$ cat new_file
if expr "$1" : "Mark" >/dev/null
     then echo Matching word is Mark
elif expr "$1" : "John" >/dev/null
     then echo Matching word is John
elif expr "$1" : "Dennis" >/dev/null
     then echo Matching word is Dennis
else echo * * * No match * * *
fi
$ _
```

Note that with **elif** only one **fi** statement is required. The output of the **expr** command is redirected to */dev/null*, which can be considered as a dumping site for the unwanted output.

## Testing Files, Quantities, and Strings **test**

The **test** command is used in conjunction with commands such as **while, if,** and **until.** These commands evaluate the **test** command and take action based on the return-value of the **test** command.

The arguments of the **test** command form an expression, which is evaluated by the **test** command. If the result is true, a value of zero is returned; if the result is false, a non-zero value is returned. The **test** command may be used to evaluate any of three different things:

- files
- quantities
- strings

### *Testing Files*

You can use the **test** command to evaluate files in any of these five ways:

| | | | |
|---|---|---|---|
| **test** | **-r** | **<filename>** | [file exists and can be read] |
| | **-w** | | [file exists and can be written to] |
| | **-f** | | [file exists and is **not** a directory] |
| | **-d** | | [file exists and is a directory] |
| | **-s** | | [file is not empty—its size is non-zero] |

In each case, **test** returns a value of zero if the test passes and a value of non-zero if the test fails.

In the example below, you can see that **if** commands are nested and that **test** commands are used to check an argument file's status.

```
$ cat copyall
num=0                                  [Set the number of
                                       unreadable files to zero]
if test -d $HOME/$1                    [Check for the existence of
                                       the directory typed]
then :                                 [If the directory exists, do
                                       nothing]
else mkdir $HOME/$1                    [If it doesn't exist, create
                                       it in your home
fi                                     directory]
for eachone in *                       [Check filenames in the
                                       current directory]
do if test -f $eachone                 [Is this a file?]
  then if test -r $eachone             [If so, is it readable?]
     then cp $eachone $HOME/$1         [If so, copy it to the
                                       directory typed]
     else num=`expr $num + 1`          [Otherwise, add 1 to the
                                       total number of
     fi                                unreadable files in the
                                       current directory]
  fi
done
echo "$num non-accessible files"
$ _
```

This program (*copyall*) allows you to copy each accessible, non-directory ordinary file from your current directory to a directory named by you in your home directory. For example, if you invoke *copyall* with the command line

```
$ copyall newdir
```

the program will copy each readable file in your current directory to subdirectory *newdir* in your home directory. If *newdir* doesn't yet exist, it will be created. If it does exist, then each file in your current directory is checked (first for an ordinary file, then for being readable). If it is both **test** (that is, if it is a readable file), it will be copied to *newdir*; if it is a non-readable file, **copyall** will add 1 to the total of unreadable files (*num*). After all files have been checked, **copyall** will display the number of unreadable files.

## Comparing Quantities

The **test** command uses a different set of expressions to check the relationship between two numbers:

| | | | | |
|---|---|---|---|---|
| **test A** | **-eq** | **B** | [Is A equal to B?] | [A = B?] |
| | **-ne** | | [Is A not equal to B?] | [A ≠ B?] |
| | **-ge** | | [Is A greater than or equal to B?] | [A ≥ B?] |
| | **-le** | | [Is A less than or equal to B?] | [A ≤ B?] |
| | **-gt** | | [Is A greater than B?] | [A > B?] |
| | **-lt** | | [Is A less than B?] | [A < B?] |

In each case, **test** checks whether or not the statement is true. A zero is returned if the statement is true; a non-zero is returned if it is false.

This shell program tests the size of all files in the current directory, then displays the names of all files that contain at least 10,000 words:

```
$ cat bigfiles
count=10000
for i in *
    do size=`wc -c < $i`
    if test $size -ge $count
         then echo "$i size: $size"
    fi
done
$ _
```

This is how the program works: first variable *count* is set to 10,000. The **for** command checks for the existence of the next file in the current directory before assigning it to variable *i*: if there are no more files, the program will exit; otherwise, the next file is selected. The expression *size=`wc -c < $i`* is a command substitution, which counts the number of characters in the file currently assigned to *i*. The value of the variable *size* is then tested against the value of *count*. The expression *test $size -ge $count* will be true only if $size is greater than or equal to 10,000. If so, the name of the file will be displayed on the screen, along with its length (echo "$i size: $size").

In some cases, the program may want to check arguments before processing, as in this example:

```
if test $# -eq 2
     then echo PROCESSING
     elif test $# -lt 2
```

```
          then echo 'missing second filename'
      else echo 'too many arguments'
fi
```

The expression *test $# -eq 2* will be true only if the shell passes exactly two arguments to this program. The expression *test $# -lt 2* will be true only if the number of arguments is less than two.

## *Comparing Strings*

Expressions that are used to test strings of characters are as follows:

| | |
|---|---|
| **test -n <string>** | [The string exists] |
| **test -z <string>** | [The string doesn't exist] |
| **test <string 1> = <string 2>** | [The two strings are the same] |
| **test <string 1> != <string 2>** | [The two strings are not the same] |

This example checks the existence of the second argument, which is passed by the shell to this program:

```
if test -n "$2"
      then echo PROCESSING
      else echo 'missing second filename'
fi
```

Note that variable $2 must be enclosed in double quotes so that the **test** command will recognize it as a character string. The following expression also checks the existence of the second argument string:

```
if test "$2"
```

Let's assign two variables for comparing strings in an example:

```
Y='    abcd'
X=abcd
```

As you may recall from Chapter 23, whenever a string of characters is enclosed in double quotes, special characters retain their meanings and spaces are treated as characters. If you don't enclose the string in quotes, spaces will be omitted from its string. That is why the following program finds strings X and Y to be the same:

```
if test $Y = $X
then echo 'they are the same'
else echo 'they are different'
fi
```

However, when variables *X* and *Y* are enclosed in **double quotes**, **test** will recognize the spaces in string *Y*, and the following program will find strings *X* and *Y* to be different:

```
if test "$Y" = "$X"
then echo 'they are the same'
else echo 'they are different'
fi
```

If variables *X* and *Y* are enclosed in **single quotes**, the dollar sign ($) loses its meaning as a special character. Therefore, in the following statement, **test** compares the two-character strings *$Y* and *$X*, rather than the assigned values of the strings *$Y* and *$X*:

```
test '$Y' = '$X'
```

Note the following points about string comparisons:

- You must surround an equal sign (=) or a not-equal sign (!=) with spaces
- The two symbols in the not-equal sign (!=) must not be separated from each other.

## Compound Testing

The primitives described above can be combined with the *not, and,* and *or* operators to obtain more flexible flow-control in shell programming:

**!** Unary "not" operator inverts the truth-value of an expression.
**-o** Binary "or" operator returns *true* if either of the surrounding statements is true.
**-a** Binary "and" operator returns *true* only if both of the surrounding statements are true.

In the following example, the "not" operator inverts a true value (zero) to a false value (non-zero):

```
if test ! true
```

which provides the same result as the following expression:

```
if test false
```

Therefore, the following expression is true if string *$2* exists:

```
if test "$2"
```

The expression below is true if string *$2* doesn't exist:

```
if test ! "$2"
```

The "and" and "or" operators can also be used to test several expressions in a single test statement, like this:

```
if test -f $1 -a -r $1 -o -w $1
   then echo "file $1 is accessible"
   elif test -d $1
     then echo "$1 is a directory"
     else echo "file $1 is not accessible"
fi
```

The message *file $1 is accessible* is displayed only if the argument file (*$1*) is a normal file that is either readable or writable. The expression *test -d $1* will be true if the argument file is a directory.

## Other Programming Techniques

### *Multi-Way Branching* **case**

The **case** command provides multi-way branching for a shell program. The general format is as follows, with "esac" ("case" spelled backwards as the final delimiter):

```
case <string> in
     S1) <command list> ;;
     S2) <command list> ;;
            . . .
     Sn) <command list> ;;
esac
```

The **case** command compares the pattern *string* to each pattern *S1, S2,.., Sn.* If it finds a match, it will execute the list of commands that follows the matching pattern, with execution ending at the double semicolon (;;). Program syntax requires a double semicolon at the end of each command list and "esac" at the end of the entire **case** command. Here is an example:

```
echo -n 'Please enter your selection (from a to d) : '
read entry
case $entry in
     A|a) echo 'You have an apple.' ;;
     B|b) echo 'Where's the beef?' ;;
     C|c) echo 'Coke adds life.' ;;
     D|d) echo 'A drop in the bucket.' ;;
     *) echo 'Please type A, B, C, or D' ;;
esac
```

The **read** command accepts input from your keyboard, then assigns this input to variable *entry*. The **read** command stops reading when you press the RETURN key. If you type *A* (or *a*), then **case** will execute **case**

```
echo 'You have an apple.'
```

by displaying *You have an apple.* on the screen. If you type *B* (or *b*), **case** will display *Where's the beef?*, and so on. The asterisk (*) (used here to indicate *any other entry*) must be placed at the end of the list. Otherwise, **case** will not be able to select one of the valid entries (A, B, C, or D).

## *Interrupt-Handling* **trap**

Interrupt signals are generated by various abnormal events. While the shell handles most of these signals itself, it passes the following signals to the shell procedure that is active at the time the interrupt takes place:

- Signal 1 generated by a hangup
- Signal 2 generated by the DEL key
- Signal 9 generated by the *kill -9* process number (kill interrupt)
- Signal 15 generated by the **kill** command itself with no option (software termination interrupt)

The shell procedure may choose to catch or ignore one of these signals (except the kill signal). If your program does not catch interrupt signals, upon receiving one of those interrupts, the shell will terminate the shell procedure currently invoked. Sometimes, this might cause inconvenience, such as leaving some temporary files that were created by this shell procedure. To avoid this inconvenience, use the **trap** command to catch interrupt signals, like this:

```
trap'<command list>' <signals>
```

The command list must be enclosed in quotes. If there is more than one command, individual commands must be separated by semicolons (;). More than one signal can be specified (separated by spaces). Here is an example:

```
trap 'rm tempfile; exit' 1 2 15              [interrupt handling]
for i in $HOME/zfile/*
     do
          if expr "$i" : "$HOME/zfile/za" >/dev/null
          then cat $i >>tempfile
          fi
     done
if test -f tempfile
     then nroff -50 tempfile >nnewfile
     rm tempfile
fi
```

In this program, whenever one of the three interrupts 1, 2, or 15 occurs, the shell removes file *tempfile* before exiting from the program.

### Debugging a Shell Procedure

As mentioned earlier in this chapter, the shell allows you to monitor your shell program so that you can see where your mistakes are. To monitor a shell program, add one of these two options to the the **sh** command when you invoke it:

- **-x** Execution option: To see commands and arguments as they are executed.
- **-v** Verbose option: To display input lines while they are being read.

For example, to debug the shell procedure *filez*, type this:

```
$ sh -x filez
```

You can also bundle the options, as shown here:

```
$ sh -vx filez
```

## Summary of Chapter 24

In this chapter you learned about the **true, false**, and **exit** commands, and the commands for looping (**while, until, break, continue**, and **for**); the commands used to form a conditional statement (**if, then, else**, and **elif**); the command used to test files, strings, and quantities (**test**, along with a number of comparators and operators); and a few other tools for writing shell procedures (the **case** command, the **trap** command, and the options **-x** and **-v** for monitoring a shell procedure being executed).

### Constructing Loops

A **loop** is a segment of a program that executes repeatedly until it is stopped by some indication that a condition has been met.

**Returning true.** The **true** command always returns an exit-status of true.

**Returning false.** The **false** command always returns an exit-status of false.

**Looping while true.** Use the **while** command to continue executing a loop as long as the exit-status is true, like this:

```
while <command list>
do [execute commands
```

**trap**

```
    between do and done]
done
```

**Looping while false.** Use the **until** command to continue executing as long as the exit-status is false, like this:

```
until <command list>
do [execute commands
    between do and done]
done
```

**Nesting.** When one loop is placed inside another, the loops are said to be "nested."

**Breaking out of a loop.** To terminate execution of an inner loop and return to an outer loop, use the **break** command, giving an optional nesting level number if desired.

**Resuming execution of a loop.** To continue execution at an enclosing **for** or **while** loop, use the **continue** command, giving an optional nesting level number if desired.

**Exiting a loop.** To abort the entire procedure, use the **exit** command.

**Looping on a variable.** To construct a loop on a set of assigned values to a given variable, use the **for**- loop construction:

```
for variable in <list>
do [execute commands
    between do and done]
done
```

## *The Conditional Statement*

The **if** command allows you to set up a number of branching options in a shell procedure:

```
if <expression>
then <command list>
fi

if <expression>
then <command list>
else <command list>
fi

elif = "else if"
```

## Testing Files, Quantities, and Strings

**Testing files.** You can use the **test** command with one of five different options to determine whether a file can be read from or written to, whether it is a directory, or whether it is empty.

**Comparing quantities.** You can also use the **test** command with one of six two-letter options to compare two quantities (equal, not equal, and so on).

**Comparing strings.** In addition, you can use the **test** command to determine whether a single string exists or whether two strings are the same or not.

**Compound testing.** Finally, you can form compound tests with symbols for "and" (**-a**), "or" (**-o**), and "not" (**!**).

## Other Programming Techniques

**Multi-way branching.** You can form a multi-way branching list with the **case** command, using pairs of semicolons to terminate individual command lists and the **esac** command to terminate the entire list.

**Interrupt-handling.** You can use the **trap** command to handle various system interrupts.

**Debugging a shell procedure.** Two **sh** command options allow you to display commands and arguments as they are being executed (**-x**) or display input lines while they are being read (**-v**).

# 25

# *Introduction to the C Shell*

In Chapters 21-24 you learned about the **Bourne shell** (the original shell developed by Stephen R. Bourne at Bell Laboratories) and the **sh** command, which is used to invoke Bourne shell procedures. In this chapter we'll talk about a newer shell called the **C shell**. The C shell, developed by William N. Joy at the University of California, is one of the major "Berkeley enhancements" to UNIX.

Some versions of UNIX may support only the Bourne Shell. If yours also supports the C shell, you can use the **csh** to invoke C shell procedures. Unless you are already in the C shell, you should ask the system administrator for your UNIX system to set up your account so that the C shell is your log-in shell. To do this, the administrator must change an item inside a file called */etc/passwd*. Somewhere in this file, there will be a line with your *login* name; the last item of this line must be changed from from */bin/sh* to */bin/csh.*

## Initialization Files

To tailor the C shell to work properly with your terminal, you must have two files in your home directory:

```
.login                         .cshrc
```

These two files will be executed by the C shell every time you log into the system (*.cshrc* first). These files will now be explained in detail.

## The Login File .login

The only time the *.login* file is executed by the C shell is when you log into the system. Therefore, this file should contain only those commands that need to be executed one time only (such as the ones for setup, command search path, and terminal type). Here is a typical *.login* file with the lines spread apart to leave room for explanations:

```
stty ff0 cr0 -tabs erase "^H"
```

[This line is to set up your tty line: no delay after a formfeed or carriage return, replace tabs with spaces, use CTRL-H to erase.]

```
set path=(/test/bin /bin /usr/bin $HOME/bin .)
```

[This line is to set up the command search path. In this case, the shell will search (in this order) */test/bin*, */bin*, */usr/bin*, and subdirectory */bin* of your home directory and your current directory for commands.]

```
setenv TERM vt52
```

[This line sets the "terminal" variable *TERM*. In this case, your terminal will be known by the system as a VT52, with all of the characteristics described under *vt52* in */etc/termcap*.]

```
echo "today is `date` "
```

[This line displays the date each time you login.]

The "set environment" command (**setenv**) is explained in Chapter 26 in the section on "Variables."

## The C shell "Read Command" File .cshrc

The **.cshrc** file is executed whenever a new C shell is created—when you first log into the system or when you invoke a C shell procedure. For this reason, this file contains mostly variables that can be reinitialized for the newly created shell. Here is a typical **.cshrc** file:

```
set prompt = "<\!> "
set history = 11
alias   h        history
alias   cdl      cd '\!*; l | more'
```

```
alias   ch      cd /usr/Mike/book/\!\*
alias   ch8     cd /usr/Mike/book/chap8
alias   ch9     cd /usr/Mike/book/chap9
alias   ch10    cd /usr/Mike/book/chap10
alias   ch11    cd /usr/Mike/book/chap11
```

These lines are explained in detail in the sections that follow.

## Explanations of Individual Items

### *Setting Your Own Prompt* — **prompt**

The C shell, like the Bourne shell, allows you to set the prompt that appears for each command line. However, the C shell allows a "dynamic" prompt, which changes for each new command line. You can create line-numbering in your prompts by using the line number of the command line, known as the "event" and indicated by an exclamation point (!). This is what has been done in the sample **.cshrc** file above, which calls for displaying the current event within a pair of angle brackets: < >. (You have to type a backslash in front of the exclamation mark (!) to prevent it from being interpreted as an "event specifier" by the shell.) Then, with your prompt set this way, this is how your prompt will look immediately after you log in:

```
<1> _
```

This event number is incremented each time you execute another command, thereby "counting" your command lines for you. If you do not assign anything to the variable "prompt," the C shell will assign a percent sign (%) by default.

### *Setting the Number of Events to Be Saved* — **history**

On the second line of the sample **.cshrc** file you find this entry:

```
set history = 11
```

This assigns a value of 11 to the variable *history*. This number determines the number of events to be saved for later reference (that is, the size of the *history* list). Thus, the C shell keeps on this list the command lines of the last 11 events, which can be recalled at your request. You can set the variable *history* to any number, as long as it does not exceed the limit for your system (typically 25). You can change the value of *history* at any time with the **set** command:

```
<2> set history = 5
<3> _
```

**.login**
**.cshrc**
**prompt**
**history**

After this, until variable *history* is reassigned again, it will record only the last five events. You can also invoke **history** as a command to display a "history list," as illustrated here:

```
<10> history
      5 cd book/xenix
      6 ls -l
      7 cp chapter23 /usr/dennis/backup
      8 vi chapter23
      9 ls /usr/dennis/backup
<11> _
```

The five most recent commands are shown after their event numbers. These event numbers can now be used to reinvoke command lines in the history list. Furthermore, by using the history substitution command (explained in the next section), you can modify a recent command before executing it.

## Reinvoking Previous Commands

Being able to reinvoke a past event means that you don't have to retype the whole command string, which may be very long and involved. To reinvoke a past event, construct a "redo" command by typing an exclamation mark (!), followed by a reference to an event. The exclamation mark tells the C shell to look for the command line on the history list. There are four ways to refer to an event:

- Double exclamation marks (the previous event)
- The actual event number
- A relative event number
- A command name

### *Reinvoking the Most Recent Event* !!

The quickest way to reinvoke the most recent event is to type double exclamation marks (!!) as the current command. (Since you entered *history* as event number 10 in the previous section, the next event number will be 11.) After you enter the two exclamation marks, the shell will first display the command string being replayed, then the results, as shown here:

```
<11> !!
history                              [The previous event: number 10]
      6 ls -l
```

```
       7 cp chapter23 /usr/dennis/backup
       8 vi chapter23
       9 ls /usr/dennis/backup
      10 history
<12> _
```

## *Reinvoking an Event by Number* **!n**

In the following example, you reinvoke an event by typing its number. Let's invoke the command identified as event number 9:

```
<12> !9                              [Reinvoke event number 9]
ls /usr/dennis/backup                [Event number 9 is recalled: ls]
micro.back      entry.back           [Results of the ls command]
changes.back    files.back
<13> _
```

## *Reinvoking an Event Relative to the Current Event* **!-i**

In **ed** and **vi** you used relative line numbers (for example, .-5 means five lines back from the current line). The concept is exactly the same with the C shell (!-5 means five events back from the current event). Here are two examples with relative event numbers:

```
<13> !-6
cp chapter 23 /usr/dennis/backup
<14> !-3
history
       8 vi chapter23
       9 ls /usr/dennis/backup
      10 history
      11 history
      12 ls /usr/dennis/backup
      13 cp chapter23 /usr/dennis/backup
<15> _
```

## *Reinvoking an Event with a Search String* ***!string***

You can also type a search string after the exclamation mark, indicating that the C shell is to search for a matching command line. If the C shell finds a match, the event is reinvoked; if it doesn't, the message

**!!**
**!n**
**!-i**
***!string***

"*string*: Event not found" will appear on your screen. Here are two examples:

```
<15> !l
ls /usr/dennis/backup
micro.back      entry.back
changes.back    files.back
<16> !s
s: Event not found
```

Since **ls** begins with *l*, the reexecution command *!l* resulted in a successful match (event number 12), so the C shell displayed the results. The next attempt (*!s*) failed because no command string started with *s*. However, the C shell provides a way to search for a match anywhere on the command line. Type a question mark after the exclamation point, as shown here:

```
<17> !?s
ls /usr/dennis/backup
micro.back      entry.back
changes.back    files.back
<18> _
```

The question mark tells the C shell to look for a match with *s* anywhere on the command line.

## Selecting Individual Arguments

Like the Bourne shell, the C shell splits every input line into words at blanks and tabs, assigning each word a number. Again, the command name is numbered zero, then the first word following is numbered one, the second word two, and so on. For example, the following command line contains a command (word 0), a first argument *-l* (word 1), and a second argument */usr/dennis/backup* (word 2):

```
ls -l /usr/dennis/backup
```

The C shell's numbering scheme allows you to select a specific word on a command line. Simply append a colon, followed by a number, to a reinvocation command (a command that begins with an exclamation point). In the following example, we first set up a command (event number 18), then select word *1* from this command line (event number 19):

```
<18> echo word-1 word-2 word-3 word-4 word-5 word-6
word-1 word-2 word-3 word-4 word-5 word-6
```

Now we select the second word from the command line of event 18:

```
<19> echo !18:1
echo word-1                [The C shell first displays the command]
word-1                     [then it displays the results of the command]
```

## Selecting the First Argument ∧

Another way to obtain the same result is by replacing *1* with a caret (∧), as shown here:

```
<20> echo !18:^
echo word-1
word-1
```

## Selecting the Last Argument $

The dollar sign ($) can be used to address the last word of a command line, as shown here:

```
<21> echo !18:$
echo word-6
word-6
```

## Selecting a Range of Arguments n-m

To address a range of words, use the hyphen, as shown in this example:

```
<22> echo !18:2-5
echo word-2 word-3 word-4 word-5
word-2 word-3 word-4 word-5
```

## Selecting All Arguments *

To address every word of a command line except zero (that is, to select every argument of the command, but not the command name itself), use an asterisk (*) to make a wildcard selection, as shown here:

```
<23> echo !18:*
echo word-2 word-3 word-4 word-5 word-5 word-6
word-1 word-2 word-3 word-4 word-5 word-6
```

## Omitting the Colon with Symbols

∧
$
n-m
*

Whenever you use a caret (∧), dollar sign ($), or asterisk (*) in place of an explicit word designator, you can omit the colon (:) between the event number and the word designator. For example, here is another way to type events 20, 21, and 23:

```
<20> echo !18^
echo word-1
word-1
<21> echo !18$
echo word-6
word-6
<23> echo !18*
echo word-2 word-3 word-4 word-5 word-5 word-6
word-1 word-2 word-3 word-4 word-5 word-6
```

# Modifying A Command Line

The C shell allows you to reinvoke an **event** in the history list (a command line) with modifications, which can spare you a lot of extra typing. To modify an event, type a modifier after the colon (:) in place of a word number. You can substitute one string for another, repeat a string, remove prefixes and suffixes, preview an event, or protect an event from further changes.

## *Replacing a Character String* **s**

Use the substitute modifier **s** the way you have used the **s** command with **ed** and **vi** to replace one character string with another. As an example, let's reinvoke event 23, then make a substitution:

```
<24> !23
echo word-1 word-2 word-3 word-4 word-5 word-6
word-1 word-2 word-3 word-4 word-5 word-6
```

Now we'll use the substitute modifier **s/w/W** to substitute *W* for *w* (first occurrence only) of the most recent event:

```
<25> !!:s/w/W
echo Word-1 word-2 word-3 word-4 word-5 word-6
Word-1 word-2 word-3 word-4 word-5 word-6
```

As with the **s** (substitute) command in **ed**, only the first occurrence of *w* in *word-1* is affected. To convert all occurrences of *w* to *W*, use the global modifier **g**, as shown here:

```
<26> !23:gs/w/W
echo Word-1 Word-2 Word-3 Word-4 Word-5 Word-6
Word-1 Word-2 Word-3 Word-4 Word-5 Word-6
```

You can modify only a selected word by including its number. The following command affects only the second word:

```
<27> echo !23:2:s/word/WORD
echo WORD-2
WORD-2
```

If you attempt to modify a non-applicable word of a string (such as "word-9", in this example), a "Modifier fails" message will be displayed.

## *Repeating the Previous Substitution* &

The & modifier allows you to repeat the last substitution without having to retype the entire command. Suppose that event 25 was just invoked:

```
<25> !!:s/w/W
echo Word-1 word-2 word-3 word-4 word-5 word-6
Word-1 word-2 word-3 word-4 word-5 word-6
```

We could use the & modifier for the next event:

```
<26> !25:&
echo Word-1 Word-2 word-3 word-4 word-5 word-6
Word-1 Word-2 word-3 word-4 word-5 word-6
```

The & modifier affects only Word-2 this time.

## *Removing the Last Name from a Pathname* h

Use the **h** modifier to remove the last name in a pathname. For example, let's create a pathname:

```
<28> echo /usr/dennis/backup.new
/usr/dennis/backup.new
```

Then we can use the **h** (head) modifier to remove *backup.new* from the pathname, like this:

```
<29> !!:h
echo /usr/dennis
/usr/dennis
```

## *Removing the Suffix* r

Use the **r** modifier to remove the suffix (in the form of *.xxx*) from a string. Let's use the **r** modifier to remove *.new* from the pathname in event 28:

```
<30> !28:r
echo /usr/dennis/backup
/usr/dennis/backup
```

### *Removing the Prefix* **t**

Use the **t** (tail) modifier to remove the prefix from a pathname. Let's use the **t** modifier on the pathname in event 28:

```
<31> !28:t
echo backup.new
backup.new
```

### *Previewing a Command Line* **p**

To display a command line without executing it, use the **p** (print) modifier to preview it. For example, let's display the command string of event 28:

```
<32> !28:p

echo /usr/dennis/backup.new
<33> _
```

### *Preventing Further Modification* **q**

Use the **q** modifier to "quote" a command line (that is, to protect it from further modification). After you execute event 33, any attempt to modify either event (28 or 33) will result in an error message ("modifier failed"):

```
<33> !28:q
echo /usr/dennis/backup.new
/usr/dennis/backup.new
```

## Aliased Commands **alias**

As explained earlier in this chapter, the C shell splits command input into words. Each of these words is checked for a match against the C shell's "alias list," which provides a list of abbreviated commands, called **aliased commands**. If the C shell finds a match, it substitutes the full command line for the aliased command; if the C shell does not find a match, no substitution takes place. (You may recall that seven of the nine lines placed in the file **.cshrc** at the beginning of this chapter were intended for the "alias list.")

## *Creating a Custom Command*

The "alias list" allows you to create either a new name for an existing or your own new command, which consists of a compound command string. For example, you can create a new **d** command to replace the **pwd** command, so that when you type *d* <*cr*>, the result will be the same as if you had typed *pwd* <*cr*>. Here's how to do this:

```
<34> alias d pwd
<35> d                                   [Invoke the new d command]
/usr/book/xenix.1
```

Note that creating a new command name does not prevent you from continuing to use the old name. You can now use either **d** or **pwd**.

## *Removing an Aliased Command*

If you want to remove the **d** command above from the alias list, use the **unalias** command, as shown here:

**t**
**p**
**q**
**alias**

```
<36> unalias d
<37> d
d: command not found
```

### Storing Aliased Commands

The most common use of the **alias** command is to allow you to type shorthand commands to replace frequently-used and excessively long commands. To preserve your aliased commands from one session to another, it's most convenient to store your own "alias list" in your **.cshrc** file, which is read every time a new subshell is created.

You can also use **alias** as a command to display your "alias list," as shown here:

```
<38> alias
alias ch8  cd /usr/Mike/book/chapter8
alias ch9  cd /usr/Mike/book/chapter9
alias ch10 cd /usr/Mike/book/chapter10
alias ch11 cd /usr/Mike/book/chapter11
```

### Invoking an Aliased Command

Once you have *ch8*, *ch9*, *ch10*, and *ch11* stored in your "alias list," you can invoke them as your own private commands. For example, you can now invoke *ch10* to move to the directory called */usr/Mike/book/chapter10.* Let's try it (you'll like it):

```
<39> ch10
<40> pwd
/usr/Mike/book/chapter10
```

### Making a "Real-Time" Selection

You can set up a variable command that allows real-time selection at the time of invocation, like this:

```
alias ch cd /usr/Mike/book/\!\*
```

The aliased command **ch** allows you to pass an argument to be used as a part of the change directory (**cd**) command. The exclamation mark and asterisk must be quoted to prevent them from being interpreted by the shell. However, they are still passed to the alias. Let's invoke **ch** with arguments:

```
<39> ch chapter10
<40> pwd
```

```
/usr/Mike/book/chapter10
<41> ch chapter9
<42> pwd
/usr/Mike/book/chapter9
```

### Combining Commands

You can combine more than one command into one aliased command, as shown here:

```
alias cdl cd '\!*; ls -l | more'
```

Because this command list contains spaces, an asterisk, and a pipeline symbol, it must be enclosed within single quotes ('). The exclamation mark (!) must be quoted (preceded by a backslash) to prevent the C shell from interpreting it and passing it to the alias. When invoked, **cdl** changes to the directory that you type after *cdl* as an argument; then all the files in this directory are piped to the **more** command to be displayed on the screen. By using **more**, instead of **cat**, you can control the display of a large directory like */etc*, as illustrated here:

```
<43> cdl /etc
total 398
    -rwx------ 1 bin     1346 Sep  4 1982 accton
    -rwxr-x--- 1 bin      157 Apr 28 1981 asktime
    -rw-r--r-- 1 bin       21 Dec 19 15:40 checklist
    -rwx------ 1 daemon  6354 Sep  4 1982 cron
    -rw-r--r-- 1 bin        0 Apr 30 1981 ddate
    drwxr-xr-x 2 bin      128 Feb 24 04:50 default
    -rws--x--x 1 sysinf  7984 Feb  3 1983 dmesg
    -rwx------ 1 roo    28432 Feb 24 04:44 dmfmt
    -rwx------ 1 root    1274 Feb 24 04:46 firsttime
    -rwx--x--x 1 bin     9228 Sep  4 1982 fixperm
    -rwx------ 1 bin     4080 Feb 15 14:30 getty
    -rw-r--r-- 1 bin       45 Feb 24 04:45 group
    -rwx------ 1 bin     4721 Feb 24 04:45 haltsys
    -rwx------ 1 bin     1438 Sep 27 1982 inir
    -rwx------ 1 bin     4736 Feb 24 04:44 init
    -rwx--x--x 1 bin     5792 Feb 22 16:23 mdmctl
    -rwx--x--x 1 root    7136 Feb 15 14:18 mffmt
    -rwx--x--x 1 sys    10496 Feb 24 04:45 mkfs
    -rwx------ 1 sys     5088 Feb 24 04:45 mknod
    -rwx------ 1 root   22720 Feb 14 1983 mkuser
    -rw-rw-r-- 1 bin      202 Dec 23 09:21 motd
    -rwx--x--x 1 bin     5404 Feb 24 04:45 mount
--More-- (23%)
```

At this point, the display stops until you press the space bar.

### *Recursive Substitutions*

You can alias commands recursively to as many levels as you like. If you do this, the C shell will substitute the aliased command over and over again until it reaches the last one in the list:

```
<44> alias com.1 com.2
<45> alias com.2 com.3
<46> alias com.3 echo last command
<47> com.1                              [Invoke com.1 command.]
last command
```

Suppose you changed the alias procedure of event *<46>* so that *com.3* is aliased to *com.1*. Then, if you invoke **com.1**, you will see how the C shell deals with this, like this:

```
<46> alias com.3 com.1
<47> com.1
Alias loop.                             [ error message ]
```

The C shell can detect that this is a infinite loop, and it warns you with an error message.

## The Logout File

**.logout**

You can arrange for a custom logout to occur each time you sign off by placing commands in a special file called **.logout**. These commands may be standard UNIX commands or custom commands that you have set up with a shell procedure. The commands may simply place a message on the screen, or they may remove all the temporary files that you have created during your session with UNIX. The file must reside in your home directory, not a subdirectory. Here is an example of a **.logout** file already created:

```
<48> cat .logout
echo You are leaving the system
echo Goodbye !
```

### *Ordinary Logout*

With these two command lines in your **.logout** file, pressing CTRL-D to log out not only allows you to exit from the system, but also to display a brief message on the screen:

```
<49>                                  [You press CTRL-D]
<49> You are leaving the system
Goodbye !
```

### Explicit Logout

You may recall that CTRL-D serves several functions in UNIX—one being a signal to log out, another being the "end-of-file" code. If a command that reads keyboard input is designed to exit upon receiving an end-of-file code (EOF), it will terminate the process. Occasionally this results in an accidental logoff. To prevent this kind of mistake, the C shell provides a mechanism that disables CTRL-D as the signal to log out and forces you to type *logout* instead. The mechanism is the variable called *ignoreeof* ("ignore end-of-file"). Just type *set ignoreeof* to disable CTRL-D as the logoff signal.

```
<49> set ignoreeof          [Set variable ignoreeof]
<50>                        [You press CTRL-D]
Use "logout" to logout.
<50> logout
```

## Summary of Chapter 25

This chapter introduces the C shell, an enhanced version of the Bourne shell. You learned about the two files frequently used with the C shell (**.login** and **.cshrc**), setting your own prompt, reinvoking previous commands, selecting individual arguments, modifying a command line, abbreviating a command string, and setting up a logout file (**.logout**).

### Initialization Files

**.login**. This file contains commands that are to be executed every time you log in, such as identifying your terminal, modifying your default command search path, and possibly providing a login message.

**.cshrc**. This file contains commands that are to be executed whenever a new C shell is created, and may be used to set your prompt, set the number of events to be saved, and set new names for command strings.

**Setting your own prompt**. Use the "prompt" variable to set your own prompt, using either words or symbols.

**Setting the number of events to be saved.** Use the "history" variable to set the number of command lines (events) to be saved for future reference.

**.logout**

## *Reinvoking Previous Commands*

**Reinvoking the most recent event.** To reinvoke the most recent event, type *!!*.

**Reinvoking an event by number.** To reinvoke any previous event, type an exclamation point, then the number, as in *!17*.

**Reinvoking an event relative to the current event.** To reinvoke an event a certain number of command lines from the current line, type an exclamation point, a minus sign, and the number, as in *!-4*.

**Reinvoking an event with a search string.** To reinvoke an event in the history list that begins with a certain string of characters, type an exclamation point, then the characters, as in *!ls*. To allow a match anywhere in the event, type a question mark between the exclamation mark and the string, as in *!?s*.

## *Selecting Individual Arguments*

**Selecting an argument by numbers.** To select an individual argument in a command string, add a colon and the number of the argument to the end of a reinvocation command, as in *echo !18:4*.

**Selecting the first argument.** To select the first argument, type one of the following alternate commands: *echo !18:1*, *echo !18:^*, *echo !18^*.

**Selecting the last argument.** To select the last argument, type a command like the following: *echo !18:$* (or *echo !18$*).

**Selecting a range of arguments.** To select arguments from a range of numbers, type a command like this: *echo !18:2-5*.

**Selecting all arguments.** To select all arguments, use the wildcard symbol (*), as in *echo !18:** (or *echo !18**).

## *Modifying a Command Line*

**Replacing a character string.** To replace one character string with another, use the substitute modifier **s**, as in this example: *!!:s/w/W* (replace *w* with *W*).

**Repeating the previous substitution.** To repeat the previous substitution, use the repeat modifier **&**, as in *!25:&*.

**Removing the last name from a pathname.** To remove the last name in a pathname, use the head modifier **h**, as in *!!:h*.

**Removing the prefix.** To remove the prefix from a pathname, use the tail modifier **t**, as in *!28:t*.

**Removing the suffix.** To remove the suffix from a pathname, use the remove modifier **r**, as in *!28:r*.

**Previewing a command line.** To display a command line (event) without executing it, use the preview modifier **p**, as in *!28:p*.

**Preventing further modification.** To protect a command line (event) from further modification, use the quote modifier **q**, as in *!28:q*.

## *Aliased Commands*

**Creating a custom command.** To create an abbreviated name for a longer command, assign the longer command to the shorter one with the **alias** command.

**Removing an alias.** To remove an alias already assigned, use the **unalias** command, like this:

```
% unalias d
```

**Storing aliases.** To store an alias permanently, place it in your **.cshrc** file along with other aliases, thereby forming an "alias list." To view this list, type **alias** as a command.

**Invoking an alias.** To invoke an alias in your "alias list," simply type the alias form as a command.

**Making a real-time selection.** To allow arguments to be passed with an aliased command, use an exclamation point followed by a wildcard character (*), both preceded by a backslash.

**Combining commands.** The C shell allows you to combine more than one command into a single aliased command.

## *The Logout File*

**Standard logout.** The C shell allows you to set up a logout file to run commands at the time you sign off the system. These commands can either perform housekeeping tasks or just display a message.

**Explicit logout.** To force you to logout by typing *logout* instead of CTRL-D, include the command **set ignoreeof** in your *.login* file.

# 26

# C Shell Variables

## Assigning a String Variable

The method for assigning a variable in the C shell is somewhat different from the method in the Bourne shell. In the following example, the string *table* is assigned as a value of variable *VAL*:

```
<1> set VAL = table
```

In the C shell, the **set** command is required, and the equal sign (=) must be surrounded by spaces in many UNIX systems. As in the Bourne, type a dollar sign ($) and variable name to recall the assigned value. Thus, *$VAL* will yield the value of variable *VAL*:

```
<2> echo $VAL
table
<3> _
```

If a value to be assigned to a variable contains spaces, it must be enclosed within single quotes, double quotes, or parentheses, as shown here:

```
<3> set var1 = '$VAL A B'
<4> set var2 = "$VAL A B"
<5> set var3 = ($VAL A B)
<6> _
```

Each pair of symbols—' ', " ", ( )—will have a slightly different meaning, as summarized here:

- *Single quotes.* Metacharacters are interpreted literally.
- *Double quotes.* Metacharacters retain their special meaning.
- *Parentheses.* Metacharacters retain their special meaning, and the characters enclosed form an array (discussed in the next section).

The following **echo** commands illustrate these differences:

```
<6> echo $var1
$VAL A B
<7> echo $var2
table A B
<8> echo $var3
table A B
```

```
<9> echo $var1[2]
Subscript out of range
<10> echo $var2[2]
Subscript out of range
<11> echo $var3[2]
A
```

## Displaying Assigned Values

**set**

By typing the **set** command by itself, you can display a listing of declared variables and their assigned values, as illustrated here:

```
<12> set
argv ()
bk /usr/book/
history 23
home /usr/work
path (/test/bin /bin /usr/bin /usr/work/bin .)
prompt <!>
shell /bin/csh
status 0
unmask 022
<13> _
```

## Removing a Variable

**unset**

The C shell keeps a list of all declared variables. To remove a variable from the list, use the **unset** command, as shown here:

```
<13> unset bk     [Remove variable bk from the list]
<14> set          [Display the variable list]
```

```
argv ()
history 23
home /usr/work
path (/test/bin /bin /usr/bin /usr/work/bin .)
prompt <!>
shell /bin/csh
status 0
unmask 22                        [Variable bk is no longer in the list]
<15> _
```

## Variables as Arrays

Improving on the Bourne shell, the C shell treats any string value of a variable as an array—provided that the string value is enclosed in parentheses . This means that, even though the entire string shares a common name, you can access individual words in the string. In the example that follows, the variable *path* is the name of an array whose value is a command search path. As in the C language, each item of an array can be addressed individually by pointer: the first item is referred to as path[1], the second one is path[2], the third one is path[3], and so on. In the following example, we recall the third item:

```
<15> echo $path            [ Recall all values of variable path]
/test/bin /bin /usr/bin /usr/work/bin
<16> echo $path[3]         [ Recall item 3]
/usr/bin                   [Third item in the search path]
<17> _
```

Since each item occupies a numbered position in the array, you can overwrite any item in a declared string variable. Type the **set** command and the array name, followed by the number enclosed in square brackets [ ]. In the following example, the first location of array *path* is overwritten with the string */usr/joe/bin* (this becomes the first name in the path):

```
<17> set path[1] = /usr/joe/bin
<18> echo $path
/usr/joe/bin /bin /usr/bin /usr/work/bin
<19> _
```

### *Declaring an Array*

You must declare an array before you can use it. To declare an array, specify the array's name and size in a dummy **set** command. The C shell will reserve the number of locations that you have requested. You can then initialize the array with an actual string. In the example shown here, seven positions of array *temp* are set aside with null strings:

**set**
**unset**

```
<19> set temp = ("" "" "" "" "" "")
<20> _
```

## Assigning Positions

Once the positions in the array have been reserved, use *temp* as a storage location, to which strings can be written and from which strings can be read. Let's fill some of these locations with actual strings:

```
<20> set temp[1] = one
<21> set temp[3] = three
<22> echo $temp
one three
<23> _
```

You can also assign the value of an element in one array to an element in another, as shown here:

```
<23> set temp[2] = $path[1]
<24> echo $temp
one /usr/joe/bin three
<25> _
```

You can also retrieve any of these strings and assign them to another variable, as shown here:

```
<25> set VAL1 = $temp[1]
<26> echo $VAL1
one
<27> _
```

## Determining Whether a Variable Has Been Declared ?

Special reserved variables are used to obtain information about assigned variables. The special variable ? is zero (false) if a variable is undeclared and one (true) if it has been declared, as shown here:

```
<27> echo $?temp     [Test variable temp]
1                    [True: the variable has been declared]
<28> _
```

## Determining the Size of an Array #

Use special variable # to determine the size of a variable (array). Let's check the size of array *temp*:

```
<28> echo $#temp      [ Test array temp]
7                     [Array temp has seven positions]
<29> _
```

## Assigning Numeric Variables

@

Just as the **set** command is used to assign **string** values to variables, the @ command is used to assign **numeric** values to variables, as shown here:

```
<29> @ VAL = 3
<30> _
```

If you attempt to assign a non-numeric value to a variable with @, a syntax error message will be displayed, like this:

```
<30> @ VAL = abc
@: Expression syntax
<31> _
```

To list all declared numeric variables, use the @ command alone, just as you did with the **set** command:

```
<23> @
val 3
num 5
integer 12
<24> _
```

### *Performing Arithmetic*

Unlike the **set** command, the @ command can be used to perform arithmetic and logical testing, like the **expr** command of the Bourne shell. You can use @ with the following arithmetic operators:

| | |
|---|---|
| + | addition |
| - | subtraction |
| * | multiplication |
| / | division |
| % | remainder |

Here are some examples:

```
<32> @ A = 2 + 4       [ Add 2 and 4 and assign the sum to A]
<33> @ S = $A - 3      [ Subtract 3 from A and assign the difference to S]
```

? # @

```
<34> @ M = $A * $S             [ Multiply A by S and assign the
                                product to M]
<35> @ R = $M % 4              [ Divide M by 4 and assign the
                                remainder to R]
<36> @ D = $M / 4              [ Divide M by 4 and assign the
                                quotient to D]
<37> echo $A $S $M $R $D       [Display all five results]
6 3 18 2 4
<38> _
```

## Increasing the Value of a Variable

**++ or +=*n***

Use the ++ operator to increase the value of a variable by one:

```
<38> @ D++                     [ Increase the value of D by one ]
<39> echo $D
5
<40> _
```

You can add any numeric value to an variable with the += operator. For example, suppose variable *R* has a value of 2. The following example shows how you could add *5* to *R*:

```
<40> @ R += 5                  [ Add 5 to the value of R]
<41> echo $R
7
<42> _
```

## Decreasing the Value of a Variable

**-- or -= *n***

Use the -- operator to decrease the value of a variable by one:

```
<42> @ D--                     [ Decrease the value of D by one ]
<43> echo $D
4
<44> _
```

You can subtract any numeric value from an variable with the -= operator. For example, using variable *D* with a value of *4*, the following example shows how you could subtract *3* from *D*:

```
<44> @ D -= 3                  [ Subtract 3 from the value of D]
<45> echo $D
1
<46> _
```

### Obtaining the One's Complement of a Variable

~

Use the tilde (~) to obtain the one's complement of the value of a variable (the opposite sign minus one), as illustrated here:

```
<46> R =~ $R        [ Assign to R its own one's complement]
<47> echo $R
-8                  [This is the one's complement of 7 (-7- 1)]
<48> _
```

### Logical Testing

Logical tests work in the C shell like the **test** command in the Bourne shell to yield true (1) or false (0) as the exit-status of a test:

| | |
|---|---|
| **A < B** | True if A is less than B |
| **A > B** | True if A is greater than B |
| **A <= B** | True if A is less or equal to B |
| **A >= B** | True if A is greater or equal to B |
| **A = B** | True if A is equal to B |
| **A != B** | True if A is not equal to B |

Here is an example of a sequence of logical tests:

```
<48> @ A = 10; @ B = 15   [ Assign values to variables A and B]
<49> @ C = ($A <= $B)     [ Test whether A is less than or equal
                            to B]
<50> echo $C              [ Display the result]
1                         [True: A is less than or equal to B]
<51> _
```

The expression right of the equal sign must be enclosed in parentheses to prevent the shell from interpreting the greater than sign (>). You can also construct more complex statements, as shown here:

```
<51> @ K = ($A + $B > $A * $B) [ Is the sum greater than the product?]
<52> echo $K
0                              [False: 25 is not greater than 150]
<53> _
```

As you can see, the return-status of the expression of event 43 is a zero, which indicates that the expression is false.

## Setting Elements of a Numeric Array

++ or += *n*
– or -= *n*
~

Arrays were discussed earlier in this chapter in connection with **string** variables. Like the **set** command, the @ command can also be used with pointers to select individual elements of a **numeric** array. Here is an example:

```
<53> @ scale = (1 2 3 4 5 6 7 8 9)
<54> @ scale[3] = 100          [Assign a value to the numeric array]
<55> echo $scale
1 2 100 4 5 6 7 8 9
<56> _
```

### Performing Arithmetic

The @ command allows you to perform arithmetic on an element of an array. In the following example, the values of positions 3 and 5 are added together, then the sum is stored in location 8:

```
<56> @ scale[8] = $scale[3] + $scale[5]
<57> echo $scale
1 2 100 4 5 6 7 105 9
<58> _
```

### Performing Logical Tests

You can also perform logical tests within a numeric array. Here, a logical test is performed on the values of positions 3 and 8 of array "scale," with the logical result stored in position 9:

```
<58> @ scale[9] = ($scale[3] > $scale[8])
<59> echo $scale
1 2 100 4 5 6 7 105 0          [False: 100 is not greater than 105]
<60> _
```

Position 9 becomes 0, indicating **false**. Once again, the expression to the right of the equal sign in event 50 is enclosed in parentheses to prevent the "greater than" sign (>) from being interpreted by the shell.

## Variables Reserved by the C Shell

The C shell uses the variables named in this section to record information and pass it to a child process. Some of the special variables are set by the C shell, and some can be changed by the user.

### Argument Number n  **$argv[n]**

The shell uses this variable to pass arguments to the C shell procedure in the same way that the Bourne shell passes positional parameters to the shell script. Therefore, $argv[0] is the name of the program being invoked, $argv[1] is the first argument, and so on. For example, suppose there is a C shell procedure *reflect* with the following contents:

```
<60> cat reflect
#                                      [# indicates that this is a C shell
                                       procedure]
echo $argv[0] $argv[1] $argv[2] $argv[3]
set argv[3] = NEW
echo $argv[3]
<61> _
```

Let's invoke *reflect:*

```
<61> reflect one two three             [Invoke the program with three
                                       arguments]
reflect one two three                  [The command line just typed is
                                       echoed]
NEW                                    [NEW replaces three as the third
                                       item]
<62> _
```

The C shell passes the positional parameters to *reflect,* and you can change any argument except the **echo** command argv[0]. However, you can still use $1, $2, . . . , $9 in place of $argv.

## *Number of Arguments* **$#argv**

The C shell uses this variable to store the number of arguments in the command just invoked. Let's change the *reflect* program so that it looks like this:

```
<62> cat reflect
#                                      [A C shell procedure]
echo $argv[1] $argv[2] $argv[3]
echo $#argv                            [Add this new line]
<63> reflect one two three
one two three                          [Only the arguments are echoed
                                       now]
3                                      [Number of arguments]
<64> _
```

The expression *argv[*]* refers to all of the positional parameters.

## *Search Path* **$cdpath**

When you type the **cd** command with an argument as the target directory, the **cd** command uses the value of *cdpath* as the search path to

**$argv[n]**
**$#argv**
**$cdpath**

search from the current directory for that target directory. If the subdirectory is found, this becomes your working directory. For example, suppose your current working directory is */usr/book* and *cdpath* is set this way:

```
<64> set cdpath = $HOME/book/xenix/chapter21
<65> _
```

and you type this:

```
<65> cd chapter21
<66> pwd                          [ Verify your current directory]
/usr/book/xenix/chapter21
<67> _
```

If *cdpath* is **not** set or the search fails, a message is displayed:

```
<67> cd xenix
cd: No such file or directory
<68> _
```

The message appears because *xenix* is not a subdirectory of your current directory (in fact, your current directory is a subdirectory of *xenix*).

## Child Process Number — $child

This variable carries the process number of a child process, which is forked in the background. The C shell unsets this variable when the child process terminates.

## Echo a Command — $echo

If this variable is set, any command you enter will be echoed (displayed on the screen) before being executed. This variable works like the -x option of the **sh** command (Bourne shell).

```
<68> set echo                     [ Declare variable echo]
<69> pwd                          [ You then type this]
pwd                               [Your command is echoed]
/usr/book/xenix                   before being executed]
<70> _
```

You can use the **unset** command to remove the effects of *echo.*

## Length of the History List — $history

This variable was explained in Chapter 25. You can set **$history** to the size of the history list.

## Home Directory **$home**

This variable, the same as the **$HOME** variable of the Bourne shell, can be abbreviated with a tilde (~). Its value is the pathname of your home directory, which is set by the shell. Here is an example:

```
<70> cp /usr/john/file.1 ~/saving
<71> _
```

This command causes *file.1* in directory */usr/john* to be copied to directory *$HOME/saving.*

## Ignore End-of-File Character **$ignoreeof**

Ordinarily, CTRL-D (or ∧D) is defined as the end-of-file (EOF) character. If this variable is set, the shell will ignore the end-of-file character from your keyboard. This prevents you from being accidentally logged off. Then you can exit with the **logout** command (for a more detailed explanation, see "Explicit Logout" at the end of Chapter 25).

## Prevent Overwriting **$noclobber**

When this variable is set, the C shell prevents you from overwriting a file as the result of redirection of output. For example, suppose file *tempfile* resides in your current directory, and you type this:

```
<71> set noclobber                 [ Declare variable]
<72> echo I WRITE THIS LINE > tempfile
                                   [Redirection of output]
tempfile: File exists              [Overwriting is not allowed]
<73> _
```

Once *noclobber* has been set, the shell also will not create a new file when you append text to a non-existent file, as shown below:

```
<73> echo I ADD NEW LINE >> newfile
newfile: No such file or dirctory
<74> _
```

## Remove Special Meanings Automatically **$noglob**

When this variable is set, filename expansions such as * , ?, and ~ are treated as normal characters, allowing you to use them literally. Here is an example:

**$child**
**$echo**
**$history**
**$home**
**$ignoreeof**
**$noclobber**
**$noglob**

```
<74> echo *
file.1 file.2 file.3 tempfile   [Files in this directory]
<75> set noglob                 [ Set variable noglob ]
<76> echo *                     [ The asterisk is now treated
*                               as an ordinary character]
<77> _
```

In event 74, the asterisk (*) is interpreted by the shell as a wildcard character, allowing all filenames in the current directory to be displayed. The variable *noglob* is set in event 70 so that the shell treats the asterisk the same as any other character, as shown in event 75.

## *Remove Special Meanings If There Is No Match* $nonomatch

When this variable is set, the C shell first attempts to find a matching file with one of the filename expansion characters such as *, ?, and ~. If the shell finds a match, it passes that name to the calling program; if it cannot find a match, it passes the argument with the special character treated literally. If **$nonomatch** is **not** declared and the C shell fails to find a match, the C shell will display an error, as illustrated here:

```
<77> echo tempfile?
echo: No match
<78> set nonomatch              [ Set variable nonomatch ]
<79> echo tempfile?             [ The echo command interprets the
tempfile?                       question mark literally]
<80> _
```

## *Search Path* $path

The C shell uses the value of this variable as the command search path, assigning to it the default value */usr/bin /bin.* Therefore, you can execute only files that reside in those directories. This variable is explained in detail in Chapters 21 and 25.

## *Prompt Symbol* $prompt

The value of this variable is your prompt symbol. If you don't set *prompt,* the C shell will set % as the default value. This variable is explained in greater detail in Chapter 25.

## *Pathname of the Shell* $shell

The value of this variable is the pathname of the shell. The variable *shell* reflects whatever is set in the file */etc/passwd,* as shown here:

```
<80> echo $shell
/bin/csh
<81> _
```

The */bin/csh* response indicates that you are using the C shell.

## *Exit-Status of the Last Command* **$status**

The value of this variable is the exit-status returned by the command most recently invoked.

## *Time to Execute a Command* **$time**

When this variable is set, the shell displays the number of seconds to execute the most recent command (user time, system time, real time, and the percentage of real time spent on user time and system time combined):

```
<81> set time
<82> pwd
/usr/xenix/book/chapter21
0.1u 0.4s 0:02 24%
<83> _
```

The numbers shown indicate user time (*0.1*), system time (*0.4*), and real time in seconds (*0:02*) required to process the **pwd** command, along with the percentage of real time spent on user time and system time ((0.1 + 0.4)/2).

## *Terminal Type* **$TERM**

This variable, which is set with the **setenv** command, indicates the type of terminal you are using. You must set this variable before you can use **vi**, **more**, or one of several other programs.

## *Process Identification Number* **$$**

The value of this variable is the process identification number of the current process (discussed in greater detail in Chapter 21).

## *Complete Messages* **$verbose**

This variable works like the **-v** option of the Bourne shell when invoked with the **sh** command. When "verbose" is set, your commands will be echoed when read by the C shell.

### *Permanent Settings*

If you want any of these variables set to a value of your choice every time you log in, place them in your **.cshrc** file, which is executed each time you log into the system and each time a new process is created.

## Summary of Chapter 26

In this chapter you learned about assigning values to string and numeric variables, working with variables as arrays, performing arithmetic and logical operations, and special C shell variables.

### *Assigning String Values*

Use the **set** command to assign a string value to a variable.

**Calling a variable.** After the string value has been assigned, call the variable preceded by a dollar sign.

**Displaying variables.** Use the **set** command by itself to display all declared variables and their assigned values. Use the **unset** command to "undeclare" a variable.

**Variables as arrays.** The C shell treats the value of a variable as an array whenever the assigned value is enclosed in parentheses. This allows you to access individual elements of the array.

**Declaring an array.** Use null strings within single quotes to declare an array.

**Assigning positions.** Once declared, an array can be filled one position at a time.

**Checking declaration.** Use a question mark between the dollar sign and the name of a variable in an **echo** command to determine whether or not a variable has been declared. The response will be either yes (1) or no (0).

**Determining size.** Use a pound sign (#) between the dollar sign and the name of a variable in an **echo** command to display the number of elements in an array.

## *Assigning Numeric Values*

Use the @ instead of the **set** command to assign a numeric value to a variable.

**Calling a variable.** After the string value has been assigned, call the variable preceded by a dollar sign.

**Displaying variables.** Use the @ command by itself to display all declared numeric variables and their assigned values.

**Performing arithmetic.** Use the operators +, −, *, /, and % to perform arithmetic with numeric variables.

**Increasing a variable.** Use the ++ and +=**n** operators with the @ command to increase the value of a variable.

**Decreasing a variable.** Use the — and -=**n** operators to decrease the value of a variable.

**Complementing a variable.** Use the ~ operator to obtain the one's complement of a variable.

**Performing logical tests.** Use the operators <, >, <=, >=, !=, and = with the @ command to perform logical test. The response will be either true (1) or false (0).

**Setting elements of a numeric array.** Use an array selector in square brackets with the @ command to assign a numeric value to an individual element in an array. You can use the @ command to perform either arithmetic or logical tests on individual elements of an array.

## *Variables Reserved by the C Shell*

The variables listed here are reserved for use by the C shell:

| **Description** | **Name** | **Type** |
|---|---|---|
| Argument number n | $argv[n] | string or numeric |
| Number of arguments | $#argv | numeric |
| Search path | $cdpath | string |
| Child process number | $child | numeric |
| Echo a command | $echo | true or false |
| Length of history list | $history | numeric |
| Home directory | $home | string |
| Ignore end-of-file | $ignoreeof | true or false |

| | | |
|---|---|---|
| Prevent overwriting | $noclobber | true or false |
| Remove special meaning automatically | $noglob | true or false |
| Remove special meaning if there is no match | $nonomatch | true or false |
| Search path | $path | string |
| Prompt symbol | $prompt | string |
| Pathname of the shell | $shell | string |
| Exit status of last command | $status | true or false |
| Time to execute a command | $time | string |
| Terminal type | $TERM | string |
| Process identification number | $$ | numeric |
| Complete messages | $verbose | true or false |

## *Permanent Settings*

You can set some of these reserved variables in your **.cshrc** file, which is executed each time you log on and each time a new process is created.

# 27

# C Shell Procedures

## Executing a File as a Shell Procedure

When used as a programming language, the C shell provides mechanisms similar to those used in the Bourne shell, but these mechanisms require slightly different program syntax. A file can be invoked as a C shell procedure in one of two ways:

- make the file executable
- execute the **csh** command with the file's name as an argument.

### *Making a File Executable*

Whenever you make a file executable with **chmod,** it becomes a command file. This means that you can execute it as a normal command within the directory where this file resides. Before executing a shell file, the C shell checks for a pound sign (#) as the first non-blank character. If this symbol is missing, the file will automatically be executed in the Bourne shell by default (see the example in the next section).

### *Executing the csh Command*

Invoking the **csh** command with the name of the desired file as an argument is the surest way to have this file executed by the C shell, as shown here:

```
<1> csh filename
```

Like the Bourne shell, the C shell passes the filename as the value of argv[0] and any following words as argv[1], argv[2], and so on.

### File Checking

The C shell has a method for checking files similar to the **test** statement of the Bourne shell. However, the format of the expressions, which may be used in **if, for each,** and **while** statements, is different. Each expression returns a status of either true (1) or false (0), depending on what is being tested:

| Option | | Meaning |
|---|---|---|
| -e | <filename> | true if the file exists |
| -z | | true if the size of the file is zero |
| -f | | true if the file is an ordinary file |
| -d | | true if the file is a directory |
| -o | | true if the user owns the file |
| -r | | true if the file is readable |
| -w | | true if the file is writeable |
| -x | | true if the file is executable |

## Forming Conditional Statements

### The Simple Conditional Statement

**if**

Like the **if** statement of the Bourne shell, the **if** statement of the C shell evaluates the status of the expression. If it is true, the shell executes the statement that follows; if it is false, the shell skips the statement that follows. Here is an example:

```
<2> cat example.1
# This program checks for the existence of the argument file
if -e $argv[1]
  echo "File $argv[1] exists"
```

The pound sign (#) is mandatory; without it, the C shell cannot execute this file. As shown in the example, the line that begins with the pound sign may also contain comments, which will be ignored by the C shell.

The **if** statement evaluates the expression *-e $argv [1],* which tests for the existence of an argument file. If an argument file exists, the shell will execute the statement

```
echo "File $argv[1] exists"
```

The message is enclosed in double quotes to preserve the special meaning of the dollar sign ($). A syntax error will result if the statement that follows the logical test is complex (that is, contains a pipeline or a group of statements).

## *The Three-Way Conditional Statement* **if . . . then . . . else**

This statement works just like the "if . . . then . . . else" statement of the Bourne shell. This allows an alternative logical path for the program, based on the status returned from the expression that follows **if**. Here is an example:

```
<3> cat example.2
# This is a modified version of example.1
if -e $argv[1] then
   echo "File $argv[1] exists"
else
   echo "File $argv[1] not found"
endif
```

If the expression that follows the **if** statement is true (1), the command list between the **if** and **else** statements is executed ; if it is false (0), the command list between the **else** and **endif** statements is executed. Notice that **endif** is used to close the **if . . . then . . . else** statement. If **endif** is missing, a syntax error will be displayed. In the example below, file *example.2* invokes itself and passes itself as its own argument:

```
<4> example.2 example.2
File example.2 exists
```

## *An Additional Alternative* **else if**

The **else if** statement provides additional alternative logical paths for a C shell program. This statement works the same way as the **elif** statement of the Bourne shell. Here is an example:

```
<5> cat example.3
# This program checks the file-type of the argument file
#
if -f $arg[1] then
  echo "$argv[1] is an ordinary file"
  else if -d $argv[1] then
    echo "$argv[1] is a directory"
  else
    echo "$argv[1] is unknown"
endif
```

The expression *-f $argv[1]* tests whether or not the first argument names an ordinary file. If it is not, the shell evaluates the expression that follows *else if* (*-d $argv[1]*) to determine whether or not the first argument names a directory. If it is not, the shell executes the command list between the **else** and **endif** statements. If any of the expressions is

**if**
**if...then...else**
**else if**

true, then the shell will execute the command list that follows immediately.

You can have more than one **else if** statement in a C shell procedure. The **else** statement is optional, and only one **endif** is needed to close the **if** control structure, no matter how many logical paths are given. Let's invoke **example.3** with *example.2* as its argument:

```
<6> example.3 example.2
example.2 is an ordinary file
```

# Forming Loops

## *The Branching Statement*

**goto**

The format of the branching statement **goto** is

goto *label*

The **goto** statement causes the C shell to search for a line within the file that contains *label:* (with a colon following), then transfers program control to this line. Here is an example:

```
<7> cat example.4
#
if -d $argv[1] then
  echo "$argv[1] is a directory"
  goto list
  else if -f $argv[1] then
    echo "$argv[1] is an ordinary file"
else
  echo "$argv[1] unknown"
endif
list:
  echo "Here are the contents of $argv[1]:"
  ls $argv[1]
  exit
```

In this program, if the expression that follows the **if** statement is true (the argument is a directory), the shell executes the *goto list* statement: the C shell will search for the line that starts with the label *list:*, then executes the commands that follow. In this case, the shell will display a list of all filenames in the directory named by *$argv[1].* For example, directory *backup* is a subdirectory that contains four files: *file1.bk, file2.bk, file3.bk,* and *file4.bk.* Let's invoke **example.4** with *backup* as its argument:

```
<8> example.4 backup
backup is a directory
Here are the contents of backup:
file1.bk file2.bk file3.bk file4.bk
```

## *The Loop Control Statement* **foreach**

The **foreach** statement controls the loop structure, performing a function similar to the **for** statement of the Bourne shell. The format of the **foreach** is as follows:

```
foreach variable (wordlist)
  command-list
end
```

The value of *variable* is initialized to the first member of *wordlist* on the first iteration, then to the next member on each subsequent iteration. If the value of *variable* is not null, the shell executes the command-list between the **foreach** statement and the **end** statement. Then the process is repeated until *variable* has a null value, indicating that there are no more words in *wordlist* to be assigned. In the example that follows, the shell copies each item in *buffer2* to *buffer1* one at a time without changing its order:

```
<9> cat cp_buff
# Copy data from buffer2 to buffer1
#
set buffer1 = ("" "" "" "" "" "")        [Initialize buffer1 ]
set buffer2 = (A B C D E F)              [Initialize buffer2 ]
set pointer = 1                          [Initialize the pointer]
#
foreach data ($buffer2)                  [Read a word of buffer2 ]
  set buffer1[$pointer] = $data          [Write a word to buffer1 ]
  @ pointer++                            [Increment the pointer]
end
#
echo "buffer1 $buffer1"                  [Display the name then the
echo "buffer2 $buffer2"                   contents of each buffer]
exit
```

As explained in the previous chapter, before an array can be used, it must be declared with the desired number of elements. In this case, *buffer1* and *buffer2* are declared with six elements each. In the first iteration of the **foreach** loop, the value of variable *data* is initialized to the first element of array *buffer2*, which is *A*.

Since variable *pointer* has been initialized at 1, the statement *buffer1[$pointer]* means *buffer1[1]*. Therefore, $data is written to *buffer[1]* **goto foreach**

on the first iteration. At the end of the loop, the statement @ *pointer*++ increases the value of *pointer* by one. So in the second iteration, *buffer1[$pointer]* becomes *buffer1[2];* in the third iteration, it becomes *buffer1[3];* and so on.

After processing character *F* (transferring it from *buffer2[6]* to *buffer1[6]*), **foreach** finds no more characters left in buffer 2. So when **foreach** attempts a seventh loop, assigment of the next character to *data* fails, and the loop terminates. This is what you will see on the screen when you invoke *cp_buff*, as shown here:

```
<10> cp_buff
buffer1 A B C D E F
buffer2 A B C D E F
```

## Looping While True

**while**

The **while** statement evaluates the expression that follows it in parentheses. If the status of the expression is true, the shell executes the command-list between the expression and the **end** statement. If its status is false, the shell halts execution of the **while** loop. The syntax of the **while** loop is

```
while (expression)
  command list
end
```

In this example, the **while** loop is used to fill the buffer (which has been declared as an array) with numbers:

```
<11> cat fillup
# Fill an array with numbers in ascending order
#
set buffer = (0 0 0 0 0)                [Initialize buffer with zeroes]
set pointer = 1                         [Initialize pointer at 1]
set count = $#buffer                    [Set count to the buffer length (5)]
#
while ($count)                          [Test whether to begin an iteration]
  set buffer[$pointer] = $pointer       [Write a number into buffer ]
  @ pointer++                           [Increment pointer by one]
  @ count--                             [Decrement count by one]
end
#
echo $buffer                            [Display the contents of the array]
```

The key to this loop is the value of *$count,* which is initialized to the number of elements in *buffer* (5), then decremented by one at the end of each loop. The **while** statement ends the loop when the value of *count* becomes zero, meaning that there are no more numbers left. The value of *count* is intialized to the number of elements in *buffer* (5).

During the first iteration, since *$count* is not a zero, the shell executes the statements in the loop: is initialized to the first element of *buffer* the value of the pointer (1) (*set buffer[$pointer] = $pointer* becomes *set buffer[1] = 1*), the pointer is increased to 2 by the statement *@ pointer++*, and the count is decreased to 4 by the statement *@ count—*.

During the second iteration, the shell assigns *2* to *buffer[2]*, the pointer goes up to 3, and the count drops to 3; during the third iteration, the shell assigns *3* to *buffer[3]*, the pointer goes up to 4, and the count drops to 2; and so on until the fifth iteration. Here is a diagram that summarizes what happens during each iteration (with "before" and "after" values for the pointer and the count):

| Iteration Number | Value at the Start | | Value Assigned to the Array | Value at the End | |
|---|---|---|---|---|---|
| | Pointer | Count | | Pointer | Count |
| 1 | 1 | 5 | buffer[1] = 1 | 2 | 4 |
| 2 | 2 | 4 | buffer[2] = 2 | 3 | 3 |
| 3 | 3 | 3 | buffer[3] = 3 | 4 | 2 |
| 4 | 4 | 2 | buffer[4] = 4 | 5 | 1 |
| 5 | 5 | 1 | buffer[5] = 5 | 6 | 0 |

At the end of the fifth iteration, the count becomes zero, indicating that there are no more numbers left. When the **while** statement attempts to begin a sixth iteration, it discovers a zero in the statement *while ($count)*, and the loop ends. This is what you will see on the screen when you invoke *fillup:*

```
<12> fillup
1 2 3 4 5
```

## Breaking Out of a Loop

**break**

The **break** statement of the C shell is similar to the **break** statement of the Bourne shell. In the C shell, the statement breaks to the nearest **while** or **foreach** loop. This example will help you with file management:

```
<13> cat backup
# Copy files from the current directory to "$home/backup"
if -d $home/backup then                [Does directory "back" exist?]
  goto COPY:                           [If so, go to COPY]
else                                   [If not, . . .
  mkdir $home/backup                   create such a directory]
endif
COPY:
set total = 'ls'                       [List all the files in total]
```

**while**
**break**

```
foreach file ($total)                    [Test whether to begin another]
  if ($#argv == 1) then                  [Is there an argument after backup ?]
    if ($#argv[1] == $file) break [If so and if it matches the current
  else                                   file, then stop here]
    cp $file $home/backup                [If not, then copy this file . . .
    echo '    $file copied'              and display a message]
 endif
end
echo '* Backup completed *'
```

This procedure lets you back up all the files in the current directory to a directory in your home directory called *backup*—with one added feature. If you include a file name as an argument, *backup* will copy up to, but not including, the file named. For example, suppose your current directory contains these files:

```
apple       date       kiwi       orange
banana      fruit      lemon      peach
coconut     grape      melon      pear
```

If you invoke **backup** without an argument, all 12 files will be copied to *backup.* If you type one of these filenames after *backup,* then only those files in the directory that precede the file named will be copied, as shown here:

```
<14> backup fruit
    apple copied
    banana copied
    coconut copied
    date copied
  * Backup completed *
<15> _
```

## *Continuing a Loop* **continue**

This statement directs program control to the nearest **while** or **foreach** loop. Here is a program that takes an argument and selects even numbers:

```
<16> cat select
# Select only even numbers from arguments entered
#
if ($#argv == 0) then                    [Are there no arguments?]
echo "Numeric arguments required" [If so, display a message and . . .
exit                                     terminate the program]
```

```
if ($argv > 10) then                 [Are there more than 10 arguments?]
echo "Only ten numbers allowed"      [If so, display a message and . . .
exit                                 terminate the program]
endif
set output = (Ø Ø Ø Ø Ø Ø Ø Ø Ø Ø) [Initialize input with ten zeroes]
set count = 1                        [Begin the counter at one]
foreach number ($argv)               [Set number to the next argument]
  if ($number % 2) continue          [Test the argument for odd or even]
  set output[$count] = $number       [If it is even, store it in output
  @ count++                           and increase the counter by one]
end
echo "Even numbers: $output"         [Display the even numbers stored]
```

You activate this program by typing *select,* followed by a sequence of no more than ten whole numbers. The first seven lines of statements take care of incorrect invocations of the command (no numbers typed after *select* or too many numbers). Then two variables are initialized (the array that will hold the numbers selected and the counter).

Finally, the main procedure begins the **foreach** statement, which begins by assigning the first number typed to the variable *number.* The **if** statement on the next line is the key to this program. It uses the remainder operator (%) to determine whether or not the number is even:

- If the number is even, the remainder that results from dividing by 2 will be zero (indicating false), the **continue** statement will be ignored, the number will be assigned to *output* on the next line, and the counter will be increased by one for the next iteration. The counter serves as a pointer to the next location in *output*—in which the number is to be stored.
- If the number is odd, the remainder will be 1 (indicating true), and the shell will execute the **continue** statement, which acts like a **goto** statement, returning execution to the **foreach** statement. This means that the number will **not** be assigned to *output* and the counter will not be increased.
- If the argument isn't a number, the shell will display an error message.

Finally, after all arguments have been processed, the resulting value of *output* is displayed. Here is what you will see displayed on the screen:

```
<17> select
Numeric arguments required

<17> select 3 4 5 11 16 17 22 31 46 63
Even numbers: 4 16 22 46 Ø Ø Ø Ø Ø Ø
```

continue

### Exiting from a Loop

**exit**

This statement works exactly like the **exit** statement of the Bourne shell: it forces a program to abort and return to the parent process. You can pass an exit-status as an argument of the **exit** statement to the parent process. See Chapter 24 for a detailed description of this statement.

## Other Programming Techniques

### Multi-Way Branching

**switch**

The **switch** statement, which is similar to the **case** statement of the Bourne shell, provides multi-way branching. End each **switch** statement with **breaksw**, which is analogous to the double semicolon (;;) of the Bourne shell. Program control will then break from the **switch** statement and resume at the **endsw** statement. The format of the **switch** statement is as follows:

```
switch (string)
case pattern1:
     command list
breaksw
case pattern2:
     command list
breaksw
default:                       [optional]
     command list
breaksw
endsw
```

The **switch** statement passes **string** to each **case** to match the pattern. After executing the command list of the **case** selected, the **breaksw** statement directs program control to the statement that follows the **endsw** statement. Without the **breaksw** statement for each **case**, the program will continue to execute the next **case**, even though there is no match. If no match is found, the command list following the **default** statement is executed. Here is an example:

```
<18> cat matchfile
#
if ($#argv == 0) then
  echo "No argument is declared"
  exit
endif
switch ($argv[1])
  case FILE1:
```

```
    echo "User selects FILE1"
  breaksw
  case FILE2:
    echo "User selects FILE2"
  breaksw
  default:
    echo "You must select either FILE1 or FILE2"
  breaksw       [optional]
endsw
```

The **if** statement is to test for the existence of an argument to be passed by the C shell before going to the **switch** structure (optional). If you leave out the **if** statement to test the existence of argv[1] in the absence of argv[1], the **switch** statement will refuse to go on, and the program will terminate with a vague message.

If the above program is invoked with an argument, The **switch** structure will try to match this argument with string FILE1 or FILE2. If there is no match, the **default** is invoked; this procedure includes error-checking to guarantee correct usage. The last **breaksw** is optional. Although it is not required, it is good practice to have it there. If you omit it, program control will go to the **endsw** statement anyway. (The **breaksw** statement will also direct program control to the **endsw** statement.) Here you see *matchfile* invoked three different ways, the first two incorrect:

Invoke *matchfile* without an argument:

```
<19> matchfile
No argument is declared
```

Invoke *matchfile* with argument *unknown:*

```
<20> matchfile unknown
You must select either FILE1 or FILE2
```

Invoke *matchfile* with argument *FILE2:*

```
<21> matchfile FILE2
User selects FILE2
```

Since the **switch** structure also accepts metacharacters such as *, ?, and so on, as expansion characters, we can change **default** to become another **case** with the statement *case* *—without changing program performance:

```
<22> cat matchfile
#
if ($#argv == 0) then
  echo "No argument is declared"
  exit
```

**exit**
**switch**

```
endif
switch ($argv[1])
  case FILE1:
    echo "User selects FILE1"
  breaksw
  case FILE2:
    echo "User selects FILE2"
  breaksw
  case *:          [Change]
    echo "You must select either FILE1 or FILE2"
endsw
```

## *Shifting Arguments* **shift**

This statement is the same as the **shift** statement of the Bourne shell. It shifts each element of *argv* to the left one position, and discards *argv[1]*. If the value of *argv* does not have at least one word, then the C shell regards *argv* as an unset variable, and displays an error message. Here is an example:

```
<23> cat moveleft
# Shift arguments to the left
foreach words ($argv[*])
  shift
  echo $argv
end
```

Let's invoke *moveleft* with three arguments (1, 2, 3):

```
<24> moveleft 1 2 3
2 3                    [Argument 1 is discarded]
3                      [Argument 2 is discarded]
<25> _                 [Argument 3 is discarded]
```

## *Interrupt-Handling* **onintr**

At times you may want to terminate a C shell program while it is running by pressing the [DEL] key. However, you also want to remove all of the temporary files that were created by this program at the time it terminates. You can do so with the **onintr** statement. This is the format of the statement:

```
onintr label
```

When an interrupt occurs, the C shell clears the interrupt and passes control to the **onintr** statement, which executes the line that starts with *label:*—as if you had given a **goto** statement. Here is an example:

```
<25> cat print.format
#
if ($#arv == 0) then                    [Does the file exist?]
  echo "Missing input file"
  exit 0
  else if -d $argv[1] then              [Is the file a directory?]
    echo "$argv[1] is a directory"
  exit
endif
onintr cleanup                          [Interrupt control]
  pr $argv[1] > $home/bin/tempfile
  cp $home/bin/tempfile $arg[1]
cleanup:                                [Interrupt-handling routine]
  if -f $home/bin/tempfile
    rm $home/bin/tempfile
exit
```

If you press the [DEL] key while this program is running, **onintr** will transfer program flow to the line labeled *cleanup.* This interrupt handling routine checks for the existence of *tempfile* in your *bin* directory and removes it before exiting.

## Built-In Commands

The C shell includes built-in commands, to which the C shell can pass control without using a search path or creating a new process. For a complete list of built-in commands, see Appendix G.

## Summary of Chapter 27

In this chapter you learned about executing a file as a shell procedure; the statements for forming conditional structures (**if, then, else,** and **else if**); the statements for forming loops (**goto, foreach, while, break, continue,** and **exit**); and a few other tools for writing C shell procedures (**switch, shift,** and **onintr**).

### *Executing a File as a Shell Procedure*

**Making a file.** To make a file executable by the C shell, you must place a pound sign (#) at the beginning of the first line, then use the change mode command with **u+x**.

**Executing the file.** To execute any file as a C shell procedure, use the **csh** command, followed by the filename. **shift**
**onintr**

**File-checking.** The C shell uses expressions to test files and directories in **if, foreach,** and **while** statements the way the Bourne shell uses the **test** to perform similar tests.

## Forming Conditional Statements

**The simple conditional statement.** You can use the **if** statement by itself to carry out a simple test.

**Three-way conditional.** For more involved tests, you can use the "if . . . then . . . else" construction.

**An additional set of alternatives.** You can use the **else if** statement to add an additional set of alternatives.

## Forming Loops

**Branching.** Use the **goto** statement to force the C shell to branch to a labeled line.

**Loop control.** use the **foreach** statement in the C shell as you would use the **for** statement in the Bourne shell.

**Looping while true.** Use the **while** statement to form a loop, and sustain execution of the loop as long as the expression being tested indicates true.

**Breaking out of a loop.** Use the **break** statement in the C shell much the way you would use the **break** statement in the Bourne shell.

**Continuing a loop.** Use the **continue** statement to direct program control to the nearest **while** or **foreach** loop.

**Exiting from a loop.** Use the **exit** statement in the C shell as you would use the **exit** statement in the Bourne shell.

## Other Programming Techniques

**Multi-way branching.** Use the **switch** statement as you would use the **case** statement in the Bourne shell to perform multiple branching, based on pattern-matching, terminating each alternative with **breaksw** (instead of ;;).

**Shifting arguments.** Use the **shift** statement in the C shell as you would use it in the Bourne shell.

**Interrupt-handling.** Use the **onintr** statement in the C shell to perform clean-up in the event that the procedure is interrupted before completing execution. It will then act like a **goto** statement.

# Appendices

# A

# Summary of General-Purpose Commands and Symbols

Here is a list of general-purpose XENIX commands and symbols. In this list, generic names are italicized.

## Basic Commands for Starting Out

| | |
|---|---|
| date | Display date and time |
| who | List logged-on users |
| @ | Erase an entire command line |
| # or ∧H | Erase a character on the command line |
| CTRL-D | Log off the system; sometimes end-of-file (EOF) |
| man | Call up on-line XENIX documentation |
| learn | Call up on-line XENIX tutorials |

## Working With Directories and Files

| | |
|---|---|
| / | The root directory |
| /bin | The directory that contains most system shell procedures and executable command programs |
| /usr | The directory that usually contains user accounts |
| . | The current directory |
| .. | The parent directory |
| >*file* | Redirect output to *file* |
| >>*file* | Redirect output and append to *file* |
| <*file* | Redirect input from *file* |

| | |
|---|---|
| *pr1* \| *pr2* | Pipe: use the output of process *pr1* as the input for process *pr2* (*pr1* must send its output to the standard output file and *pr2* must take its input from the standard input file) |
| cat *file* | Display the contents of *file*<br>CTRL-S: halt scrolling of screen output<br>CTRL-Q: resume scrolling of screen output |
| more *file* | Display the contents of *file* one screen at a time |
| head *file* | Display the opening lines of *file* |
| tail *file* | Display the last lines of *file* |
| cat f1 f2 > *file* | Concatenate files *f1* and *f2* into file *file* |
| mv f1 f2 | Change the name of file *f1* to *f2* |
| mv f1 f2 DIR | Move files *f1* and *f2* to directory *DIR* |
| cp f1 f2 | Make a copy of file *f1* and call the copy *f2* |
| cp f1 f2 DIR | Copy files *f1* and *f2* to directory *DIR* |
| rm file | Remove *file* from the current directory |
| ls | List the names of all files and subdirectories in the current directory |
| ls −l | Display a *long* directory list |
| pwd | Display the name of your working directory |
| cd dir | Change your working directory to *dir* |
| mkdir dir | Create directory *dir* |
| rmdir dir | Remove directory *dir* (which must not contain any files) |
| rm −r dir | Remove directory *dir* and every file in it |
| mv d1 d2 | Change the name of directory *d1* to *d2* |
| chmod . . . *file* | Change the access permissions to *file,* using the following abbreviations: |

| | | | | | |
|---|---|---|---|---|---|
| **u** | user | + | add | **r** | read |
| **g** | group | − | remove | **w** | write |
| **o** | others | = | absolute | **x** | execute |

## Searching: Forming Regular Expressions

| | |
|---|---|
| ^ | Beginning of line |
| $ | End of line |
| ? | Match a single character in a search |
| * | Match any character in a search |
| [ ] | Match any of the characters enclosed in a search |
| \ | Interpret the following special character literally |

## Setting Basic Features

| | |
|---|---|
| passwd | Change your password |
| newgrp *name* | Switch to working group *name* |
| newgrp | Switch back to your default group |
| stty | Set your terminal options |
| tabs *term* | Specify tab settings for terminal *term* |

## Working With Processes

| | |
|---|---|
| & | Run a process in the background (placed at the end of a command line) |
| DEL | Abort a foreground process |
| kill *nnnn* | Abort background process with PID number *nnnn* |
| ps | Display the status of active processes associated with your terminal |
| time *process* | Display the amount of time required to run *process* |

## Processing Information

| | |
|---|---|
| dc | Call up the desk calculator |
| bc | Call up the high-precision calculator |
| echo | Echo a string on the screen |
| sort *file* | Sort *file* by the sequence specified |
| grep 'p' *file* | Search for pattern *p* in *file* |
| awk *file* | Select lines in *file* and process them |
| wc *file* | Count the number of lines, words, and characters in *file* |
| spell *file* | Check spelling of words in *file* |
| diff *f1 f2* | Display the differences between files *f1* and *f2* |
| cmp *f1 f2* | Compare files *f1* and *f2* |
| comm *f1 f2* | Display lines common to files *f1* and *f2* |
| tr *s1 s2 file* | Translate from string *s1* to *s2* in *file* |
| lpr *file* | Send contents of *file* to the line printer to be printed |
| nroff *file* | Format and print the contents of *file* |

## Other Basic Commands

| | |
|---|---|
| mail *user* | Send electronic mail to *user* |
| mail | Read your electronic mail |

| | |
|---|---|
| calendar | Display events stored in the file $HOME/calendar by date as a reminder |
| write *user* | Write directly to *user*'s terminal |
| cu | Call up another system |
| uucp | Communicate with another UNIX system |

# B

# Summary of **ed**

## Commands

The general form of an **ed** command is a letter, preceded by one or two line numbers (generally optional). Two **ed** commands, **e** (edit) and **r** (read), must be followed by a filename, and **w** (write) may be. Only one command is allowed per line, but **p** (print) may follow any command except **e** (edit), **r** (read), **w** (write), or **q** (quit). A backslash (\) may be used at the end of each line to continue a long command string on the next line.

**a** **Append** lines to the editing buffer, starting at the current line, unless another line is specified. Appending continues until a period appears by itself as the first character on a separate line. Once appending is completed, the last line appended is considered the current line.

**c** **Change** the lines specified to the text that follows. The text must be terminated with a period on a separate line. If no lines are specified, replace only the current line. The last line changed becomes the new current line.

**d** **Delete** the lines of text specified. If no lines are specified, the current line is deleted. Generally, the first line following the deleted text becomes the new current line. However, if the last line is deleted, then the new last line becomes the new current line.

**e** **Edit** a file. If the editing buffer contains text when **e** is issued, it will be overwritten by the contents of the new file. To avoid loss of text, use the **w** (write) command for the buffer before using **e**.

**f** **File**. Recall the name of the active file. If you type a filename after **f**, that is the name that will become the new active file. It will aslo be recalled the next time you issue **f**.

**g** **Global search.** Execute the command specified for all lines in the editing buffer.

**i** **Insert** the text that follows in front of the current line (or in front of the line specified). The text to be inserted must be terminated by a period on a separate line. The last line inserted becomes the current line.

**m** **Move** the lines specified to the location immediately following the line specified after **m**. The last line moved becomes the current line.

**p** **Print** (that is, display) the lines specified. If no lines are specified, display the current line. Press RETURN to display the line following the current line.

**q** **Quit ed.** Exit the editor and return to the shell. Unless you first issue w (write), **q** will discard the editing buffer.

**r** **Read** a file into the editing buffer, beginning at the end of the buffer, unless another line is specified. The last line read becomes the new current line.

**s** **Substitute** the first occurrence of one string for another in the lines specified. If no lines are specified, the substitution takes place only in the current line. The last line in which a substitution takes place becomes the new first line. If no substitution takes place, the current line remains unchanged.

**v** **Reverse global search.** Execute commands on those lines that do **not** match the string indicated.

**w** **Write** text from the editing buffer to a file. The file may be named either here or in an earlier **ed** or **e** (edit) command. The current line remains unchanged.

**/** **Context search.** Search for the next line that matches the string indicated by */string/*. The search begins at the line following the current line, and continues all the way through the editing buffer back to the current line if necessary. The line where the string is matched becomes the new current line.

**?** **Reverse context search.** Search backwards for the line that matches the string indicated by *?string?*. The search begins at the line preceding the current line, and continues all the way through the file—wrapping back around to the current line if necessary. The line where the string is matched becomes the new current line.

**.=** **Current line.** Display the number of the current line.

$= **Last line.** Display the number of the last line of the editing buffer.

! **Escape.** Execute a XENIX command without leaving **ed.**

## Special Characters for Searching

In search and replace commands, the following special characters have the meanings given here, except when preceded by a backslash (\). In those instances they are interpreted literally.

^ Beginning of line

$ End of line

\ Turn off special meaning

. Match a character

* Repeat a character

[ ] Match one of the characters enclosed

& Use the search string as the replacement string

The following special characters are fixed, and do not change in meaning:

/ Delimiter for search strings and replacement strings. (In a replacement string, you can also use any other character not found in the replacement string itself).

\( \) Tag a substring (in a search string)

\n Insert substring **n** (in a replacement string)

# C

# Summary of **vi** and **ex** Commands

You enter **vi** commands from **vi command mode.** These commands are never displayed on the screen. To enter an **ex** command, type a colon (:) to enter **ex command mode,** type the command, then type **ESC** or RETURN to return to **vi command mode.** The search commands begin with either / or ? and end with a RETURN. Commands that begin with :, /, and ? are displayed at the bottom of the screen.

## Moving the Cursor

**h** Move the cursor one space to the left
**j** Move the cursor one space down
**k** Move the cursor one space up
**l** Move the cursor one space to the right

**b** Move to the first character of the previous word
**B** Move to the first character of the previous word (ignore punctuation)

**w** Move to the first character of the next word
**W** Move to the first character of the next word (ignore punctuation)

**e** Move to the last character of the next word
**E** Move to the last character of the next word (ignore punctuation)

**(** Move to the beginning of the current sentence
**)** Move to the end of the current sentence

**{** Move to the beginning of the current paragraph
**}** Move to the end of the current paragraph

**[** Move to the beginning of the current section
**]** Move to the end of the current section

**^** Move to the first visible character of the current line
**0** Move to the beginning of the current line
**$** Move to the end of the current line

**H** Move to the top of the screen
**M** Move to the middle of the screen
**L** Move to the bottom of the screen

**nG** Move to line **n** (last line if *n* is omitted)

**%** Move to the matching bracketing symbol: ( ), { }, [ ]

**^U** Scroll up (CTRL-U)
**^D** Scroll down (CTRL-D)

**^B** Page back (CTRL-B)
**^F** Page forward (CTRL-F)

## Adding New Text

**a** Append text after the cursor
**A** Append text at the end of the line

**i** Insert text before the cursor
**I** Insert text at the beginning of the line

**o** Open a new line of text below the current line
**O** Open a new line of text above the current line

## Changing Text

All of the commands shown here may be used with multipliers (for example, c5w, 5cc, c5), c5}, and so on).

**cw** Change text to the end of the current word
**cW** Change text to the end of the current word (ignore punctuation)

**c^** Change text to the first visible character of the current line
**c0** Change text to the beginning of the current line
**c$** Change text to the end of the current line
**cc** Change the entire line

**c(** Change text to the beginning of the current sentence
**c)** Change text to the end of the current sentence

**c{** Change text to the beginning of the current paragraph
**c}** Change text to the end of the current paragraph

## Shifting Text

All of the commands shown here may be used with multipliers (for example, 5>>, >5), <5}, and so on). Shift left is <; shift right is >.

<< or >> Shift the entire line a distance of one **shiftwidth**
<( or >( Shift text to the beginning of the current sentence
<) or >) Shift text to the end of the current sentence

<{ or >{ Shift text to the beginning of the current paragraph
<} or >} Shift text to the end of the current paragraph

## Deleting Text

All of the commands shown here may be used with multipliers (for example, d5w, 5dd, d5), d5}, and so on).

**dw** Delete text to the end of the current word
**dW** Delete text to the end of the current word (ignore punctuation)

**d^** Delete text to the first visible character of the current line
**d0** Delete text to the beginning of the current line
**d$** Delete text to the end of the current line (same as D)
**dd** Delete the entire line

**d(** Delete text to the beginning of the current sentence
**d)** Delete text to the end of the current sentence

**d{** Delete text to the beginning of the current paragraph
**d}** Delete text to the end of the current paragraph

## Searching and Replacing

| | |
|---|---|
| **tx** (or **Tx**) | Move the cursor forward (or back) to the character before (or after) *x* on the current line |
| **ctx** (or **cTx**) | Change from the cursor to the character next to *x* |
| **dtx** (or **dTx**) | Delete from the cursor to the character next to *x* |
| **fx** or **Fx** | Find character *x* on the current line |
| **cfx** or **cFx** | Change from the cursor to character *x* on the current line |
| **dfx** or **dFx** | Delete from the cursor to character *x* on the current line |
| ***/word*** | Search forward for *word* in the work area |
| ***?word*** | Search backwards for *word* in the work area |

| | |
|---|---|
| **r** | Replace the character under the cursor with another |
| **R** | Replace several characters one after another as you type |
| **s** | Replace one character with several |
| **S** | Replace an entire line (same as **cc**) |

| | |
|---|---|
| **:n,Ns/old word/new word/g** | Substitute **new word** for **old word** in every occurrence from line **n** to line **N**, searching forward in the work area. |
| **:n,Ns?old word?new word?g** | Substitute **new word** for **old word** in every occurrence from line **n** to line **N**, searching backwards in the work area. |

## Invoking the Editor

| | |
|---|---|
| **$ vi *file*** | Begin an editing session with *file,* starting on the first line. |
| **$ vi +*line file*** | Begin an editing session with *file,* starting on line *line.* |
| **$ vi +/*word/file*** | Begin an editing session with *file*, starting on the first line that contains *word.* |
| **$ vi + *file*** | Begin an editing session with *file*, starting on the last line. |
| **$ vi −r *file*** | Begin an editing session to recover *file* after a system failure. |
| **$ vi −R *file*** | Begin an editing session to make *file* read-only. |
| **$ vi −t tag** | Edit the file that contains **tag**. |
| **$ vi −x *file*** | Edit an encrypted file (or edit a cleartext file and have it encrypted when writing it to disk). |

## Exiting the Editor

| | |
|---|---|
| **:wq <CR>** | **Write and Quit.** Write the text in the work area to a file and end the editing session. |
| **:x <CR>** | **Conditional Write and Quit.** Write the text in the work area only if there have been changes, then end the editing session. (Same as **ZZ**.) |
| **:q! <CR>** | **Abandon Text.** Abandon the text in the work area (along with any changes made to it) and end the editing session. |

## Moving Text

The general procedure for moving text within the buffer is to move the cursor to the beginning of the text, delete the text, move the cursor to the new location, and then "put" the text either in front of the cursor (**p**) or ahead of the cursor (**P**). If you are moving text to another file, you must delete the text to a buffer (a-z) and then "put" it from the same buffer. You must begin editing the other file (**:e**) with no other operators intervening between the delete and the "put." Some of the many variations of the basic procedure involve the following combinations (where **p** means either **p** or **P**):

| | | | |
|---|---|---|---|
| **x** and **p** | Move a character | **nx** and **p** | Move **n** characters |
| **dw** and **p** | Move a word | **dnw** and **p** | Move **n** words |
| **d)** and **p** | Move a sentence | **dn)** and **p** | Move **n** sentences |
| **d}** and **p** | Move a paragraph | **dn}** and **p** | Move **n** paragraphs |
| **dd** and **p** | Move a line | **ndd** and **p** | Move **n** lines |

## Copying Text

The general procedure for copying text within a file is to move the cursor to the beginning of the text, "yank" the text, move the cursor to the new location, and then "put" the text either in front of the cursor (**p**) or ahead of the cursor (**P**). If you are copying text to another file, you must "yank" the text to a buffer (a-z) and then "put" it from the same buffer. You must begin editing the other file (**:e**) with no other operators intervening between the "yank" and the "put." Some of the many variations of the basic procedure involve the following combinations (where **p** means either **p** or **P**):

| | | | |
|---|---|---|---|
| **yw** and **p** | Copy a word | **ynw** and **p** | Copy **n** words |
| **y)** and **p** | Copy a sentence | **yn)** and **p** | Copy **n** sentences |
| **y}** and **p** | Copy a paragraph | **yn}** and **p** | Copy **n** paragraphs |
| **yy** and **p** | Copy a line | **nyy** and **p** | Copy **n** lines |

# Customizing vi

You can customize **vi** by setting options, assigning abbreviations, and assigning command sequences to keys on the keyboard.

## *Setting Options* **set**

| | |
|---|---|
| `:set aw` | Set auto-write mode |
| `:set report=3` | Set **report** to 3 |
| `:set dir=files` | Set your directory to **files** |

## *Assigning Abbreviations* **ab**

| | |
|---|---|
| `:ab unx UNIX operating system` | Assign **UNIX operating system** to the abbreviation **unx.** |

## *Defining Keys* **map**

| | |
|---|---|
| `:map * { >}` | Assign the sequence { >} to the * key. |

## *Making Assignments Permanent*

To make assignments permanent, place the commands (without colons) in the **.exrc** file, which will be read each time you call up **vi**. Here is a sampling of line entries you could place in **.exrc**:

```
set aw report=3 dir=files
ab xen XENIX operating system
map * { >}
```

# D

# Summary of vi Options

This appendix lists all **vi** (and **ex**) options that can be set with the **:set** command. The options are grouped as toggled, number-valued, and stringvalued. For each option, you will find its name, abbreviation (if any), default setting, and description.

## Toggled Options

These options may be set only as on or off. To turn an option off, type "no" in front of its name (or abbreviation).

### *Automatic Indentation* **ai**

The **autoindent** (**ai**) option allows you to achieve the indentation desired in structured programming. For each line entered during text entry mode, **vi** matches the indentation with the previous line, using the spacing between tab stops specified by the **shiftwidth** option. The only way to back the cursor up to the previous tab stop is to type *CTRL-D*.

When this mode is set, certain lines are processed in a different way:

- A line with no characters in it is turned into a blank line
- The input for a line that begins with a caret (), followed immediately by CTRL-D, is placed at the beginning of the line, but the indentation for the previous line is retained for the line that follows
- The input for a line that begins with a zero (0), followed immediately by CTRL-D, is placed at the beginning of the line, along with input for subsequent lines.

The **autoindent** option is not in effect for global commands. Default for **autoindent: noai.**

## *Automatic Printing* **ap**

The **autoprint (ap)** option causes the current line to be printed after any **ex** command that changes the buffer. This is the same as appending **p** to each command. The **ap** option applies only to the last of a sequence of commands on a single line, and is not in effect for global commands. Default: **ap.**

## *Automatic Writing* **aw**

The **autowrite (aw)** option causes the contents of the editing buffer to be written automatically to the current file if you have made any changes to it before giving one of the following commands:

| | |
|---|---|
| **:n** (next) | :! (escape) |
| **:rew** (rewind) | **CTRL-^** (switch files) |
| **:tag** (tag) | **CTRL-]** (go to tag) |

Default for **autowrite: noaw.**

## *Beautifying Text* **bf**

The **beautify (bf)** option prevents all control characters except tab, newline, and formfeed from being entered into the editing buffer during text entry. The first time a backspace is discarded, there is a message. The **bf** option does not apply to command input. Default: **nobf.**

## *Compatibility with ed* **edcompatible**

The **edcompatible** option retains the global **(g)** and confirm **(c)** suffixes during multiple substitutions, and causes the read **(r)** suffix to work like the **read** command, instead of like the repeat string (&) suffix. Default: **noedcompatible.**

## *Ignore Case* **ic**

The **ignorecase** (**ic**) option maps uppercase characters in text to lowercase for the purpose of matching regular expressions—except for characters enclosed within brackets. Default: **noic.**

## *LISP Operation* **lisp**

The **lisp** option allows indentation appropriate for writing programs in the LISP language, and modifies the meanings of the following symbols to conform to standard LISP usage:

( )          { }          [[ ]]

Default: **nolisp.**

## *List All* **list**

The **list** option displays text the way **ed**'s list command (**l**) does, with tab stops and new line characters shown on the screen as "I" and "$". In addition, **list** folds any line longer than 72 characters. Default: **nolist.**

## *Special Meanings for Characters* **magic**

The **magic** option allows metacharacters to retain their special meanings. When this option is turned off, only the caret () and dollar sign ($) retain their special meanings. However, you can still evoke the special meanings of other special characters by preceding each with a backslash (\). Default: **magic.**

## *Allowing Messages* **mesg**

The **mesg** option allows other UNIX users to write to your screen with the UNIX **write** command while you are using **vi**. The usual setting **nomesg** prevents others from interfering with your screen display during editing. Default: **nomesg.**

## *Line-Numbering* **nu**

The **number** option displays line numbers with text. Default: **nonu.**

## *Optimizing Output*

**optimize**

The **optimize** option is used to speed up the operation of terminals that lack cursor-addressing by eliminating automatic returns when displaying more than one line. This is especially helpful if the text contains quite a bit of indentation at the start of each line. Default: **optimize.**

## *Redrawing the Screen*

**redraw**

The **redraw** option allows **vi** to simulate the operation of an intelligent terminal on a dumb terminal by redrawing the screen each time a deletion takes place and refreshing text continuously during insertion. Since this option requires considerable processing, it is useful only at very high transmission speeds. Default: **noredraw.**

## *Displaying Matching Symbol*

**sm**

The **showmatch** option allows you to display the matching symbol of a pair of parentheses or braces. When you type *)* or , for example, the cursor moves to the matching ( or { and waits for one second before returning—if the matching symbol is on the screen. Default: **nosm.**

## *Allowing Brief Messages*

**terse**

The **terse** option allows an experienced user to revert to briefer messages on the screen (for example, *15/297* instead of *15 lines 297 characters*). Default: **noterse.**

## *Warning to Save*

**warn**

The **warn** option makes **ex** give a warning before allowing you to execute a shell command via the escape command (!) (''[No write since last change]''). Default: **warn.**

## *Allowing Wrapping During Searches*

**ws**

The **wrapscan (ws)** option allows a search for a string to wrap from the end of the editing buffer to the beginning, rather than stop at the end. Default: **ws.**

### *Allowing Any Write* **wa**

The **writeany** (**wa**) option allows you to write to any file allowed by UNIX file access permissions, inhibiting the checks usually made before executing a **write** command. Default: **nowa**.

## Numbered Options

These options are set to numerical values using an equal sign to indicate the assignment.

### *Hardware Tab Stops* **ht**

The **hardtabs** (**ht**) option indicates the spacing between terminal hardware tab stops. Default: **ht**=8.

### *Report on Commands* **report**

The **report** option indicates the number of repetitions of a command needed to cause a message to be displayed on the screen. For commands that may have extensive consequences (global commands and the undo command), the message is saved until completion of execution. Default: **report**=5.

### *Lines to Be Scrolled* **scroll**

The **scroll** option indicates the number of logical lines to be scrolled during execution of scroll down (CTRL-D) and scroll up (CTRL-U). Default: **scroll=1/2 window**.

### *Software Tab Stops* **sw**

The **shiftwidth** (**sw**) option indicates the number of spaces between software tab stops, which is used by the shift commands, **autoindent**, and CTRL-D for indenting text and moving back to previous indentations. Default: **sw**=8.

### *Editor Tab Stops* **ts**

The **tabstops** (**ts**) option indicates the amount of space between tab stops when a file is displayed on the screen. Default: **ts**=8.

### Tag Length **tl**

The **taglength (tl)** option indicates how many characters in a tag name are significant. A value of zero (0) means that all characters in the name are significant. Default: **tl=0.**

### Window Height **window**

The **window** option indicates the number of lines to be displayed in one window of text, with the default value based on the transmission speed to the terminal. Defaults: **window=8** (up to 600 bit/s), **window=16** (1200 bit/s), **window=23** (9600 bit/s) (the variables **w300, w1200, w9600** may be used in place of the numbers **8, 16,** and **23**).

### Wrap Margin **wm**

The **wrapmargin (wm)** option indicates the margin for automatic wordwrapping to the following line. A value of zero (0) means no margin (and therefore no wrapping). Default: **wm=0.**

## String-Valued Options

These options are set to string values using an equal sign to indicate the assignment.

### Directory **dir**

The **directory (dir)** option names the directory that is to contain the editing buffer. If this directory is write-protected, **vi** will exit immediately, since it won't be able to maintain an editing buffer. Default: **dir=/tmp.**

### Paragraphs **para**

The **paragraphs (para)** option gives the delimiters for the "beginning of paragraph" ({) and "end of paragraph" (}) commands, using the names of **nroff** macros for starting paragraphs. Default: **para= IPLPPPQPP LIbp** .

Note: The default string represents an abbreviation for seven macros—four **ms** macros (.IP, .LP, .PP, and .QP), two **mm** macros (.P and .LI), and one **nroff** macro (.bp).

## *Sections*

**sections**

The **sections** option gives the delimiters for the "beginning of section" ([[) and "end of section" (]]) commands, using the names of **nroff** macros for starting paragaraphs. Default: **sections=SHNHH HU.**

Note: The default string represents an abbreviation for four macros— two **ms** macros (.SH, and .NH) and two **mm** macros (.H and .HU).

## *Shell*

**sh**

The **shell (sh)** option gives the pathname of the shell to be used whenever you execute a shell escape command (!) or a **shell** command. If SHELL has been assigned a value, then this becomes the default. Default: **sh=/bin/sh**.

## *Tags*

**tags**

The **tags** option gives the pathnames of files to be used as tag files by the **tag** command. Any time a tag is requested, this tag is searched for sequentially in the files designated. Default: **tags=/usr/lib** and the current directory.

## *Terminal*

**term**

The **term** option gives the type of the terminal. Default: **term=$TERM** (the value of the shell variable **TERM**).

# E

# Summary of Formatting Requests

## ms Requests

### Forming Paragraphs

| | | | |
|---|---|---|---|
| **.PP** | Standard paragraph | **.QP** | Quotation paragraph |
| **.LP** | Block paragraph | **.IP** | Indented paragraph |
| **.RE** | Shift left | **.RS** | Shift right |
| **.1C** | Single column | **.2C** | Double column |

### Displaying Text

| | | | |
|---|---|---|---|
| **.DS** | Standard display | **.DS B** | Blocked display |
| **.DS C** | Centered display | **.DE** | End of display |

### Keeping Lines Together

| | | | |
|---|---|---|---|
| **.KS** | Standard keep | **.KE** | End of keep |
| **.KF** | Floating keep | | |

### Using Footnotes

| | | | |
|---|---|---|---|
| **.FS** | Start of footnote | **.FE** | End of footnote |

### Using Headings

| | | | |
|---|---|---|---|
| **.SH** | Unnumbered heading | **.NH** | Numbered heading |

## Emphasizing Text

| | | | |
|---|---|---|---|
| .I | Underlining (italic) | .R | End of underlining (roman) |

## Page Layout

| | | | | | |
|---|---|---|---|---|---|
| .ND | | Remove the date | .DA | | Change the date |
| .ds | (LH<br>{CH<br>(RH | Change the header | .ds | (LF<br>{CF<br>(RF | Change the footer |

# nroff Requests

## Page Adjustment

| | | | |
|---|---|---|---|
| .pl | Page length | .po | Page offset |
| .ll | Line length | .pn | Page number |
| .bp | Page break | .ne | Need vertical space |

## Displaying Lines

| | | | |
|---|---|---|---|
| .fi | Turn on filling | .nf | Turn off filling |
| .ad | Adjust text | .nd | No adjustment |
| .ce n | Center next n lines | .ls n | Line spacing n |
| .hy n | Hyphenation | .nh | No hyphenation |
| .in n | Indent to n | .ti n | Temporary indentation |

## Displaying Characters

| | | | |
|---|---|---|---|
| .ul | Underline | .cu | Continuous underline |
| \u | Superscript | \d | Subscript |
| % | Page number | | |

# F

# Summary of the Bourne Shell

## Shell Variables

These variables may be set in the login file (**.profile**):

| | | | |
|---|---|---|---|
| **PSI** | Primary prompt | **PATH** | Command file search path |
| **PS2** | Secondary prompt | **MAIL** | Mail file |
| **TERM** | Terminal type | **HOME** | Login directory |

## Standard Input, Output, and Diagnostics

| | | |
|---|---|---|
| Standard input | File descriptor 0 | From terminal |
| Standard output | File descriptor 1 | To terminal |
| Standard diagnostic output | File descriptor 2 | To terminal |

### *Redirection of Input and Output*

| | |
|---|---|
| < | Redirect command input |
| > | Redirect command output |
| > > | Append to an output file |

### *Redirection with File Descriptors*

Use the file descriptors to redirect standard output to one file and standard diagnostic output to another.

## Background Commands

| | |
|---|---|
| **&** | Run a process in the background |
| **ps** | Monitor the status of background processes (−l for long list) |

| | |
|---|---|
| **PID** | Process identification number |
| **TTY** | Terminal number |
| **TIME** | Cumulative execution time |
| **CMD** | Name of the command |

**nice** Change the priority of a process
**kill n** Terminate background process number **n**

## Connecting Processes

| | |
|---|---|
| **p1 \| p2** | *Pipeline:* Connect p1 to p2 (that is, use the output of **p1** as the input of **p2**). |
| **p1 \| tee file** | Tee: View the output of **p1** as it is being written to file. |

## Giving Directives to the Shell

### *Command Grouping*

| | |
|---|---|
| **(p1 p2)** | Create a subshell to read commands **p1** and **p2**. |
| {1 p2} | Cause the shell to read commands **p1** and **p2**. |
| **p1;p2;p3** | Command list with three commands. |

### *Conditional Execution*

| | |
|---|---|
| **p1 \|\| p2** | OR-IF: Invoke command **p2** only if **p1** fails. |
| **p1 && p2** | AND-IF: Invoke **p2** only if **p1** succeeds. |

### *Pattern-Matching*

| | |
|---|---|
| * | Match any string of any length. |
| ? | Match any single character. |
| [ ] | Match any of the characters enclosed. |

## Shell Procedures

### *Preliminary Commands*

| | |
|---|---|
| **echo** | Display text at the standard output (terminal screen). |
| **read** | Receive text from the standard input (terminal keyboard). |

### *Shell Variables*

| | |
|---|---|
| **$ var=string** | Assign **string** to the variable **var**. |
| **$ echo $var** | Display the contents of the variable. |
| **string** | The value of **var** is displayed on the screen. |

| | |
|---|---|
| ' ' | Use single quotes for a string that contains spaces. |
| " " | Use double quotes for a string that also contains special characters whose meanings need to be retained. |
| **eval** | Evaluate a command string. |
| **{$P}s** | Distinguish variable P from the surrounding text. |

### Command Substitution

| | |
|---|---|
| **$ files=\`ls\`** | Assign the result of the **ls** command to **files**. |
| **$ y=\`expr $x + 5\`** | Evaluate the arithmetic expression and assign the result to **y**. |

### Conditional Substitution

| | |
|---|---|
| **${var−sub}** | If **var** has a value, use it; if not, use **sub** and leave **var** unassigned. |
| **${var=sub}** | If **var** has a value, use it; if not, assign the value of **sub** to **var**. |
| **${var?sub}** | If **var** has a value, use it; if not, display the message **var:sub** and abort the process. |
| **${var+sub}** | If **var** has a value, use the value of **sub** instead; if not, use a null string and leave **var** unassigned. |

### Positional Parameters

| | | | |
|---|---|---|---|
| $0 | Command | $3 | Third argument |
| $1 | First argument | $4 | Fourth argument etc. |
| $2 | Second argument | $5 | Fifth argument etc. |

### Reserved Shell Variables

| | |
|---|---|
| # | Number of arguments in a command line |
| ? | Return code for the command |
| $ | PID of the current process |
| ! | PID of the most recent background process |
| − | Status of shell flags |

## Constructing Loops

### Looping While True

```
while <command list>
do [execute commands
    between do and done]
done
```

### Looping While False

```
until <command list>
do [execute commands
    between do and done]
done
```

### Nesting Loops

```
while <command list>
do [execute commands
    between do and done]
    until <command list>
    do [execute commands
        between do and done]
    done
done
```

Nest the **until** loop within the **while** loop

### Looping Statements

| | |
|---|---|
| **break** | Exit from a loop |
| **continue** | Resume execution at the start of the nearest loop |
| **exit** | Exit from the shell procedure |

### Looping on a Variable

```
for <variable in list>
     do [execute command list
          from do and done
done
```

## The Conditional Statement

```
if <expression>
   then <command list>
fi

if <expression>
   then <command list>
   else <command list>
fi

elif = "else if"
```

# Testing Files, Strings, and Quantities

## *Testing Files*

| | | | |
|---|---|---|---|
| test | -r | <filename> | [file exists and can be read] |
| | -w | | [file exists and can be written to] |
| | -f | | [file exists and is an ordinary file] |
| | -d | | [file exists and is a directory] |
| | -s | | [file is not empty—its size is nonzero] |

## *Comparing Quantities*

| | | | | |
|---|---|---|---|---|
| test A | -eq | B | [Is A equal to B?] | [A = B?] |
| | -ne | | [Is A not equal to B?] | [A ≠ B?] |
| | -ge | | [Is A greater than or equal to B?] | [A ≥ B?] |
| | -le | | [Is A less than or equal to B?] | [A ≤ B?] |
| | -gt | | [Is A greater than B?] | [A > B?] |
| | -lt | | [Is A less than B?] | [A < B?] |

## *Comparing Strings*

| | |
|---|---|
| `test -n <string>` | [The string exists] |
| `test -z <string>` | [The string doesn't exist] |
| `test <string_1> = <string_2>` | [The two strings are the same] |
| `test <string_1> != <string_2>` | [The two strings are not the same] |

## *Compound Testing*

**!** Unary "not" operator inverts the truth-value of an expression.

**-o** Binary "or" operator will return "true" if either of the surrounding statements is true.

**-a** Binary "and" operator will return "true" only if both of the surrounding statements are true.

# Other Shell Programming Techniques

## *Multiple Branching*

```
case <string> in
     S1) <command list> ;;
```

```
     S2) <command list> ;;
           . . .
     Sn) <command list> ;;
esac
```

## Interrupt-Handling

Signal 1: Hangup
Signal 2: Quit signal
Signal 3: Interrupt
Signal 15: Software termination

trap '<command list>' <signals>

## Debugging a Shell Procedure

`$ sh -x <filename>` [execution option: display commands]
`$ sh -v <filename>` [verbose option: display input lines]

# G

# *Summary of the C Shell*

.login
.cshrc

## Initialization Files

### *A Sample Login File* .login

| | |
|---|---|
| **stty** | Set up your terminal (tty) |
| **set path** | Set up your command search path |
| **setenv TERM** | Select a terminal name from those already described |
| **echo** | Select an opening display |

### *The Shell "Read Command" File* .cshrc

| | |
|---|---|
| **set prompt** | Set your prompt |
| **set history** | Set the number of events to be saved |
| **alias** | Set an alias |

## Reinvoking Previous Commands

**!!** Reinvoke the most recent event
**!17** Reinvoke event number 17
**!-4** Reinvoke the fourth event back from the current event
**!ls** Reinvoke the event that begins with **ls**
**!?s** Reinvoke the event that contains **s** (anywhere in the line)

## Selecting Individual Arguments

**!18:4** Select the fourth argument of event 18
**!18:^** Select the first argument of event 18 (also **!18**)
**!18:$** Select the last argument of event 18 (also **!18$**)
**!18:2-5** Select arguments 2, 3, 4, and 5 of event 18
**!18:*** Select all arguments of event 18 (also **!18***)

## Modifying a Command Line

**!!:s/w/W** Replace w with **W** in the previous event
**!!:&** Repeat the previous substitution in the previous event
**!!:h** Remove the last name from a pathname in the previous event
**!!:t** Remove the prefix from a pathname in the previous event
**!!:r** Remove the suffix from a pathname in the previous event
**!!:p** Preview the previous event
**!!:q** Protect the previous event from further modification

## Assigning an Alias to a Command String

% **alias d pwd** Use **d** as an abbreviation (alias) for **pwd**
% **unalias d** Remove **d** as an abbreviation (alias)
% **alias ch cd /usr/Mike/book/ \ ! \ * (dynamic aliased command)**
% **ch chapter10** Invoke **ch** with a real-time selection
**$ alias cdl cd ' \ !*; ls -l more ' (complex aliased command)**

## The Logout File

### *Standard Logout*

% **^D** [Press CTRL-D]

### *Explicit Logout*

**set ignoreeof** (placed in **.login**)

## Assigning String Values

| | |
|---|---|
| % **set VAR = value** | Assign **value** to variable **VAR** |
| % **echo $VAR** | Retrieve the value of **VAR** |
| % **set** | Display all declared variables and their values |
| % **echo $path** | |
| /usr/peter/bin /bin /usr/clan/bin | |
| % **echo $path[2]** | Display the second argument of "path" |
| /bin | |
| % **set array = (' ')** | Declare "array" with four elements |
| % **set array[2] = two** | Assign the second element |
| % **echo $?array** | Test whether "array" has been declared |
| **1** | [True: "array" declared] |
| % **echo $#array** | Display the number of elements of "array" |
| **4** | |

## Manipulating Variables That Contain Numeric Values

| | |
|---|---|
| % @ **val = 5** | Assign **5** to the variable **val** |
| % **echo $val** | Display the value of **val** |
| 5 | |
| % @ | Display all numeric variables and their assigned values |

| | | |
|---|---|---|
| + Add | * Multiply | |
| − Subtract | / Divide | % Remainder |

| | |
|---|---|
| % @ **Y++** | Increment "Y" by one |
| % @ **X+=5** | Increment "X" by five |
| % @ **Y--** | Decrement "Y" by one |
| 3% @ X-=3 | Decrement "X" by three |
| % @ **X = ~ $X** | Assign the one's complement of **X** to **X** |
| % @ **M = 9;** @ **N = 10** | |
| % @ **T =($M < $N)** | Test whether "M" is less than "N" |

| | | |
|---|---|---|
| < Less than | <= Less than or equal to | = Equal to |
| > Greater than | >= Greater than or equal to | != Not equal to |

## Variables Reserved by the C Shell

| **Description** | **Name** | **Type** |
|---|---|---|
| Argument Number n | $argv[n] | String or numeric |
| Number of Arguments | $#argv | Numeric |
| Search Path | $cdpath | String |
| Child Process Number | $child | Numeric |
| Echo a Command | $echo | True or false |
| Length of History List | $history | Numeric |
| Home Directory | $home | String |
| Ignore End-of-File | $ignoreeof | True or false |
| Prevent Overwriting | $noclobber | True or false |
| Remove Special Meaning Automatically | $noglob | True or false |
| Remove Special Meaning If There Is No Match | $nonomatch | True or false |
| Search Path | $path | String |
| Prompt Symbol | $prompt | String |
| Pathname of the Shell | $shell | String |
| Exit Status of Last Command | $status | True or false |
| Time to Execute a Command | $time | String |
| Terminal lType | $TERM | String |
| Process Identification Number | $$ | Numeric |
| Complete Messages | $verbose | True or false |

You can set some of these variables in your **.cshrc** file, which is executed each time you log on and each time a new process is created.

## File-Checking

The C shell uses the following expressions in **if**, **foreach**, and **while** statements the way the Bourne shell uses **test** to performs similar tests:

| | | |
|---|---|---|
| -e | | true if the file exists |
| -z | | true if the size of the file is zero |
| -f | | true if the file is an ordinary file |
| -d | | true if the file is a directory |
| -o | *file* | true if the user owns the file |
| -r | | true if the file is readable |
| -w | | true if the file is writeable |
| -x | | true if the file is executable |

## Forming Conditional Statements

```
if . . . then

if . . . then . . . else

if . . . then . . . else . . . else if
```

## Forming Loops

| | |
|---|---|
| `goto label` | Branch to the line with label *label* |
| `foreach variable (wordlist)`<br>`  command list`<br>`end` | |
| `while (expression)`<br>`  command list`<br>`end` | |
| `break` | Exit from a loop |
| `continue` | Continue execution at the start of the nearest loop |
| `exit` | Exit from the shell procedure |

## Other Programming Techniques

```
switch (string)
case pattern1:
     command list
breaksw
case pattern2:
     command list
breaksw
default:                    [optional]
     command list
breaksw
endsw
```

| | |
|---|---|
| `shift` | Shift all arguments to the left one position |
| `onintr label` | Branch to the line with label *label* if an interrupt occurs |

## Built-In Commands

Built-in commands are commands whose code is part of the C shell. When a built-in command is invoked, the C shell doesn't need to use a command search path to locate this command, since the command isn't in a separate file. The C shell gives control to an invoked built-in command without creating a new process. Following is a list of built-in commands. Most of them are explained in greater detail in Chapters 25-27.

**alias** This command is used to substitute a new name for a command string. When **alias** is invoked alone, a list of aliased commands is displayed. Refer to Chapter 25 for more details of this command.

@ This command is used to initialize a numeric variable, and to perform a logical or arithmetic operation on a variable. The list of declared variables is displayed when this command is invoked alone. Refer to Chapter 26 for details on this command.

**break** This command is used to abort the nearest **while** and **foreach** loop. The execution will resume after the closest **end** statement. Refer to Chapter 27 for details.

**breaksw** Use this command to break the **case** of the **switch** structure. This command is explained in greater detail under the **switch** command in Chapter 27.

**case** This command is used in the **switch** structure; refer to **switch** structure in Chapter 27.

**cd** or **chdir name** Change the shell working directory to an argument directory (name). If no argument is given, your home directory will be the working directory. The argument can be a pathname.

**continue** This command directs the program flow to the nearest **while** or **foreach** command. Refer to the **continue** command in Chapter 27 for details.

**default** This command is used in the **switch** structure to handle a case when no match is found for any **case**. This command should appear after each **case** command. Refer to Chapter 27 for details.

**echo string** This command is the same as the **echo** command of the Bourne shell. When invoked with \c, **echo** will cause the newline to be withheld from the end of the output string.

**else** This command is used in the **if** structure. Refer to the **if** command in Chapter 27.

**end** This command is used in **while** and **foreach** structures. Every **while** or **foreach** must have a matching **end** command. Refer to the **while** command for an example.

**endsw** Like the **end** command above, this command is to close the **switch** structure. Refer to the **switch** command for details.

**exec** This command executes the command argument in the current shell without returning to the calling program. Here is an example:

```
% cat example
#
if -d $argv[1] then
  cd $argv[1]
  exec pwd
  echo 'This line is never displayed'
```

In the program shown above, the last line will never be executed because the **exec** command after executing the **pwd** command will exit to the C shell and never return to program **example.**

**exit** This command will terminate the program flow and return the calling program (the parent process).

**foreach** Refer to the **foreach** command in Chapter 27.

**goto** Refer to the **goto** command in Chapter 27.

**history** Refer to the **history** command in Chapter 25.

**if** Refer to the **if** command in Chapter 27.

**login** This command is invoked automatically by the **getty** process during the log-in sequence. When invoked by the user, it logs out the current user from the system.

**logout** When variable **ignoreeof** is set, this command is the only way for you to logoff from the system. If **.logout** file exists the shell will execute this file before it exits.

**set** This command is used to initialize variables. Refer to Chapter 25 for details.

**setenv** This command allows you to initialize variables such as TERM and export definitions of these variables to the environment.

**shift** This command shifts the arguments one position to the left. Refer to Chapter 27.

**source** This command is similar to the . command of the Bourne shell. When invoked, this command will execute the argument file without creating a new process. The difference between this command and the **exec** command is that this command will return to the calling program upon finishing its execution.

**switch** This is the multi-way branching command. Refer to Chapter 27.

**time** When this command is invoked with another command as its argument, the amount of time needed to process the command argument will be displayed after it has been executed. The displayed information is the same as that stored in the variable **time**.

**unalias** This command removes an aliased command from the alias list.

**unset** This command removes a variable definition from the variable list.

**while** Refer to the **while** command in Chapter 27.

# H

# Describing a Terminal for *vi*

## Preliminary Setup Procedures

In the major directory */etc* there is a file called *termcap* (short for "terminal capability"). This file contains abbreviated descriptions of all the terminals capable of running on your UNIX system. Each description provides alternate names for a given terminal, the size of its screen, whether or not it supports basic functions like backspacing and automargins, and the codes required to clear the screen, home the cursor, move the cursor in different directions, and so on. A description may contain only one line for a simple terminal or over 30 lines for a sophisticated terminal.

For example, to describe the Lear Siegler ADM-3 terminal, */etc/termcap* will contain an entry that looks something like this:

```
Names for terminal
↓                 ↓
l3|adm3|3|lsi|adm3:bs:am:li#24:co#80:cl=^Z
                  ↑                       ↑
                  Capabilities of terminal
```

This one-line entry (with descriptions added here) gives four alternate names for the terminal (separated by vertical bars):

`l3 (el three)` `adm3` `3` `lsi adm3`

It also gives five basic capabilities of the terminal (separated by colons):

| | |
|---|---|
| **bs** | Backspacing (ability to move the cursor back and erase) |
| **am** | Automargins ("wrapping" from the edge of the screen) |
| **li#24** | 24 lines of display |
| **co#80** | 80 columns per line |
| **cl=^Z** | Clearing (erasing the screen) with CTRL-Z |

## *Entry in termcap*

If */etc/termcap* already contains an entry for your terminal, all you have to do is identify your terminal to the UNIX shell. This involves setting the shell variable TERM (short for "terminal"). For example, if you are using a Lear Siegler ADM-3, all you have to do is select one of the alternate names and assign it to the shell variable TERM:

| Bourne shell | C shell |
|---|---|
| `$ TERM=adm3; export TERM` | `% setenv TERM adm3` |

Alternately, use **ed** to call up a file in your home directory called either *.profile* (Bourne shell) or *.login* (C shell) and place this statement on a line by itself in that file. Then the UNIX shell will automatically treat your terminal as a Lear Siegler ADM-3 every time you log in.

## *No Entry in termcap*

If */etc/termcap* does not contain an entry for your terminal, then (sigh) you will have to add an entry yourself. The "sigh" has been added because, with certain exotic terminals, this task can sometimes get very involved. In rare instances, it has even been known to result in "wailing and gnashing of teeth.'' If it becomes necessary for you to write your own terminal description, read the rest of this appendix. As soon as you have done that (and assigned your terminal), you are ready to start using **vi**.

### *Summary of Setup*

Before you can even think about using **vi**, you have to make sure that two things have been done:

- Someone has placed an entry in the file */etc/termcap* that describes your terminal to UNIX
- You have assigned the terminal described in */etc/termcap* to the shell variable TERM (either at the command line or in your directory's "log-in file") and also **exported** this variable.

## Designing an Entry

Suppose you check */etc/termcap* on your system and find that there is no entry for your terminal. Now what do you do? If you're really adventuresome, you can write one yourself. Otherwise, you can ask someone else for help. You may find that *etc/termcap* is a read-only file on your system. If so, you will have to ask the system administrator at some point to allow you temporary permission to write your entry to the file. In the mean time, you can set up your own little private *termcap* file while you are developing your entry for the main file.

You may find that your system won't allow you to use the name */etc/termcap* within your directory. However, you can choose another name that resembles it. Let's say you decide to call your one-entry file *tcap*. Begin an editing session with this file and enter the information for your terminal. How does the shell know that your entry is there instead of in the main public file? The answer is simple: you tell the shell. You have to name to the shell the file that contains the description of your terminal (*tcap*)—unless the description is in */etc/termcap*. You also have to name to the shell the description itself (wherever it may be located).

Here are the commands to type at your terminal:

| *Bourne shell* | *C shell* |
|---|---|
| `$ TERMCAP=/usr/robin cap` | `% setenv TERMCAP /usr/robin cap` |
| `$ export TERMCAP` | |
| `$ TERM=newterm` | `%setenv TERM newterm` |
| `$ export TERM` | |

In this pair of examples, you are placing a description called *newterm* in a file called *tcap.* In the C shell, the **setenv** command includes assigning the shell variable and exporting it in a single command.

Typing these commands on the command line like this allows the assignments to remain in effect only for the duration of your current session with UNIX. As soon as you log off, the assignments are lost. If you would like the assignments to go into effect every time you log in, you can place them in your "log-in file" (**.profile** in the Bourne shell, **.login** in the C shell). Just add the command statements shown above to this file, and they will be activated automatically.

As long as you're looking at your "log-in file," make sure it contains a statement that looks like this:

```
stty erase "^H" kill "^D"
```

This statement assigns to your terminal one character for backspacing and erasing the character to the left of the cursor (CTRL-H in this example) and one character for "killing" a process from your terminal (CTRL-D in this example). You will not be able to use **vi** properly if these statements are missing from your "log-in file."

The process of actually describing your terminal in a *termcap* entry involves looking at the manual that describes the operation and finding the codes that are used for various actions on your terminal. Then you find the name of the appropriate **termcap** variable and type an assignment statement (separated from other assignment statements by colons). For example, suppose your terminal manual tells you that the code that clears your terminal's display to the end of the line is CTRL-N. Looking under *termcap* in Section 5 of the **UNIX Programmer's Manual,** you find that the name of the variable that describes this action is *ce.* So you type this:

```
ce=^N
```

Suppose your terminal's code to clear to the end of the screen is CTRL-O. Since **termcap's** variable is called *cd,* you add another assignment to your string of beads:

```
ce=^N:cd=^O
```

When you type these entries, type the caret symbol (∧), followed by the character. To type an escape sequence (such as ESC L), use capital E preceded by a backslash to represent the ESC character:

```
\EL
```

This is about all we can say about the process of constructing a **termcap** entry. For a more detailed discussion, see the series of three excellent articles by Bill Tuthill in the first three issues of **UNIX/ WORLD:**

Vol. 1, No. 1 (Jan/Feb 1984): "Introduction" (pp. 59-61)
Vol. 1, No. 2 (Mar/Apr 1984): "Intermediate" (pp. 53-56)
Vol. 1, No. 3 (May/Jun 1984): "Advanced" (pp. 53-56)

The second article gives actual **termcap** entries for the Televideo 925 and Heath/Zenith 29. The third article gives entries for TRS-80, TRS-80 II, Apple II, Apple IIe, Heath/Zenith 89, Osborne 1, IBM PC with Kermit communications package (VT52 emulation), along with the Freedom, Micro Decision I, and Ann Arbor Ambassador.

UNIX/WORLD
444 Castro Street, Suite 1220
Mountain View, California 94041
(415) 964-0900

You may also be interested in the **Termcap Reference Manual,** which you can buy for $19.95 from

Independent UNIX Bookstore
520 Waller Street
San Francisco, California 94117
(415) 621-1593

# I

# Different Versions of UNIX

## Commands for Different Versions

This appendix lists the commands found in the most widely-used versions of UNIX: Version 7, System III, 4.1 and 4.2BSD, and XENIX 2.3.

### *Version 7 Commands*

| | | | | |
|---|---|---|---|---|
| ac | deroff | ln | pubindex | tr |
| adb | df | login | pwd | tee |
| ar | diff | look | quot | test |
| arcv | diff3 | lookall | ranlib | tk |
| as | du | lorder | ratfor | time |
| at | dump | lpr | rm | tp |
| awk | dumpdir | ls | rmdir | tr |
| bas | echo | m4 | refer | troff |
| basename | ed | mail | restor | true |
| bc | egrep | make | rev | tsort |
| cal | enroll | man | roff | tty |
| calendar | eqn | mesg | sa | uniq |
| cat | expr | mkdir | sed | units |
| cb | factor | mv | sh | uucp |
| cc | false | ncheck | size | uulog |
| chkeq | fgrep | newgrp | sleep | uux |
| chgrp | file | nice | sort | wall |
| chmod | find | nm | spell | wc |
| chown | fsck | nohup | spline | who |
| clri | f77 | nroff | split | write |

| cmp | graph | od | strip | xget |
|---|---|---|---|---|
| col | grep | passwd | struct | xsend |
| comm | icheck | plot | stty | yacc |
| cp | iostat | pr | su | |
| crypt | join | prep | sum | |
| cu | kill | primes | sync | |
| date | ld | prof | tabs | |
| dc | learn | ps | tail | |
| dcheck | lex | pstat | tar | |
| dd | lint | ptx | tbl | |

## System III Commands

System III includes most of the commands of Version 7, plus the following:

| acctcom | delta | kun | rsh | unpack |
|---|---|---|---|---|
| admin | dfl | line | sact | uuname |
| banner | diffmk | logname | sag | uupick |
| bdiff | dircmp | mm | scc | uustat |
| bfs | dirname | mmcheck | sccsdiff | uuwhat |
| bs | env | mmt | sdb | vpmc |
| cdc | errpt | news | sdiff | vpr |
| checkcw | get | nl | send | 300 |
| comb | getopt | pack | sno | 300s |
| cpio | greek | paste | split | 4014 |
| cref | help | pcat | timex | 450 |
| csplit | hp | prs | tplot | |
| ct | hyphen | reform | typo | |
| cut | id | regcmp | uname | |
| cw | kas | rjestat | unget | |

## Berkeley 4.1BSD Commands

4.1BSD includes most of the commands of Version 7, plus the following:

| | | | | |
|---|---|---|---|---|
| clear | ex | more | ssp | vi |
| csh | freq | num | strings | view |
| ctags | head | reset | tra | whereis |
| e | last | script | tset | whoami |
| edit | mkstr | see | ul | xstr |

## Berkeley 4.2BSD Commands

4.2BSD includes most of the commands of Version 7 and most of the commands of 4.1BSD (all except freq, num, see, ssp, and tra), plus the following:

| | | | | |
|---|---|---|---|---|
| addabib | ftp | newaliases | soelim | uusend |
| apply | gprof | page | sortbit | vgrind |
| apropos | groups | pagesize | spellin | vlp |
| arl1 | hostid | pc | spellout | vmstat |
| biff | hostname | pdc | style | vplot |
| chsh | indent | pi | symorder | vpq |
| colcrt | indxbib | pix | sysline | vprint |
| colrm | install | pmerge | t300 | vprm |
| compact | lastcomm | print | t300s | vtroff |
| dbx | leave | printenv | t450 | w |
| diction | lib | prmail | talk | whatis |
| error | lisp | pti | tek | which |
| expand | liszt | px | telnet | whois |
| explain | lock | pxp | tftp | yes |
| eyacc | lookbib | pxref | tip | |
| f | lpq | quota | trman | |
| fed | lprm | rcp | u | |
| finger | lptest | rlogin | uncompact | |
| fmt | lxref | roftbib | unexpand | |
| fold | mail | ruptime | unifdef | |

| | | | |
|---|---|---|---|
| force | mailq | ruusend | uptime |
| fp | mesg | rwho | users |
| fpr | mt | score | uudecode |
| from | netstat | secs | uuencode |
| fsplit | new | sendbug | uupoll |

# Description of XENIX

## *Improvements*

XENIX was developed by Microsoft in the late 1970s and early 1980s to fill the need for a commercial version of UNIX. Evolving as it did in the world of research and academics, UNIX lacked some of the features required for use in a business environment. XENIX has added some of these features, along with some other general improvements.

First, the improvements. XENIX takes advantage of the unique features of each of the major microprocessors used in the more recent microcomputers (the Intel 8086 and 8088, the Motorola 68000, and the Zilog Z8000). For example, in the 8086 and 8088, XENIX avails itself of memory segmentation, dynamic relocatibility of code, separation of data and instructions, input/output via memory-mapping, and multiprocessing.

On the minicomputers on which UNIX was developed, central processing and memory resources were scarce, while disk input/output was fast. On today's personal computers, however, the reverse is true, with central processing and memory abundant and disk input/output relatively slow. XENIX accommodates these differences by, for example, increasing the data transfer rate and reducing the amount of swapping of programs to and from disk.

Other improvements over UNIX include avoidance of bad disk sectors, interactive system configuration, built-in floating-point arithmetic, logging of device errors, automatic file system recovery, optimization of the C compiler, and a number of miscellaneous bug fixes.

## *Enhancements*

Next, the enhancements (largely to facilitate the implementation of network and database applications). XENIX offers record- and file-locking. With this feature, a program can gain exclusive access to a single record, a group of records, or an entire file, thereby avoiding the errors that can result when more than one program attempts to access and update the same record at the same time.

To coordinate the activity of different tasks in progress, XENIX provides semaphores and a message buffer. Semaphores allow two different tasks to achieve synchronization with simple signals to each other. The message buffer allows unrelated tasks to communicate with each other.

Other enhancements include "scatter-loading" (placing segments of a program in non-contiguous areas of memory), synchronous writing of records to disk, and non-blocked reading of records to avoid unnecessary waiting.

## *XENIX VERSION 2.3 Commands*

XENIX Version 2.3 contains most of the commands of Version 7, plus the following:

asktime
config
copy
ctags (BSD)
disable
enable
finger (BSD)
head (BSD)
l
lc
mkfs
mknod
mkstr (BSD)
mkusr
more (BSD)
printenv (BSD)
random
rmusr
sddate
settime
shutdown
strings (BSD)
touch
tset (BSD)
vi (BSD)
wait
xstr (BSD)

# Index

*This index was prepared by using the procedures described at the end of Chapter 20.*

## RELATED RESOURCES SHELF

### Mastering FORTH *Anita Anderson, Martin Tracy, Micromotion*

Here's a step-by-step tutorial that covers the new standard FORTH-83 International Standard. Offers exctensive coverage of other dialects, stack manipulations, variables, loops, strings, and more.

☐1985/220pp/paper/D6609-4/$17.95

### The C Programmer's Handbook *Thom Hogan*

Handy and well organized for quick access to information, it defines complete C language clearly and understandably with examples and explanations of restrictions and defaults.

☐1984/288pp/paper/0-89303-365-0/D3650-1/$19.95

### The C Programming Tutor
*Leon A. Wortman, Thomas O. Sidebottom*

Here is a tutorial text that goes beyond the standard guides to C language by exploring the programming aspects of the language. Contains a wide variaety of programming examples in a complete, self-study format.

☐1984/228pp/paper/0-89303-364-2/D3642-8/$19.95

TO ORDER, simply clip this entire page, check off your selection, and complete the coupon below. Enclose a check or money order for the stated amount. (Please add $2.00 postage and handling per book plus local sales tax.) Or call TOLL-FREE 800-638-0220. (In MD, 301-262-6300)

Mail to: **Brady Communications Co., Inc., Dept. TS. Bowie, MD 20715**

Name ________________________________

Address ________________________________

City/State/Zip ________________________________

Charge my credit card instead: ☐ MasterCard ☐ Visa

Account# ________________ Expiration Date ________________

Signature ________________________________

Dept. Y Y0510-BB(5)

*Prices subject to change without notice.*